THE LEGACY OF CHERNOBYL

# THE LEGACY OF CHERNOBYL

## Zhores A. Medvedev

W· W· Norton & Company
New York   London

*Library of Congress Cataloging-in-Publication Data*
Medvedev, Zhores A., 1925–
The legacy of Chernobyl / Zhores Medvedev.
p. cm.
Includes bibliographical references.
1. Radioactive pollution—Environmental aspects.
2. Chernobyl Nuclear Accident, Chernobyl, Ukraine.
1986–
Environmental aspects. I. Title.
TD196.R3M418 1990 89–39757
363.17'99—dc20
ISBN 0–393–02802–X

W·W· Norton & Company, Inc.
500 Fifth Avenue, New York, N.Y. 10110

Printed in Great Britain.

1 2 3 4 5 6 7 8 9 0

# Contents

# Preface and Acknowledgements

CHERNOBYL was certainly not the most tragic accident of the last decade. But it was the most frightening catastrophe of modern industrial history. Two workers were killed immediately by the reactor explosion, and the loss of life directly caused by the Chernobyl accident was about the same as in the fire at London's King's Cross underground station in 1987, where 30 commuters and one fireman died.

Economically, however, Chernobyl was the most expensive accident in human history and the price the Soviet Union has to pay for it will continue to mount for decades. A young, tired and inexperienced operator, Leonid Toptunov, who died three weeks later in great pain, moved the control rods of Reactor No. 4 to only slightly below the correct position. This seemingly minor oversight resulted in a giant plume containing millions of curies of deadly radioactive aerosol being released. It moved towards the north and west and within a few days had reached nearly every country in the northern hemisphere.

The number of people who may die in the next 50 years from cancer and other health problems related to the Chernobyl accident cannot be accurately measured by health and mortality statistics even in the countries that were most affected. But millions of people who do contract a fatal cancer will believe that they might have remained alive had it not been for Chernobyl. People's perceptions of nuclear power have been changed forever and this will affect our future energy policies and, consequently, our history. The imagination often plays a more important role in history than simple facts.

Many books have already been published about the Chernobyl accident and many more will probably be written. 'Chernobylogy' has become a special branch of science which will remain important for some time. It was almost inevitable that, after writing a book more than ten years ago on the nuclear disaster in the Urals, which was the most serious nuclear accident before Chernobyl, I would be tempted to write about Chernobyl. In the mid-1970s I was working alone and writing about a disaster that no one knew anything about. In fact, few people seemed to want to know. This time I have been writing about an accident that everyone knows about and I have had generous assistance and help from many experts. If I have been able to offer some new facts and insights about developments since the fateful night of 26 April 1986, I have to thank all those people who have sent me unpublished documents and reports, newspaper and magazine cuttings, and who have directed my attention to specific problems or invited me to give lectures and talks about the environmental and medical impact of Chernobyl.

As a biologist with a background in agriculture and radiobiology, it is natural that I have paid particular attention to the environmental, agricultural and health impact of the accident. But my experience of more than 20 years of research work in Soviet scientific centres, however, made it possible for me to try to offer an objective analysis of the Soviet nuclear establishment. The ten years during which I lived and worked in Obninsk, a town which was built to serve the research and design needs of Soviet nuclear energy and development, were particularly useful and contributed to my understanding of some of the complex problems which are important in discussing technical details.

Over the course of many years, living and working both in the Soviet Union and Britain, I have tried to prove that an open and co-operative society is much better protected from serious industrial accidents and other human-made calamities like hunger, malnutrition and epidemics, than are closed societies. We have known so little about accidents in communist countries because in the past even trivial problems were kept secret. Accidents were covered up and unpleasant social phenomena were hidden from the public eye. But an artificial paradise, agitprop prosperity and Potemkin villages can only be maintained for a certain length of time. And true *glasnost'* began to emerge gradually after the Chernobyl accident.

It was not only the explosion of the reactor that made Chernobyl the turning point. It was also weather and chance. If the winds had blown in an easterly direction at the end of April 1986 rather than north-westerly, or if the reactor explosion had occurred not near Kiev, but somewhere in the Urals or Siberia, it is unlikely that the International Atomic Energy Agency (IAEA) would have been able to discuss it in detail four months later. More than 10,000 reactor accidents are known to have occurred in the rest of the world since the first reactor became critical in 1942. But for the Soviet public, Chernobyl was the first officially acknowledged nuclear accident that they were told about. And it was the first nuclear accident in the Soviet Union that Soviet officials eventually reported to the rest of the world.

In our age of high technology, supersonic speed, nuclear energy and computer-made decisions, we cannot afford too many secrets. I wanted to write this book not only to show the real scale of this particular catastrophe, but also to demolish a few more secrets and deliberate misconceptions. My intention was to be neither pro- nor anti-nuclear. I wanted to present objective and valid facts. I would like to thank the many people who have helped me search for these facts. The list of people who gave me valuable assistance in my research is very long. I shall name here only those whose contribution was most essential, even if they themselves do not immediately recognize from the text how valuable their assistance was.

First, I must thank my brother, Roy A. Medvedev, who has supplied me with cuttings and other materials from Soviet newspapers, magazines and journals, many of them very useful for this study. I am particularly grateful to James Daglish and Yasuhiko Yoshida from the Division of Public Information of the IAEA, who kindly sent me Russian and English copies of the official Soviet Chernobyl report, prepared for the post-accident meeting in Vienna in August 1986, the reports of the IAEA conference on Chernobyl in September 1987 and other IAEA materials. Dr Walter C. Patterson's book on nuclear power and his comments on the technical problems of nuclear reactors were of great value. Henry Hamman and Stuart Parrot, the authors of one of the first books on Chernobyl published in 1987, kindly supplied me with copies of many documents on the Chernobyl fallout in Europe which reflect the monitoring work carried out by the offices of the World Health Organization and other agencies. Dr Martin Dewhirst of Glasgow University also kindly sent me cuttings and copies of many articles on Chernobyl published in little-known Soviet publications like *Sel'skaya Molodezh* (Rural Youth) and *Sotsialisticheskaya Industriya* (Socialist Industry). His help is greatly appreciated. Professor Marvin Goldman of the University of California, Davis, who provided me with the report of the US Department of Energy Team Analyses of the Chernobyl Accident Sequence and other reports on Chernobyl by American experts helped me to understand more clearly the main design faults of the RBMK reactor models. I would also like to thank Dr Brian Wade of Harwell Laboratory, UKAEA and Mary Morrey of the National Radiological Protection Board for sending me reprints, reports and other NRPB materials relevant to the impact of Chernobyl on the United Kingdom and Western Europe. I am grateful to Dr Lennart Devell of Studsvik Nuclear Laboratory in Sweden, who sent me the reports of his laboratory and of the Swedish National Institute of Radiation Protection about

Chernobyl fallout in the Nordic countries, to Wieland Eschenhagen, who provided me with the official government report on the Chernobyl fallout in the FRG, and to Kazuhisa Mori, Executive Director of Japan Atomic Industrial Forum, for giving me materials on the Chernobyl fallout in Japan and the Japanese nuclear programme.

The Landsat photographs of the Chernobyl exclusion zone as seen from space, sent to me by Mats Thoren of Space Media Network, Stockholm, were particularly useful. I also benefited from the advice, discussion and materials provided by Professor Richard Wilson of Harvard University, Professor John H. Fremlin of the University of Birmingham, D. Dixon of Weymouth, Roger and Bella Belbeoch of Paris, Anthony Tucker, Science Correspondent of the *Guardian*, Ze'ev Wolfson, of the *Environmental Policy Review*, the Hebrew University of Jerusalem, Mark Thompson of *END Journal*, Dr John F. Potter of the *The Environmentalist*, Theodor Shabad of *Soviet Geography*, New York, and Dr Arent Schuyler of the University of California, Santa Barbara. Finally, I would like to express my particular gratitude to Dr Margot Light of the London School of Economics and Political Science for her linguistic, editorial and bibliographic assistance.

It should be added that despite *glasnost'*, no one has yet been able to bring samples of dust or local soil from the Ukraine or Byelorussia. The Environmental Studies Group of the Harwell Laboratory of the UK Atomic Energy Authority was involved in a project to collect soil samples from all the countries of the northern hemisphere during the post-Chernobyl period in order to assess global fallout. It acquired samples from such distant places as the Bahamas, Alaska and Cameroon. Samples of soil from Bucharest, Sofia and Warsaw were taken from diplomatically protected embassy gardens. The British Embassy in Moscow also sent a sample which gave similar readings of radioactive caesium to samples from Ulan Bator in Mongolia and Beijing in China. It was not therefore surprising that the British assessment of the Chernobyl global fallout was later shown to be an underestimate. But what the reader might find surprising from this book is that Soviet experts themselves did not know the accurate figures. The true picture of the Chernobyl radioactive fallout in the Soviet Union, as well as of the economic and political fallout, is emerging only now, several years after the accident.

Zhores Medvedev

# Plate Acknowledgements

The author and publisher would like to thank the following for their kind permission to reproduce plates: *The Independent* (photograph: Dr Vladimir Shevchenko) 15; Novosti Press Agency 5, 6 (photograph: I. Kostin), 7 (photograph: V. Zufarov); Popperfoto 8; Society for Cultural Relations with the USSR 1, 2, 4, 9; Tass 3 (photograph: V. Zufarov), 10, 13 (photograph: A. Klimenko), 14 (photograph: V. Solovyev); Professor Richard Wilson 11, 12.

# I

# A Post-mortem of the Catastrophe

## INTRODUCTION

THE post-accident review meeting of the International Atomic Energy Agency (IAEA) held in Vienna 25–9 August 1986 produced a remarkable calm in one of the most heated technological debates of recent times. The Soviet delegation presented a very frank and comprehensive preliminary report entitled *The Accident at the Chernobyl Nuclear Power Plant and its Consequences*. The Soviet authorities had previously been notorious for their reticence about industrial accidents, concealing their causes and, where possible, denying their occurrence. For four months after the Chernobyl nuclear plant accident on 26 April 1986 the future of the world nuclear energy industry seemed uncertain. The most serious feature of the accident, the graphite fire, threatened the future of those Western reactors that use graphite in the core as a moderator to control the energy of fast neutrons, such as the British magnox and advanced gas-cooled reactors (AGR), as well as some old American nuclear power stations and plutonium-producing military reactors. All reactors work on the basis of nuclear fission of uranium fuel elements which generate neutrons, with moderators to slow down the fast neutrons and help to sustain a chain reaction and to transform fission energy into thermal energy. But most modern reactors use water rather than graphite as a moderator. An explanation of the causes of the graphite fire at Chernobyl would probably indicate potential problems in all graphite core reactors and lead to the end of graphite moderator models. The first major nuclear reactor accident had caused a graphite fire at the UK Windscale plant in 1957. But the nuclear energy programmes in Japan, West Germany, Canada and France would not necessarily be adversely affected.

However, an analysis of the Chernobyl fallout radionuclides also indicated that the ultimate nightmare of the nuclear industry – a meltdown of the core – had occurred. Monoelemental particles of pure ruthenium (Ru-103 and Ru-106) were identified in the Chernobyl plume when it passed over Sweden. Ruthenium has a melting point of 2,250°C. This proved that the reactor core must have reached this temperature. Meltdown must, therefore, have occurred, because zirconium which is used for nuclear fuel cladding melts at 1,852°C (uranium melts at 1,132°C). Meltdown is the most serious possible reactor accident. Most reactors are situated inside a huge metal or concrete containment structure to prevent the escape of radionuclides from melting down fuel elements in case of an accident. Only one previous core meltdown accident had earlier occurred in the nuclear power industry, in Pennsylvania in 1979. The solid, hermetic containment structure surrounding the reactor had limited the extent of the damage caused by the accident. But the Chernobyl reactor and other reactors of what is known as the RBMK-1000 type did not have protective containment structures (in Russian, the initials RBMK stand for 'reactor high-power boiling channel type'). This was considered their most serious short-coming. Several old British magnox reactors and American graphite moderated plutonium-producing reactors without appropriate contain-ment domes were also still in operation. It was inevitable after the Chernobyl accident that they would be shut down and eventually dismantled. It seemed to be the only way to calm public anxiety and to save more advanced nuclear energy programmes.

It soon became clear from the Soviet Report presented to the IAEA post-accident review meeting that the Chernobyl accident had been far worse than a simple core meltdown which may occur due to the heat from residual fission radionuclides. It had occurred as the result of a runaway chain reaction of uranium-235. In effect, a slow nuclear explosion had occurred so powerful that it had destroyed the reactor instantly. It would probably have breached any modern containment vessel; there is no effective protection against a nuclear explosion. However, the accident was presented as the result of a sequence of so many improbable and incomprehensible human errors that the incompetence and irresponsibility displayed by the Soviet operators and engineers seemed to be irrelevant to nuclear energy in the rest of the world. The Chernobyl accident appeared to be a Soviet phenomenon from which only the Soviet establishment could learn. The authorities in most other countries that use nuclear energy concluded that their own nuclear plants were not prone to this type of accident. The nuclear energy industry was saved.

In the years since the accident many government-sponsored analytical works have been published to support this basic conclusion. However, independent researchers have published no fewer studies to challenge this view. As far as Soviet studies of the accident are concerned, apart from the draft of the 'Working Document' presented to the IAEA meeting in August 1986, most of the studies of the accident have remained classified information. General media and popular science descriptions, three novels and one play have tried to minimize the scale of the disaster and the seriousness of the long-term consequences. There were three other Soviet unofficial books, two written by journalists (A. Illesh and Y. Shcherback) and one by a former official in nuclear industry (G. Medvedev) (which I will often quote in this study) which did try to go beyond the Soviet official version and to uncover some new information. But these authors did not receive any co-operation from officials and did not have access to figures and documents. Two investigative documentary films on Chernobyl also provided valuable information. However, these few attempts to find the real picture did not replace the need for a comprehensive and open national or international inquiry in which all the technical, environmental and health aspects of this accident should be analysed by independent experts. Unfortunately, revealing the true story of Chernobyl is not in the interests of most nuclear energy or state officials who know, or could discover, the truth. Half-truths or a plausible cover-up serve their interests much better. A number of Western and Soviet experts do not trust the official story, but they do not have sufficient evidence to dispute it.

I am sceptical about the official, now almost universally accepted, version of the Chernobyl accident. Like other sceptics, I do not have access to many of the facts which would contradict or modify it. But I have some knowledge of the way 'pseudo-facts' and misinformation are created in the Soviet Union to serve political and institutional interests. I also understand the limits of *glasnost'*. This experience and some new facts, which do not fit the official version, that I have unearthed by extensive detective analysis of the published documents and numerous reports in the general Soviet media over several years have enabled me to retell the story of the Chernobyl accident in a different light.

## THE CHERNOBYL RBMK-1000 REACTOR

The first serious accident in a modern 1,000 MWe reactor occurred in the United States in 1979. It involved a technologically advanced model of a pressurized-water reactor (PWR). The environment did not become contaminated because the reactor was contained in a hermetic, dome-shaped protective structure made of reinforced concrete. There was a danger during the accident that the hydrogen accumulating inside the structure would explode. If that had occurred, the containment structure would probably have been breached and a vast number of radionuclides would have been released into the environment. In other words, a containment structure is an important safety element but it does not afford absolute protection.

The Chernobyl RBMK-1000 model is an example of the technology of the 1950s, which is now obsolete elsewhere, as far as the physics of its nuclear cycle is concerned. And it is precisely the outdated way in which it generates electricity that makes it unsafe in principle. But reactor safety does not depend entirely on the latest state of the art in physics. The quality of the engineering is vital in all parts of the basic equipment such as the pumping stations, pipes, heat exchangers, valves, steam generators, welding, the quality of the alloys, the purity of the graphite, the sophistication of the computers and the automatic controls. The new generation of fast-breeder reactors may be based on more advanced nuclear physics, but they are less safe than old-fashioned nuclear-fission reactors. Although readers probably understand the basics of reactor technology and why nuclear power is used to produce electricity, a brief outline of the principles of RBMK, PWR and AGR helps to explain the accident at Chernobyl.

The heaviest natural element, uranium, has several isotopes. The main isotope, uranium-238, is slightly radioactive but it cannot support what is known as a nuclear chain reaction. The only atom found in nature which can support a nuclear chain reaction is uranium-235. In natural deposits of uranium, U-235 represents about 0.7 per cent of uranium-238 (for every 140 atoms of U-238 there is one atom of U-235). When a neutron collides with the nuclei of uranium-235 it splits. As a result, pieces of uranium-235 form new elements with smaller nuclei which are often unstable. They are called fission products or radionuclides. In addition, a few more neutrons are released which can split more than one new atom of uranium-235 if they are very close. It is this release of new neutrons which can split more and more new atoms of uranium-235 that is called a chain reaction. If there is a critical mass of pure uranium-235, the chain reaction is so fast that it produces an instant explosion (Hiroshima was destroyed by this kind of explosion in 1945). But if the atoms of uranium-235 are separated and if the speed of the neutrons is regulated by a moderator, the chain reaction can be slowed down so that the huge energy of fission is released gradually. This process of *controlled fission* is used in nuclear reactors. The fission of 1 lb of uranium-235 produces as much heat energy as 1,500 tonnes of coal. The possibility of generating so much energy from so little uranium makes it both economical and rational to use uranium in nuclear reactors (140 lb of natural uranium which contains 1 lb of U-235 had a market price in 1989 of $18,000). However, very large amounts of highly radiotoxic and often very volatile fission radionuclides are produced at the same time, making the use of uranium very dangerous. In the process of fission of uranium-235 nearly 100 highly radioactive and hot substances accumulate in the fuel rods.

When neutrons collide with the nuclei of uranium-238 in a mixture of uranium-235 and 238 some of them transform it into a new element, Plutonium-239. Plutonium is also fissionable and it is more suitable than uranium for making bombs. In fact, the first reactors were designed to manufacture plutonium, not to generate electricity. To transform a nuclear reactor into a power station the principles that apply to any thermal station are used. The heat from the reactor is used to create steam from water. The steam power rotates turbogenerators which, in turn, generate electricity. But the technology used to execute this task varies in different reactors.

The difference between the design of RBMK-1000 reactors and the PWR will become clear when the history of the Soviet nuclear energy programme is examined. What is important here are the engineering features of the Chernobyl RBMK-1000 reactor which affected the accident on 26 April 1986.

In RBMK-1000 reactors neutrons are moderated by graphite blocks. Slightly enriched uranium (in other words, uranium containing 2 per cent U-235 rather than 0.7 per cent) is used as fuel. The graphite blocks slow down the speed of the fast neutrons that are released during the fission of U-235. Slow neutrons are more efficient in sustaining a chain reaction, since they are more likely to hit the new nuclei of uranium-235. In the shutdown position the large reactor core consists of 2,488 graphite columns (the total weight of graphite is 1,700 tonnes). The graphite columns separate about 1,660 fuel channels or pressure tubes, each about 10 m long. Each channel contains specially prepared uranium assemblies and space for the cooling system. Thus each channel is a complex system that generates heat and steam. The intensity of the chain reaction is regulated by neutron-absorbing rods which have separate channels in the graphite core. There are 211 control rods made of elements like boron carbide which absorb neutrons and prevent the generation of new neutrons. When they are withdrawn from the core the chain reaction is activated. When they are pushed into the core the chain reaction is inhibited. By varying the number of rods withdrawn or left in the core and by changing their position, the intensity of the chain reaction and therefore of the power of the reactor can be controlled. But the control rods do not prevent the emission of alpha, beta and gamma radiation (see Glossary) of the fission radionuclides.

The control rods in the RBMK-1000 reactor can be moved at a speed of 40 centimetres per second. It therefore takes 20 seconds to move them from their top position to their lowest point. By modern standards this is very slow (in the CANDU reactors used in Canada which use heavy water as a moderator and in PWRs in the USA and Japan this operation takes 1 second).

The nuclear reaction generates heat in order to produce high pressure steam to rotate the turbogenerators. All parts of the reactor are thus normally very hot. The temperature of the graphite columns, for example, reaches 700°C. The core contains many independent water cooling circuits and only one water circulation system (in other words, the water that circulates inside the fuel channels to produce steam for the turbogenerators). An important feature of the RBMK-1000 reactor is that high-pressure steam for the turbogenerators is produced directly in the first water circuit inside the fuel channels. In the PWR, on the other hand, steam is produced in a second independent circuit which is heated by a heat exchanger. The boiling water, therefore, does not have direct contact with the uranium fuel elements. But in the RBMK-1000 system each fuel channel is also a channel of boiling water, with an independent water-circulation system, and a pressure and temperature regime which is recorded in the control room. This means that thousands of pipes and welded joints are used. It also means that each reactor is an assembly of smaller reactors, vulnerable to innumerable small leaks and faults. This is why RBMK systems have become unpopular in the West.

Other specific technical details of the RBMK will become clear in chapter 7 on the development of the Soviet nuclear energy programme. For present purposes this is sufficient detail to understand the fatal safety test, which was the cause of the explosion, and the subsequent attempts to stop the graphite fire and a complete meltdown of the fuel elements.

Figure 1.1 is a simplified representation of a RBMK-1000 reactor.[1] It can be seen that it does not have the single, large, steel pressure vessel typical for PWR reactors. Instead it consists of 1,600–1,700 individual fuel channels or pressure tubes. Each tube is 10 m high, with a diameter of 9 cm and a wall thickness of 4 mm. It is made of zirconium alloy in the middle part and of corrosion-resistant steel in the lower and upper parts. Since it cannot withstand significant increases of pressure, it has safety valves. Each pressure tube can generate about 3,000 kW of thermal energy per hour and it requires a flow of 28 tonnes of water per hour.

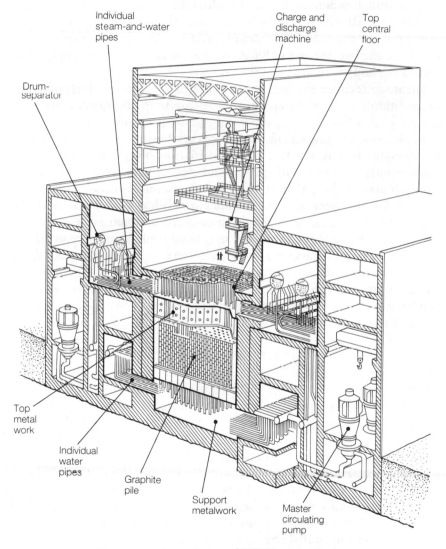

**Figure 1.1** General view of RBMK-1000 reactor.

The reactor is divided into two sections, each linked to a turbogenerator. This design allows one half of the reactor to be shut down and one 500 MWe turbogenerator to be used. However, the complexity of the individual channels and the numerous independent cooling-water circuits inside the core make it essential that the water circulation through the reactor is uninterrupted. The 'rundown unit' which was to be tested on 25 April 1986 was one of the safety systems to ensure uninterrupted water circulation. Although Soviet experts did not consider the RBMK reactor to be particularly safe, they did not worry about the danger of an explosion of the core or about a serious accident involving the whole reactor. Since the reactor is so large and complex, if something happened in one of the pressure tubes it would be easy, it was thought, to localize the accident by inserting control rods around the damaged tube and removing it from the core without shutting down the whole reactor.

At the time of the accident, the reactor contained about 75 per cent of the original fuel which had been loaded in 1983. The fuel was not entirely burnt out, but had spent about 70–80 per cent of its potential energy.[2] About 25 per cent of the fuel channels (nearly 400) were fresher. In other words, pressure tubes which had become defective or had begun to leak had probably been replaced between 1984 and 1986. They may even have been removed so that plutonium could be extracted from them at reprocessing plants. Since one of the advantages of the RBMK system is its usefulness for military purposes, spent reactor fuel elements are easier to remove when they are small, separable and easily transportable (the more compact reactor cores of the PWR are more difficult to handle to extract plutonium).

## THE DESIGN PROBLEM

Numerous fission products or radionuclides are accumulated in all operational nuclear power stations. Some of them are extremely hot (up to 3,000°C), others are volatile. They may be short- or long-lived and, until they decay, they emit lethal gamma, beta and alpha radiation. This is why nuclear stations are far more dangerous than other types of power station. Coal, oil or hydropower stations do not become more dangerous with time nor does their fuel change its quality during the fuel cycle. The uranium fuel load used in nuclear power stations does not change its weight, but it changes its isotope composition. As a result, fresh fuel is easier to handle than spent fuel. Each fuel cycle might last several years, but the reactor becomes more and more dangerous as new radioactive isotopes form and accumulate in the fuel. At the end of its normal fuel cycle the standard 1,000 MWe reactor contains nearly three billion curies of radionuclides in its spent fuel rods. If these radionuclides were to be spread evenly over the land surface of the planet, each square kilometre would receive at least 20 microcuries ($\mu$Ci) or 800,000 becquerels (Bq), making it temporarily dangerous for farming and fishing.

Because of the increasing danger caused by accumulated radionuclides, safety systems are the most important part of the design of nuclear reactors. The only way to ensure a reasonable level of safety is to provide multiple, normally redundant, protective devices which can be switched on rapidly one after the other. Economic constraints, however, make it impossible to achieve absolute safety: although we need safe power stations, we also need cheap, or comparatively cheap, electricity. A high degree of accuracy and efficiency in the execution of all operational procedures therefore represents a vital extra element of nuclear plant safety.

Minor mishaps, accidents and 'unusual occurrences' are frequent in all complex and sophisticated high-risk technologies. They occur in nuclear reactors as well (some of them are discussed in chapter 8). Core meltdown, the ultimate accident, is the result of a sudden loss of cooling water through the reactor core, preventing the removal of heat from the fuel rods. The two technical faults most likely to cause a meltdown are, first, burst main circulation pipes (these pipes are always subject to high temperature and pressure), and secondly, a failure of the electrical system leading to a station blackout or to the loss of the power plant's internal source of electricity. Most of the safety systems depend on electricity. If reserve supplies are not provided almost instantly, the continuing chain reaction or the residual heat of the accumulated radionuclides could destroy the reactor core within a very short time. The experiment which the engineers at the Chernobyl power station were conducting at the time of the accident concerned this problem.

It is rare, but not unknown, for electrical failure to cause a station blackout. The Soviet Working Document for the IAEA briefly mentioned a blackout which had occurred in 1980 at the Kursk RBMK nuclear power station. Although no water was pumped through the core for 80 seconds, core meltdown did not occur.[3] The slow natural circulation of water was sufficient to prevent serious overheating. The sudden loss of water which would result from damage to the main circulation pipes is potentially more dangerous for RBMK-1000 reactors. In the PWR model, water not only removes heat, it also serves to moderate the energy of fast neutrons. If the cooling water is lost, the chain nuclear reaction is inhibited. The rapid introduction of neutron-absorbing control rods acts as a second level of safety. When graphite blocks serve as the moderator, however, the sudden loss of cooling water does not stop the chain reaction. The rapid introduction of neutron-absorbing control rods is vital to prevent a nuclear explosion. But the speed at which the neutron-absorbing control rods (211 solid absorbers in specially separated channels cooled by water from an autonomous circuit) can be inserted depends on electric power, and the sudden loss of water can itself cause a blackout. Thus a crucially important part of the safety system of RBMK-1000 reactors is an independent supply of electricity for each group of control rods (there are 30 to 36 rods in each group) which can be provided rapidly in the case a of serious accident. A few seconds delay will prevent a safe shutdown and cause an explosion due to an uncontrollable burst of power (known as a 'power excursion').

Nuclear plants normally run their equipment off their own power. But if there is a problem, their electrical systems can be switched over quickly to an outside power grid (electricity produced by other power plants). In some circumstances the switch may be difficult because the electrical system is damaged or it may fail. To cover this possibility, emergency power must be available from special diesel generators on the site of the plant. Because diesel generators may prove slow or unreliable, some reactor designs provide for redundant diesel systems (in other words, two diesel generators in case one fails). If both fail, a major accident is unavoidable. Judging by the description of the 1980 blackout in Kursk, the diesel generators were not switched on for 90 seconds (probably they were not switched on at all).[4] According to the description of the technical characteristics of the Leningrad nuclear power stations with two RBMK-1000 reactors: 'In the case of a total power shutdown, the supply can be fed from a hydrostation generator and Diesel generators, switched on automatically 3 minutes after the main power supply is cut off. Users who cannot tolerate a power supply interruption are switched over to an accumulator bank'.[5]

A three-minute delay would be totally unacceptable in Western reactors. Some Western diesel generators are expected to provide the necessary power within 10 seconds, but it is commonly known that this cannot be taken for granted. An accumulator bank can provide electricity for computers and other similar equipment but it cannot provide enough energy to operate emergency water pumps which need

5,500 kW of power each. The new Chernobyl RBMK-1000 reactors are provided with diesel generators which are said to require only 15 seconds to start up, but they take 60–75 seconds to reach their full capacity of 5,500 kW.[6] A 50–60 second interruption in the power supply is unacceptable in several possible emergencies. The attempt to solve this problem was at the centre of the tests which led to the fatal accident.

In the general description of the accident offered in the Soviet report, the authors presented the experiment as an attempt 'to test the possibility of utilizing the mechanical energy of the rotor in a turbogenerator cut off from the steam supply to sustain the unit's own power requirements during power failure'.[7] In other words, the residual mechanical energy of the rotating turbine was to be used. In previous tests and experiments the voltage had fallen too quickly. According to the Soviet report a new solution had been found and a special generator magnetic field regulator had been added to the system which was to be tested on 25 April 1986. It was expected to eliminate earlier problems.[8]

This explanation of the rationale of the safety test is plausible but not entirely convincing. It does not answer the question which even a technically not very competent person would ask: why was a comparatively simple test planned for the end of the reactor cycle when it would be most dangerous and when it could not be repeated? Any experiment of this kind requires repetition. It would have been much easier to perform the test when the turbine itself was tested during the reactor launching period.

More serious doubts about the explanation arise from the fact that the use of the inertia mechanical energy of the rundown turbogenerator is already considered to be a major safety system of the RBMK-1000 reactor. It is designed to maintain the proper voltage to run the cooling pumps for 45–50 seconds, to bridge the gap between the shutdown (which in a RBMK reactor needs 20 seconds) and the beginning of the full operation of the diesel generators. If this is a standard feature of the RBMK safety system, the engineers could not have wanted to *improve* it but to install it. In other words, they must have been trying to install a safety device which should already have been tested and installed when the reactor was first certified for commercial operation in 1984. This makes the Soviet claim that safety tests on an operational power plant are both possible and permissible far more controversial.[9] Why was so vital a system not properly tested and installed from the very beginning?

## THE INADEQUACY OF THE INITIAL SAFETY TESTS

Reactor No 4 at Chernobyl was a new unit. On 25 April 1986 it had reached the end of its first cycle. According to the Soviet report it had begun operating in December 1983. But this is only partly true. The construction of the reactor and all its systems was completed in December 1983. It was physically launched on 20 December 1983. In the Soviet Union 22 December is a day of celebration for workers in the energy industry (most professional groups in the Soviet Union have an annual day of celebration when the profession is given press publicity, awards are announced and bonuses paid). On 21 December 1983 it was decided that it would be appropriate to report the successful launch the previous day of Unit 4 at Chernobyl. But there is usually a long interval between the physical launch of a new reactor (which normally runs for a brief period and for a fraction of its projected power) and its full commercial operation. The schedule normally prescribes up to 6 months of tests and repairs. It often takes even longer than this to test all the systems. The RBMK-1000 model has up to 1,700 independent fuel channels and thousands of different pipes and valves, each of which must be tested under different regimes and replaced if faults are found. For purely political reasons (which certainly have nothing to do with safety), the administration, engineers, workers, operators and scientists engaged in running the launching tests of Unit 4 publicly undertook to reduce the time taken for the tests (or to accelerate them) and to put the reactor into full commercial operation ahead of the official schedule. Such undertakings are usually made under pressure from ministerial and Party officials.

At the beginning of March 1984 it was reported that the 1 million kilowatt energy Unit 4 of the Chernobyl plant had been introduced into commercial operation two months ahead of schedule, 'with significant reduction of the time necessary for the mastering of the project norms allocated for tests and launching the new energy unit to full power'.[10] On 10 March 1984 the Central Committee and Council of Ministers of the USSR congratulated all workers, engineers and operators of the Chernobyl plant for reducing the period between the physical launch and full commercial operation. There had been delays in putting most other nuclear power plants into operation and the 'labour victory' at Chernobyl was therefore particularly welcomed. But it appears that the special government commission which normally inspects and tests all nuclear power systems had not completed all the necesssary tests.

Completing a project ahead of schedule is a rare event in Soviet industry and it brings enormous rewards and benefits. It is likely that the desire to report 'overfulfilment' led to corners being cut in the scheduled programme of tests. The Soviet report to the IAEA acknowledged that turbogenerator tests to use rotation energy had been done – and had failed – at Chernobyl before. The original tests were probably done during the launching period from 20 December 1983 to March 1984, when they were much safer and when they could more easily be repeated. The only way that the time allocated by the design requirement for testing a new reactor can be shortened is by reducing the number of tests and postponing some of them.

Certifying that a nuclear power station is ready to operate is not a single act. Each system must be tested and officially accepted by the administration of the power station from the construction and assembly teams. On 20 December 1983 the first physical launch had been made and publicized in the press. In July and August 1987, at the trial of six senior administrators of the Chernobyl station (the director, Viktor Bryukhanov, the chief engineer, Nikolai Fomin, the deputy chief engineer, Anatoly Dyatlov, shift manager Boris Rogozhkin, the manager of Reactor No. 2, Alexandr Kovalenko and the inspector of the committee for reactor safety, Yuri Laushkin) it was admitted that Reactor No. 4 had been cleared for operation, although safety tests relating to the turbogenerator had failed. In the published extract of the sentence it was said that:

> On 31 December 1983, despite the fact that the necessary tests had not been conducted on reactor No. 4, Bryukhanov signed an act accepting into operation the launching complex of the reactor and certifying that it had been completed. Aiming to bring the safety systems into working order, tests were conducted on the turbogenerator between 1982 and 1985. These tests were unsuccessful and remained incomplete.[11]

The trial was held in camera and the full text of the sentence was not published. But it seems obvious that the acceptance document was signed on the last day of 1983 under pressure, in order to be able to declare that the works planned for 1983 had been fulfilled. In the Soviet system of planning there are annual targets based on a calendar year. If Bryukhanov had not signed the act on 31 December 1983 thousands of workers, engineers and his own superiors in the ministries and committees would have lost bonuses, awards and other extras (which often amount to as much as two or three times a monthly salary). Since salaries rarely increase in the Soviet Union, the bonuses paid for fulfilment or overfulfilment of the plan become an increasingly important part of the average industrial income. This is one reason why output figures are often falsified (and why the usefulness of Soviet statistics has declined).

It is now known that the experiment that was attempted on 25 April 1986 was part of the tests which had been left incomplete at the end of 1983 and beginning of 1984. Using the mechanical energy of the inertia of turbogenerators to produce extra electricity makes sense. As long as the generator rotates, it goes on generating electricity. According to the Soviet report it had been found (probably in the tests during the launching period in 1984) that the inertia rotation was insufficient to provide high-voltage electric current for long enough to fill a certain gap,[12] probably between the loss of internal load and the beginning of the reserve production of electricity from standby diesel generators (or perhaps to move the control rods back into the shut down position). It is not clear why this was true of the turbogenerator of this particular unit nor is it clear what the rationale was for the extra tests (which are crucial before commercial operations commence). It seems likely that the engineers responsible for the electrical parts of the project suggested some alterations to the magnetic field regulator. It would take time to make the alterations but a promise had already been given that the time taken to do the introductory launching tests would be reduced. The people in charge probably made a simple but irresponsible decision – to postpone the tests until the next cycle.

This kind of practice is not unusual in Soviet industrial construction. Many industrial objects are accepted by the relevant government commission with a long list of incomplete elements and operations which the construction team promises to complete after the object has been officially licensed. If the commission takes a strict line and refuses to sign an act of acceptance, no one receives a bonus and basic salaries may be delayed. Everyone, including the government, is unhappy if the plan is registered as unfulfilled. The result is that it has become normal practice to accept as fully operational industrial objects that have not been completed to specification.

Using the inertia rotation of turbine rotors is an important safety device of RBMK systems. The three emergency diesel generators, each of 5,500 kW, cannot be started instantly. The three-minute time lag reported for the Leningrad RBMK-1000 built in the 1970s is clearly unacceptable (Western diesel generators require only 10 seconds to reach full power although some sceptics maintain that such diesels are 'notoriously unreliable' even in the United States[13]). Cold weather probably affects the time it takes to start diesel generators and this explains why the specifications of the Chernobyl diesel generators, situated in a warmer part of the country, maintain that they require 15 seconds to switch on and a further 30–40 seconds to produce the energy necessary to run the emergency pumps.[14]

A 50-second gap in the circulation of cooling water through the core might be acceptable if large amounts of fission products have not accumulated in the reactor fuel. But fission products generate residual heat even in the shutdown position. The problem is that the RBMK-1000 is a system with 'on load' refuelling. In other words, individual fuel channels can be removed and replaced if necessary without shutting down the whole reactor. And this means that in a mature reactor there are likely to be both fresh fuel channels and many that are approaching the end of their natural life and have accumulated fission products. The cooling system serves each channel individually. If the water pumps are stopped older fuel channels may overheat and sustain damage very quickly. Thus anything that interrupts the pumping of cooling water through the reactor core is very dangerous. The intention of the engineers to complete the work that should have been done before Unit 4 was put into commercial operation and to provide the turbogenerators with an important safety device is perfectly understandable. But it is less easy to understand why the work was planned for the very end of the first cycle when the station was due to be shut down for maintenance, repairs and the reloading of some fuel channels. It allowed only a very short time for the test. It would have been much safer to do it after the old fuel elements had been replaced and the maintenance repairs had been done, when the reactor would, in any case, need testing before its second two-year working cycle.

My conviction (later confirmed by some media stories) that the test planned for 25 April 1986 was part of the incomplete 1984 programme is based on the description of the reactor given in Annex 2 of the Soviet report. Most of the published comments about the Soviet report to the IAEA are based on a careful reading of the short Part I of the report, which describes the accident. Few commentators have examined the details given in the 'technical' annexes. It is clear even from Part I, that the use of power from the running down turbogenerator was necessary because 'this regime is in fact used in one of the reactor's fast-acting emergency core cooling systems (ECCS)'.[15] In the case of a 'maximal project accident' where the core cooling system is damaged, emergency cooling water is required immediately. The emergency cooling system must consist of several parts which are switched on independently. The first such system consists of two cylinder parts each comprising six vessels of 25 m$^3$ volume. Water in these vessels is under pressure (pressurized nitrogen) and can start to supply the damaged part of the reactor within 3.5 seconds without pumps. The duration of this emergency cooling depends on the scale of the coolant leak from the primary cooling system in the event of an accident, but it is designed to work for not less than 100 seconds. Although theoretically it can work without active pumping, it is not clear whether it requires electricity. The description makes it plain that: 'In the event of a maximum design-basis accident coinciding with a loss of power to users of the own-requirement supply from the power unit, the supply of water from the electric feed pump is assured for a period of 45–50 sec. as the pump runs down in tandem with the turbogenerator'.[16]

A second emergency system envisages using electricity generated by the rundown turbogenerator for 45–50 seconds to bridge the gap between the beginning of the accident and the availability of electricity provided by the emergency diesel generators. It requires extra transformers to short-circuit the unit transformers and provide energy in case the main system has broken down. In theory the inertia of the rundown generator can provide electricity and the necessary cooling for at least 45 seconds. Since the generator voltage varies in proportion to its rpm (revolutions per minute), a 'rundown unit' connected to the generator excitation regulator ensures that the rotor current in the generator is maintained at a constant level as the rpms decrease.[17] The 'rundown unit' is switched on when the signal is given that a design-basis accident has occurred and the turbine shut-off valves close.

The 'rundown unit' was the key element of the test planned for 25 April 1986. The Soviet report and other statements of Soviet officials in 1986 made it seem that the fatal test was designed to introduce a new invention which would improve the safety characteristics of the reactor. Information that a *new* voltage regulating system was to be tested was repeated in some international documents about the Chernobyl accident. In fact, it was a design requirement of the RBMK-1000 that turbogenerator inertia should be capable of producing electricity of the necessary voltage during rundown following the closure of the turbine emergency stop valve. If a test was required in 1986, it must mean that this important safety feature had been found defective in the pre-launch testing of the 'rundown unit' in 1982–5 and that the inertia of the turbogenerator had been found insufficient to provide the necessary voltage for 50 seconds. If this assumption is correct, it was highly irresponsible to certify the reactor for commercial operations in 1984.

Moreover, it seems likely that other RBMK-1000 reactors suffer from the same defect, since Reactor No. 4 at Chernobyl was not the only reactor to undergo this test.

After the Chernobyl accident the only people openly held responsible were local plant officials and engineers. However, the government commission which must have been created to supervise the completion of the project, and which was obliged to check all the necessary tests before signing the licensing documents, must have consisted of competent high officials representing relevant branches of industry, for example: the State Committee on Atomic Energy, the Ministry of Power and Electrification, the State Committee for Safety in the Atomic Power Industry, the Ministry of Medium Machine Building responsible for the design of reactors and the reactor fuel cycle, officials of the fire protection services, representatives of the ministries which manufacture turbogenerators, computer and control systems, representatives of the design bureaux and institutes which designed the project. The director and chief engineer of the Chernobyl Power Station were members of the commission. One section of the commission represented those who had designed and built the project (they would have wanted an early completion date). Other members represented the people who would operate the new project after it had been tested and declared safe (they would normally want as little unfinished and untested work as possible to avoid future problems). If the relationship between the two groups (which, in fact, represent producers and consumers) was purely commercial, it would be impossible to cut too many corners or to cheat. But in the Soviet Union the groups represent different ministries but the same owner – the state. And it is normally state and Party officials who try to find a compromise solution when there is disagreement between the two groups. The compromise usually takes the form of an 'act of acceptance' which includes a list of incomplete tasks which the design and construction section promise to complete. All too often, however, the incomplete tasks are forgotten by the producers and must be finished by the consumers who were persuaded to accept the incomplete object. This is the rule throughout Soviet industry, from the building of apartment blocks or silage towers to the building of very sophisticated industrial projects.

The team which arrived at the Chernobyl station in April 1986 to conduct tests and to install equipment for the new turbogenerator 'rundown unit' represented the Ministry of Power and Electrification. In other words, it represented not the producers but those who were obliged to exploit the turbogenerators and reactors. The experts who prepared the test were not criticized in principle for conducting the test. They were criticized because their test programme 'was not properly prepared and had not received the requisite approval'.[18] This supports the conclusion that the problem was a residue of the launching period in 1983–4 and that there were no clear instructions about the reponsibilities of the design and construction side for the tasks which had been left incomplete in order to put the nuclear plant into commercial operation two months ahead of schedule. There had been a collective cover-up in 1982–4 of the fact that important safety tests had been left uncompleted.

The team of experts that prepared the report for the IAEA meeting in Vienna in 1986 must have been aware of the cover-up. That is probably why the report concentrates on the human errors which occurred in carrying out the test without offering any explanation about why the test was required and what relation it had to the similar system which is an integral part of the RBMK-1000 safety system and which should have been tested before the reactor was licensed for commercial operation. The ambiguity of the general part of the report (later published in a Soviet professional journal and presented to the government[19]) gives the false impression that the test was designed to improve safety standards with a new invention. In fact, it was the completion of the initial programme of tests. For more than two years Reactor No. 4 had operated with one important element of its emergency core cooling system faulty or absent. The 'Working Programme for Experiments on Turbogenerator No. 8 of the Chernobyl Station' seems to have been prepared as a compromise for the acceptance commission in 1983. If the reactor had developed problems and required an earlier shut down for checks and repairs, the programme would probably have been completed sooner. But Reactor No. 4 worked very well. As a result there was no option but to wait until the end of the cycle to repair the fault and remove the possibility of a meltdown in the case of a 'maximum design accident'.

However misguided, the decision to license the reactor for commercial operation at the beginning of 1984 was predictable in the Soviet context. The rewards for fulfilling the plan ahead of time were high. The danger of a serious accident seemed remote, particularly with fresh uranium fuel. The water in the reserve tanks could prevent meltdown for long enough for the diesel generators to be switched on. Unfortunately, once the reactor was operational hot fission products began to accumulate and by 1985 the first line of defence against meltdown was already inadequate. The safety tanks contain about 250 tonnes of water, while an operational reactor requires 37,000 tonnes per hour for cooling. The station managers and ministry officials must have waited anxiously to fix the fault during the scheduled shutdown for maintenance. This is the only possible logical explanation why they were so determined to carry out the test when the opportunity arose. It also explains why they did not attempt to obtain the requisite approval – it would have meant acknowledging a cover-up which had occurred more than two years previously. When permission was received to put the reactor into operation in March 1984 the General Secretary of the CPSU was Konstantin Chernenko and the country was in a state of pessimism, apathy and mismanagement. By April 1986 Mikhail Gorbachev had become General Secretary and his *perestroika* and *glasnost'* had begun to take effect.

## THE SET-UP FOR THE ACCIDENT

The technical aspects of the accident and the sequence of errors made by the operators were described in the draft Soviet report to the International Atomic Energy Agency (IAEA) and in the separate report of the International Nuclear Safety Advisory Group (INSAG). These documents claim to be preliminary reports. No definitive, final version of the accident has ever been made public. Some of the details of the preliminary reports have been repeated in Western books and anti-nuclear pamphlets. Paradoxically, Soviet people know far less about the technical details of the accident and have much less access to the relevant literature than people in the West.

One Soviet expert did begin to write a book about Chernobyl in 1987. Academician Valery Legasov had every opportunity to prepare an accurate account. As head of the scientific team in the government commission sent to Chernobyl on 26 April 1986, he was given the task of presenting the Soviet report to the IAEA post-accident meeting in Vienna. Since he was First Deputy Director of the Kurchatov Institute of Atomic Energy, where RBMK reactors were invented, designed and developed, he was clearly the most qualified man in the world to compile the documentary record of the causes and consequences of the accident. He began to dictate his memoirs about Chernobyl at the end of 1987, but only a small section (in the form of a personal introduction) has been published so far.[20] It does not add much to what is already known. For reasons that are not yet clear, Legasov committed suicide on 27 April 1988, a day after the second anniversary of the Chernobyl accident.

In the brief published section of his account, Legasov compared the historical significance of Chernobyl to the eruption of Mount Vesuvius which buried Pompei in AD 79. The comparison is justified. The hot ashes from Vesuvius completely covered Pompei; the hot debris of the Chernobyl reactor covered an area more than 5,000 km$^2$ with nearly 20 million curies of radionuclides, making human life impossible. Well beyond that area 30 million curies of debris, aerosol and gaseous radionuclides were dispersed, creating spots of serious radioactive contamination in Sweden, Germany, Northern Italy, Poland, Austria, Yugoslavia, Greece and many other countries. Like Vesuvius, the eruption of the Chernobyl radioactive volcano will be remembered for many thousands of years. The giant sarcophagus which surrounds the destroyed reactor core containing nearly 1,000 kg of plutonium must remain intact for far longer even than the Egyptian pyramids. When the current structure begins to decay it will have to be rebuilt many times (unless future robots are sophisticated enough to be placed inside to fragment and pack debris for burial elsewhere).

Legasov maintained that no single person was responsible for the accident. The operators made mistakes, but the whole programme of the experiment was poorly prepared. It had not been approved and corrected by the proper experts. The mere fact that the operators were carrying out an experiment that had not been approved by higher officials indicates that something was wrong with the chain of command. The State Committee on Safety in the Atomic Power Industry is permanently represented at the Chernobyl station. Yet the engineers and experts in that office were not informed about the programme. In part, the tragedy was the product of administrative anarchy or the attempt to keep everything secret.

A detailed description of the sequence of errors which led to the explosion is given in the Soviet report prepared for the IAEA meeting in Vienna 25–9 August 1986. An accurate, but not very full description of the technical aspects of the accident is also given. At the meeting, attended by more than 500 qualified experts from 62 countries and 21 international organizations, the report was discussed and new facts and observations were extracted from the Soviet delegation. The discussion was confidential but INSAG prepared and published a 'summary report'. It included material from the Soviet report and new information acquired from questions, clarifications and comments. It was made available to anyone interested in problems of nuclear safety. It is more critical than the Soviet report of the design flaws of the RBMK reactors which exacerbated the errors made by the operators and transformed a serious accident into a disaster.[21] Although it is an official document of the IAEA and contains highly specialized technical details, it leaves many questions unanswered.

It is obvious to people like myself, who may not be highly qualified experts on nuclear safety but who have some experience of working in Soviet research establishments and in studying more general aspects of Soviet science and technology, that the post-accident review meeting in Vienna could not give a convincing explanation of how such an improbable sequence of errors could occur at Chernobyl. The nuclear energy experts who took part in the discussion did not ask certain important questions and seemed satisfied with some inadequate answers given by the Soviet delegation. In the account that follows the technical details of the events that led to the accident are based on the original Soviet and INSAG reports and mention is made of important aspects of the tragedy which were omitted or which were presented in a misleading form.

The Soviet report was intent on minimizing problems of reactor design and placing the blame for the accident exclusively on the operators. There is no reason to doubt the correctness of the facts offered or the sequence of events. The participants in the post-accident meeting were interested in technical aspects that might be relevant to the nuclear reactors in their own countries. They were also interested in design faults of the RBMK which could be corrected or modified to make Soviet nuclear plants safer. The Chernobyl disaster had made a huge impact on the nuclear energy industry world-wide. No one would want a repetition of the disaster in other Soviet nuclear plants. But if the post-accident meeting had been a more open enquiry in which not only nuclear energy experts had participated, but also economists, planners, ecologists and experienced journalists, the picture of the accident which emerged might have contained details that explained both the sequence of errors and also the causes of the errors. Unfortunately, it is still impossible to hold such an enquiry in the Soviet Union and the vested interests of the international nuclear energy industry make it unlikely that it will be held elsewhere.

The nature of the test planned for 25–6 April 1986 has already been described and the reason why it was planned for such an inconvenient period of the reactor fuel cycle has been suggested. Foreign experts at the post-accident meeting were surprised by the determination of the Chernobyl operators to conduct the test despite the many problems that began immediately to emerge. However, they did not probe the reasons for this blind determination. The INSAG report repeats the Soviet claim that the preparations for the test were inadequate:

The test was intended as a purely electrotechnical one which was thought to have no impact on nuclear safety. As a result, the initiative and direction of the test were left to electrical experts. Little emphasis was put on nuclear safety, and proper authorizations were not obtained. The scene was thus set, but, as will be clear from what follows, the accident would not have occurred without a wide range of other interrelated problems and major violations.[22]

Although this depiction of the first crucial error is accurate, it was caused not just by an oversight on the part of the Chernobyl plant managers, but by the way in which nuclear energy is administered in the Soviet Union. All commercial nuclear power stations are strictly subordinated to the Ministry of Power and Electrification of the USSR (which also administers thermal and hydroelectric power stations). The Chernobyl station was administered by the Ukrainian branch of that ministry. It is inconceivable that a new voltage-regulating system on the turbogenerator could be tested at Chernobyl without the knowledge and authorization of both that ministry and the Ministry of Power Machine Building (which probably designed and built the turbogenerator in Unit 4 at Chernobyl). The more secretive Ministry of Medium Machine Building supervises reactor design and the fuel cycle. The State Committee on the Utilization of Atomic Energy functions within the Ministry of Medium Machine Building. The administration of the Chernobyl station would not deal directly with either the Ministry of Medium Machine Building or its design institutes, since they operate as classified organizations engaged in the production of plutonium, the reprocessing of spent fuel, the disposal of nuclear waste products, military nuclear reactors and the manufacture of nuclear weapons. The co-ordination of various aspects of the operation of nuclear reactors can only be done at ministerial level. It would have been the responsibility of the Ministry of Power and Electrification to arrange for the proper authorization of the test and the participation of other relevant organizations.

The State Committee for Safety in the Atomic Power Industry was created at the end of 1983 (possibly as a result of some accident which has remained secret). It was probably involved in supervising the final stages of launching Unit 4 from December 1983 to March 1984 and therefore issued the documents certifying the unit as safe, despite the failure of the initial test on the 'rundown unit'. This would explain why Evgenii Kulov, the chairman of the committee (who had previously worked in the Ministry of Medium Machine Building), was dismissed soon after the Chernobyl accident. According to the Soviet report, there was a 'Working Programme for Experiments on Turbogenerator No. 8 of the Chernobyl Nuclear Power Plant' but it had not been properly prepared and had not received the requisite approval.[23] Neither the author of the programme nor those whose approval should have been sought is given. It appears that a special team of engineers and physicists, some from Moscow, came to Chernobyl to do the test. It may have been this group that pressed the local operators to continue the test despite all the alarm signals.

Administrative changes that have occurred since the accident suggest that it can be explained in part by bureaucratic malfunction at a high level. In July 1986 a new Ministry of Atomic Power Stations took over all the functions related to nuclear power stations previously exercised by the Ministry of Power and Electrification and other ministries and state committees. The functions of the Committee on Safety in the Atomic Power Industry, the watchdog of the industry, have also been modified. The Soviet report is less than frank and explicit, however, about general organizational and management problems.

It has already been mentioned that similar unsuccessful tests had already been conducted on the turbogenerator in 1983 and 1984. Who conducted them? Were they done by the same operators or by the people who constructed the station and the turbogenerators? Who was in charge of the turbogenerator during the previous tests? Was the programme the same as in 1986 and did the reactor respond in the same way? It has recently been admitted that the operator crew on duty on the night of 26 April had no previous experience of conducting tests.[24] According to both Soviet and INSAG reports the test was planned for the scheduled shutdown of the reactor for routine maintenance work. The shutdown carried out by the day shift began on time, at 13.00; at 13.05 turbogenerator No. 7 was switched off.[25] Unit 4 had two identical turbogenerators but only one was to be tested. By switching off turbogenerator No. 7 reactor thermal power was reduced to 1,600 MW, half its normal power. This reduced the generation of electricity by 500 MW. Since it was a scheduled shutdown, the Ukrainian electric grid system had probably been informed well before that there would be a reduction of power by 1,000 MW during the early afternoon of Friday 25 April. It seems, however, that at 14.00 the manager of the local grid asked for a postponement of the shutdown. Why? The English translation of the Soviet report makes a strange error. According to the Russian version, 'because the grid manager demanded it, the process of taking the turbogenerator out of operation was delayed'.[26] The English translation, however, maintains that 'because of control room requirements the removal of the unit from operation was delayed'.[27] The post-accident review meeting, as reflected in the INSAG report, tried but failed to find out the reason for the delay. The INSAG report offered a third version: 'After delays initiated by the system dispatcher the further conditioning of the plant for the test recommenced late on the night of 25 April'.[28]

The test was resumed at 23.10. The day shift (which worked from 08.00 to 16.00) had been instructed in advance about the test and was familiar with the procedures. A special team of electrical engineers was on the spot to test the generator magnetic field regulator which appears to have been a large, complex piece of equipment that had been brought to the station to eliminate the problem that had been left unresolved two years before. The ten-hour delay had serious consequences. By 23.10 the day shift had long since departed. Moreover, the evening shift which operated the reactor from 16.00 was also preparing to leave. At midnight, while the experiment was under way, it was replaced by the night shift.[29] We now know that the night shift consisted of fewer experienced operators and that it had not been prepared for the test. It could not therefore respond properly to the situations that developed. A deputy chief engineer took over administration of the station. The special test team of electrical engineers had waited ten hours for permission to conduct the test. An exhausted test team, an unprepared night crew and a new manager was obviously a poor combination for a dangerous and complex experiment. These are the circumstances that set the scene for the accident.

The decision to carry out the test in the middle of the night could not have been taken lightly. It seems certain that instructions to continue with it must have come from higher authorities. Since the station was expected to be shut down, the main work that would be necessary that night would be to cool the reactor core. The night crew, therefore, could not have expected a busy night. Only one member of the evening shift who knew something about the test, Yuri Tregub, decided to stay on to help with the procedures.[30] In Legasov's posthumously published article, he maintained that the operators did not understand what the test was about:

> I have in my safe a transcript of the operators' telephone conversations on the eve of the accident. Reading the transcript makes one's flesh creep. One operator rings another and asks: 'What shall I do? In the programme there are instructions of what to do, and then a lot of things are crossed out'. His interlocuter thought for a while and then replied: 'Follow the crossed out instructions'. The level of preparation of serious documents

for something like an atomic station: someone has crossed something out, and the operator could decide whether what was crossed out was correct or not. He could take arbitrary actions. One cannot lay all the blame on the operator because someone composed the plan . . . someone signed it and someone did not approve it.[31]

Western experts were also very critical of the reactor crew. Some of them wondered why it was necessary to carry out the test during the scheduled shutdown, when it would be difficult to repeat it if the first attempt failed. (Providing for a possible repetition, which required keeping the reactor operating at low power, was one of the causes of the accident.) In principle, the test could have been done at any time but 'the crew seems not to have realized that they could have carried through a single test at any time, simply by allowing the safety system to close down the reactor'.[32] But it is possible that the reactor crew did not really want to conduct the test. At a press conference in Moscow for foreign journalists, just before the Soviet delegation departed for Vienna, Academician Legasov partially explained why the experiment had been delayed: the Kiev regional controller asked that the planned shutdown of Reactor No. 4 be delayed for some hours to accommodate an unexpected demand for electric power.[33] Both he and Professor A. A. Abegyan insisted that the delay had not contributed to the accident. Some experts, however, have suggested that the delay might have created problems even if only because a less knowledgeable control room shift had taken over.[34]

The delay needs more investigation. Why should there have been an unexpected demand for electric power on Friday afternoon? This is the least difficult question to answer, but no one even asked it. In fact, Friday 25 April seems an odd choice for a scheduled shutdown and a complex test. The following two days were the weekend; 1 and 2 May are always national holidays. Ukrainian mines, plants and factories could be expected to work very hard during the week 20–5 April to fulfil their monthly production plans. Many workers would be likely to take days off from 28 to 30 April. This would make the usual rush to fulfil the plan even more intense. Many Soviet factories produce about half their monthly targets during the last week of the month (the practice is known as *shturmovshchina*). All Soviet administrators know that the last week of the month is crucial for the monthly plans, particularly just before 1 May, when reports have to be given about fulfilment and when rewards are distributed. On Friday 25 April 1986 many workers would have been asked to work overtime. Moreover, Soviet industry was in the midst of a drive for higher productivity. Part of the campaign consisted of closing down obsolete factories and transferring the workers to more modern ones which operated two or three shifts per day. Since industry is the main consumer of electricity in the Ukraine, the high demand for electric power in the afternoon and evening of 25 April should not have come as a surprise.

Does the local grid manager have the authority to postpone a scheduled shutdown? It seems unlikely, unless his request is supported by higher officials. Besides, even if the supply of electricity fell after 13.00 when turbogenerator No. 7 was switched off, there must have been more than enough electricity left for the need of industry. The total electrical power available in the Ukraine is 53,000 MW; 500 MW could hardly have made much difference, particularly at the end of April when the hydroelectric systems of the Dnieper and other rivers are working at maximum capacity after the spring thaw (the huge water reservoirs which feed the hydroelectric power stations are full then, although by the end of the summer their level has fallen).

It seems likely, therefore, that someone more powerful than the local grid manager must have ordered the postponement. But we do not know where the order came from. Chief engineer Fomin received it and complied with it, but he had the authority to refuse to continue the test. Since the decision to conduct the test at night was irrational, something more important than research curiosity must have been behind the decision to start it at 23.10. It is clear, however, that no one expected trouble. The commander of the local fire brigade, Major Telyatnikov, was off duty until Sunday. At 01.30 he was woken by the emergency alarm telephone in his flat.

Hundreds of reports (many of them highly classified) have been written about the events inside Unit 4 of the Chernobyl station between 23.10 on Friday and 01.24 on Saturday 26 April. Each member of the test team and the operator crew prepared a report (some of them were written in hospital a few days or weeks before the authors died). Dozens of experts have reconstructed the events. Some of the reconstructions have been modelled by computer. The station's own measuring and computer equipment was destroyed in the explosion and fire – one of the design faults was the location of the control rooms in the same building as the reactor.

## THE CATASTROPHE

At 23.10 on 25 April, after a ten-hour delay, the scheduled shutdown was resumed. It would normally have been a straightforward operation.

All the neutron-absorbing rods had to be moved down and some of the residual steam had to be redirected into the condensers. The cooling of the fuel elements had to be continued because of the hot fission radionuclides they contained. The turbine would continue to rotate for some time through inertia. The mechanical and electrical power could be measured at this point with the new 'rundown unit' which would change the electromagnetic loading of the generator. However, when a reactor containing fission products in its core is shut down entirely, a process known as xenon poisoning takes place. It is a major problem in an emergency or scheduled shutdown in reactors of various types.

Xenon-135 is a normal by-product of the fission process formed from iodine-135 and tellirium-135, the main isotopes produced by the fission of uranium-235. Xenon-135 absorbs neutrons and changes into xenon-136. This process inhibits the chain reaction. The xenon-135 that is not changed into xenon-136 is unstable and has a half-life of only 9.2 hours when it transforms into caesium-135. Caesium-135 is less voracious and eventually transforms into caesium-134 which remains in the core. The transformation of xenon-135 into xenon-136 requires neutrons which are generated by the fission of uranium-235. In a working reactor some of the fission neutrons are lost to this process of transformation, although enough are left to generate heat to produce steam. But when a reactor is shut down, the transformation of xenon-135 into xenon-136 declines. Moreover, iodine-135, which has a half-life of 6.7 hours, is transformed into xenon more rapidly than xenon-135 decays. As a result, xenon begins to accumulate. Since it absorbs neutrons, it makes it difficult to restart the reactor. It takes about three days for the iodine-135 and xenon-135 to decay sufficiently for the reactor to be restarted.

What all this means is that if the first turbine test had not been successful on 25 April, it could not have been repeated. Provision was therefore made for the test to be repeated a second and possibly even a third time by keeping the reactor active at reduced power. According to the Soviet report 'the rundown of the generator with simultaneous provision of unit power requirement was to be carried out at a reactor power of 700–1000 MW (thermal)'.[35] This is slightly less than half the thermal power required for one turbogenerator to work normally (1,600 MW). It is possible that the test did not require the rotation of the generator at full speed and it was safer to switch it off steam. However, once the test had started, the reduction of electrical supply would resemble an emergency blackout and would therefore automatically trigger the diesel generators and other emergency systems to operate the cooling system. This would interfere with the test and make it impossible to repeat it. It was therefore decided to isolate the turbo-generator from its emergency safety systems. Later, of course, it was obvious that this was one of the most serious errors made by the operators and those who designed the test. If the emergency cooling system had operated, the scale of the accident would probably have been much reduced. The test programme was not presented for discussion in Vienna, but it appears that imitating a proper, full blackout and inertia test for 50 seconds was considered too dangerous since the cessation of electrical supplies to the main pumps could cause loss of coolant and result in a real accident. Instead, it was expected that half the water pumps would continue working from the general electric grid.

Reducing reactor power is a slow but routine process which takes more than an hour. For some unknown reason the operator made an error at this stage. Nuclear power plants do not always work at maximum power. Their power is regulated by moving the neutron-absorbing control rods up and down. There are 211 control rods modifying the power output in a RBMK-1000 reactor. According to the Soviet report, the operator did not reset the parameters of the automatic control system properly. As a result, the control rods moved down further than expected and the power output of the reactor fell to below 30 MW (thermal), almost to complete shutdown level. At this point the turbine was rotating slowly and the electrical output was only about 10 MW, insufficient to support the cooling system pumps, each of which needs 5 MW. When this happened the test should have been aborted, the reactor should have been shut down completely and an immediate switch should have been made either to the emergency diesel generators or to the general electrical grid so that the cooling system would continue operating. The Soviet delegation insisted at the Vienna meeting that the decision to continue the test violated both standard operating procedures and the written test programme. But neither the standard operating procedures nor the test plan were presented for the scrutiny of foreign experts. It is possible that the test programme did not cover this contingency or that it had never been properly explained to the night crew. According to the Soviet delegation, the reason why the test was continued was that the test crew realized that if it was not done then, they might have to wait another year for a scheduled shutdown of the reactor before they could test whether their modified equipment could sustain the voltage of a decelerating turbogenerator.[36]

It is difficult to understand why the test could not have been conducted at the beginning of the new cycle rather than at the end of the old. During the shutdown a significant part of the fuel elements, 75 per cent of which dated from the original loading, would be replaced.[37] The test crew should have known that xenon poisoning was accelerated in a reactor working at reduced power. Whatever the reason, the crew decided to raise the reactor power and to accelerate the turbine so that they could continue the test. At 01.00 exactly the operator succeeded in raising the power to 200 MW (thermal). It could not be raised further because xenon-135 was absorbing the neutrons and reducing the reactor's 'reactivity'. Thermal power of 200 MW was insufficient for the experiment. To raise it still higher, the crew decided to raise the control rods so that more neutrons would be released to overcome the xenon inhibition. To do this they had to use manual controls to override the automatic system. They also prepared for the test by increasing the circulation of cooling water through the reactor core, switching on an additional main pump at 01.07 which was supplied with electricity from the general grid. The total coolant flow through the reactor core rose to 56,000–58,000 tonnes per hour. This, too, violated the standard operating procedures. The amount of steam formed declined, causing a consequent fall in steam pressure and changes in other parameters of the reactor. At this point the automatic system should have shut the reactor down completely. But to avoid this happening, the staff had blocked the emergency signals relating to these parameters.[38] This is incomprehensible. At a press conference in Vienna, Legasov pointed out that the permission of the chief engineer of the station or his deputy had not been sought, despite the requirements of the station regulations.

When the steam pressure fell, the rotation speed of the turbogenerator was reduced. The proper conditions for the test no longer existed. Legasov suggested later that the operators were still determined to carry on with the test, considering it a 'matter of honour'.[39] This is not very convincing. It is far more likely that whoever was in charge pressed the operators to continue. The person in charge was later identified as the deputy chief engineer of the station, Anatoly Dyatlov. In the first Chernobyl trial in July–August 1987 he was sentenced to prison for ten years.[40]

The reactivity of the reactor began to decline again. Normal Soviet safety procedures forbid the operation of a reactor below the level of 700 MW (thermal) because of thermal-hydraulic instability. The operators also infringed safety procedures by removing more control rods from the reactor core than the regulations allow in an effort to compensate for the 'negative reactivity' produced by the increased flow of coolant. According to Legasov, 'the station regulations require that operators should never, in any circumstances, operate with less than the equivalent of 15 control rods of reactivity up their sleeves'.[41] At this stage of the test, the reserve reactivity could have been no more than the equivalent of six to eight rods. At 01.22.30 'the operator saw from a printout of the fast reactivity evaluation program that the available excess reactivity had reached a level requiring immediate shutdown of the reactor'.[42] Nevertheless, the experiment began.

Here again, it is difficult to understand the decision even from the point of view of the electrical engineers who were dealing with the turbogenerator. The reactor power was at a level of about 12 per cent of the power needed for the maximum speed of turbogenerator rotation. The rotation had already been slowed down by the drop in steam pressure. There was no point in proceeding with a test which, apart from being dangerous, would now be useless. But at 01.23.04 the emergency regulating valves of turbogenerator No. 8 were shut, disconnecting the turbine from steam. According to the test programme, four of the pumps were to be driven by the decelerating turbogenerator during the test and it was planned that they would remain in use after the completion of the first test. In fact, it is difficult to see how this would be possible. Each pump of the RBMK-1000 reactor needs 5.5 MW electric power (with pump shaft power 4.3 MW).[43] Four pumps therefore need more than 20 MW. The pumps in other circulation systems probably need a further 10 MW. The total electrical output of the turbine at that moment was only about 60 MW of electricity. The test was originally planned for the turbogenerator working at half its power of 500 MW and able to keep the pumps working for 50 seconds. With the turbogenerator working at only 12 per cent of its power, the new modifier of the electromagnetic loading of the turbogenerator could not be tested properly. The experiment would be too short and too dangerous. Even if the test team did not know the reactor, the station's own operators must have realized that they could not imitate a blackout at this very low energy output.

Once the test had begun the turbogenerator began to run down. Apparently its electrical output also began to decline sharply. When the steam flow to the turbine ceased at this very unstable moment (with the feedwater circulation also declining) steam voids rapidly formed in a large part of the core.[44] The Soviet report indicates that 'the reactor power began to rise slowly'.[45] Steam voids are very poor coolants and the fuel elements began to overheat. A positive void coefficient (more steam equals more power, more heat and higher steam pressure) began to show itself with accelerating speed. The total flow of water through the reactor continued to decline because four of the eight circulation pumps were working off the running-down turbogenerator.[46] When the power began to rise the operators finally realized that they were dealing with a real emergency. The shift foreman (later identified as engineer Leonid Toptunov) pressed the special panic button for an immediate emergency shutdown of the reactor at 01.23.40, 36 seconds after the beginning of the test. But it was too late. Almost all the neutron-absorbing control rods were in the upper part of the core. The panic button should have sent them back into the core in order to stop the chain fission process. However, even in an emergency, the rods only reduce the power by 5 per cent per second. This was too slow to prevent disaster (in modern PWRs only 1 second is required for this operation). The power continued to rise dramatically. Within 3 seconds it rose above 530 MW. It has been calculated that it must have reached 100 times the normal full power of the reactor within four seconds of 01.23.40. The rods moved down but after a few seconds a number of shocks were felt. The operator saw that they had halted half way. He cut the current to the sleeves of the servo-drives so that they would fall into the core under their own weight.[47] But they did not move. The sharp increase of steam pressure had destroyed the fuel channels (in any case, the fuel channels were probably too long). If the neutron moderator had been heavy or light water, the rods would have reached the bottom, but it was solid graphite and the destruction of the fuel channels blocked the passage for the control rods. As the nuclear chain reaction continued without being inhibited or cooled, the temperature of the core and the steam pressure inside it continued inevitably to rise and the destruction also continued.

A computer model of the accident made later showed that the overheating caused by the runaway fission reaction had destroyed the fuel, causing a 'rapid and abrupt increase of steam pressure in the fuel channels, destruction of the fuel channels'.[48] Before this had happened the pressure in the core had risen to the point where an abrupt reduction of water supply from the main circulation pump occurred as the check valves closed. The rupture of the fuel channels partially restored the flow of water from the main circulation pumps. However, at this stage the water was no longer being pumped into intact channels but into the reactor space filled with pieces of overheated fuel. This produced the first powerful steam explosion. At 01.24, only 20 seconds after the panic button had been pressed, there was a steam explosion which damaged the roof of the reactor hall and ejected fragments of material. The reactor space had been designed to withstand a possible rupture of one or two of the 1,600 fuel channels. The increased pressure lifted the upper plate which weighed 1,000 tonnes.[49] The shifted plate ruptured further fuel channels, lifted the control rods and sheared off the horizontal pipes. A second, more powerful explosion occurred about two or three seconds after the first.

The second explosion was caused by the hydrogen which had been produced either by the overheated steam–zirconium reaction or by the reaction of red-hot graphite with steam that produce hydrogen and oxygen. According to observers outside Unit 4, burning lumps of material and sparks shot into the air above the reactor. Some of them fell onto the roof of the machine hall and started a fire.[50] About 25 per cent of the red-hot graphite blocks and overheated material from the fuel channels was ejected. The inventory of the system was blown into the reactor core, reactor hall and the space below the core. Parts of the graphite blocks and fuel channels were blown out of the reactor building. The tanks containing the water for emergency cooling broke. As a result of the damage to the building an airflow through the core was established by the high temperature of the core.[51] The air ignited the hot graphite and started a graphite fire.

This was the worst ever disaster in the history of nuclear reactors. But the two explosions which blew millions of curies of radioactive products into the environment and the graphite fire were only the beginning of the catastrophe. Worst-case scenarios of reactor accidents envisage overheating and explosions or meltdowns caused by loss of coolant because of the presence in the fuel elements of the fission products which remain in the reactor even after the chain fission reaction of uranium-235 has been stopped. The thermal power of these residual radionuclides can reach as much as 4 per cent of the total working reactor power at the end of the fuel cycle. But it drops rapidly after shutdown. In a PWR the loss of coolant means that there is also a loss of neutron moderator. As a result, a chain or criticality reaction is impossible. But the accident in the Chernobyl RBMK-1000 was worse than any possible PWR accident. All the neutron-absorbing rods were outside the core, the coolant was lost but the graphite moderator remained inside the destroyed core. This meant that the chain reaction of nuclear fission could continue in some parts and the neutrons would add to the heat produced by the accumulated radionuclides and contribute to the meltdown.

The first vital step was to extinguish the fires on the roof and elsewhere. Next, the graphite fire and the remaining pockets of chain fission reaction had to be stopped. It had previously been considered that a meltdown was more likely when coolant was lost in a PWR than in a RBMK – it was thought that the large size of the RBMK core made overheating of the residual radionuclides less likely. In the event, during the Chernobyl accident, heat was generated in the core not only by the radionuclides but by the continuing fission of uranium-235. At the Vienna meeting it was postulated that the chain reaction stopped after the second explosion because the core had been destroyed.[52] But a lot of fuel mixed with graphite remained within the core and the chain reaction might have continued in those parts. This was the initial conclusion of physicists who arrived at the site and tried to measure the neutron radiation. Meltdown (molten core debris burning through the foundations of the reactor building) was considered probable for a number of days after the accident. Desperate preventive measures were taken, which are described in the next chapter. Because at the time of the accident the reactor core contained 1,659 fuel assemblies separated by 1,700 tonnes of solid graphite, it was not expected that the meltdown would create a single molten mass. Each fuel assembly could melt separately. Fresh fuel assemblies (with a higher concentration of uranium-235) were more prone to a continuing chain reaction, whereas the older channels could overheat because of their high concentration of fission radionuclides.

The first two explosions were great disasters, but the continuing emission for many days of fresh radionuclides represented an even graver danger to the population and to the environment. A meltdown of the core would lead to unimaginable damage. If it could not be prevented half of the Ukraine and Byelorussia would have to be evacuated. The land would be contaminated for many years. The Dnieper and other rivers in the area would be affected for decades. The three other reactors on the Chernobyl site (which were still working and producing electricity) would be destroyed, causing untold further damage. There were about 3,000 kg of accumulated plutonium and 700,000 kg of uranium in the fuel elements of the four reactors in Chernobyl and vast amounts of other radionuclides. Everyone who was involved in the emergency operations around Chernobyl recognized the gravity of the situation but no one knew how to prevent the catastrophe of a meltdown.

## CONCLUSION

For several months after the Chernobyl accident the Soviet nuclear establishment was generally successful in promoting a cover-up story about the test of an entirely new safety device. The accident thus appeared to be the result of a concern for safety which, because of the negligence and incompetence of local operators and administrators, had terrible consequences. Western experts stressed that, in addition to the human errors which occurred during the test, certain design flaws made the accident possible.

The main defects in the design were thought to be the absence of a containment vessel (which would have prevented the release of radionuclides into the environment in the case of a meltdown) and the existence of a 'positive void coefficient' which meant that the increase in the steam pressure formed during overheating could lead to further overheating and to larger steam voids, which in turn lead to a drop in the cooling water levels in the fuel channels. The latter flaw is found in reactors in which the steam for the turbogenerators is produced directly inside the reactor core. American 'boiling water reactors' (BWR) use the same method, but the water also serves as the moderator.

The formation of steam is a very effective additional way to remove heat and BWRs were considered economical and simple. However, the formation of steam bubbles (or voids) was recognized to be a danger. They create instability and unpredictable local effects on reactivity. In BWRs the steam voids not only reduce the cooling. They also reduce the transformation of fast neutrons into slow neutrons and inhibit the chain reaction. In the Soviet RBMK model, however, the combination of a graphite moderator and the formation of steam bubbles or voids is much more dangerous. The cooling is reduced but the chain reaction is accelerated. A second difference between BWRs and the RBMK is the control of boiling. In both models the primary coolant supplies steam directly to the turbine. But in the BWR system the coolant circulates through a comparatively compact reactor core. In the RBMK it circulates through nearly 1,700 individual pressure tubes which makes control over the proper regime much more difficult.

There is no doubt that both these defects of the RBMK reactor contributed to the scale of the disaster. Soviet officials did not deny them but they insisted that the RBMK design has many extra safety systems and normally operates under strict regulations. This makes it generally safer and more reliable than reactors with a single core and a single pressure vessel like the PWR and the BWR. It is obvious, however, from an analysis of the safety test and other major features of the Chernobyl RBMK reactor that the main liability of the system was (and still is) the absence of protection from station blackout – in other words, the loss of on-site electrical power. The detailed description of the electrical system of the RBMK-1000 given in Annex 2 of the Soviet report does not describe how off-site power can be used in an emergency; moreover, the general scheme of the electrical system which was attached to the report was absolutely illegible.[53] Of course, Chernobyl and other Soviet nuclear power stations must be able to use electricity from the general grid in the case of an emergency. But the speed with which the switch can be done has not been described and it seems that the ability of the running-down turbogenerator to provide emergency power supplies for at least 50 seconds represents the main safety feature of the RBMK system. These 50 seconds of power are crucial not only to bridge the time needed to start the diesel generators and to support the circulation of cooling water but also to effect the shutdown of the reactor itself. The large size of the reactor core, the large number of control rods and the length of time necessary to reinsert them into the core (20 seconds) make the availability of inertia, rundown electricity essential. The rods require considerable force to be reinserted because they move down against the strong upward circulation of the cooling water. As a result, electric batteries are insufficient as a source of energy; proper power is required.

This problem had been solved in the RBMK blueprint, and perhaps even in the prototypes. But it does not appear to have been solved in the real RBMK-1000 reactors which have been built. Reactor No. 4 at Chernobyl was probably not the only RBMK with this fault in its safety system. It is likely that all the other RBMK-1000 reactors in the Soviet Union, which provide nearly 60 per cent of nuclear-generated electricity in the country, have the same fault. The fault was covered up and the cover-up was not the responsibility of the operators. In 1986 and the first part of 1987 the cover-up was not clear to many Soviet government officials outside the nuclear establishment. Many statements were made maintaining that the construction of RBMK reactors had not been affected by the Chernobyl accident. Reactors No. 5 and 6 at Chernobyl itself were expected to be completed once the area had been deactivated. But the dismissal by the Politburo of four very senior officials in July 1986 indicated that the fate of the RBMK-1000 reactor was in doubt. No one at that time publicly blamed the RBMK reactor for the accident. An order was given that existing RBMK reactors should be operated with all their control rods partly inserted into the core. This reduced their power but it also reduced the time required for an emergency shutdown. Some unspecified automatic systems were also added to the reactors.

The main fault of the RBMK could not remain hidden for long. The competition within the USSR between two reactor systems, the RBMK and the VVER (PWR), would sooner or later expose the basic lack of safety of the RBMK reactor. Classified technical enquiries and investigations were undertaken in 1987 and 1988. The inevitable decision was finally made in 1988 to cancel the programme of constructing new RBMK reactors and to freeze those that were already under construction. The RBMK reactor programme was dead.

Given all the problems, the Chernobyl accident should neither have been unexpected nor improbable. The only surprising thing is that a major accident did not occur sooner. If the Kursk accident in 1980 had not been covered up and if there had been an open enquiry, the RBMK programme would probably have been cancelled much sooner, long before the tragic accident at Chernobyl. The Chernobyl catastrophe was born of secrecy and the habit of covering up unpleasant news.

The picture of the accident given in this chapter has, to a large extent, been based on my interpretation of the official Soviet report for the IAEA and of additional material which I have extracted from Soviet experts and the Soviet press. It has been evident that most Soviet and foreign experts have tried their best to blame the reactor operators for the accident. It is only fair to add, as a postscript to this chapter, the explanations of what happened and who was to blame given by the operators who survived the accident.

### POSTSCRIPT: THE REACTOR OPERATORS' VIEW

The trial of some officials and engineers of the Chernobyl power station for 'criminal negligence' held in Chernobyl town in July–August 1987 was designed specifically to find them responsible for the mistakes that had occurred, not the people who had designed and licensed a reactor with so many faults. Many operators and experts were called as witnesses. The trial did not add much to our knowledge of the accident. It was held in camera (except for the opening and the final days) and neither Soviet nor foreign journalists were able to find out much about the substance of the two-week court proceedings for some time afterwards. But at the end of 1988 Yuri Shcherbak, a Ukrainian writer, interviewed some of the operators and engineers who had been present at the trial and who had resumed work at the repaired and deactivated Units 1, 2 and 3. They expressed strong reservations about the official attempt to blame the accident on the incompetence of the operators.

Shcherbak named the two operators who made fatal mistakes in carrying out the tests: Aleksandr Akimov, the chief of the night shift in Unit 4 and Leonid Toptunov, the operator responsible for the movements of the control rods and the operational regime of the reactor. In

Legasov's report in Vienna in August 1986 they were described as extremely careless and incompetent. It was Toptunov who first reduced the power of the reactor too much and then pressed the panic button to shut down the reactor too late. Both of them were in the block for several hours after the accident and both participated fully in the rescue operations. They both died two weeks later from acute radiation sickness. They had been exposed to the highest doses of radiation and were considered hopeless cases right from the beginning. They had been given bone marrow transplants in an final attempt to save their lives.

Shcherbak's interviews confirmed that the night crew had not been prepared to carry out the experiment. The task and procedures had only been explained to the day and evening shifts. Igor Kazachkov, Yuri Tregub and A. G. Uskov were the operators in the earlier shifts who were initially responsible for the procedures which Toptunov and Akimov then had to carry out because of the delay. In trying to establish whom they held responsible for the errors, Shcherbak asked Kazachkov for his opinion about what had happened:

> We didn't have any foolproof safeguards against that particular thing happening . . . And we still don't have. There are lots of safeguards, but nothing that controls the number of rods. I'll say this: we have often had less than the required number of rods and nothing has happened. No explosion, everything proceeded normally.
>
> The chaps who were there that night said that Lenya Toptunov couldn't cope with shifting from automatic controls and let the power fall. There are so many instruments there, that he could have failed to see what was happening . . . the more so because he was probably nervous. It was the first time this situation had occurred, that the power had to be reduced. After all, he had only worked as senior engineer of the reactor control for four months and in that time the power of the reactor had never been reduced.
>
> I sometimes think now about what we need to prevent it happening again. I'm not talking about technology . . . but about people. There should not just be highly qualified people at the control panels, but freer people. Free from fear. People who aren't afraid of the sword constantly hanging over their heads. You know . . . what does it mean to be fired from work at Pripyat? That's it, the end. That's awful, isn't it . . . If Sasha Akimov had been free, then he would have been able to take the correct decisions. The operator of an AES must be like a pilot. Or more than a pilot or cosmonaut. If a cosmonaut dies, it's a tragedy, but it doesn't have terrible consequences like here . . . [54]

Tregub was less certain that the operators were to blame. He told Shcherbak:

If one starts from the instructions that existed before the accident, everything the personnel did was correct. They are not to blame . . . If they had been told that it was particularly dangerous, it would be a different matter.

Lenya Toptunov was a young fellow. I am sorry for him. I think that if I had been in his place it would simply not have happened . . . Toptunov had only worked independently as a senior engineer for 2 to 3 months.[55]

Uskov was even more certain that the blame lay not with the operators, but higher up. He told Shcherbak:

I never would have thought it would be so difficult to answer a seemingly simple question: 'If you had been in the place of the engineers at the controls of panel 4 on the night of 26 April 1986, would you have infringed the regulations to conduct that experiment?' If I'm completely honest, then I have to reply that I may have infringed them. If I had been working at the control panels, I might perhaps have protested to the chief engineer, *but I would not have had enough spirit to refuse categorically to carry out his command.*

Why? Let me try to explain . . . Firstly, we often don't see the need to observe our laws to the letter because these laws are broken all around us before our eyes – and quite often! . . . Can it really be that the Government Commission that accepted block 4 as ready for operation did not know that it was accepting it incomplete? Of course they knew . . . If you look more deeply, then the accident started not at 1.23 on 26 April 1986, but in December 1983, when the director of the AES, Bryukhanov, put his signature on the document of the Government Commission . . . without seeing the necessity of insisting that the run-down unit of the turbogenerator was tested . . . And our Moscow comrades needed that run-down unit even less. They said 'The fourth block has been put into operation and will go into the report for this year. That's good'. . .

There would have been a completely different picture if they had conducted that ill-fated experiment then . . . But the main reason why the personnel on that night infringed the regulations (regulations are also law!) was because there was no clear and categorical instruction about not working with an operating store of reactivity of fewer than 15 rods. The chaps couldn't even imagine that they were in a regime of nuclear danger.

Nowhere has a line of this been mentioned. And already in the classrooms of their institutions they had beaten into their heads: a reactor cannot explode. It was only after the accident that the operating store was set at 30 (!) rods and no less. And it was only in October 1986 that the regulations were changed to include the grim warning: 'When there are fewer than 30 rods the reactor goes into a situation of nuclear danger'.[56]

The fatal mistake of the night crew was to try to raise the power of the reactor after the young inexperienced operator, Toptunov, had reduced the reactor's reactivity to too low a level by mistake. The order to raise the power was given by the deputy chief engineer, Anatoly Dyatlov, an experienced and knowledgeable physicist. At the trial Dyatlov, who was in overall charge of the experiment, insisted that he did not give this erroneous order and that he did not know about the temporary loss of power caused by Toptunov's error. He claimed that he had left the room at this particular moment to go to the toilet. When he returned, the operators were already raising the power. With Akimov and Toptunov in their graves, the court never had the chance of proving who was right and who was wrong.

# 2

# Radioactive Volcano

## INTRODUCTION

THE ten days from 26 April to 6 May 1986 have become known in Soviet literature as the 'Battle of Chernobyl'. Despite the many accounts that have been published, some important details remain obscure. There were no direct reports from Chernobyl in those first ten days. The news blackout was partially lifted on 6 May when Soviet journalists were allowed to send 'heroic' reports from Chernobyl, including some details of the 'great battle' which, it was claimed, had already been won. However, no technical details were given. At this stage the people who were directly or indirectly responsible for the accident controlled the emergency measures. They had nothing to gain and a great deal to lose from *glasnost'*.

Attempts to cover up inconvenient information and a tendency to shift responsibility were immediately apparent. They became even stronger later, particularly during and after the trial in July 1987 of the director of the Chernobyl station and his deputies and engineering team. The proceedings of the trial were kept secret not because classified technical information was divulged, but because they were too embarrassing. It was feared that public trust in nuclear energy would be undermined. Both the Soviet government and the nuclear industry itself wanted to preserve the momentum of the nuclear energy programme. It was not only a crucial element of the Soviet Five-Year Plan and of the long-term plan to the year 2000, it was also the cornerstone of plans to integrate the economies of the Soviet Union and the countries of Eastern Europe. The draft of the Five-Year Plan had been approved by the XXVIIth Party Congress in February. It was due to become law during the Supreme Soviet session in June 1986. The Chernobyl accident had serious repercussions for the Plan, but the government was unwilling to reconsider it at such short notice. No changes were made to the nuclear energy programme.

From 1987 to 1989, when the real debate about the future of nuclear energy in the Soviet Union began to take shape, many new details about the accident became known. Many of them contradicted the 'heroic' reports published in 1986, including the official Soviet 'Working Document', prepared for the IAEA post-accident review meeting in Vienna 25–9 August 1986. The tremendous human, ecological, agricultural and economic costs of the accident became known and public resistance to the construction of new nuclear stations began to mount.

The future of nuclear energy does not depend only on the ability of scientists and engineers to design and build safer reactors, it also depends on their ability, and that of the emergency services, to deal efficiently with accidents and to minimize their hazards and consequences. This means that a competent analysis of the emergency measures taken after the Chernobyl accident is no less important than establishing the causes of the accident. The emergency measures include the initial response to the accident in the first ten days when officials were acting under the protection of the news blackout. They also include the attempts to decontaminate the area, to construct a 'sarcophagus' around the reactor in order to isolate it from the environment, to establish hydrological isolation of the plant site and to set up effective dosimetric control of food.

## FIGHTING THE FIRE

The fact that the accident took place at night had one obvious advantage: there were few people in the immediate vicinity. The first concentrated cloud of radioactive debris, aerosol and gases which formed over the reactor passed over parts of the town of Pripyat, Yanov station and some villages. But most people were asleep indoors, protected from the radiation to some extent by the walls of their houses. Moreover, the night shift in the station was smaller than the day shifts. During the day shifts, for example, more than 2,000 workers normally worked on the construction sites at Units 5 and 6 at Chernobyl. There were far fewer people around at one o'clock in the morning, however. According to the Soviet official report for the IAEA, there were 176 duty operational staff at the plant at the time of the accident and 268 builders working at the construction site nearby.[1]

The runaway chain reaction which destroyed the core of Unit 4 was localized in the upper part of the reactor core. A second, more powerful hydrogen gas explosion shot burning lumps of graphite and reactor fuel into the air above the reactor. Some of these lumps landed on the roof of the machine hall and started a number of fires. The roofs of the reactor building and machine-turbine hall (which served Units 3 and 4) were made of bitumen, an inflammable material. The explosion caused more than 30 fires in different parts of the plant in addition to the graphite fire inside the reactor crater. These fires were the first emergency.

Valerii Khodomchuk was on duty in the reactor hall just over the reactor plate. He was the only immediate victim of the blast. A second operator, Vladimir Shashenka, was close to the reactor hall. He was still alive when he was found by the firemen but died about an hour later in the local hospital. The fire-alarm went off in the local fire station about one minute after the second explosion. The fire service in the area consisted of several crews and stations. Station No. 2, with several duty crews commanded by Lieutenant Vladimir Pravik, was responsible for the Chernobyl plant. The night crew, in three fire-engines, was the first to arrive at the scene of the accident. Lieutenant Pravik realized immediately that his crew was too small to deal with the fire. He sent a coded emergency radio signal to mobilize the fire brigades in Pripyat, Chernobyl town and the whole Kiev region.

The roof of Reactor No. 4 had collapsed into the reactor hall. Part of Pravik's team climbed into the machine hall to fight the fire there. The Pripyat fire brigade arrived a few minutes later and tackled the fires in the reactor building. Many of the firemen who died were members of this crew. Pravik left his crew in the machine hall and joined the Pripyat team in the reactor. He was among the earliest victims. Major Leonid Telyatnikov, the commander of Station No. 2, was on holiday, but he lived in Pripyat and had received the alarm signal by telephone. He arrived at the reactor site about 10 minutes after the firemen had begun their battle and took overall command. He climbed onto the roof of Reactor No. 3. Although there were at least five fires on the roof, the reactor was still operating. The priorities of the firemen were clear – they had to extinguish the fires on the roof of the undamaged reactor and in the machine hall. They used mainly water to do this. Despite their efforts, they could not prevent the fire from spreading before the Kiev fire brigade arrived to replace them.

The historic fight against the fire has been described in great detail (in some cases a minute by minute timetable is given[2]). By 06.35 37 fire crews consisting of 186 firemen and 81 engines had managed to put out all the fires with the exception of the graphite fire inside the reactor crater.[3] The first reports of the fight against the fire were published in

Soviet newspapers ten days later. By then almost all the local firemen had been admitted to the Moscow radiological hospital. Major Telyatnikov was interviewed in his special sterile cubicle in this hospital. Readers were, of course, proud that the firemen had been ready to make such great sacrifices to prevent new tragedies (which would have occurred, for example, if the burning roof of Unit 3 had collapsed inside the reactor hall while the reactor was still operating – it had only been shut down at 05.00). But, at the same time, the description of the conditions in which they had worked, surrounded on all sides by the 'molten lava of the blazing bitumen',[4] raised a number of questions. Why, most people asked, were the roofs of the reactors made of an easily inflammable material that was banned from use in industrial buildings?

A second question that arose later concerned the inadequate equipment used by the firemen. Their clothing did not protect them from radioactive particles. Firemen in nuclear power stations in other countries have special protective clothing and respirators. Soviet firemen did not have even the simplest type of respirator. As a result, they suffered from inhalation of radioactive and hot debris and from radioactive skin burns. It was also apparent that there had never been a fire-drill in Chernobyl. The instructions for fighting fires at nuclear power stations were practically identical to those for fighting other industrial fires. No account was taken of the possibility of radiation. At the IAEA meeting in August 1986, the Soviet authorities were advised to provide systems for 'fire-fighting with specific provisions for nuclear safety', to use less inflammable construction materials and to supply firemen with clothing to protect them not only from high temperatures but from radioactive contamination.[5]

It also became clear that the local fire service did not have dosimetric equipment to check the radiation levels. Moreover, the fire brigades that came from further afield were totally ignorant about the danger of radiation and they paid for this with their lives. Those who worked on the roof of the machine hall and Unit No. 3 suffered later from acute radiation sickness but most of them, including Major Telyatnikov, survived. But the firemen who tackled the fire in Reactor No. 4 died. They had not realized that the graphite in the reactor core was burning nor had they known that the core was exposed. They tried to quench the fire by pumping water into the crater. This was both useless and dangerous since the temperature inside the crater was high enough to split the water into oxygen and hydrogen. Grigorii Khmel, the driver of one of the fire-engines, later described what happened:

We arrived there at 10 or 15 minutes to two in the morning . . . We saw graphite scattered about. Misha asked: 'What is graphite?' I kicked it away. But one of the fighters on the other truck picked it up. 'It's hot', he said. The pieces of graphite were of different sizes, some big, some small enough to pick up . . .

We didn't know much about radiation. Even those who worked there had no idea. There was no water left in the trucks. Misha filled the cistern and we aimed the water at the top. Then those boys who died went up to the roof – Vashchik Kolya and others, and Volodya Pravik . . . They went up the ladder . . . and I never saw them again.[6]

By 05.00 the fire had been localized to the area of Reactor No. 4. The deputy chief of the Kiev fire service, J. Kozura, reported that the fire emergency was over.[7] Two hours later the collapsed roof had burnt out and the visible fire in Reactor No. 4 had been extinguished. Major Telyatnikov and his men had reported earlier that the inside of the crater was red hot, but nobody knew that this was caused by the exposure of the reactor core and a graphite fire. A report was sent to Moscow that the fire had been extinguished. It probably seemed that the worst emergency was over. In fact, it was only beginning.

Reactor No. 3 continued working despite a severe increase in radio-activity caused by the penetration of radionuclides through the ventilation system. The chief of the night shift, Yuri Bagdasarov, wanted to shut down the reactor immediately, but chief engineer Fomin would not allow this. The operators were given respirators and potassium iodide tablets and told to continue working. At 05.00, however, Bagdasarov made his own decision to stop the reactor, leaving only those operators there who had to work the emergency cooling systems.

However, the most serious danger had been avoided by the firemen who extinguished about 40 fires on the roof of the turbine hall building (which served Reactor No. 3 as well) and by the workers inside the turbine hall itself. The oil system of the turbine was damaged by falling masonry. Red hot graphite and pieces of reactor core fell through the holes in the roof and started a fire in the hall. People working in the turbine hall urgently removed the reserve oil from the storage facilities and replaced it with water. They prevented an explosion of the hydrogen in the generator by replacing it with nitrogen. If this had not been done, the fire in the machine hall would certainly have spread to the other three reactor buildings which were connected to the turbine hall of Unit 4 by many communication systems. The whole power station with all four reactors would have gone up in flames. It took the people working in the turbine hall several hours to fight the fire. At about

05.00, when the danger was over, the whole shift of eight men was taken to hospital. Four of them died later.

If the roofs of the reactors and other buildings had not been constructed of bitumen the fires would probably have been far less severe. The official documents did not, however, list this as a mistake or a violation of industrial safety precautions. There was an indirect suggestion of this in a play by V. Gubarev based on the events of the accident. One of the characters, the procurator, interrogates the man who had signed the fire-safety certificate in 1983 when the reactor was in the process of being commissioned for commercial use. The procurator tells him that bitumen has been banned in industrial buildings for the past 12 years. In the play the man replies: 'I objected . . . I informed my ministry . . . but the decision was made at a higher level'. And the character who plays the director of the nuclear power station also admits that he knew the regulations and explains that there was a lot of bitumen in storage and the station had to be completed three months ahead of schedule.[8]

In the aftermath of the accident questions were asked by the public about the roofs of other reactors and industrial sites. Official replies to these questions have never been given.

## THE NATIONAL EMERGENCY

It is now known that the explosion which destroyed the reactor core in the early hours of 26 April 1986 blew nearly 20 million curies of radioactive materials and several million curies of the inert radioactive gases, xenon-133 and krypton-85, into the atmosphere.[9] The gases and aerosol formed a plume about 2 km high which began to move north and north-west. Nearly 10 million curies of radioactive debris in the form of large particles and lumps of destroyed core (graphite, fuel elements, etc.) fell within a 2–3 km radius of Reactor No. 4. Soviet publications have never, however, given even approximate figures of the level of radioactivity on the site close to the fire. The level was well in excess of the scales on the available dosimetric equipment. During the trial of Bryukhanov, the director of the station, he was accused of failing to organize radiation control. The station lacked the equipment which would have made this possible. Although the reports of the trial do not disclose the actual level of radiation, Bryukhanov, it was alleged, 'deliberately reduced the levels of radioactivity by several orders of magnitude' when he reported the situation to his superiors.[10]

This attempt to lay the blame for the initial cover-up on the local administrators (who, it is implied, thereby made it difficult for Moscow officials to assess the disaster immediately) is misleading. There is an extensive network of radiation monitoring stations in the Soviet Union. They work around the clock, measuring radioactivity in the air at different levels. Normally situated in very tall meteorological towers (the one I knew in Obninsk is 300 m high), they are supervised by the State Committee on Hydrometeorology and Environmental Control. They have a dual function: to measure radioactivity in the air (partly to monitor the nuclear test ban treaty) and to co-ordinate the release of radioactive gases from nuclear power stations. All nuclear power stations periodically discharge some gaseous radionuclides (iodine-131, xenon-133, krypton-85 and others) into the air. That is why they are equipped with high chimneys. Iodine, which is easily absorbed and hazardous, is filtered out first. But inert gases like xenon and krypton cannot be absorbed and they are short-lived. They are commonly accumulated within the station and released into the air when the meteorological conditions ensure that they will move in a safe direction (towards the sea or towards deserted, uninhabited parts of the country). In the case of Chernobyl, the wind must be blowing in a westerly or easterly direction for it to be safe to release the gases (Kiev is situated south of Chernobyl and Pripyat, Gomel and Minsk are to the north).

Because of its dual function the radiation monitoring service is partly under military control. As a result, its activities are classified information and no information has been given about how it reacted to the Chernobyl accident. It provided the maps which were included in the Soviet report for the IAEA in Vienna in August 1986 showing the distribution of radioactive plumes inside the Soviet Union between 26 April and 5 May. They are rather crude and indicate the absence of computer analyses or projections. But it was this service and the special military radiological service which took over the task of monitoring radiation levels around the Chernobyl station (using specially equipped planes and helicopters) after 26 April.

During the trial of station officials in July 1987 it was reported that:

> Bryukhanov and the former shift foreman, Boris Rogozhkin, were responsible for not taking the measures envisaged in the evacuation plan (all nuclear power stations have such plans for accidents of various magnitudes). Moreover, almost the entire shift which came to work at eight o'clock in the morning remained unnecessarily at the station.
>
> The population of Pripyat was not warned about the accident, nor were the civil defence headquarters informed. Since the civil defence staff had

no information about the situation, they took no measures. As a result, the usual rhythm of life on a Saturday proceeded . . . The evacuation began only 36 hours later and was conducted according to a newly worked-out plan.[11]

This description is not entirely accurate and it is not fair to blame Bryukhanov and Rogozhkin alone. Some important details about the initial reactions of the officials only became known in 1989, when Grigory Medvedev's 'Chernobyl Notebook', written in 1986, was published.[12] Medvedev was a nuclear power station inspector and he participated in the government commission as an adviser.

According to Medvedev, the fatal test programme was approved by the chief engineer, N. M. Fomin. The night shift supervisor, A. Akimov, sent two young probationary operators, Kudryavtsev and Proskuriakov, to the reactor hall to find out what had happened. It was a suicidal mission. They found that the top protective plate of the reactor had become displaced and that the core was visible through red and blue flames. They just had time to report to Akimov and his superior, Diatlov, that the reactor had been destroyed before, brown from 'radiation tan', they were taken off to hospital where they died soon after. However, Akimov and Diatlov did not believe their report.

Bryukhanov, the director of the Chernobyl station, arrived at 02.30. Akimov told him that there had been a serious radiation accident and fire, but that the main part of the reactor core was apparently intact. There were no proper dosimeters to establish what the level of radiation was. The existing monitors could not register more than 1 milliroentgen per second (3.6 roentgens per hour). After this report Bryukhanov left Block 4 for his office. From there he telephoned Vladimir Mar'in, the head of the atomic energy sector of the Central Committee of the CPSU, at home in Moscow at 03.00. He was probably acting according to emergency rules that Party leaders should be the first to be informed about major industrial accidents.

The local chief of civil defence also arrived at Block 4 at about 03.00. (his name is altered in Medvedev's notebook because of secrecy). He had a radiometer which could measure radiation up to 250 roentgens per hour. But even this was not enough to detect the real level in the machine hall, which was much higher. He realized the seriousness of the accident, but he reported to Bryukhanov, not to his own superiors. The civil defence network in town was not alerted. Between 03.00 and 04.00 the Minister of Power, A. I. Maiorets, and all other top administrators of the nuclear energy system in Moscow and Kiev, were informed about the accident. The Kiev regional Party Secretary, Revenko, was also woken with the news. They were all told that there had been a minor steam explosion and that two people had been killed, but that the reactor core had not been destroyed. The main task was thought to be controlling the fire.

At 09.00 the deputy chief engineer, Anatoly Sitnikov, also climbed up to Block 4 and reported to Bryukhanov and Fomin that the reactor had been destroyed. His reports was ignored. Neither the director nor the chief engineer believed that this could be possible. Sitnikov also died later from radiation exposure. During all this time the fire brigades continued pumping water into the reactor hall. This was a useless remedy because the temperature inside the core was too high.

By 06.00 Kiev officials were in direct control of the situation in Pripyat. The Kiev Party committee sent its second secretary to take charge. The medical aspects of the accident (including the evacuation) are discussed in chapter 5, since they reflect the reaction of the local health services and the decisions of health authorities in Kiev, Minsk and Moscow. The Pripyat department of the Ministry of Internal Affairs (MVD) held an emergency meeting at 02.15, less than an hour after the accident. It decided to set up roadblocks to prevent cars from entering the town (this also prevented people from leaving town by car). Like the firemen, the local police asked for assistance from Kiev and more than a thousand policemen were sent to Pripyat immediately. One police post was set up near the burning reactor. The policemen were as ignorant as the firemen about radiation. They too had neither respirators nor protective clothing. Nor did they have individual radiation monitoring equipment. Some were on duty for ten to twelve hours during the first day.[13] It is not surprising that the group later found to have the third highest risk of radiation exposure (after the firemen and plant operators) were the police. From 05.00 law and order on the site and in Pripyat were the responsibility of Deputy Minister of Internal Affairs of the Ukraine, Major General Gennady Berdov, and the Chairman of the Political Department of the Kiev MVD, General A. Borovik.

In 1988, when the 'heroic stage' of the 'Battle of Chernobyl' was over and the health problems were accumulating, it was disclosed that 16,500 policemen from the Ukrainian branch of the MVD had taken part in the emergency operation at Chernobyl. Of these 57 suffered acute radiation sickness, 1,500 developed chronic respiratory or digestive problems and more than 4,000 showed other symptoms;[14] 355 policemen received more than the maximum permissible emergency dose of 25 rem. The high incidence of respiratory and digestive problems was probably caused less by total exposure than by the inhalation and consumption of 'hot particles' or radioactive dust and debris from the reactor core (which causes local biological damage disproportionate to the total-body irradiation which is usually used in working out the permissible emergency exposure).

In the literature about the accident there is some confusion about when Moscow received the first report and how it responded. The confusion probably arises from the fact that there were several independent lines of communication with Moscow and the various services (medical, nuclear energy, administration, Party and military) did not co-ordinate their responses immediately. A reconstruction of the events suggests that the swiftest response came from the military administration.

In an article written in December 1986, the Commander of the Chemical Service of the Soviet Army, Colonel General Vladimir Pikalov, reported that all units of the chemical troops in the central and western parts of the Soviet Union were aroused by emergency alarm signals at 03.12, less than two hours after the accident.[15] In other words, the military professionals took two hours to assess the situation and report to the General Staff and Ministry of Defence (they did not yet know about the graphite fire and were thinking only of decontamination). Some time early in the morning, Marshal Sergei Akhromeev (Chief of General Staff) and Marshal Sergei Sokolov (Minister of Defence) ordered Pikalov to send chemical troops to Chernobyl immediately by air. The first to arrive at Pripyat were military units of the chemical defence section of the Kiev military district. They were also the first people there with proper protective clothing and masks. General Pikalov and his unit landed their giant transport AN-26 plane at Kiev and unloaded their equipment at 14.00.

A special government commission was set up to deal with the disaster. The most reliable source of information about the timing of this commission is Academician Valerii Legasov, the key member of the atomic science establishment on the commission. His notes about Chernobyl were published in May 1988, three weeks after he had committed suicide on 27 April 1988, at the age of 52 (several contradictory suggestions have been made about why he committed suicide; one obvious reason may have been delayed health problems caused by radiation exposure).[16] Legasov is credited with major decisions about how to deal with the reactor fire and prevent meltdown. He also headed the Soviet delegation at the IAEA meeting in August 1986. He was the first deputy director of the Kurchatov Institute of Atomic Energy, where the RBMK-1000 reactors were designed. Although a key figure in the government commission sent to Chernobyl, he only heard about the accident at noon, more than 10 hours after it had occurred. He attended a party organizational meeting in his ministry from 10.00 (the name of the ministry is not given). A break was announced at about mid-day, during which he was informed that he had been included in a government commission. The commission was to assemble at Vnukovo airport at 16.00. He went to his institute to seek advice from a reactor specialist:

> With great difficulty I managed to find the chief of the section which worked on stations with RBMK reactors . . . Aleksandr Konstantinovich Kalugin. He already knew about the accident since the signal 'one, two, three, four' had arrived from the station during the night. This meant that a dangerous situation had arisen at the station with nuclear, radiation, fire and explosive implications . . .
>
> At Vnukovo I was told that the leader of the government commission was Deputy Chairman of the Council of Ministers of the USSR, Boris Evdokimovich Shcherbina . . . he was busy with a Party economic aktiv out of town. We would board the plane which was already ready as soon as he arrived . . .
>
> When we disembarked in Kiev the first thing we saw was a large cavalcade of black government cars and an anxious crowd of Ukrainian leaders. They did not have detailed information, but told us that the situation was bad. We loaded ourselves into the cars quickly and drove to the nuclear station. I must say that it did not even enter my head that we were driving towards an event of global magnitude . . .[17]

Legasov's account makes it clear that the officials in Moscow did not understand that they were dealing with a catastrophe of global dimensions. There are signs, too, of an initial attempt to hide what had happened. The coded message arrived during the night. The decision-making process seems to have been deliberately slow to preserve a façade of 'business as usual'. The Chairman of the commission, Shcherbina, was allowed, for example, to complete a routine, rather un-important meeting. It was probably hoped that if there were no sign of crisis, rumours of the accident could be prevented. Another indication that Moscow did not comprehend the seriousness of the accident was the low status of the commission. Normally, when an industrial or natural disaster is considered to be nationally or internationally important, an emergency commission is set up under a member or candidate member of the Politburo. Few people, even in the Soviet Union, knew Boris Shcherbina. He was one of more than a dozen deputy Prime Ministers and had previously been a minister of construction in the oil and gas industry. When it became clear a few days later that the Shcherbina commission lacked the necessary power to deal with the accident, a parallel, superior commission was set up under Nikolai Ryzhkov, Chairman of the Council of Ministers of the USSR and a member of the Politburo.

If the plane left Moscow at 16.30 it must have arrived in Kiev at about 17.40. By 20.00 the government commission must have arrived at its headquarters in the Pripyat party committee. Local officials reported that:

> in the course of conducting an irregular experiment . . . two consecutive explosions had occurred in the fourth block of the station, the reactor building had been destroyed and several hundred people had received radiation injuries . . . two people had died and the others were in the town hospitals . . . The radiation level in Pripyat was significantly raised, but it did not yet represent a grave danger to the population.[18]

Grigory Medvedev who, like Legasov, took part in the work of the government commission as an expert (he was not, however, a member of the commission), maintains that an advance party of the commission left Moscow (from Bykovo airport) at least two hours earlier. Boris Shcherbina was 5,000 km away, in Barnaul, Altai region, when he was appointed chairman of the commission. The first group of officials left Moscow for Kiev while he was still on his way back. It included the assistant of the Procurator General, Yu. N. Shchadrin; the Minister of Power and Electrification, A. I. Maiorets; his deputy, A. N. Semyonov; the head of the atomic energy sector of the Central Committee, V. V. Mar'in; the Deputy Minister of Medium Machine Building (the ministry that deals with nuclear reactors and reprocessing), A. G. Meshkov; the head of the atomic energy construction committee, M. S. Zvirko; the Deputy Minister of Health, E. I. Vorob'ev; and some other officials. In Kiev they were joined by several Ukrainian officials.

It is clear that the Moscow officials did not expect to stay in Pripyat for more than two or three days and that they knew very little about the accident. Even when the first meeting of the entire commission was held at the office of the local party committee secretary, A. S. Gamanyk, in Pripyat, it was still not known that the reactor had been destroyed. This was 16 hours after the accident had occurred and water was still being pumped into the reactor space in order to keep it cool. Some of the officials inspected block 4 in person and were surprised to find a number of graphite blocks lying around. Medvedev reported the following conversation:

'Anatoly Ivanovich', Mar'in interrupted in his stentorian bass voice, 'Gennady Aleksandrovich and I have just been at block 4. It's an awful sight . . . there is a smell of burning and there is graphite lying around . . . Where does the graphite come from? . . .'

The minister turned to the director of the AES. 'Bryukhanov, you reported that the radiation situation is normal. What is this graphite?'

'It's hard even to guess . . . The graphite that we got for building the fifth block is all in place, whole. At first I thought that it was this graphite, but it's all in place. We can't therefore exclude an eruption from the reactor' . . .

'We can't measure the radioactivity accurately', Shasharin explained . . . 'we had one radiometer, but it was buried somewhere'.

'It's outrageous! Why does the station not have the necessary instruments?'

'The accident wasn't in the plan. The unthinkable has happened . . . We've asked civil defence and the chemical troops for help. They are due to arrive soon'.[19]

When the radioactivity was measured later in the places Mar'in had visited the graphite turned out to be mixed with pieces of nuclear reactor fuel elements. The radioactivity was about 2,000 R/h; 15 minutes there was enough to give a lethal dose of radiation.

Boris Shcherbina arrived in Pripyat at 21.00, about three hours after this conversation. It was already dark by the time he, Legasov and the remaining members of the commission who had not arrived earlier approached their destination. Shcherbina assumed leadership and divided the commission into groups, each charged with a particular task. Legasov headed the group which aimed to work out measures to localize the accident.

By then it was already too dark to inspect the site. From the description of the findings of the helicopter military units, it is clear that they began making observations at daylight on the next day, Sunday 27 April:

It was evident on the first flight that the reactor was completely destroyed. The top cover which hermetically seals the reactor compartment was almost vertical, but at something of an angle . . . The top part of the reactor hall was completely destroyed. Pieces of the graphite blocks, either whole or in bits, were scattered about on the roofs of the machine hall and over the whole area . . . From the nature of the destruction it was clear . . . that an extensive explosion had taken place. A white column several hundred metres high consisting of the products of the fire (apparently graphite) was constantly being emitted from the reactor crater. Inside the reactor space one could see separate huge spots of crimson incandescence.[20]

The chemical troops under General Pikalov (whose command post was in the same building as the government commission) had begun measuring surface radioactivity on the evening of 26 April. They reported the results to the Shcherbina commission. The situation deteriorated hourly. Throughout the night of 26 April the level of radioactivity in the air continued to increase. General Pikalov decided to inspect the destroyed reactor. Although heavy armoured personnel carriers, which offered some protection from external radiation, were later used to move about the area, ordinary cars were used in the first few days. As Pikalov and his driver drew closer to the reactor building, they noticed that the air above the ruins was fluorescent. There were no flames, just the eerie light. Pikalov understood the cause, but did not know how to deal with it.[21] He decided to try something desperate. He took a special armoured car equipped for radiological reconnaissance and drove to the plant. The gates were closed. Dismissing his driver, Pikalov took the wheel himself and smashed through the gates. He stopped near the destroyed building to take measurements. It was only then, more than 20 hours after the original explosion, that it was finally and definitely established that the graphite of the reactor core was burning, that the core was still melting and that the reactor continued to release enormous quantities of radioactivity and heat.

At 07.00 on Sunday 27 April, Pikalov and the group of nuclear experts who had spent the night discussing his findings reported the situation to the government commission. The commission in turn reported to the Kremlin. Pikalov probably also reported to his military superiors in the Ministry of Defence. This was the first proper information received by the leaders of the Soviet Union about the scale of the disaster and its possible consequences.

As a nuclear physicist, Legasov was particularly concerned about the state of the nuclear fuel in the core. It could not be excluded that the chain reaction of the uranium-235 was continuing in parts of the core. This could lead to meltdown and to new explosions caused by the rising temperature inside the core. He knew that attempts to lower the control rods had failed. He also knew that the core was not being cooled. The mixture of destroyed uranium fuel elements and graphite moderator could allow the chain reaction to continue. This was the most dangerous possibility. Legasov decided to check whether there was neutron radiation. This would indicate whether the chain reaction was continuing.[22]

By the time the government commission arrived in Pripyat it was clear that if the reactor was still releasing enormous amounts of radioactive material, the danger to the local population was mounting rapidly.

Evacuation was clearly indicated. The medical officials on the commission wanted to delay the evacuation, however, on the grounds that the radiation level in Pripyat was not high enough to warrant it. One of these specialists was Professor L. A. Il'in, director of the Institute of Biophysics (to which Hospital No. 6 was attached), chairman of the Soviet National Radiological Protection Board and the main author of the instructions about how to deal with the medical emergency resulting from a nuclear accident. Legasov later reported that:

> The physicists felt that the situation would become worse and they insisted on immediate evacuation. The medical experts then gave in . . . and at about 10 or 11 o'clock in the evening of April 26, Boris Evdokimovich [Shcherbina] took the decision to evacuate the population.
> It was to take place next day. Unfortunately, the information was passed around verbally . . . and evidently it did not reach everyone, because on the morning of the 27 April one saw mothers wheeling prams outside, children playing in the streets and, generally, all the signs of an ordinary Sunday.[23]

It appears that Professor Il'in refused to agree with the decision, arguing that the radiation level might improve. Two years later the writer, Ales' Adamovich, who reported the accident from the Byelorussian side of the future exclusion zone, wrote bitterly:

> the most disgraceful thing that was illuminated by the Chernobyl explosion . . . was the behaviour of some of our medics. There are many doctors who . . . honourably lived up to their high calling. But it is also a fact that it was only the medical representative on the government commission who did not sign the decision about the belated evacuation of Pripyat. Perhaps he wanted to wait until the wind turned and blew enough 'rads' onto the town as were envisaged in the instructions.[24]

Although by Sunday 27 April, the authorities knew how grave the situation was, they did not realize that the radioactive plume had crossed the Soviet border and that the accident had therefore acquired international dimensions. The radiation monitoring service had probably not yet been able to summarize the contours of the plume and to offer computer predictions of its movements. There was still some hope that the accident could be covered up. And as long as there was that chance, local radio and television could not be used to advise people to stay indoors. Thus people in Kiev were not informed of the accident and the evacuees from Pripyat were moved only a short distance, to villages in the Polessky district, 40 km south-west of Chernobyl.

Although the whole site was heavily contaminated, Reactors No. 1

and 2 had continued operating throughout 26 April. When the Shcherbina commission arrived there were no local plans to shut them down. Reactor No. 3 had been shut down, but operators were still inside the building, supervising the cooling system (after an emergency shutdown cooling of the reactor core has to continue for a number of days to prevent overheating of the fuel elements caused by residual fission products which could produce a meltdown and explosion). According to Legasov, the contamination of Reactors No. 1 and 2 was exacerbated by the ventilation system which had not been switched off after the accident.[25] Curiously the commission did not immediately order that Reactors No. 1 and 2 should be shut down. The Soviet Working Document for the IAEA records that 'units 1 and 2 were shut down at 01.13 and 02.13 respectively on 27 April'.[26] The delay may have been caused by ignorance or negligence. But it is more likely that the electricity supplied by Units 1 and 2 was required for Pripyat and for the emergency work. It is not clear why electricity could not be supplied from the standby diesel generators or the general grid of the Kiev region. The most likely explanation is that it required a decision by someone higher in the decision-making hierarchy.

## THE SECOND MELTDOWN OF THE CORE

The next stage of the emergency was to extinguish the graphite fire and stop the continuing release of large amounts of radioactive material from the reactor crater. The physicists suggested plugging the crater by dropping heavy, heat-resistant materials onto it from the air. The Ukrainian Ministry of Energy, however, which had sent its own commission to the site and which acted independently on 26 and 27 April, tried to use water to quell the graphite fire. Three unsuccessful attempts were made. Late in the afternoon of 27 April the first helicopter drops of sand and other materials began. At first the pilots simply dropped sacks of sand through the open doors of their helicopter:

> The command was given to cover the reactor with sacks of sand. For some reason the local officials could not immediately organize sufficient people to prepare the sand and the sacks. With my own eyes I saw the helicopter crews, young officers, loading sacks of sand onto the helicopters, taking off, dropping them on the object, then returning and repeating the task.[27]

This method proved far too slow and inaccurate. Moreover, the pilots were exposed to great risk. Although the pace increased on the following day, it would clearly take weeks to do the job. On April 27, 93 sorties were made and about 50 tonnes of material was dropped. On April 28, 186 sorties were made and several hundred tonnes of material was dropped. By now it was not only sacks of sand that were being dropped. Scientists had selected several types of material, each for a specific purpose. Sand and clay were designed simply to quench the fire and it was expected that they would absorb radioactive particles. Large amounts of boron carbide, lead and dolomite were also used. Boron materials are the most efficient absorbers of neutrons. It was hoped that they would inhibit or prevent further chain reactions in parts of the core. The lead was designed to cool the core. If the temperature inside the core was higher than 2,000°C (which was the case), the lead would boil at 1,744°C and absorb some of the heat. The dolomite ($MgCaCO_3$) would be broken down at higher temperatures into MgCa and $CO_2$. This would both absorb heat and generate inert gas which would blanket the fire.

The commander of the helicopter operation, Major General Nikolai Antoshkin, asked the chief helicopter designer, M. Tishchenko, and his engineering team to modify the helicopters which would be used for the task. They attached a device which enabled several tonnes of material to be carried in nets outside the machine. When the command to drop was given by radio from an outside observation post, a button inside the cabin released the material. There was no need to open the hatches and doors. These modifications improved the accuracy of the drops and increased the rate to over 1,000 tonnes per day. Each day the release of radioactivity from the reactor declined (from 4 million curies on 27 April to 2 million curies on 1 May).[28] During the six days of helicopter sorties more than 5,000 tonnes of material were dropped onto the core: 2,600 tonnes of sand, clay and dolomite, 2,400 tonnes of lead and 40 tonnes of boron.[29]

The first brief public report about the accident was made on Monday 28 April, during the evening television transmission. But even this brief announcement occurred only because of pressure from Sweden which was already covered by the radioactive plume. Swedish scientists had established the source of the plume and its radionuclide composition. The latter indicated a massive accident at a working reactor and partial meltdown of its core. From 29 April, US intelligence was able to take pictures over Chernobyl with its KH-11 military reconnaissance satellite. They showed that the reactor roof had blow off and the walls had been pushed out. The inside of the destroyed building was visible and so was the burning graphite. The helicopter sorties were also identified. Pictures from the disaster area were published all over the world. None the less, the Soviet government continued its news blackout from the site. Limited information was released centrally in the form of brief daily statements. The disaster was treated as a minor incident. Main attention on Soviet news was given to the traditional 1 May celebrations of mass demonstrations and festivities all over the country, including in Kiev, Minsk, Gomel and other towns around Chernobyl which were already suffering significant radioactive contamination. The brief statement issued on 1 May acknowledged, without giving the number of people, that the population from the nearest town had been evacuated. But it also stated that 'the radiation situation in the power station and the surrounding area is stabilized'.[30] This was completely untrue: 2 million curies per day of radionuclides in the form of gases and aerosol were being released and the wind, which had changed direction, was blowing the radioactive cloud in the direction of Kiev.

As soon as the reactor crater was filled and capped with sand, clay and other materials, the physical situation inside the reactor core began unexpectedly to deteriorate. The sand cap was not sufficiently hermetic to stop a chimney-type circulation of air. On the other hand, it was large enough to reduce the exchange of heat between the core and the environment. Part of the heat was generated by the graphite fire. But a significant part of it was caused by fission radionuclides which did not depend on the availability of oxygen from the air. None of the material dropped into the crater could prevent the fission radionuclides from generating temperatures far higher than any conventional fire. The temperature inside the reactor began to rise and the amount of very fine radioactive aerosol and gases which filtered through the sand cap began to increase (from 2 to 4 million curies between 1 and 2 May to 5 million curies on 3 May).[31] A new fear arose: the heavy load of sand, clay, lead and dolomite had increased the pressure on the reactor foundations. The drops had been made from a height of about 200 m and no one knew how much structural damage had been caused by these heavy blows from the air. The situation rapidly became critical. Scientists and engineers in charge of the operation were well aware that a meltdown had become possible. The red-hot reactor core with a temperature of about 2,500°C was pressed hard against the concrete foundations. It could burn down and drop into the large bubbler pool of water which was below the reactor vault. This would cause a new, more powerful explosion and complete dispersal of the full inventory of uranium, plutonium and large quantities of other radioactive products. By 3 May only about 3 or 4 per cent of the total inventory of radionuclides had been released into the environment and contributed to the formation of the plume of airborne radioactive particles. Probably not less than 10 per cent of the core was blown out and scattered close to the reactor, together with pieces of graphite. However, the main part of the destroyed reactor core was still trapped inside. The constant measurements of the radioactive release were relevant only for the gases and aerosol produced by the burning core. The amount of the reactor core material blown out in the form of larger pieces which were scattered around the destroyed unit was not reported. However, both the descriptions of the site by eye witnesses and the evidence of many photographs show that, judging from the amount of hot graphite lying around, not less than 10–20 per cent of the reactor core was blown out.

The basement of the reactor building had been flooded during the accident when the pipes from the main circulation pumps were destroyed by the explosion and the reserve water tanks breached. The initial fight against the fire on 26 and 27 April and the attempt to extinguish the graphite fire with water had added vastly to the radioactive contamination of the flooded basement. The helicopter sorties were halted on 2 May when the temperature inside the reactor began to rise. Although it would have been sensible to continue dropping lead, since it would melt down through the sand cap and protect the foundations from overheating, the scientists were afraid of the consequences of hammering the foundations further with heavy drops. To prevent a second, even greater catastrophe there were now two urgent tasks: to drain the bubbler pool and to freeze the earth beneath the reactor building to make it solid.

The bubbler pool was a pressure suppression pond beneath the reactor. It normally acted as a safety system in case of burst steam pipes – the most likely type of accident in a RBMK-1000. As we have seen, there are about 1,700 small pressure channels and steam pipes in each RBMK reactor. Their small diameter means that they are not very strong. The bubbler pool makes it possible to condense steam from a broken pipe, it also serves as a large water reserve for the emergency pumps which work off the diesel generators. After the accident, the bubbler pool and flooded basement represented a grave danger so it was essential to drain them. The bubbler pool could be drained by opening its slide valves. In spite of the hazards of doing this (the water was already radioactive), volunteers in diving suits managed to open them. Fire brigade pumps were used to begin draining the basement. It was a long and dangerous operation which has been described in reliable detail in two works available in both Russian and English.[32] It took until 8 May for the task to be completed, by which time some 20,000 tonnes of highly radioactive water had been pumped out.

Removing the water made a powerful steam explosion less likely, but it did not eliminate the danger of a meltdown. It meant that the molten core would need to burn through two foundations before it could reach the water table underneath the building. But once it reached the water table an explosion could still take place. The second emergency measure to reduce the danger of meltdown was to freeze the earth beneath the reactor building. Solid frozen soil would, it was thought, provide stronger support for the foundations. Using equipment normally used by oil engineers, drilling was begun so that liquid nitrogen could be pumped into the earth. It was calculated that 25 tonnes of liquid nitrogen per day would be required to keep the soil underneath the reactor frozen solid at a temperature of 100°C below zero. Well before the drilling was complete, workers began pumping liquid nitrogen into all the spaces around the reactor vault to cool the foundations and walls of the vault. The operation began on 4 May, when the temperature of the core was rising rapidly and the amount of radioactivity emitted into the air through the sand cap had risen from 5 to 7 million curies. In other words, the situation was critical.

By now a second government commission under Prime Minister Ryzhkov had been set up. Thousands of miners from the Donbass, metro-workers from Kiev and Moscow, firemen and servicemen had been mobilized. Several projects were undertaken simultaneously. It was decided to fill the drained bubbler pool and basement with concrete. It was also decided to insert a new, thick foundation underneath the reactor in the form of a concrete dish lined with lead. But these were long-term projects. By now the exclusion zone had been increased to a radius of 30 km around the reactor and a further 60,000 people had been evacuated between 2 and 5 May. None the less, the government continued to publish misleading statements. Until 2 May it was reported that the emission of radioactive substances had decreased and that 'enterprises, collective and state farms are functioning normally'.[33] In fact, the collective and state farms were evacuated a few days after this report. On 3 May there was no communiqué about Chernobyl. The government did not know how to report the increase of radioactivity or the fact that the exclusion zone had been extended. The statement on 4 May claimed that the graphite fire was diminishing and that work to deal with the accident was proceeding in an organized manner.[34] The short and misleading daily reports about Chernobyl were probably intended to prevent panic in Kiev and other towns near the reactor.

In fact, the situation regarding meltdown was unpredictable and the government was helpless. The rise in the temperature of the core revived the fear that a fission reaction was taking place under the pressure of the heavy cap. Special equipment to monitor neutrons was located close to the core. To the relief of the physicists, no neutron radiation was registered.[35] Frantic activity of every possible kind continued, frequently arousing new fears. There was some anxiety, for example, that powerful drilling too close to the foundations would cause structural damage. Miners and metro-workers were instructed to use manual equipment to dig the tunnel under the reactor. Liquid nitrogen was brought to the site from every nitrogen plant in the Ukraine (there is normally a small plant producing liquid nitrogen and other gases at large nuclear power stations because nitrogen and other inert gases are used for the aeration and gas cooling of some systems). It was injected into every possible space around Reactor No. 4. A cloud of cold nitrogen rose around the reactor. This proved to be an effective remedy. The temperature of the lower part of the reactor began to fall. At the same time, the air drawn by the chimney effect through the reactor core was gradually replaced by nitrogen, which suppressed the graphite fire. This was more effective in damping the fire than sand or dolomite. The fire at last began to die down.

But this was not the end of the problem. Heat continued to be generated by the fission products in the reactor core which were not being cooled and were producing a temperature far higher than that of an ordinary fire. Thus, although the graphite fire was dying down, the temperature of the core continued to rise alarmingly. And, as the temperature rose, so the release of radioactive products increased. The changing radioisotope composition of the released materials made it clear that something was happening inside the core. The amount of volatile isotopes like iodine-131 and caesium-137 declined, whereas the amount of zirconium-95 and ruthenium-103 and 106 rose sharply. On 2 and 3 May the trend had been the opposite – the amount of volatile isotopes increased and the non-volatile isotopes decreased.[36] The increase in zirconium and ruthenium caused intense alarm because they were isotopes of elements with extremely high melting points. Zirconium melts at 1,852°C and ruthenium at 2,250°C. Their increase indicated that the temperature of the core had probably risen to above 2,250°C. This signified meltdown. At such high temperatures radioactive materials are released not by air circulation (which had played an important part before the graphite fire had been extinguished when the convection of the fire had sucked in the debris of the nuclear fuel) but by vaporization.

The vapours are swept away from the fuel because of the immense heat and vapour pressure. On 5 May, 8–12 million curies of radioactive material was released from the reactor. This was almost as much as on the first day of the accident.

The presence of ruthenium particles in the initial plume which reached Sweden on 28 April had indicated to Swedish scientists that the reactor core was exposed and that meltdown had occurred. In the initial release the ruthenium isotopes were mostly carried by fuel fragments, although there were some monoelemental hot particles of pure ruthenium. The fragmented particles indicated that the core of the reactor was dispersed by the explosion, while the pure, monoelemental particles were the result of meltdown. In subsequent releases the size of the ruthenium particles became smaller and both isotopes of ruthenium were eventually released in the form of a volatile oxide.[37] Larger particles had probably been unable to filter through the sand and clay cap. But the appearance of volatile ruthenium oxide signified that a second meltdown, with temperatures even higher than 26 April, was taking place.

Suddenly, later on 5 May, the release of radionuclides from the reactor core dropped sharply and the volcanic eruption of radioactive vapour and aerosol began to decline rapidly. On 6 May, 150,000 curies were released into the atmosphere, almost 100 times less than on 5 May.[38] The decline continued. Nuclear scientists have not really been able to explain this sudden drop. It was relatively easy to explain the heat-up period from 2 May. The sand and clay cap served to reduce the heat exchange of the core. Moreover, once the helicopter drops were discontinued, the heat exchange produced by melting lead and pyrolysis of dolomite ceased. As a result the temperature inside the core rose and the vaporization of radionuclides was enhanced. But why did this process end? Some tentative explanations have been offered. It has been suggested, for example, that the substantial release of fission products from the fuel on 4 and 5 May could itself have caused a sudden reduction in the heat produced by their decay and, therefore, the temperature of the core began to fall. It is also possible that the amount of radioiodine and radiocaesium released in the last few days of the heat-up period fell because 100 per cent of the total inventory of these radionuclides had already been released from the core. The Soviet figures of the released voltaile radionuclides which account for 20 per cent of the iodine-131 and 13 per cent of the caesium-137 are based on the deposition inside the Soviet Union only. Later studies of the global distribution of these isotopes indicate that the major proportion was distributed world-wide (see chapter 6).

A third plausible explanation for the sudden decrease in radioactivity is that it was caused by a meltdown of a major part of the debris of the reactor fuel elements. The temperatures of 2,300–2,700°C which occurred inside the reactor core produced liquefaction of zirconium, the main material from which the pressure tubes were made. During liquefaction vaporization of materials accelerates. But the liquefied debris relocated itself in the lower pipe runs of the reactor vault. There they solidified again, because this part of the reactor vault had been effectively cooled by the injections of liquid nitrogen. In this meltdown the large size of the core was an advantage. If the meltdown had occurred in a pressurized-water reactor, the fuel elements would have formed a large concentrated mass of extremely hot material (known as the 'China Syndrome' effect). But a graphite moderated reactor with numerous individual pressure tubes has a very low energy density and the graphite, the steel and zirconium prevented the uranium fuel elements from melting into one large hot ball which could burn through the reactor foundations. The continuing cooling with liquid nitrogen prevented the debris from melting again and destroying the concrete and steel structure of the reactor vault.[39] At this stage the danger declined day by day because the radioactive decay of radionuclides also reduces the amount of heat which is generated. As soon as the chain reaction is over, the generation of heat declines rapidly because many radionuclides have a short half-life. Molybdenum-99, for example, which was present in the inventory of the reactor radionuclides in larger quantities (4.8 × $10^{18}$ Bq) than all the iodine-131, caesium-134 and 137 and strontium-90 put together, has a half-life of only 2.8 days.

Later, when the main danger was over, some physicists claimed that a second meltdown had been prevented by a scientifically selected strategy. Academician Evgenii Velikhov, a member of the scientific team on the government commission, later maintained, rather simplistically: 'No one in the world has ever been in such a difficult position. It was necessary to judge the situation very exactly and not to make a single mistake. The further development of the situation showed that the correct method was chosen to struggle with the raging reactor.'[40]

In fact, a number of errors were made and the final fortunate outcome was the result of many contradictory measures with unpredictable consequences. The attempt to use water to put out the graphite fire, for example, was a dangerous mistake which was made because there was no one qualified to tell the firemen what the temperature was inside the core. The fact that nuclear physicists were brought to the site with considerable delay, arriving 18 hours after the explosion had taken place, was a gross error. Competent physicists from Kiev (with their equipment) should have been sent to Chernobyl immediately. They could have arrived at the same time as the Kiev fire brigade. They would have prevented the pumping of thousands of tons of water into the reactor core. If ruthenium had been identified in the radioactive release (which could have been done very quickly with gamma spectrometry), it would have indicated that the temperature inside the core was about 2,300°C. At that temperature water not only evaporates immediately but, in contact with overheated graphite, it produces inflammable carbon monoxide which acts to fuel flames. And when overheated or melting metals like steel and zirconium react with water or steam, they oxidize and release hydrogen which also fuels flames. At a temperature of 2,500–2,700°C water itself begins to dissociate into hydrogen and oxygen, forming an explosive mixture.

The decision to cover the reactor core with sand and clay was also a mistake. It did not prevent the release of radionuclides. Moreover, it reduced the release of heat sharply. It was this that eventually produced the second meltdown. If lead, dolomite and boron had been dropped on the reactor without sand and clay, the temperature might have continued to fall. Lead melts easily and boils at a temperature of 1,744°C, which is lower than the melting point of the zirconium alloys (1,852°C) from which the nuclear cladding and pressure tubes had been made. After the initial explosion, radionuclides were released because of the process of vaporization caused by the very high temperatures inside the fuel channels. The graphite fire was less dangerous than a meltdown. In itself it did not generate the kind of temperatures that can produce zirconium meltdown. On April 26 a partial meltdown had occurred because of the runaway chain reaction of uranium-235. But it had been restricted to the upper part of the working half of the reactor core. The sand and clay cap could have caused a meltdown of the whole core because of the accumulated heat of the residual fission radionuclides. If liquid nitrogen had begun to be pumped on 26 or 27 April (or if dry ice or liquid $CO_2$ had been unloaded) rather than on 4 May, the heat-up would not have occurred and the second meltdown would have been prevented. Moreover, it would have been possible to extinguish the graphite fire sooner, because the oxygen which sustained the fire would have been absent. In other words, a better strategy would have been to reduce the temperature inside the core rather than concentrating on plugging the crater which raised the temperature and created a critical situation.

It may seem unfair now to criticize the desperate actions which were underaken at great risk to human life. Velikhov's statement that no one had ever previously faced similar problems is, of course, true. There were no tried and tested remedies and this explains some of the errors. But it does not excuse all of them. And Velikhov's claim that the outcome was a triumph of accurate scientific strategy is nonsense. In fact, the secrecy exacerbated the problems. Although the scientists at the site were competent, they had limited expertise in dealing with such critical problems. If *glasnost'* had reigned from the beginning, correct solutions might have been found sooner. Unofficially, through diplomatic channels, some experts tried to solicit advice from their foreign colleagues about the best way to deal with the graphite fire. But the Soviet government expected its few top scientists (in effect, the top bureaucrats of the Academy of Sciences) to find their own solutions. Competent computer analyses of the situation would have accelerated the finding of a better strategy. If the Chernobyl catastrophe itself was born of secrecy, many of the mistakes and miscalculations which were made afterwards and which significantly increased the human and economic cost were also the result of secrecy and cover-up.

From Legasov's posthumous notes it seems clear that the scientists on the site could not predict the outcome of events and that they often reacted without any really scientific strategy:

> At some time on 9 May it seemed to us that unit 4 had ceased to breathe, burn, live. Externally it seemed to be calm. We wanted to celebrate on the evening of Victory Day [9 May is the anniversary of the victory over Nazi Germany] . . . Unfortunately a small, but brightly burning crimson spot inside unit 4 was discovered on that day. This indicated that a high temperature still existed. It was difficult to determine whether the parachutes with which the lead and other material had been dropped were burning. In my opinion this is unlikely. It is more likely that there was a hot burning mass of sand, clay and everything else that had been dropped. The holiday was spoiled and the decision was taken to drop a further 80 tonnes of lead into the reactor crater. After that the burning ceased.[41]

This story about the fire inside the reactor core on 9 May and how it was dealt with has recently been challenged by another competent witness, Grigory Medvedev. He took part in the work of the government commission. In 1989 he published the most comprehensive technical description of the accident and the post-accident measures that has appeared so far. According to Medvedev:

> At about 20.30 on 9 May part of the graphite in the reactor started burning through. Under the huge loads that had been dropped onto the

reactor a vacuum formed. The vast bulk of five thousand tonnes of sand, clay and boron carbide crashed down, throwing out from underneath a huge amount of radioactive dust. The radioactivity at the station, in Pripyat and in the thirty-kilometre zone rose sharply. The increase was felt as far away as 60 kilometres . . .[42]

This sudden new eruption of radioactive material on 9 May 1986 was not reported in any documents or papers about Chernobyl until June 1989. There was no mention of it in the IAEA documents. Medvedev believes that it was a serious mistake to use helicopters to drop sand and other materials into the reactor crater. According to his calculations, even after the drops the graphite fire only ceased when all the graphite which had remained inside the core after the initial explosion had burnt out entirely. In other words, the fire ceased when there was nothing left to burn. This also means that pumping liquid nitrogen was not as useful as the INSAG report suggested. Perhaps a future open inquiry into all aspects of the disaster will clarify the problem.

Despite the absence of neutron radiation outside the reactor the possibility that a chain reaction continued in some parts of the core or that it could resume was not excluded. When the core debris relocated itself during the second meltdown on 5 May it could have created conditions for chain reactions, because of the changed position of uranium-235 and plutonium in the destroyed fuel elements. The composition of the releases had to be monitored to be sure that isotopes with very short half-lives (measured in hours and minutes) did not reappear. The results of the monitoring have not been published, but radiologists who were asked to check whether there was sodium-24 in the blood of irradiated people claim that they should be credited with finding the absence of neutron radiation (Na-24 appears as a result of neutron irradiation).[43]

Whatever the cause, the drop in temperature of the reactor core and the sharp decrease in the release of radionuclides on the evening of 5 May was a great relief to everyone involved in the emergency operation. The general public still knew little about the danger that had ended. But now that there was good news to report there was no further need for a new blackout. A news conference was called for Soviet and foreign journalists on the evening of Tuesday 6 May.

## THE FIRST SIGNS OF *GLASNOST*'

The ten-day news blackout about Chernobyl harmed the reputation of the Soviet government and its new policy of *glasnost*'. But it did not surprise anyone who lives and works in the Soviet Union. *Glasnost'* was new. It had not yet become a trend that could be trusted. Thousands of people had to be mobilized to work on the site in dangerous conditions. The government probably thought that it would be easier to persuade people to help if they did not know the extent of the danger. In fact, this short-sighted attitude eventually made the emergency work more costly, particularly in terms of human health. But there was probably also a reluctance to appear helpless, and the Soviet government *was* helpless until the inferno of the graphite fire and the huge releases of radioactive products were controlled. The reasons for the news blackout were thus primarily domestic.

Although Western experts did not know why the accident had occurred, they certainly knew what was happening. The radioactive cloud which moved across most of Europe was closely monitored. Speedy analyses of its isotope composition (the ratio between caesium-134 and 137, or between ruthenium-103 and 106) and other measurements told them that the stage of the reactor cycle was somewhere between 500 and 600 days. This information could be used to calculate the total inventory of radionuclides in the reactor core – between 2 and 3 billion curies. This huge figure gave rise to a great deal of worry. If the whole inventory, or even 50 per cent of it, was being released into the environment, the human and economic costs of the accident, not only for the Soviet Union but for many other countries of Europe, would be extremely high. The Soviet government was under great pressure to lift the news blackout and allow experts of the IAEA to supervise the accident. It was part of the legitimate obligation of the IAEA. Once the massive emission of radioactivity from the reactor had ceased, it was an obvious and timely occasion to end the news blackout.

The TASS report on Chernobyl published on 6 May was still very terse. But it included an announcement that the Director-General of the IAEA, Dr H. Blix, would visit Moscow. As a member state of the IAEA, the USSR was obliged to report all relevant details of even minor accidents. The IAEA was required to discuss such reports and to distribute materials to other member nations, particularly those with nuclear energy programmes. Before 1986 the Soviet Union had never reported any reactor accidents to the IAEA. Now the IAEA was pressing for information.

On 6 May TASS also reported that the three other units of the Chernobyl power station were under control. They had been shut down, but their cooling systems were functioning normally, supervised by operators who were also cooling the nuclear waste sections of the plant, where spent fuel rods were cooled permanently for a year before they could be shipped to a reprocessing plant or to waste burial ground. In fact, the operators could not work full shifts because of the level of contamination. The permissible annual radiation dose was temporarily raised for workers on the site from 5 to 25 rems. But the level of radioactivity was so high in many places that the annual dose could be received within a very short time. Operators and engineers from other nuclear power stations in the Soviet Union were mobilized and sent to Chernobyl to work in short shifts during the emergency. To compensate for the hazards, they were paid from three to five times their normal salaries. Immediate cash bonuses were paid for executing particularly dangerous tasks. Two journalists, A. Illesh and A. Pral'nikov, who reported regularly from Chernobyl for *Izvestiya*, later published a book based on their reports. They claimed that the firemen who were involved in draining the flooded basement of Unit 4 were given immediate cash rewards of 1,000 roubles each as soon as the job was completed.[44]

The news conference organized by the Ministry of Foreign Affairs on 6 May was the turning point in the dissemination of news from Chernobyl. But only a small part of it was shown on Moscow television and, as a press conference, if left a lot to be desired. Called at very short notice, it was very tightly controlled. Soviet and East European journalists were allowed to ask oral questions, but Western journalists had to submit written questions. In the introductory statement A. G. Kovalev, a deputy Foreign Minister, criticized Western attitudes to the accident. Boris Shcherbina's statement contained little information and no explanation of how and why the accident had occurred. He made no mention of the experiment that had caused it. Neither he nor any other Soviet official would confirm that the graphite fire had been extinguished. They reported only that the release of radioactivity had declined sharply in the last 24 hours. The chairman of the Committee on the Peaceful Use of Atomic Energy, A. M. Petrosy'ants, a deputy Minister of Health, E. I. Vorob'ev, the deputy head of the Committee on Hydrometeorology and Environmental Control, Yu. S. Sedunov, and a corresponding member of the Academy of Sciences, I. Ya. Yemel'yanov, were also present at the news conference, representing organizations and groups responsible for the Soviet nuclear energy programme and safety precautions (many violations of which had been exposed by the accident). Later in 1986, Petrosy'ants, Vorob'ev and Yemel'yanov who was identified as the scientist responsible for the design of this particular model of the RBMK-1000 reactor) were dismissed from their positions.

The news conference was intended as a damage-control exercise and

an attempt to calm the public. It did not succeed in either aim. Neither
domestic nor international demands for information (for example,
about levels of contamination of the territory, or of water and food
products) were satisfied. Dr Hans Blix arrived in Moscow on 7 May and
was allowed to fly to Kiev and to inspect the Chernobyl site by
helicopter. Afterwards he held a press conference in Moscow, but he had
nothing new to report. He and his assistants took their own portable
dosimeters with them, and through them accurate levels of radiation in
the vicinity of the reactor became known. During their flight over the
reactor on 8 May, their dosimeters 'had registered 350 mrem an hour at
a height of 400 m above the plant and at a distance of 800 m'.[45] These
readings indicated very heavy contamination – taken inside the helicopter,
the level must have been much higher outside it. It is worth noting that
the *Pravda* correspondent who accompanied Dr Blix on the trip,
B. Dubrovin, reported that their dosimeters had registered 10 milliroentgen (about 10 mrem), 35 times less than the figure made public by
Dr Blix.[46] Presumably Dubrovin did not realize that Dr Blix's figures
were public knowledge in the West.

Although the amount of radioactivity released from the damaged
reactor had declined sharply on 6 May, the reactor remained a considerable source of radioactive contamination of the atmosphere and environment for some time. On 6 May the release was about 150,000 curies
(which was more than the total release after the Windscale accident in
Britain in 1957). On 9 May, the day after Dr Blix's journey, the release
was 12,600 curies, still a very large amount by any standards. It dropped
to 8,700 curies on 11 May and continued to fall.[47] The IAEA experts
were concerned that the reactor core, insulated with more than 5,000
tonnes of sand, clay and other materials, remained very hot, probably in
molten form and that it could still burn through the concrete foundation.
Liquid nitrogen continued to be pumped into the basement and the
creation of a layer of solidly frozen soil underneath the reactor was
proceeding. The danger of meltdown receded day by day as the shorter-
lived (and therefore hottest) radionuclides decayed.

Only now that the worst danger was over were officials in Kiev and
Minsk allowed to take action to protect the population. Before 6 or 7
May it was feared that the whole population of big cities like Kiev (with
a population of 2.5 million) or Gomel (with 478,000 inhabitants) would
need to be evacuated in case of new explosions. This was no longer
thought necessary. But Kiev and other towns and cities were severely
contaminated, and children were in particular danger. For ten days
officials insisted that there was no danger in Kiev. But on 5 May the

Ukrainian and Byelorussian Ministries of Health decided that children should be evacuated. All schools in Kiev were to close on 14 May. The evacuation of children up to the age of 14 years would begin on 15 May. In order to explain away the fact that the evacuation was so delayed (it would have been more beneficial if it had been done 29–30 April), Kiev residents were told that it was a prophylactic measure and did not mean that the children were in danger. While it took some time to prepare the summer camps to accommodate the children and also mothers of infants and pregnant women, the preparation would have been done far more quickly if there had been *glasnost'* before 6 May. And because of the delay, the danger in the middle of May had to be downplayed.

The temperature inside the reactor finally began to fall on 10 May. It was measured through a special hole made in the wall between Unit 3 and Unit 4 and on the basis of several other physical indicators. The news was received with great relief. It indicated that the graphite fire had been extinguished. The release of radioactivity also continued to decline. But the use of liquid nitrogen to cool the reactor vault and foundations remained necessary for many weeks. Concrete, which consists of a mixture of cement and ordinary water, is a heat-resistant material but no one had ever tested the thermal stability at very high temperatures of the particular type of concrete from which the walls of the reactor pit had been made. Urgent tests were conducted in the Kurchatov Institute of Atomic Energy, but the results were never reported. On 11 May the Moscow television programme *Vremya* reported that the danger was over. Decontamination of the site and of other parts of the exclusion zone had now become the priority. It was considered appropriate now for Gorbachev to address the nation and the world.

For Gorbachev the Chernobyl accident was a particularly painful misfortune. Any development programme in a large industrial country depends on energy. Lenin had maintained that electrification was the way forward to socialism. Stalin and Khrushchev had concentrated on developing hydroelectric energy. Brezhnev had expanded the extraction of Siberian gas and oil. But Soviet oil production had begun to decline in 1985 and 1986. Gorbachev hoped that nuclear power would be the main source of the rapid growth in the supply of electricity. The new Five-Year Plan adopted at the XXVIIth Party Congress in February 1986 called for the production of nuclear generated electricity to double, from 11 to 22 per cent of the total. Now this target was in doubt.

Many people expected that Gorbachev would reassess the role of nuclear power in his television address. He was also expected to explain the cause of the accident more fully. In fact, his rather sombre television broadcast on 14 May 1986 was disappointing. As expected, he reported the latest number of casualties but he said little about the cause of the accident, merely stating that: '. . . the reactor capacity suddenly increased during a scheduled shutdown . . . the considerable emission of steam and subsequent reaction resulted in the formation of hydrogen, its explosion, damage to the reactor and the associated radioactive release.'[48] A large part of his address consisted of traditional agitprop. He criticized Western reporting and Western leaders who had used the tragedy to launch 'an unrestrained anti-Soviet campaign with mountains of lies, most dishonest and malicious lies'.[49] He promised that the entire truth would be told in due course when the accident had been analysed, and he suggested that an appropriate forum would be a 'highly authoritative specialized international conference in Vienna under IAEA auspices'.[50]

It was an important promise. It was the first time in Soviet history that an offer was made to put records of Soviet technology and details of an accident before the international scientific community for analysis and judgement. The reports which the Soviet delegation eventually presented to the IAEA conferences in 1986 and 1987 and to other bodies of the United Nations still represent the main information known about the technical aspects of the Chernobyl accident.

It was not in the Soviet interest to delay the IAEA analysis of the accident. There were probably some people in the government who realized that the international nuclear community could help Soviet planners resolve a vital problem about the feasibility of constructing further reactors of the RBMK-1000 type. Some were already under construction; others were at the planning stage. They represented about half the programme for nuclear construction until the end of the century. All those involved in the RBMK-1000 programme and who worked at Chernobyl were ordered to have their reports ready in July 1986. The IAEA conference was expected to take place in August and the final report would need to be considered and approved by the Politburo.

The reports of the government commission and of the various expert groups were discussed at an extraordinary special session of the Politburo on Saturday 19 July 1986. In a statement afterwards the Politburo blamed the accident on crude violations of the safety regulations and on the experiments which were carried out at night. The administration and experts working at Chernobyl were not properly prepared for the experiments and did not co-ordinate them with their superiors. The Politburo also criticized the Ministry of Power and

Electrification and the State Committee on Safety in the Atomic Power Industry for poor control of the situation at Chernobyl, for the absence of effective safety measures and for violations of discipline and rules at the station. Lack of responsibility, negligence and lack of discipline were considered the main causes of the disaster. In other words, according to the Politburo human error was the sole cause of the accident.

The radioactive contamination which resulted from the accident extended over 1,000 km$^2$. Agriculture had ceased in this area and the population had been evacuated. The accident had also affected the national economy by reducing the supply of energy. The direct costs of the accident were said to be about 2 billion roubles.[51] But even at this stage the Politburo was not ready to acknowledge the real scale and cost of the disaster. The 2 billion roubles represented only the direct cost of the destroyed building, lost equipment and loss of electricity up to July 1986 from four 1,000 MW reactors. It did not include the loss of towns and villages in the exclusion zone, the loss of agricultural produce, the cost of decontamination, nor the medical costs and the cost of radiological control. By the end of 1987 the official cost of the accident had risen to 8 billion roubles and in May 1988 it was said to be 11 billion roubles (£10 billion).[52] The figure of 1,000 km$^2$ indicated by the Politburo was wrong. The area from which the population was evacuated by July 1986 measured more than 5,200 km$^2$.

The Politburo dismissed four very senior officials: Yevgenii Kulov, the chairman of the State Committee on Safety in the Atomic Power Industry; G. A. Shasharin, the Deputy Minister of Power and Electrification; Aleksandr Meshkov, the First Deputy Minister of Medium Machine Building; and Professor Ivan Yemel'yanov, deputy director of a research and design institute and one of the main designers of the RBMK reactors. These four officials also received severe Party reprimands. The former director of the Chernobyl Nuclear Station, Bryukhanov, was expelled from the Communist Party. Many other officials also received reprimands and the Committee of Party Control and the Central Committee of the Ukrainian Republic were instructed to start investigating the responsibility of other workers for the accident. The Politburo demanded that all relevant ministries and committees should develop and urgently introduce additional safety measures in nuclear power stations, strengthen technological discipline and organize additional training of personnel. Nuclear power stations were placed under the supervision of a new Ministry of Atomic Energy.

The Politburo decision implied a radical change of attitude. The face-saving policy was more or less over and the disaster ceased to be considered a mere 'misfortune'. The question of responsibility was raised. Inevitably wider problems of nuclear energy came under scrutiny. Nikolai Lukonin was appointed the new Minister of Atomic Energy. He had previously been the director of the Leningrad nuclear power station (before that he was the director of the Ingalina nuclear power station near Vilnius, in Lithuania). The director of the Beloyarsk nuclear power station near Sverdlovsk, in the North Urals, Vadim Malyshev, was appointed the new chairman of the Committee on Safety in the Atomic Power Industry. The main scientist behind the original design of the RBMK reactors in the early 1950s and the main proponent of locating nuclear power stations near large cities, Academician Anatoly Aleksandrov, was by then 83 years old and he retired from his position of President of the USSR Academy of Sciences.

It was unlikely that the new administration of nuclear science and technology would exonerate the RBMK design, even though it was the main type used in the Soviet nuclear programme. Although the government would not be able to afford the massive loss of electricity implied by shutting down all the existing RBMK reactors, new RBMK nuclear power stations would not be built. Institutional support for the RMBK model had declined and the new administration could not guarantee the complete safety of RBMK reactors in future. The most likely outcome is that RBMK reactors will be phased out gradually and quietly and without embarrassing publicity.

## CONCLUSION

The general conclusion by the Soviets and Western press is that the measures which were applied to extinguish the graphite fire and stem the uncontrollable release of radioactivity from the reactor core were successful. It was the first task of this kind since the Windscale disaster in Britain in 1957 and it seemed to have been carried out with more efficiency and determination. But if one judges from its final results the operation, which involved the army, airforce, the best nuclear scientists and engineers and many thousands of workers, was not entirely successful.

The strategies used to deal with the graphite fire in the reactor core were misguided. The first, difficult attempts to use water (at one stage the fire-hose was held above the crater by helicopter) were useless and served only to flood the basement and increase the contamination of the site. In Legasov's posthumous notes he acknowledges the mistake. But he also makes it clear that the graphite fire was considered highly dangerous:

> By the evening of April 26 all possible means of using water had been tried, but they achieved nothing apart from a high rate of steam formation and the distribution of water via various transport corridors to the neighbouring blocks.
> The next question arose when it became clear that a very powerful stream of aerosol and gas radioactivity was being emitted from the damaged block. The graphite was burning and each particle of graphite carried a large amount of radioactivity. Dealing with it was a difficult task. Graphite normally burns at the rate of a tonne an hour. In unit 4 there were about 2.5 thousand tonnes of graphite. It followed therefore that at a normal rate of burning in 240 hours the radioactivity would be distributed over a vast area which would become intensely contaminated with various radionuclides.[53]

In fact, the reactor contained 1,700 tonnes of graphite and a substantial part of it had already been blown out of the reactor. No one knew how much was left inside, and how intense the fire was (in other words, whether it was burning at the rate of 1 tonne per hour or more intensely). But the graphite burnt actively for 240 hours or longer, sucking a great deal of radioactive debris into the air. The first period of cooling was registered only on 10 May. It is possible that well above half or more of the total graphite was burnt out.

As we shall see from the following chapters, the figures given by the Soviet authorities of the amount of radionuclides released were based on the deposition of airborne particles inside the Soviet Union. They are therefore inaccurate. Careful calculations were carried out in 1987 in various countries. It became clear from them that nearly 100 per cent of the reactor inventory of volatile radionuclides (iodine-131, caesium-134 and 137, and others) was released. The amount of less volatile isotopes released has also been reconsidered and increased, although most of them were deposited inside the Soviet Union. Most of the uranium fuel is still trapped inside, together with significant amounts of plutonium. Metallic uranium has a rather low melting point, but the uranium oxide which is used as fuel melts at temperatures above 3,000°C. The temperature of the core did not reach this level, even at the critical period. The state of the uranium fuel is unclear and the amount of graphite moderator which is still inside the core is unknown. No one knows what is left inside the sarcophagus and whether the Chernobyl radioactive volcano is really dead. Nor do they know whether it will be safe for future generations.

# 3

# The Environmental Impact

## INTRODUCTION

ON 25 April 1986 Reactor No. 4 was near the very end of its first full fuel cycle. Its core contained fission products which had accumulated for more than two years. Two-thirds of the original uranium-235 had been transformed into spent fuel – a complex mixture of radionuclides. RBMK reactors of the Chernobyl type are designed for on-load refuelling but only about 25 per cent of its 1659 fuel channels had been replaced since the reactor had gone into operation on 20 December 1983. At the time of the accident, Reactor No. 4 had 75 per cent of the fuel channels of the original first load with a burn-up up to 70–80 per cent of the full design burn-up of the uranium fuel.[1] The initial fuel enrichment (2 per cent) corresponds to 20 kg/t of the uranium-235, whereas in normally unloaded spent fuel the amount of uranium-235 is 4.5 kg/t. Unloaded fuel also contains large amounts of plutonium (4.9 kg/t) in a mixture of its different isotopes (239, 240 and 241).

As we have seen, the xenon poisoning in Unit 4 during the test resulted in many operational errors which, in the end, led to the explosion. If a similar explosion had occurred in a freshly loaded reactor the environmental and health consequences would have been less serious. Unlike coal or oil power stations which carry a constant risk throughout their work cycles, risk factors in nuclear reactors increase and become progressively more dangerous towards the end of their cycle in direct proportion to the accumulation of fission radionuclides. The proportion of nuclear energy which remains in these radioactive isotopes grows towards the end of the nuclear cycle. This is why it is incomprehensible that the most dangerous point in the reactor cycle was selected for the 'experimental blackout' test, a simulation of the most serious potential mishap.

The total core inventory of Unit 4 of the Chernobyl Atomic Electric Station (AES) before the accident was at the level of 1,100–1,200 MCi or $4 \times 10^{19}$ Bq.[2] Fortunately only about 5 per cent of the total core inventory was released into the environment before the graphite fire in the reactor core was finally extinguished after ten days of immense effort. None the less, the release was large enough to reach every country in the northern hemisphere. It was only in the Soviet Union, however, that the contamination of some geographically significant areas rose to a level incompatible with human habitation, agricultural cultivation or the commercial use of some reservoirs. As a result it was necessary to resettle permanently about 130,000 people. It was also necessary to undertake a large-scale decontamination programme which included the removal of topsoil, the destruction of forests and bushland, the construction of dams to ensure the hydrological isolation of the most contaminated areas and the creation of a fenced exclusion zone (which had to be extended to an area far larger than originally expected).

The disaster resulted in varying levels of contamination by radionuclides depending on the type of soil and the ecological system. Large-scale research programmes had to be initiated immediately, not only in the medical and genetic fields of radiology and radiobiology but also in radioecology. More than three years have elapsed since the accident, yet very few scientific papers have been published in Soviet radiobiological, ecological, environmental or radiological literature. The first Soviet Report about the accident, which was prepared for the IAEA meeting in Vienna in August 1986,[3] was only slightly updated in the papers which various officials and scientists presented to the IAEA in 1987. There were several scientific conferences in Kiev to discuss environmental problems relating to Chernobyl, but their proceedings have not yet been published. It is known that the exclusion zone around the plant has been transformed into an experimental area for radioecologists, radiobiologists and experts on the use of radiation in agriculture. But not even their preliminary findings have been published.

The Chernobyl exclusion zone is the second geographically sizeable area heavily contaminated by radionuclides to levels which could have visible genetic and biological effects on plants and animals. The first such exclusion zone, about 1,000 km$^2$ in area, has existed since 1957 in the Cheliabinsk region of the Urals. It was the result of the Kyshtym accident in which nuclear waste from many years of processing spent reactor fuel to extract plutonium for military purposes was dispersed over an extensive area.[4] In the Kyshtym accident strontium-90 was the main long-lived contaminating radionuclide. My analysis of the 'secret' Kyshtym disaster (at first to prove that it occurred and then to document it with ecological, radiobiological and genetic data[5]), together with my work in the fields of radiobiology and radiology in the Soviet Union from 1952 to 1969 has given me the knowledge and experience to approach this research on Chernobyl. It should be possible, at some point in the future, to make a scientific comparison between the environmental and other kinds of impact of the two accidents.

## THE AMOUNT, COMPOSITION AND DYNAMIC OF RELEASE OF RADIONUCLIDES INTO THE ENVIRONMENT

The emergency services of the Soviet nuclear industry had contingency plans for possible reactor accidents, but the plans envisaged a single release of radionuclides into the environment, rather than a protracted eruption.[6] The details of the plans were secret and had never been revealed in the open literature. The American Atomic Energy Commission sponsored a special study of a 'worst case' reactor accident well before the massive American programme began of nuclear generated electricity. Published in 1957, it was called *The Brookhaven Report, WASH-740*[7]. The 'worst case' envisaged in the report concerned an explosion in a pressurized water reactor of 200 MWe size nearing the end of its 180-day cycle. Its inventory would be about 400 MCi, less than half the inventory of Unit 4 of the Chernobyl RBMK-1000 reactor on the day of the accident. It would be expected that about half of all the radionuclides would be released and the plume would be blown towards a large city with a population of 1 million people situated 50 km from the reactor. Like the Soviet contingency plans, the American scenario presumed a single release and the formation of a plume in one direction only. It was calculated that such a cloud containing 200 million curies of fission radionuclides would result in 3,400 deaths, 43,000 injuries and property damage of $7 billion (at 1957 prices).

The financial cost of the Chernobyl accident, which has been officially estimated (the unofficial estimates are higher) as more than 8 billion roubles (or $14 billion) at the end of 1987 and 11 billion roubles (or $19 billion) in 1988, tallies with this.[8] The release of radioactivity was four times less than in the theoretical scenario of WASH-740 and the nearest large city (with a population of 2.5 million) was 130 km away. However, the accident proved more complex than the expectations of the Soviet contingency plans or WASH-740 because the release of radio-activity was extended over ten days. It therefore affected all directions out from the reactor. It was also accompanied by an intense graphite fire and high temperatures. As a result, the radioactive cloud rose high into the atmosphere and travelled far from the explosion. About 50 million curies of different radioactive isotopes were discharged from the damaged reactor, in addition to larger amounts of the radioactive inert gases krypton-85 and xenon-133, which are generally not considered to harm the environment (xenon and krypton are released into the environment during normal reactor operations although not, of course, as a single event).

Soviet estimates of the release of radionuclides were made by aerial gamma-ray measurement using special helicopters and airplanes of the Air Force and by some other methods employed by the radiological service of the USSR State Committee on Hydrometeorology and Environmental Protection. The report to the IAEA admitted that these measurements were very inaccurate and could have an error up to 50 per cent, mostly as an underestimation. More accurate measurements were apparently carried out later on the basis of samples of soil, water and vegetation, but they have not been published. However, some results of the analysis of samples relevant to the contamination of the exclusion zone were published in the Soviet report for the IAEA. They indicate that as much as 20 MCi of fission and transuranic (plutonium, neptunium, curium) isotopes may have been deposited within the 30 km radius area which was evacuated. Other heavily contaminated spots (by primary and secondary contamination) were located in May and June 1986 west, north, north-east and north-west of the exclusion zone. These included the small towns of Bragin (about 60 km from Chernobyl) and Elsk.[9] Later studies, in 1987 and 1988, also found significant contamination in several districts of the Mogilev and Gomel regions at a distance of between 100 and 300 km from the Chernobyl plant, in the Briansk and Zhitomir regions and in some spots south of Kiev.[10]

In September 1986 the International Nuclear Safety Advisory Group (INSAG) of the IAEA published a summary report. On the basis of the Soviet report, extensive discussions in Vienna in August and a recalculation of the figures of the Soviet Working Document (from curies to becquerels), a table[11] of the core inventories and total releases of different radionuclides was presented (see table 3.1).

It should be stressed that the figures in table 3.1 reflect the amounts of radioactive isotopes which were released and deposited *inside* the Soviet Union. The Soviet experts who prepared the report for the IAEA meeting did not speculate on the amount of volatile isotopes (primarily radioiodine and radiocaesium) deposited outside Soviet borders. The Soviet government has not acknowledged any liability for radioactive contamination of the environment in other countries and maintains that

# The Environmental Impact

Table 3.1 *Core inventories and total releases*

| Element | Half-life (d) | Inventory[a] (Bq) | Percentage released |
|---|---|---|---|
| Krypton-85 | 3,930 | $3.3 \times 10^{16}$ | ~ 100 |
| Xenon-133 | 5.27 | $1.7 \times 10^{18}$ | ~ 100 |
| Iodine-131 | 8.05 | $1.3 \times 10^{18}$ | 20 |
| Tellurium-132 | 3.25 | $3.2 \times 10^{17}$ | 15 |
| Caesium-134 | 750 | $1.9 \times 10^{17}$ | 10 |
| Caesium-137 | $1.1 \times 10^{4}$ | $2.9 \times 10^{17}$ | 13 |
| Molybdenum-99 | 2.8 | $4.8 \times 10^{18}$ | 2.3 |
| Zirconium-95 | 65.5 | $4.4 \times 10^{18}$ | 3.2 |
| Ruthenium-103 | 39.5 | $4.1 \times 10^{18}$ | 2.9 |
| Ruthenium-106 | 368 | $2.0 \times 10^{18}$ | 2.9 |
| Barium-140 | 12.8 | $2.9 \times 10^{18}$ | 5.6 |
| Cerium-141 | 32.5 | $4.4 \times 10^{18}$ | 2.3 |
| Cerium-144 | 284 | $3.2 \times 10^{18}$ | 2.8 |
| Strontium-89 | 53 | $2.0 \times 10^{18}$ | 4.0 |
| Strontium-90 | $1.02 \times 10^{4}$ | $2.0 \times 10^{17}$ | 4.0 |
| Neptunium-239 | 2.35 | $1.4 \times 10^{17}$ | 3 |
| Plutonium-238 | $3.15 \times 10^{4}$ | $1.0 \times 10^{15}$ | 3 |
| Plutonium-239 | $8.9 \times 10^{6}$ | $8.5 \times 10^{14}$ | 3 |
| Plutonium-240 | $2.4 \times 10^{6}$ | $1.2 \times 10^{15}$ | 3 |
| Plutonium-241 | 4,800 | $1.7 \times 10^{17}$ | 3 |
| Curium-242 | 164 | $2.6 \times 10^{16}$ | 3 |

[a] Decay corrected to 6 May 1986 and calculated as prescribed by the Soviet experts.
Source: INSAG-1 Report, p. 34.

the amount was negligible. In fact, as shown in chapter 6 on the global impact of Chernobyl, larger amounts of some volatile isotopes were distributed outside the Soviet Union than inside. Only one-third of the radiocaesium released (caesium-134 and 137) was deposited in the Soviet Union (about 1.5 MCi). A similar amount was deposited in the rest of Europe and the remaining third was deposited world-wide in the northern hemisphere.[12] The total release of radioiodine and radiocaesium has been calculated to be three times higher than that indicated in table 3.1. The figures given in table 3.1 of other isotopes released by the accident also need correction if the global fallout is considered and not just Soviet fallout.

It should also be emphasized that the radioactive substances were not discharged in a single event. The release continued for ten days (from 26 April to 5 May 1986) and the pattern of discharge (the initial release caused by the explosion, the cooldown period and the heat-up period) was linked to very different conditions of distribution of radionuclides into the atmosphere. The general pattern of the release is represented in figure 3.1.[13] The cooldown period reflects the measures taken by the Soviet authorities to extinguish the graphite fire with massive drops of sand, clay, lead and dolomite. The reactor core, however, covered with about 5,000 tonnes of these substances, began to heat up due to the reduction of the heat exchange of the fission materials. The temperature of the core increased to at least 2,500°C and this caused the renewed release of radioactive particles, mostly in the form of gases, vapours and a very fine aerosol.

The radioactive plume which moved towards Finland and Sweden and later contaminated other parts of Western Europe came from the

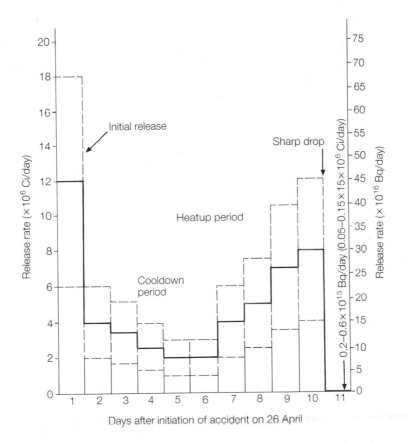

**Figure 3.1** The daily release of radioactive substances to the atmosphere during the Chernobyl accident (excluding inert gases). The values shown are calculated for 6 May 1986 taking into account radioactive decay up until then. The radioactivity released on 26 April 1986 was $75-80 \times 10^{16}$ Bq ($20-22 \times 10^6$ Ci). The range of uncertainty is ± 50 per cent (from INSAG Report, p. 35).

release during the first three days of the accident. After 29 April the radioactive cloud moved in a southerly direction towards Kiev and south-westwards to Moldavia. The fallout from this cloud later contaminated Greece and Turkey. The radionuclides discharged during the last three days of the heat-up were blown to the eastern parts of the Soviet Union. The Soviet Working Document presented a draft map which showed that the areas towards Kuibyshev (in the Volga basin) and close to the South Urals were also affected.[14] Figure 3.1 shows that the large-scale release of radionuclides decreased dramatically during the eleventh day after the accident. However, the subsequent release is only insignificant by comparison with the initial massive releases; by any other standard it was very high.

During the last day of the heat-up period about 8 MCi were released into the environment. The next day, when the situation was reported to be 'under control', only 150,000 Ci were released. This was more than during the 1957 Windscale accident in the UK. On 9 May the total release was about 12,600 Ci. Twenty days after the accident, on 16 May, 1,680 Ci of radionuclides were released into the surrounding areas.[15] At the very end of May the daily releases were still much higher than the *total* release of the Three Mile Island reactor in 1979. On 5 June 1986 a specially equipped plane tested the air over the reactor to estimate the radionuclide composition of continuing releases. The calculations made on the basis of only 8 radionuclides which became fixed to the filters (because they occurred in particles, not in gaseous form) indicated that the daily release from the reactor was at the level of 135 Ci.[16] It was only in October, about six months after the accident, when the stricken reactor was finally entombed in a specially built protection containment structure using about 400,000 m$^3$ of reinforced concrete (the 'sarcophagus'), that it stopped contaminating the environment.

### THE LEVEL AND PATTERN OF RADIOACTIVE CONTAMINATION OF THE ENVIRONMENT

Only a very approximate, rather crude map of radioactive contamination of the area around Chernobyl was presented in the Soviet Report at the Vienna IAEA post-accident meeting in August 1986. It is reproduced in figure 3.2. It did not show the position of villages and other rural settlements (there are about 250 within the area covered by the map). The report represented a study of the distribution of contamination over a period of about 60 days after the accident. More legible maps of the contamination, based both on aerial and surface measurement, must have been available (presumably local health and agricultural officials have access to them) but they were not published in 1986 or in 1987–8. In 1989, however, when the original very high level of contamination had declined by more than tenfold, maps of the contamination of the Ukraine, Byelorussia and the RSFSR (Russian Soviet Federated Socialist Republic) were finally published.[17]

The initial exclusion zone declared on 27 April was only 10 km in radius around the damaged ractor. It was extended to a 30 km radius on 2 May when it became clear that there was contamination in a much wider

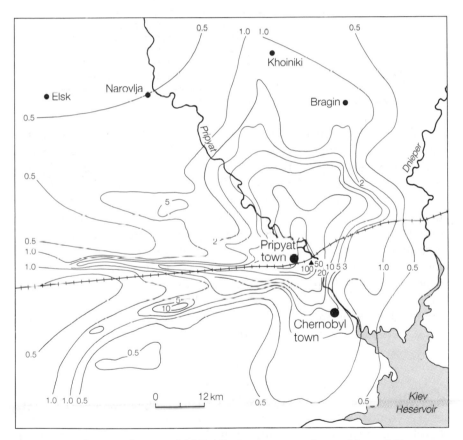

**Figure 3.2** The map of gamma field distribution as measured on 29 May 1986 in an area of about 10,000 km² around Chernobyl nuclear plant. Isolines indicate the levels of radiation in milliroentgens per hour (mR/h) (from *The Accident . . . Soviet IAEA Report*, Part II, Annex 5, figure 5.4).

area as a result of the protracted release of radionuclides. However, during the heat-up period from 2 to 5 May about half of the total release of 50 MCi was discharged over an even more extensive area. Thus the area considered heavily contaminated in the tables presented in the Soviet Working Document included more than 5,000 km².

Table 3.2 *Estimated surface activity in 30 km zone of the damaged reactor on 26 June 1986*

| Range of the activity (mR/h) | Area of zone (km²) | Activity | |
|---|---|---|---|
| | | Absolute (MCi) | Relative (%) |
| >20 | 870 | 5–8.7 | 63.0 |
| 10–20 | 480 | 0.8–1.4 | 10.2 |
| 5–10 | 1,100 | 1–1.7 | 10.8 |
| 3–5 | 2,780 | 1.3–2.2 | 16.0 |
| Total | 5,230 | 8–14 | 100.0 |

*Source: The Accident . . . Soviet IAEA Report*, Part II, Annex 4, table 4.1.

Table 3.2, taken from the Soviet Working Document,[18] presents the approximate distribution of this contamination on 26 June 1986. It shows that from 6 to 9 MCi of radionuclides (more than 20 mR/h) was deposited in an area of 870 km². A further area of 1,580 km² absorbed 2–3.1 MCi (a radiation level ranging from 5 to 20 mR/h). Further away from the site of the accident about 1.3–2.2 MCi of radionuclides (with a radiation exposure of 3–5 mR/h) was deposited over 2,780 km². A total area of 5,230 km² was calculated to contain between 8 and 14 MCi at the end of June, by when the amount of radioactive iodine in the deposited radionuclides was already insignificant (about 97 per cent of radioiodine was lost through decay). This area of 5,230 km² is still classified as being in the 30 km exclusion zone around the Chernobyl plant, although it clearly extends well beyond it.[19] It is clear from table 3.2 that only those settlements that were located in areas contaminated with more than 300–500 Ci/km² were evacuated in 1986.

The radiometric measurements of soil samples carried out during the first half of May[20] within the exclusion zone (table 3.3) showed a very heavy contamination well above the 'Derived Emergency Reference Levels' accepted in the United Kingdom and other EEC countries. Among the radioactive isotopes indicated in the table only ruthenium-106, caesium-134 and 137 can be considered long-lived (368, 750 and $1.1 \times 10^4$ days half-life respectively), with certain ecological effects.

Table 3.3 *Data from radiometric measurements of soil samples on 17 May 1986 on the northern path of fallout within the limits of the 30 km zone*

| Radionuclide | Specific activity | | Content in sample (%) | Content in irradiated reactor fuel (%) |
|---|---|---|---|---|
| | (Bq/g) | (Ci/km²) | | |
| Cerium-141 | $3.2 \times 10^3$ | $5.1 \times 10^2$ | 15.8 | 18.3 |
| Tellurium-132 | $3.4 \times 10^2$ | $5.4 \times 10^1$ | 1.7 | 0.22 |
| Iodine-131 | $3.1 \times 10^3$ | $5.1 \times 10^2$ | 15.8 | 2.8 |
| Ruthenium-103 | $3.5 \times 10^3$ | $5.6 \times 10^2$ | 17.3 | 21.4 |
| Ruthenium-106 | $9.6 \times 10^2$ | $1.5 \times 10^2$ | 4.6 | 16.9 |
| Caesium-134 | $1.6 \times 10^3$ | $2.5 \times 10^2$ | 7.7 | 4.5 |
| Caesium-137 | $1.7 \times 10^3$ | $2.7 \times 10^2$ | 8.3 | 3.4 |
| Zirconium-95 | $4 \times 10^3$ | $6.4 \times 10^2$ | 19.8 | 23.0 |
| Barium-140 | $1.8 \times 10^3$ | $2.9 \times 10^2$ | 9.0 | 9.6 |

1 Ci = $3.7.10^{10}$ Bq
Source: *The Accident . . . Soviet IAEA Report*, Part II, Annex 4, table 4.2.

However, strontium-90 and cerium-144 (with long half-lives) which were also released in rather large amounts and deposited primarily inside the Soviet Union should also be taken into account. The Soviet radiological services acknowledged the problems of measuring strontium-90 and plutonium levels because most of the facilities available during the initial period were for measuring gamma radiation.

The Chairman of the Soviet State Committee on Hydrometeorology and Environmental Protection, Yu. A. Israel and several of his colleagues, who were members of the Government Commission (and who were, in any case, directly responsible for monitoring radioactive contamination in the Soviet Union), published two articles in a professional journal in 1987.[21] They indicate how little information about the radioactive contamination of the environment the Soviet government is ready to disclose (more scientific papers have been written about the Chernobyl fallout in Japan than in the Soviet Union). None the less, they are the most reliable source of information we have about the general pattern of distribution of radionuclides inside the Soviet Union. They indicate that radioactivity was transferred in different directions at different altitudes. Although experimental measurements made it possible to follow the distribution of radioactivity in western, northern and southern directions, the movement of the cloud in a north-eastern, eastern and south-eastern direction was analysed only later, on the basis of meteorological models. In the first five days after the accident (from 26 to 30 April) the direction in which radioactive particles were transferred in different plumes at different altitudes (from surface to 1.5 km) changed through 360° and made a full circle. However, the most serious fallout was registered during the first few days, apparently because the plume consisted of larger pieces of debris and hot particles at this time, which fell down more quickly and created a so-called 'close track', no further from the reactor than 60–80 km in western and northern directions, in which nearly 30 per cent of the total Chernobyl release came down to the surface.

If Soviet measurements made it possible to estimate that about 3.5–4 per cent of the total inventory of the reactor was contained in the fallout within the Soviet Union, the extended exclusion zone (up to 40 km from the reactor) contained about 40 per cent of this amount on 10 May 1986.[22]

The map of the 'gamma field' as it was estimated in May 1986 was updated in 1987, about a year after the accident.[23] The gamma radiation close to the damaged reactor was still very high (between 50 and 100 mR/h). But just inside the perimeter of the heavily contaminated zone (Elsk–Narovliya–Bragin), the radiation level declined from 0.5–1.0 mR/h to 0.1–0.5 mR/h. This was still much higher than the natural background radiation which was 0.015 mR/h in that district before the accident. As was to be expected, the proportion of long-lived radioisotopes in the environment was higher in 1987 than in 1986. The report maintained that special maps were made for each remaining isotope, but no examples of the maps were presented. It merely mentioned that the caesium contamination was 'patchy'; partly because of the dynamic of the eruption, partly because of the unevenness of rain in the areas through which the radioactive cloud passed. In places, the contamination with caesium-137 and caesium-134 was as low as 20–30 Ci/km$^2$ and in other places it was as high as 80 Ci/km$^2$.[24] In the 'close track' the contamination with plutonium reached 0.1–1.0 Ci/km$^2$, but it reached a level higher than 10 Ci/km$^2$ very close to the reactor.[25]

The isotope composition of the contaminated areas varied in different directions and at different distances from the reactor. In Western Europe only a few volatile isotopes (mainly radioiodine and radiocaesium) were closely monitored. In the Soviet Union the situation was very different. In the exclusion zone and areas close to it less volatile radionuclides, such as molybdenum-99, tellurium-132, zirconium-95 and neptunium-239 dominated over caesium-137. But these isotopes have relatively short half-lives (between 2 and 60 days) and were therefore not considered particularly dangerous. Only two isotopes, cerium-144 (half-life 284 days) and ruthenium-106 (half-life 368 days) caused problems in 1987 and 1988, particularly because the fallout in the exclusion zone and around it contained more of them than of caesium-137 and strontium-90, two long-lived isotopes. There was comparatively little radiostrontium in the first plume, but far more in the heat-up release of 2–5 May. As a result, the southern 'track' was more heavily contaminated with strontium-90 than the western or northern tracks.[26] Even in 1987, a year after the accident, the total amount of caesium-137 was estimated at 800,000 curies. One-quarter of this amount was localized in the 'close track'.[27]

In 1989, because of medical concern and public pressure, it was acknowledged that there were many other heavily contaminated spots in several other regions, often very far from the exclusion zone. They were mainly caused by local rain which washed down radioactive particles. The map that had been presented to the Politburo commission in 1986 was published (see figure 3.3). It showed the location of areas and spots with radioactive levels above 2 mR/h (which corresponds to about 80 Ci/km or 3,000,000 Bq/m$^2$).[28]

Figure 3.2 represents the pattern of gamma fields as estimated from aerial measurements on 29 May 1986. It shows an area of about 10,000 km$^2$ around the Chernobyl plant. However, some other areas of European Russia were heavily contaminated because of rain and needed special decontamination measures, restrictions on the consumption of locally produced food and other measures. In 1986 the government was not prepared to disclose the real scale of the contamination. Many later publications on the environmental consequences of the accident only covered the contamination around the exclusion zone, as depicted on this map. However, the accumulation of radiation by people living in districts which had not been included in the evacuation in 1986 reached a critical level in some places by 1989. It was this (and local public pressure) that forced the publication of more comprehensive maps. By 1989 the level of contamination had already declined tenfold.

Maps published in *Pravda* in 1989 were rather approximate and not very informative. They are reproduced in figure 3.3a–c. They included one rather crude map (figure 3.3a) which was presented to the government on 10 May 1986 and which served as the basis for decisions about the final stage of evacuating the population (doses of ground radiation above the level of 5 mR/h) and about the zones of strict radiological control (3–5 mR/h) from which children and pregnant women would have to be temporarily evacuated. The two other maps (figures 3.3b and c) show the pattern of contamination of two areas with caesium-137 as estimated during 1988.

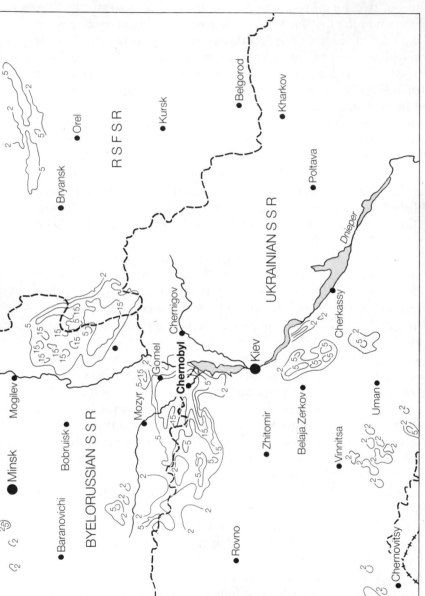

**Figure 3.3a** The gamma field pattern in the affected regions of the European parts of the USSR as measured on 10 May 1986 but disclosed only on 20 March 1989. The level of contamination in north-western and north-eastern directions give the reading of 5 mR/h as far as 300 km from the Chernobyl plant. There are spots of very high activity (15 mR/h) as far as 250–300 km from the reactor and spots of substantial contamination at distances of 300–500 km (Bryansk and Kaluga regions, Minsk region, Uman region). The total area with levels more than 2 mR/h is about

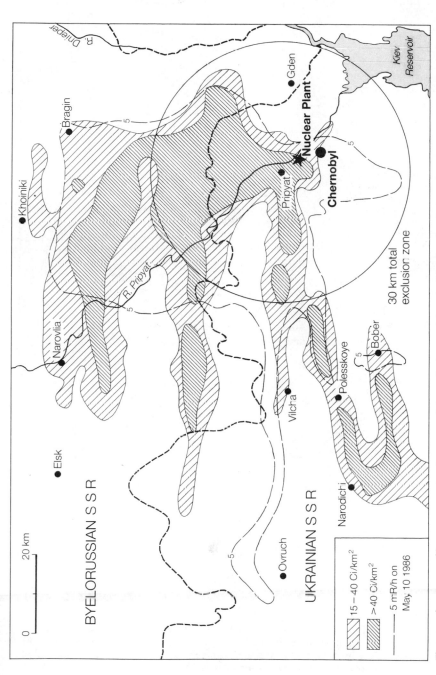

**Figure 3.3b** Areas of heavy contamination around the exclusion zone (marked by a 30 km radius circle) with the caesium-137 as measured during 1988. Only two levels are indicated. The contour marked by isolines indicates the territory which was contaminated above 5 mR/h of gamma radiation on 10 May, 1986.

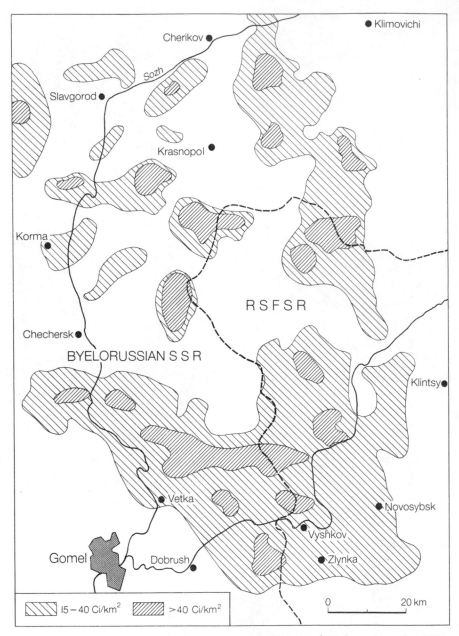

**Figure 3.3c** Map of the heavily contaminated districts of Byelorussia and RSFSR (Gomel, Mogilev and Bryansk regions) which was not disclosed until March 1989. The contamination was by caesium-137 and was probably caused by local rain at the end of April 1986. The total contaminated territory (levels above 15 Ci/km$^2$) is larger than the area in and around the exclusion zone. About 1,500 km$^2$ contained more than 40 Ci/km$^2$.

When the map in figure 3.3a is compared with the map presented for the IAEA meeting in Vienna (figure 3.2) it is clear that radioactivity on the ground declined by about tenfold between 10 May and 29 May 1986. This was the result of the decay of short-lived radioisotopes, primarily iodine-90 (half-life 8 days). In addition to the area of heavy contamination around the plant (the exclusion zone), the newly published map shows several other areas of heavy contamination. The most serious of these were in the Gomel, Mogilev and Bryansk regions, about 100–300 km north-east of Chernobyl. Some spots here registered more than 5 mR/h of radioactivity (and some reached 15 mR/h). They should, therefore, have been included in the evacuation plans. Large areas of heavy contamination which required strict measures of control and the evacuation of children and pregnant women were located as far as 300–400 km from the Chernobyl plant; for example, spots in Kaluga and Orel regions, north-east of Chernobyl; in the western parts of the Minsk region; and in many districts south and south-west of Kiev, some of them close to Moldavia. However, the two main zones of contamination which are shown in figure 3.3b and c still contained comparatively large territories with caesium-137 levels between 15 and 40 Ci/km$^2$ (or from 555,000 to 1,500,000 Bq/m$^2$) and above in 1989.

## ENVIRONMENTAL AND ECOLOGICAL EFFECTS OF THE RADIOACTIVE CONTAMINATION AND DECONTAMINATION MEASURES

The average level of ground contamination within the 30 km exclusion zone (8–10 mCi/m$^2$) was high enough to produce obvious and immediate ecological changes, such as damage to the rodent population and the more sensitive species of plants. The Soviet press reported rather casually that the pine trees around the Chernobyl plant died within a few days after the accident.[29] Later it was acknowledged that 400 hectares of pine forest had died.[30] Birch, oak and other leafy species survived the first year.

The pine forest was situated in the path of the first, most lethal, cloud formed by the initial explosion which blew out parts of the reactor core. The first two explosions threw out large particles and pieces of the reactor core. Their weight determined their distribution outside the reactor. Heavier particles were deposited close to the reactor and lighter particles further away. Very small particles formed an aerosol which remained airborne for days. They were raised to high altitudes partly by the heat and fire from the reactor, but also because many particles were composed of pure radioactive isotopes which were hot and which generated hot air around themselves. Each such particle behaved like a tiny hot balloon. These small microscopic hot particles were brought down by rain. As their radioactivity was reduced by the decay of the isotope their ability to remain airborne diminished and they fell as radioactive dust. Fortunately the Pripyat marshes absorbed a significant part of the first eruption of radionuclides. If it were not for this, the medical consequences would have been much more serious.

The decontamination measures which were carried out from May until the beginning of the winter in 1986 included the removal of topsoil from the most contaminated parts of the exclusion zone. The total area of decontamination and the way in which the contaminated top soil was buried remain unknown. Bush land could be cleared fairly easily but removing the contamination from the marshes common in that area was impossible. The geographical region which was most seriously affected by the Chernobyl fallout is known as Polyes'ye (which means 'woodland' in Russian) in Soviet geography or as the Pripyat Marshes in Western literature. *Polesye* is the largest swamp in Europe and it consists mostly of soggy forests. Ecological systems of this type have a very high retention capacity for radioactive caesium, because it moves very quickly into the plants. It was, therefore, expected that most of the radioactive caesium which contaminated the regions (in the north of the Ukraine and the south of Byelorussia) would remain there for decades. During 1960–85 many parts of the area were transformed into agricultural land through large-scale reclamation projects. The Chernobyl nuclear plant was built in the south-east part of Polyes'ye. The area around the plant was primarily agricultural and was not densely populated. In the medical section of the Soviet Working Document a 100,000 km$^2$ area of *Polesye* was stated to be the most seriously affected by fallout.

Caesium isotopes, to which main attention continues to be given in the Western literature, are relatively volatile and they were evenly distributed and contributed to the global fallout. Isotopes of strontium, the shorter-lived $^{89}$Sr (half-life 53 days) and $^{90}$Sr (half-life $1.02 \times 10^4$ days), are less volatile. They fell mostly inside the Soviet Union. The Soviet Working Document did not indicate the pattern of strontium distribution. By 1987, strontium-89, which formed the greater part of the release of strontium (about 2.2 MCi), had ceased to be important. But the 220,000 Ci of strontium-90 which were released will remain a problem for decades. There have been occasional reports in the Soviet general press that the decontamination methods for strontium included the massive distribution of calcium materials (for example, lime) which fix strontium, and deep ploughing to turn down the topsoil and bury the strontium isotopes well below it. This technique will apparently prevent the further distribution of strontium-90 through surface erosion but it could still cause difficulties for the agricultural use of the contaminated land.

If 100,000 km$^2$ of Polyes'ye which are mentioned in the Soviet Working Document as the second most heavily contaminated area (after the exclusion zone) absorbed about 10 per cent of all radioactive caesium released from the damaged reactor and also significant amounts of radiostrontium, external and internal radioactivity will not be high enough to affect the ecological situation directly. However, the isotopes were not distributed evenly. Many more heavily contaminated 'hot spots' were caused by rain. In June 1986 about 110 new villages were evacuated. In September 1987, in the Soviet report to the IAEA International Conference on Nuclear Power Performance and Safety which also discussed the measures taken to reduce the exposure of the population to radioactive fallout from Chernobyl, the authors, L. A. Il'in and O. A. Pavlovsky, acknowledged that intensive decontamination was continuing in 1987:

> The decontamination of more than 600 population centres, the removal and subsequent burial of contaminated soil, the suppression of dust over large areas, the asphalting or covering of contaminated sectors with gravel, chippings, sand or fresh earth, the designation of exclusion zones and the restriction imposed on productive activity and other similar measures enabled the average public exposure in these regions to be reduced by a factor of 2–3.[31]

The 'more than 600 population centres' (usually villages and small towns) mentioned here are *in addition* to the 186 which were evacuated in May and June 1986. It became known that new restricted zones, which were called 'areas of strict control' and 'areas of periodic control', were established in addition to the exclusion zone around the Chernobyl plant. But the general geography of this contamination was made known only in 1989 (figure 3.3a). In 1987 it was only acknowledged that the areas are located inside the Gomel'skaya, Kievskaya, Bryanskaya and Mogilevskaya regions.

Some reports published in the general media suggested that in the area of approximately a 200 km radius around Chernobyl (and which included the Kiev, Gomel and Chernigov regions) special attempts to reduce the surface contamination would involve collecting grass and autumn leaves which would then be buried as nuclear waste. Periodic mowing and burying the cut grass can reduce the amount of radioactive caesium very substantially over a period of two to three years, but it is not very effective in reducing the levels of strontium-90 and plutonium.

Several aquatic ecosystems are located in the 30 km exclusion zone. RBMK reactors release far more radionuclides into the environment during their normal operation than PWR and other types of reactors. Cooling ponds which are located near most Soviet RBMK reactors act both to cool the water and as decontamination reservoirs since the radionuclides normally accumulate in the sediment at the bottom. Special monitoring stations measure this accumulation from time to time and Soviet ecological literature periodically reports on the distribution of radionuclides in such cooling ponds.

The Chernobyl cooling pond is constructed from the waters of the Pripyat river. It is very large, with a water surface of 22 km² and forms a lake deep enough for navigation. Because of its warmer water and profuse aquatic vegetation, it was rich in fish reserves and was used for commercial fishing. Some fish species do not accumulate significant amounts of radionuclides if they are fed artificially with 'clean' food. After the accident, part of the Pripyat river flowed through the exclusion zone. The northern part of the 1,000 km² Kiev reservoir, behind the Kiev–Dnieper dam, also lay within the exclusion zone.

The Chernobyl cooling pond was heavily contaminated by the reactor disaster not only from the fallout of aerosol and reactor debris caused by the accident but from the water in the emergency cooling systems which had been used to cool the reactor and from the water used by the fire brigades. The radioactivity monitored by aerial measurement did not include this contamination. The total amount of contaminated water which was discharged into the cooling pond remains unknown. It was reported that the operators tried for about 12 hours to flood the reactor core with the help of the auxiliary feedwater pumps and water from the emergency storage tanks. The flow rate of this unsuccessful operation was said to be about 200–300 tonnes of water per hour.[32] Later the water from the flooded foundations and the 'bubbler pool' was also drained into the cooling pond. It seems that a lot of the water used in the initial decontamination measures was discharged into the cooling pond which became a contamination store. Protective dams were constructed in an attempt to prevent the discharge (also possible via rains and spring flooding) of radionuclides into open waters such as the Pripyat river and Kiev reservoirs. About 80 km of dams and underground walls were built for this purpose before the spring thaw in April 1987.[33]

It proved impossible to protect the 22 km² cooling pond adjacent to the plant. Most of the contamination, particularly the reactor debris and 'hot' particles, was insoluble and it contaminated the sediment at the bottom of the pond. The radioactivity of the cooling pond was monitored in May. The Soviet Working Document reported that the level of radioactivity of the water was $10^{-8}$ Ci/litre, whereas that of the bottom sediment was $10^{-3}$ Ci/kg.[34] In June, measurements of gamma radio-activity near the bottom of the cooling pond revealed a level of about 8 rad/h. It was calculated that radioactive decay and other processes would reduce this to 0.5 rad/h in one year. The level of internal exposure for aquatic plants for June 1986 was about 10 rad/h, according to the Soviet Working Document. The daily dose of radiation for fish species which live and breed in the undergrowth of aquatic vegetation reached the level of 100–200 rad. Soviet experts acknowledged that this would have both a direct and indirect biological effect.[35] Cold-blooded vertebrates (fish, reptilian and amphibian species) have at least a ten times higher resistance to radiation exposure than mammalian species. None the less, the mortality of the fish population in the lake will increase sharply and reproduction will be impossible for some time. It would be very interesting to compare the 1986 levels with the situation in later years in this unique 'hot' artificial lake. No observations have been published in the Soviet scientific literature, however, and the total amount of radioactive products in the cooling pond has not been reported. From the contamination level of the water and bottom sediment it is clear that about 2 MCi of radioactivity was fixed in the 10 cm of bottom silt (that is, about 10 per cent of the total fallout within the exclusion zone).

Among the soluble radionuclides which mainly contaminated the waters of the cooling pond and Kiev reservoirs, iodine-131 represented the most obvious problem in May and June 1986. In May 1986 the concentration of $^{131}$I in the water of the Kiev reservoir was $10^{-9}$ Ci/litre or 37 Bq/litre which was not higher than the level permitted by Soviet standards. The concentration of radionuclides in the bottom sediment of the Kiev reservoir was $10^{-7}$ Ci/kg (the level in the bottom sediment of the Pripyat river close to the exclusion zone was $10^{-5}$ Ci/kg).[3] If only 10 cm of the bottom sediment is considered to be contaminated, this would mean that the Kiev reservoirs contained about 100,000 Ci of radionuclides in June. Despite preventative measures, significant injections of soluble caesium salts from ground water were inevitable in the spring of 1987. The dams built along the river could offer protection only from surface flooding.

The Kiev reservoir was built in the 1960s for the Kiev dam and hydroelectric station. The location of a huge amount of water so close to the city was a permanent source of worry to Kiev residents, particularly after a flooding disaster in 1969, when residential areas in the Baby Yar districts were washed away with a significant loss of life (the number of victims was never disclosed but it is thought to be in the hundreds). The northern part of the Kiev reservoir was located inside the contaminated exclusion zone and the Ukrainian government had to build alternative water supplies for Kiev. To prevent the accumulation of radionuclides in the reservoir it was emptied in May 1987, despite the damage it caused to the fish population and the problems created for the water pressure of the hydroelectric station during the summer months. The Kiev reservoir and four other reservoirs in the Dnieper hydroelectric cascade took most of the contaminated flood water during the spring. This spring water normally creates high water levels in reservoirs which can be used as a source of energy (more than 2,000 MWe) for several hydroelectric stations during the summer. In 1987, it had to be ejected into the Black Sea because of environmental considerations. The result was an acute energy shortage in the Ukraine in 1987. It is not known whether the operation was repeated in 1988 but the contamination level had probably fallen enough to make it unnecessary. Most of the long-term contamination, particularly of radiocaesium and radiostrontium, remains fixed in the bottom sediment.

The concentration of radiocaesium declined in water reservoirs more sharply than on the surface of the soil. In the reservoirs of the Dnieper and the Pripyat it was about 20 times lower in May 1987 than in May 1986.[37] The bottom sediment was still absorbing very large amounts of various isotopes and there was a danger that strong gales might suspend some part of the sediment in shallow parts and create problems. The spring floods in 1987 were very modest and did not increase the concentration of radioisotopes higher than the permissible level.

The Chernobyl cooling pond, which absorbed more than 2 MCi of radionuclides, is not entirely isolated from the Pripyat river and Kiev reservoir. At least 5 per cent of its water evaporates annually and the loss is compensated from the Pripyat river. The part of the river alongside the pond was heavily contaminated and the northern part of the Kiev reservoir contained about 100,000 curies of radionuclides in its sediment. Reactors No. 1 and 2 at Chernobyl had resumed operations at the end of 1986 and the water of the cooling pond had to be used again for the reactor pumps and other systems. Although the radionuclides had been absorbed in the bottom silt, there is a natural turnover between the silt and the water which would continue contaminating the water for many years. Some means had to be found of fixing the radionuclides in the Kiev reservoir, Pripyat river and Chernobyl cooling pond. A single brief report was published in July 1986 about an experiment using active absorbents like ashes from coal burnt in thermal stations, lime or synthetic materials. Thus 7,200 tonnes of absorbent material was dropped into the Pripyat river. At several control points lower down the river the concentration of radioactivity was measured. The concentration decreased, confirming 'that it was possible in principle to decontaminate large volumes of water'.[38]

It is known that when water becomes contaminated the radioactivity, particularly caesium-137, is quickly fixed in the bottom sediment which acts as a giant absorber. This process was monitored by several institutes co-ordinated by the Ukrainian Academy of Sciences. About 100 scientists held a special conference in May 1987 to discuss the results, but no report was published. Indirect evidence that artificial hydroelectric reservoirs played the role of safety buffer was given in an interview by Academician Konstantin Sytnik, Vice President of the Ukrainian Academy:

> In nature there is a mighty process of dilution and dispersion of radionuclides and this saved us . . . I am referring to the trees, earth and the water of the Kiev reservoir which received and absorbed the main ejection of radioactivity. How many times have we cursed the Kiev reservoir . . . in this situation, however, it turned out to be very useful, absorbing part of the radionuclides in its silt which then settled on the bottom of the lake . . . we hope that . . . dilution of the radionuclides to an insignificant concentration will take place.[39]

The spring thaw and floods finally reduced the surface contamination of the exclusion zone. The main hazard of 1986 – the existence of very fine surface dust containing hot radioactive particles with a high concentration of radionuclides – was significantly reduced. Most of the radionuclides were washed into the soil and, although they will create future problems in the food chain, they will no longer affect external radiation and breathing. The dust hazard had almost been resolved when snow covered the Ukraine and Byelorussia in November 1986 and reached a depth of about 1 m in February 1987. Professor Richard Wilson of Harvard University was invited to visit Chernobyl in February 1987 and was allowed to take his personal dosimeter. He described what he found:

> Radiation was not evident until we reached the outskirts of the district centre of Chernobyl, where I measured 0.05 mR/hour, down from 1 mR/hour

on 29 May 1986. I measured 0.4 mR/hour near the village of Lelev (down from 10 mR/hour on 29 May) with a high spot of 0.7 mR/hour just north of the village, and 0.4 mR/hour in the power station parking lot just to the east of the turbine hall. The road from Kiev has been damaged by trucks, but it has not been scraped or resurfaced – only washed with chemicals.

From the north side of the plant the road runs west to a junction with the Chernobyl–Pripyat road by the railroad bridge just south of Pripyat. This area was under the first radioactive plume. I was not taken along this road; the reason given was that snow was not yet cleared. However, I was told that the road surface has been scraped both there and in the town of Pripyat, and that the topsoil has been removed and replaced by clean soil on either side of the road.[40]

His measurements were below those which were published later at the IAEA meeting in September 1987. This seems to be because there was about 1 m of snow cover in February which reduced the external radiation. Despite the improvement in the environmental situation, roadblocks remained in place around Kiev in 1987 to check the radioactive contamination of all incoming cars. There were probably similar roadblocks around other towns in the area.

The discovery of new high spots of contamination produced problems. For economic rather than health reasons the government was reluctant to evacuate the population. Instead they tried emergency decontamination measures which were carried out by special chemical units of the army. One such operation in Bragin, about 70 km north of Chernobyl in Byelorussia with a population of 7,000 was described in *Izvestiya* in June. According to the report, the level of radiation in the town was not dangerous but it was too high for people to live there for a protracted period. It can be assumed from this that it was well above the artificially raised 'emergency permissible level' and high enough to cause clinical effects within a period of months. The *Izvestiya* article reported that it was too difficult to disperse 7,000 people in regions that had already absorbed evacuees from the exclusion zone. The decision was made 'to deactivate' the town without removing the people. *Izvestiya* called this 'an unexpected, bold decision'.[41] Hundreds of tip-up lorries, scrapers, bulldozers, asphalt layers and excavators were used in the operation. Local inhabitants worked alongside the army units to save the town. A. T. Bezludov, the Ukrainian Minister of Communal Works who was in charge of the operation, explained that the most difficult problem was water:

A lot of [water] is required for deactivation. Two boreholes were quickly drilled and connected to the town water supply. The second problem was to . . . ensure that the radiation 'washed' from the town in the surface flow did not penetrate down to the water bearing level. All 169 wells were cleaned (in the damaged zone there are about 13 thousand wells) and hermetically sealed. The third problem was the main source of radiation danger – ordinary dust. We are trying to get rid of it urgently. That is why we are laying asphalt in the town on all the streets, on the pavements, the squares, around the schools and kindergartens.[42]

Decontamination measures are complex and take a long time. Apart from laying asphalt, several thousand houses, garages and other buildings had to be washed with special liquids. Between 10 and 20 cm of topsoil had to be removed from the streets, gardens, allotments and the area around the town, and buried somewhere. Old houses were demolished and many roofs were changed. But this was only part of the problem. The agricultural land around deactivated towns could not be used and all food had to be brought in from 'clean' regions. The surrounding forests were heavily contaminated and there was a particularly high level of radioactivity in turf soils and marshes. It was impossible to remove the topsoil from larger agricultural areas. Bush land was cleared, but the soil was simply ploughed very deeply to turn the radioactive surface down.

The numerous villages in these heavily contaminated areas were left untouched for several more weeks. Resettling 135,000 people from the exclusion zone was not an easy task and the government and local authorities decided that the radiation hazard would have to be tolerated in smaller villages where the ignorant population did not wish to move. The journalists who described the deactivation of Bragin observed in amazement that:

> Returning to Khoiniki from Bragin . . . we saw that herds of cows were grazing next to notices stating that 'Stopping by the side of the road is forbidden'. At another place a group of about 12 people were carelessly mowing the grass. It seemed inconceivable . . . On the one hand there is a dosimeter in practically every pitcher of water; on the other cows are grazing and grass is being cut . . .[43]

Khoiniki is about 30–40 km north-west of Bragin, in the same contamination zone (see map of the exclusion zone, figure 3.2). Notices warning against cars leaving the road were common in the area because the verges were particularly heavily contaminated. Radioactive particles from the asphalt surfaces of the roads had been washed into the earth by rain and by the trucks that washed the roads.

By the end of 1986 about 500 villages and towns had been decontaminated in the same way as Bragin. A further 100 were decontaminated in 1987.

The release of radioactivity from the reactor was not significant during the summer of 1986 (about 50–200 Ci per day), but the exclusion zone and areas close to it represented a huge source of hot radioactive dust. It was distributed by the winds raising this dust, which was then washed down from the clouds by rain. Attempts were made around the Chernobyl plant and on the busiest roads to use chemical sprays to fix the dust to the ground. Most of it remained volatile, however, and each time the wind blew in a southerly direction there was alarm in Kiev, where the streets were being washed constantly. The rural areas were more vulnerable. The air masses above the plant were highly radioactive throughout the summer. The Soviet Report gives the level of airborne radioactivity above the Chernobyl plant until 6 June 1986. It varied from a minimum of 10 and 8 Ci/km$^3$ on 29 May and 4 June to 300 Ci/km$^3$ on May 25, 200 Ci/km$^3$ on May 30 and 100 Ci/km$^3$ on June 6.[44] Such a high concentration of radionuclides in the air can create a surface contamination of up to 3–6 million Bq/m$^3$ when it rains. This level makes the land absolutely unusable for agriculture.

The reason why new heavily contaminated spots continued to appear outside the exclusion zone during the summer of 1986 was rain. Each time it rained within a radius of about 100 km around the exclusion zone heavy radioactive contamination occurred. Moreover the wind constantly increased the area of heavy contamination. It was difficult to monitor this distribution of radioactivity. Optimistic reports in the media that 'normal agricultural work' had been resumed were false. Nothing normal was taking place. The borders of the exclusion zone were altered several times after June 1986 and a 'restricted zone' from which children and pregnant women were evacuated until the end of 1986 was established around the exclusion zone. The size of the restricted zone was not known in 1987 but if, as Il'in and Pavlovsky reported at the IAEA conference in September 1987, deactivation was carried out in 'more than 600 population centres' the area probably extended to about 30,000 km$^2$. The spread of radioactive dust by wind and rain ceased only when the winter snow fell.

In Western Europe the main source of contamination was initially radioiodine. Later radiocaesium began to cause concern. Plutonium, the most dangerous and most radiotoxic (because it produces alpha radiation) radionuclide with the longest life, was never a threat because it is not volatile. Although traces were found in Sweden, it did not move far from the accident site. In the Soviet Union, however, plutonium isotopes (238,

239, 240, 241, 242) represented a serious problem. Nearly 200,000 Ci of plutonium were released, 3 per cent of the core inventory. The highest concentration of plutonium and other transuranium elements was in a 2 km radius around the reactor. In some spots alpha radioactivity was as high as 2,000 Bq/g of soil.[45] This level of contamination poisons the soil for millennia. Apparently such contaminated soil was buried as nuclear waste. At a distance of 50–100 km from the plant the concentration of plutonium in the air and on the surface was reported to be 'below the maximal permissible level'. But no information was given about the plutonium level in the area from 2 to 50 km from the reactor. Tables of plutonium concentration at certain distances from the plant are given only for the north-eastern, south-eastern, western and south-western directions. The north-western direction which was affected by the first plume containing the highest proportion of reactor core particles is omitted.[46] At a distance of 105 km north-east of the plant, the plutonium level was registered at 10–15 Bq/m$^2$. This level rose to 180 Bq/m$^2$ at a distance of 48 km from the plant in the same direction.[47] In the western direction the levels are similar. This seems to indicate that the levels in the omitted north-western direction were much higher and well above permissible levels even outside the exclusion zone. This must be why the figures are missing from the Soviet report.

The topsoil, bushland, fallen leaves, water and other liquids collected during the decontamination measures had to be buried properly like nuclear waste. But the enormous volume of waste that was collected created a problem. Each nuclear plant has storage space for nuclear waste but not for such vast amounts. Newspaper reports and unpublished discussions at the IAEA post-accident meeting indicate that concrete pits which had been prepared for the construction of two more reactor units at Chernobyl (Nos 5 and 6) were used to store the waste, but they were too small to accommodate all of it. The seriousness of the problem of removing and disposing of large amounts of earth was acknowledged at the post-accident meeting, but no indication was given about how it was carried out.[48] The only way that contaminated earth containing several million curies of radioactive products can be disposed of is by transforming the most contaminated spot into a giant burial ground for nuclear waste and isolating it from the Pripyat river basin.

One project that attempted to deal with the problem was the construction of a deep waterproof wall in the earth which reached the waterproof geological layer beneath the plant. A waterproof wall would prevent ground water from the most contaminated area leaking into the Pripyat river and other water sources. Geological tests showed that the water-resistant layer of clay was located 30 m below the surface. A giant trench was dug more than 32 m deep around the plant site and was filled with special waterproof bentonite concrete and other water-insoluble compounds. It formed a huge waterproof panel with extra drainage control. The area that had to be isolated from the hydrological environment had to extend far beyond the sarcophagus which was to enclose the reactor (a 2–3 km radius was probably required). The engineering works and concrete required to complete the project were enormous. Work was begun in June 1986. It is not clear whether it was completed before the spring thaw began: 'The so called 'wall in the earth' . . . was meant to create what the construction people called a 'saucepan' so that the contaminated water could not penetrate beyond the borders of the station. (Special holes will be bored to pump the liquid from the 'saucepan' . . . straight into cleansing vessels)'.[49]

This project was less visible than the sarcophagus which was built around Reactor No. 4 and aroused less publicity. Only one report has appeared about it in a little known popular science weekly *NTR* (the initials stand for Scientific and Technical Revolution). It was not maintained in the Soviet IAEA Report or in the proceedings of the IAEA Nuclear Safety Advisory Group report which appeared later.[50] This was probably not an oversight, but a deliberate attempt to avoid an embarrassing problem. The entombment of the damaged reactor unit was a complex engineering construction which was built to certain specific recommendations. Creating a waterproof dam deep under the ground was equally complex but far less predictable. It may not have met the technical requirements for the permanent disposal of radioactive waste in underground repositories. Current international regulations require that underground disposal sites are constructed on rock formations. They should be capable of retaining radionuclides without any leakage for up to 10,000 years after disposal. The 'wall in the earth' built under Chernobyl plant is almost certainly a temporary solution and it is uncertain how well it serves for the disposal of radioactive materials from the surrounding areas. The surface of this repository of nuclear waste is probably increasing and new sections were probably added in 1987 and 1988.

However adequate the 'saucepan' is, it was built around the site of the nuclear plant to contain and isolate hydrologically the most contaminated spot (probably about 10 km$^2$) which contained much of the larger-sized debris from the reactor core. It was technically impossible and far too expensive to attempt to isolate the whole exclusion zone hydrologically or to bring contaminated topsoil from other parts of the exclusion zone into the isolated area. Topsoil, roofs, bushes and trees were removed from the villages and towns outside the exclusion zone that were decontaminated (Bragin, Khoiniki and others). Many thousands of tons of contaminated material were moved to clearings in the fields into fenced temporary disposal sites. Nobody knows what was done with this nuclear waste later. Repositories for long-term storage should have been built very quickly, but the work was not started in 1986 and nothing was reported in 1987–9. Considerable amounts of radioactivity seem to have leaked into the ground water in the spring of 1987.

Removing debris from and around the damaged reactor was an extremely hazardous operation. Some spots were so heavily radioactive that people could only work there for a few moments before they had received the emergency permissible dose of radiation. It was decided to use radiocontrolled bulldozers which had been designed and tested at the Cheliabinsk tractor plant before the Chernobyl accident. At the end of April only a few experimental models were available and they were brought urgently to Chernobyl by military cargo planes. Pictures of them removing contaminated soil in an apparently rural environment were published in many magazines and newspapers. Three weeks after the accident *Pravda* published an article describing the bulldozers:

> There are still only a few of these bright yellow robots designed to struggle with the terrible nuclear force. The first huge 19 ton bulldozer must now move in to attack the damaged reactor . . . the multi-ton giant bulldozer responds to a radio order to move towards the pile of debris . . . it scoops up the remains of the structure, clears away the asphalt, leaving behind it a deep furrow. Gradually it moves closer and closer to the centre of the dangerous 'volcano'. Because of the high level of radiation work can only be done here with the help of radiocontrolled machines.[51]

Many new robots of this kind were assembled urgently, but the final result of their work was not particularly successful. In September 1986 *Izvestiya* correspondents were surprised to find some radiocontrolled bulldozers abandoned in the fields. They were told:

> Unfortunately they don't work . . . they break down very quickly . . . Our chaps have already started joking that if you count all the robots about which articles have been written it would seem that there is no work left for us to do here. In fact, the amount of help we've had from them has been minimal.[52]

In the end the decontamination work had to be done by people, not by robots.

Whether another new method of decontamination – the absorption of hot radioactive dust by a special lignosulphonate spray which quickly forms a film – was successful is not known. It was developed very quickly and put to use by the end of the second week after the accident. There was a report that about 200,000–300,000 m² was sprayed each day from 10 to 20 May (in other words more than 1 km² in a few days).[53] It was originally intended that the films would be rolled up together with the attached and fixed radioactive dust. It could then be disposed of as nuclear waste. But rolling up the film proved to be difficult. Instead, the spray was used to fix hot particles in the soil in order to prevent the formation of dust and secondary radiation contamination. The method seems to have been abandoned later because the surface waterproof film made it difficult to decontaminate by washing, and washing remained the main method of decontamination, particularly in villages and towns.

The most successful method of decontamination was time. Most radionuclides have a short life span and eventually disappear without human assistance. By July radioiodine (which has a half-life of eight days), the main danger at the end of April and in May and June, no longer caused serious problems. Strontium-89 has a half life of 53 days. It was more prevalent than strontium-90 at the end of 1986. By 1988 it had practically disappeared.

The existence in the exclusion zone of substantial amounts of long-lived radionuclides (mainly caesium-137, strontium-90 and plutonium) made the idea of real decontamination, repopulation and rehabilitation of agricultural land impractical. Only about 500,000 m³ of the topsoil was scraped off and buried as nuclear waste.[54] In other words, only about 1,000 hectares or 10 km² were actively decontaminated. This was the land closest to the nuclear plant and to some population centres. If the exclusion zone was to be rehabilitated properly, nearly 600 million tons of topsoil would have to be removed. This was considered impossible. Finally, in 1988 the decision was made to designate the area in a 10 km radius from Chernobyl nuclear plant an ecological reserve that will be used to carry out scientific studies of the impact of radiation on the natural environment.

By its very nature such a research project is for long-term study. It is probable that many of the findings in the first few years will be treated as classified information. The political sensitivity of the problem makes it difficult for objective studies to be done. This is clear from a statement by Dr Boris Prister, chairman of the radiology co-ordinating council of the southern branch of the Lenin Academy of the Agricultural Sciences. Dr Prister told the Soviet news agency TASS that: 'Regardless of the tragic nature of the event, scientists have gained a unique laboratory which makes it possible to study the effects of radiation on living nature'; but he added that 'so far no real influence on the genetic apparatus of organisms has been observed'.[55] This is not only scientifically incorrect, it is incompetent. If the intensity of radiation was so high in some spots that it killed 400 hectares of pine forest within a matter of days, short- and long-term genetic effects on other organisms are inevitable. Pine trees may be more sensitive to radiation than oak trees, but they are much more resistant than rodents and vertebrates in general.

The scale of the contamination of the environment was so enormous in 1986 that it is not surprising that the task of protecting the population was not entirely successful. The resulting health impact requires special analysis. But before this can be done the agricultural consequences of the Chernobyl accident must be considered. The long-term health effects of the radioactive contamination of the environment are only partly due to external radiation. Nearly 60–70 per cent of future health problems will be caused by the consumption of contaminated agricultural products.

# 4

# The Impact on Agriculture

## INTRODUCTION

IN both East and West Europe, where the Chernobyl fallout required neither medical intervention nor evacuation and resettlement, agriculture bore the main direct economic cost of the accident. Large quantities of milk contaminated by radioiodine and radiocaesium were destroyed in Poland, Hungary, Austria and Sweden. At the end of April and in May vast amounts of green, leafy vegetables were also destroyed in countries as far away from the Soviet Union as Greece, Italy and France. The European community banned the import of agricultural products from Eastern Europe for several months, inflicting severe financial losses on the countries of Eastern Europe. The most prolonged effect of the Chernobyl fallout was on reindeer meat in Sweden and on lamb in parts of the United Kingdom, Sweden, Germany and Eastern Europe.

In the Soviet Union attention was naturally concentrated on the health impact of the accident and on the fate of the 135,000 people who were evacuated from the exclusion zone and other contaminated areas around it. Although the loss of agricultural produce from the evacuated zone and from other contaminated areas (the sale of milk, meat, many vegetables and fruit was forbidden or restricted in the markets of Kiev, Chernigov, Minsk and several other major cities and smaller towns in 1986 and in 1987) was included in the 11 billion roubles estimated to be the cost of the accident up to May 1988[1] (some Western estimates put the cost much higher[2]), there have been no estimates that break down the losses specific to agriculture. But if one considers the future long-term effects of the Chernobyl fallout in the Soviet Union, the most obvious impact for decades will be on agriculture. As far as health is concerned, the impact will be felt mainly in the late effects of radiation, particularly in various forms of cancer which will begin to emerge in 20 to 40 years time. The damage to agriculture has the opposite pattern. The greatest effect was felt in 1986. The effects in 1987, 1988 and 1989 were still serious, but they will continue to decline slowly with time as the shorter-lived radioisotopes disappear and the longer-lived ones continue to decay or are eroded, diluted and actively removed by decontamination measures.

The rural agricultural population will suffer more from the health effects of the accident than will the urban population. About 40 per cent of the population affected in the Ukraine, Byelorussia and the RSFSR is rural. More than half the evacuees were farmers. The population of that area is and will be at most risk both from environmental external radiation and from radioisotopes in the food chains. The centralized food trade and distribution systems in the Soviet Union are designed to reach cities and towns, not villages. Most farmers depend on locally produced food, often from their own small private plots. And dosimetric control of locally consumed food is still very poor.

For these reasons it is useful to consider the impact of the accident on agriculture separately from other problems. It will also make it easier to consider the overall health impact which, outside the exclusion zone, was mostly caused by the consumption of contaminated food products.

### THE CONTAMINATION AND LOSS OF AGRICULTURAL LAND

When the 30 km exclusion zone was established around Chernobyl on 2 May 1986 no proper dosimetric measurement of the land in the area had been done. It was assumed at that time, when the massive releases of radionuclides from the reactor caused by the second meltdown was just beginning, that 30 km would provide a sufficient safety margin. All agricultural work had ceased in the area and the evacuated local rural people were instructed to take their cattle with them. In the first phase, completed on 5 and 6 May, 73 villages were evacuated. Most of the evacuees were resettled in the republic (Ukraine or Byelorussia) from which they were evacuated, in villages close to the exclusion zone. The local agricultural administration was given the task of absorbing these families. They had abandoned their domestic animals and poultry, but had brought their cattle, pigs, sheep and horses with them. The fields, meadows, vegetable and fruit gardens in the exclusion zone (about 70,000 hectares) were, of course, lost.

The collective and state farmers outside the exclusion zone and even in areas close to it, were told to continue their normal spring work of ploughing and sowing. Pastures and meadows were used as if nothing had happened. Soviet television transmitted special programmes about agricultural work in Khoiniki and Bragin districts (north and north-west of the exclusion zone) to reassure the public that everything outside the exclusion zone was safe and working normally. Milk production in these districts, the programmes reported, had not been interrupted. Even when, at the beginning of June, extensive decontamination work was undertaken in the district towns, Bragin and Khoiniki, normal work continued in the farms and villages around them.[3]

In June, proper measurements were taken of the surface contamination outside the exclusion zone. Projected radiation doses were calculated from these measurements, resulting in the evacuation of a further 113 villages in Byelorussia and the Ukraine, as far away as 80 km west, north and north-west of the reactor site. This brought the total number of evacuated settlements to 186 (2 towns and 184 villages).[4] It also meant that a total of 100,000–150,000 hectares of agricultural land outside the official exclusion zone were abandoned. In many cases people living in these villages had gone on working in the fields up to the day of their evacuation. About 2 million hectares of agricultural land was so contaminated that special decontamination measures had to be undertaken and the system of farming had to be changed.[5] The area was predominantly a dairy farming area. Meadows formed 50 per cent of the agricultural land (although potatoes, feed vegetables, grain and flax were cultivated on 25 per cent of the agricultural land). Farms in the area owned on average 60 head of cattle per 100 hectares.[6]

According to the second Soviet report to the IAEA, written in 1987, no further farming had been permitted on land with a concentration of caesium-137 higher than 40 $Ci/km^2$ (the equivalent of 1,500,000 $Bq/m^2$). The fields would be left purely for scientific observations. Land contaminated below this level would not be written off permanently, but agriculture would only resume after decontamination measures had been taken.[7] The report did not indicate how much land was contaminated at different levels but, according to an earlier report, 5,230 $km^2$ contained 300 $Ci/km^2$ of radiocaesium on 26 June 1986 (see table 3.2). This means that in 1987 this entire area would have contained more than 40 $Ci/km^2$ of radiocaesium. In fact, livestock farming should be banned temporarily on any land which has a level of caesium-137 higher than 100,000 $Bq/m^2$ because meat and milk would be seriously contaminated (in the United Kingdom there are restrictions on selling lamb and mutton from any area with a surface contamination of more than 10,000 $Bq/m^2$). If a million hectares of agricultural land outside the exclusion zone contained levels of caesium-137 higher than

100,000 Bq/m$^2$, it must have been necessary to relocate nearly 600,000 head of cattle and similar numbers of sheep and pigs.

The second Soviet report says very little about the agricultural effect of strontium-90 and plutonium, two other serious sources of pollution which were deposited inside the Soviet Union. It was more difficult to make detailed maps of the distribution of these isotopes. The periodic updating of the maps of radioactive contamination was done on the basis of powerful gamma radiation and by specially equipped helicopters and planes. Strontium-90 (which emits beta radiation) and plutonium (which emits alpha radiation) can only be identified through closer contact between the dosimeters and the sources of radiation. The dosimetrists would need to walk around the territory to identify contamination with radiostrontium and to take plant and soil samples to identify plutonium. Although the report claims that maps of contamination for strontium-90, plutonium, zirconium-95, ruthenium-103 and other longer-lived radionuclides were made, it does not give the actual pattern of their distribution outside the exclusion zone. Inside the zone the level of plutonium was 10 Ci/km$^2$ in areas close to the nuclear plant and between 0.1 and 1.0 Ci/km$^2$ in the area called the north-western 'close track', the length of which is about 80 km.[8] Volatile radioisotopes like iodine and caesium were vaporized by the high temperatures and contributed to the formation of the original plume in gaseous form or as a very fine aerosol. Strontium and plutonium fallout, on the other hand, was mostly in the form of the larger hot particles of the dispersed debris of the nuclear core which fell closer to the reactor. Strontium and plutonium are more dangerous to health than iodine and caesium and they cannot easily be washed from plants or soil surfaces. The level of plutonium indicated by the Soviet authorities (between 3,700 and 37,000 Bq/m$^2$) is far from harmless because of the very high level of radiotoxicity of emitters of alpha particles. Moreover, comparatively large amounts of vaporized strontium-90 were released from the reactor during the heat-up period from 2 to 5 May 1986.

Figure 3.2 in the last chapter shows the gamma radiation field distribution in milliroentgens for the area of about 20,000 km$^2$ around the Chernobyl plant approximately one month after the accident, on 29 May 1986. At that time radioiodine still represented a problem, despite its short eight-day half-life. If one considers that beta and alpha radiation which was not registered by aerial measurement contributes about a third of the overall radioactivity of the soil, then all the land inside the 0.5 mR/h contours is unsuitable for agricultural use. The second Soviet report showed the results of aerial measurement of gamma radiation in the same area a year later, in May 1987.[9] Although the levels had declined considerably, the whole area was still too contaminated for agriculture. The contours which had shown 0.5– 1.0 mR/h in 1986, showed between 0.1 and 0.5 mR/h in 1987. The natural radioactivity in this region had been about 0.01 mR/h before the accident.

In January 1988, the 'Space Media Network', an organization in Sweden which uses commercial Landsat satellite pictures of different parts of the earth for news analysis, asked me to comment on some pictures of the Chernobyl exclusion zone. The pictures show an area of about 50,000 km$^2$ around the Chernobyl plant, first on 11 May, 1987 and, second, on 21 July 1987. The plant, the cooling pond, the towns of Pripyat and Chernobyl, the Dnieper river and the northern part of the Kiev reservoir are all easily recognizable.[10]

A very clear idea is given of how much land was lost to agriculture, at least in 1987. The collective and state farm fields are very large. Cultivated fields have clearly defined borders and are easy to distinguish from fallow fields. The pictures show the blurry, hazier shapes of the fields that were not cultivated in the autumn and spring ploughing periods, but that have been disturbed by bulldozers and other machinery probably used to remove the topsoil and the heavily contaminated trees and bushes in the forests close to the nuclear plant. Judging from the pattern shown on these pictures, the area that has been abandoned by farmers is much larger than the 30 km exclusion zone. In the north and north-west parts of the area there are blurred fields as far away from Chernobyl as 100 km. Nothing has been cultivated in the large triangle between the Pripyat river and the Dnieper from the Kiev reservoirs to the Bragin district in the north (about 2,000 km$^2$). Properly cultivated fields appear only about 20 km east of the Dnieper. In the west there are disturbed fields well beyond 60–70 km from the plant. In other words, practically the whole area shown on the map (figure 3.2) with contours of gamma radiation remained uncultivated in 1987.[11] If, as is likely, about 30 per cent of this area was covered with forests and bushes, about 6,000 km$^2$ of arable land (nearly 600,000 hectares) seems to be seriously affected and disturbed by decontamination measures in and around the exclusion zone.

Decontamination was necessary not only to rehabilitate the land for agriculture, but also to protect the surrounding, more economically important areas and cities from radioactive surface dust and wind erosion. Although many statements have been made about the importance of recovering the land for agriculture, ploughing and cultivating, contaminated land causes dust erosion from which radioactive dust could be blown towards Kiev, Gomel and other big cities. It was apparently more important in 1986 and 1987 to protect these cities and the areas around them than to cultivate the land.

For nearly three years after the accident, the public (including the population in the Ukraine and Byelorussia) knew very little about the real scale of the contamination and the loss of agricultural land. The figures which have been given here were reported at the IAEA meetings in Vienna and at other international gatherings, but they were not published in the Soviet press. Most people knew that there was a 30 km exclusion zone, but they were told nothing else. It seems that the Ministry of Health and local officials expected that the radioactive decay of shorter-lived isotopes, together with erosion, leaching and ecological migration of longer-lived isotopes (primarily caesium-137 and strontium-90) and the decontamination measures would reduce the level of radioactivity rapidly so that further radical measures would not be required. In fact, in many districts of the Kiev, Zhitomir, Gomel, Mogilev and Bryansk regions the consumption of locally produced milk and meat still needed to be severely restricted in 1987–9. In many villages women were advised against pregnancy or advised to have abortions. Increased abnormalities among new-born farm animals were reported unofficially. When it became clear that significant groups of the rural population were approaching the maximum permissible whole-life exposure of 25 rem, a new wave of evacuation became inevitable. Increasing the permissible level to 35 rem in 1988 did not help matters.

In the political debates associated with the elections to the Congress of Deputies in March 1989, the real truth about the scale of the radioactive contamination turned out to be the most burning issue in the affected regions. Public pressure forced the authorities to publish maps of the contamination outside the exclusion zone and to disclose some figures. The Byelorussian local papers were the first to publish maps showing the contamination in Byelorussia. A few weeks later, the Ukrainian press followed suit. Finally, *Pravda* published maps of the contamination in the European part of the Soviet Union and made some figures public.[12] It became widely known for the first time that agricultural land had been lost not only in and close to the exclusion zone, but also in parts of the Mogilev, Zhitomir, Bryansk and Kiev regions, between 100 and 300 km from Chernobyl.

In these areas rain had fallen at the end of April and beginning of May 1986, bringing down particles of the radioactive plume which had formed in all directions around the burning reactor core. In 1988 about

10,000 km$^2$ of territory, 60 per cent of it outside the exclusion zone, had a concentration of caesium-137 above 15 Ci/km$^2$ (from 15–40 Ci/km$^2$) and of strontium-90 above 3 Ci/km$^2$. Of this area, 2,000 km$^2$ was in the RSFSR, the rest was in the Ukraine and Byelorussia. There were 640 villages and towns in the territory with a total population of more than 230,000. Clean food had to be brought in from outside the area and restrictions were imposed on the people. An even larger territory (21,000 km$^2$) was contaminated with between 5 and 15 Ci/km$^2$ of caesium-137 and between 1 and 3 Ci/km$^2$ of strontium-90. This was the equivalent of 200,000–600,000 Bq/m$^2$, far too high for agriculture. Despite this, the land was not abandoned. Many spots (Fig. 3.3c) which contain more than 40 Ci/km$^2$ of caesium-137 were still used for cultivation. Some fields were reported to have between 80 and 150 Ci/km of radionuclides. But this was an expensive exercise, since the products were unsuitable for direct consumption. The Chairman of the Byelorussian Council of Ministers acknowledged in 1989 that the republic produced hundreds of thousands of tons of contaminated grain annually which was procured by the state but which could not be used for any purpose.[13]

If 21,000 km$^2$ of land was contaminated with 5–15 Ci/km$^2$ of caesium-137, this means that at least 100,000 km$^2$ of land must have contained between 1 and 5 Ci/km$^2$ of caesium-137 in 1989. This gives a level of 37,000–200,000 Bq/m$^2$, which is too high for livestock agriculture. In the United Kingdom, the sale of lamb was restricted at a contamination level of 10,000 Bq/m$^2$. However, this also means that, in 1986, the level of radioactivity must have been ten times higher and in 1987 three times higher than in 1988, the year for which figures were given. If international standards were being applied for the use of agricultural land, nearly 1 million hectares would be considered lost for a century, and about 2 million hectares would be lost for 10–20 years. There was no economic rationale to the attempt to continue using heavily contaminated land for the production of food at the expense of public health. Whatever was saved in the agricultural economy will be lost in future health bills.

## THE EFFECT ON LIVESTOCK AGRICULTURE

During the evacuation of the exclusion zone in May 1986, 86,000 head of cattle were moved out of the contaminated area.[14] Some of them contained so much radioactivity (particularly iodine-131) that it was easier to slaughter them than to wait for a decline in radioactivity. By May, very little hay and other kinds of transportable rich, coarse fodder remained in the Soviet Union, so there was not enough to feed clean fodder to the evacuated cattle. In most regions of the Ukraine, Byelorussia and the RSFSR farm animals are kept outdoors for feeding. As a result of radioiodine emission in May 1986 significant quantities of milk were contaminated above the permissible level. According to the 1986 Soviet report for the IAEA, milk and other livestock products were monitored in 15 regions with a total population of about 75 million people.

The 1986 Soviet report reflected the situation in the two months following the accident. During this period the main concern was radioactive iodine, which represented nearly 50 per cent of the overall contamination of food products in May 1986. Iodine-90 moves most rapidly through the food chain. It is a gamma emitter and therefore can easily be detected by the military dosimeters which were the only ones available to the medical food inspectors in May. The monitoring was done not on the farms, in individual households or in the fields where the food was produced, but at such delivery points as slaughter houses, milk-processing factories and town food markets. Centralized supplies of meat and milk from collective and state farms were put under control. A blanket ban on selling milk and dairy products through the open markets was introduced in Kiev, Gomel, Chernigov and several other regions; these products could only be sold in state shops and supermarkets. The ban was in force more than a year after the accident. It affected about 6–7 million rural households (20–25 million people). But the extent of the contamination and shortages of dosimetric equipment and qualified personnel made it impossible to monitor the contamination in most villages outside the exclusion zone. The rural population in the Soviet Union is still very large (about 30–40 per cent of the total population of Byelorussia and the Ukraine). As a rule is it self-sufficient in milk, dairy produce, meat and vegetables. Each family has at least one milk cow and other livestock. The state did not have the resources to replace this source of food, even temporarily.

The World Health Organization (WHO) sets 2,000 Bq/litre for adults and 1,000 Bq/litre for children as the maximum acceptable level of radioiodine in milk during an emergency. It is not considered suitable for long-term consumption. Radioactive caesium (which was present in the Chernobyl plume in a ratio of almost 1:1 with iodine in the middle of May 1986) is considered less dangerous than iodine in the short term because it does not concentrate critically in any organ in the way that iodine concentrates in the thyroid. But caesium isotopes represent a longer-term danger because of their long half-life and persistence in the environment. Since June 1986 caesium-134 and 137 have caused most concern for agriculture in Europe.

The level of contamination of food permitted by Soviet authorities in an emergency is higher than the WHO level. In the case of a reactor accident, local consumption of food products is permitted if the initial content of iodine-131 in daily rations is lower than 7,400 Bq. Milk can be consumed if it has less than 3,700 Bq/litre of iodine-131. The permissible level of caesium-137 allowed in daily rations is far higher at 370,000 Bq (or $1 \times 10^{-5}$ Ci).[15] The permissible level of strontium-90 is similar to that of iodine because it is considered more radiologically dangerous (strontium is leukogenic, accumulating in the bones where it remains until the end of life). But these rules did not envisage an accident of the magnitude of Chernobyl; they were expected to apply to limited groups of people for a short time. New emergency rules for caesium, which are discussed in chapter 5, were introduced at the end of May 1986.

The contamination of milk by radioactive iodine and caesium was a serious problem over an extensive area. Figure 4.1 (from the Medical Annex of the Soviet Working Document[16]), shows that the contamination of milk by iodine-131 was well above the Soviet 'action level'. This level was registered in many areas throughout the central part of the Ukraine, Byelorussia, Moldavia, and several regions of the RSFSR, including the Kaluga regions which is only 100 km from Moscow. In many regions 30–50 per cent of all the milk and meat produced was contaminated above the permissible level. As a rule these products were not destroyed. The Soviet authorities, always concerned about shortages of agricultural products, advised food processing plants to use contaminated milk to make cheese and butter which could be stored for some time. However, if the contamination of milk by iodine-131 was as high as 10–20 microcurie per litre (which was the case in central parts of the Ukraine (400,000–600,000 Bq/litre) or even close to 100 μCi/litre (in north-western Byelorussia or Polyes'ye), the milk would also contain enough caesium-134 and 137 to make it unsuitable for consumption in any form for a very long time.

If the milk was so contaminated, the level of contamination in meat from all sources must have been far higher than the permissible levels. The Soviet Working document gave only fragmentary information about the contamination of meat: 10 per cent of meat in the Minsk region, 40 per cent in the Gomel region and 20 per cent in the Mogilev and Brest regions were reported to be above the permissible level. There were no data for most other regions of the affected area.[17] It was acknowledged that, although the centralized sales of meat and other food products had been put under radiological control, the consumption of locally produced food by the rural population could not always be controlled. This affected millions of rural families but there are no reports of how the problem was tackled in 1986 and 1987. Occasional articles were published suggesting that 'clean' milk should be produced for children living in rural areas.[18] But apparently the consumption of locally produced milk and dairy products was common.

According to some reports in the Soviet press, the Ukrainian and Byelorussian agricultural authorities prepared special maps showing contamination (and the levels of external radiation) by different radionuclides (for example, there were separate maps for caesium and strontium).[19] These maps and other data were used for a special long-term programme called 'On Rational Organization of Agro-industrial

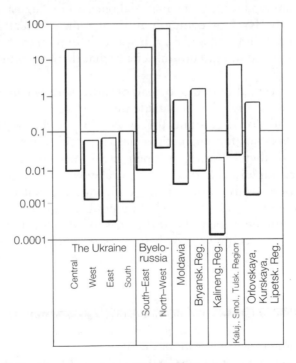

**Figure 4.1** Iodine-131 concentrations in cows milk in microcuries per litre for different regions of the European part of the USSR in the first half of May 1986 (from *The Accident . . . Soviet IAEA Report*, Part II, Annex 7, p. 64).

Works on Territories which were contaminated as a result of the Chernobyl Accident'. Neither the maps nor the programme appears to have been published. There have been occasional remarks about the recommended methods of using contaminated products (for example, contaminated grain could be used as animal feed until at least two months before slaughter, so that the slaughtered meat would not be contaminated by radioactive caesium). Even now, several years after the accident, Soviet agricultural literature has not discussed the overall effect on agriculture. The Soviet State Committee for Agro-industry has not published anything similar to *Radionuclide Levels in Food, Animals and Agricultural Products* published by the UK Ministry of Agriculture, Fisheries and Food in 1987.[20]

Radioiodine remained a serious danger until July 1986. But the contamination of milk and other livestock products by radiocaesium continued in 1987, 1988 and 1989. Unfortunately the second Soviet report presented to the IAEA in September 1987 summarized the situation in Chernobyl and around it a year after the accident but did not include any updating of the material released in August 1986. It did not disclose the level of contamination of milk or meat in different regions with caesium-134 and 137. It was only in publications in 1987–9 entirely unrelated to agricultural science that there were indications of serious problems.

As we have seen, about 86,000 head of cattle were evacuated from the exclusion zone. Many villages outside the zone were contaminated to a level which did not necessitate the evacuation of the population but which made livestock farming impossible. The problem was that animals, particularly if they pasture in open areas, accumulate radioactive isotopes very rapidly. Neither the central government nor the local authorities were ready, however, to reorientate the collective farms in 1987. In December 1987 an article in a popular agricultural magazine for rural youth described the difficulties of the local procuracy in Khoiniki district. Khoiniki is a district centre situated about 100 km north-west of the Chernobyl plant. The local procurator, V. I. Kachura, complained that:

> After the events in Chernobyl we weren't given any documents or normative acts regulating the relations between citizens and organizations, particularly collective and state farms on the one hand, and the government in connection with the accident.
>
> In the state farm 'Strelichevo' seven and a half thousand oxen were being fattened which should long before have been delivered to the state. They had reached a weight of more than 500 kg. But the state purchase

organizations would not take them because they were contaminated with radioactivity. The oxen were consuming the farm's food reserves, and no one knew what to do with them . . .

Another example: a cow which had broken its leg would normally have been delivered to the slaughter house. Now this could not be done; it was contaminated. It had to be buried (which was also a problem). The collective farmers posed the fair question: why should they shoulder the loss? Let the government buy it . . . The procuracy had to take judicial measures to compensate for damages. But this required a legal basis. In the case of a state farm, the state bears the loss. So should the state be sued? It's absurd. How should the problem be resolved? A year has passed and there is still no solution.[21]

Experts advised that contaminated animals should be transferred to clean regions at least two months before slaughter. But no one seemed able to organize this. The problem was that the contaminated animals belonged to particular farms. Once transferred, they would require special treatment and care, such as indoor feeding and the collection and disposal of their manure (which had to be treated as low-level nuclear waste).

It was senseless for Khoiniki and other contaminated *Polessky* districts to retain a speciality in livestock farming. In theory everyone knew what should be done. But the practical difficulties of changing the agricultural orientation of collective farms consisting, for the most part, of elderly peasants, are not easily overcome. The state did not tackle the problem (and in state farms it was only the state that could do so). If the situation is similar in other agricultural districts around the exclusion zone (in a radius of 200 km, particularly north, north-west and west of Chernobyl), and in some areas in Mogilev and Bryansk regions there are probably between 500,000 and 1 million head of cattle that cannot be slaughtered. With the procurement price for meat at a level of 1 rouble per kilogram of live weight, the state and collective farms will lose hundreds of millions of roubles. It is, of course, essential that slaughterhouses check the radioactive contamination of animals and refuse to process carcasses that are heavily contaminated. But the local population has not been properly supplied with alternative sources of clean milk, meat and dairy produce for adults or, more importantly, for children.

A very specific problem was reported in 1989 in some districts of the Zhitomir region of the Ukraine, particularly in Narodichi district, situated 50–90 km from the Chernobyl plant. In 1988 the contamination of soil in this district was 80 Ci/km$^2$ in some places. Vladimir Kolinko, the correspondent of *Moscow News* visited farms in this district and reported later:

> At the animal farm of the Petrovsky collective farm I was shown a suckling pig whose head looked like that of a frog: instead of eyes there were large tissue outgrowths with no cornea or pupil.
>
> 'One of the many freaks of nature', said Pyotr Kudin, the collective farm veterinary surgeon, 'They usually die soon after birth, but this one has survived'.
>
> The farm is small: 350 cows and 87 pigs. During the five years leading up to the accident at the Chernobyl APS there were only three cases of freak suckling pigs, calves were always born normal. During the first year after the accident the birth of 64 freaks was registered at the farm, 37 suckling pigs and 27 calves. During the first nine months of 1988 – 41 pigs and 35 calves. Most often, calves are born without a head or limbs, without eyes or ribs. The pigs are distinguished by exophthalmus, deformation of the skull and so on.
>
> 'And what do scientists say? After all, a special Institute of Agricultural Radiology has been set up in Kiev'.
>
> 'They have shown no particular interests in our farm', Pyotr Kudin replied. 'They examined several corpses of new-born freaks and said that there could be a hundred causes totally unrelated to radiation. I am a veterinary surgeon and I know this. But the statistics concerning freak animals point to one definite cause. Cattle feed is grown in fields contaminated with radionuclides. Even procurers refuse to accept the cattle for slaughter – the radiation levels do not meet the norm'.[22]

## OTHER FORMS OF AGRICULTURE AND THE RURAL POPULATION

The *Polessky* regions of the Ukraine and Byelorussia are particularly well suited for livestock farming because nearly half the arable land consists of rich, flooded meadows. Field crops were developed to serve the livestock farms and they occupy 35–40 per cent of the cultivated land. Grain crops (barley, rye and wheat) are also grown, taking up about 45 per cent of the cultivated land. The remaining cultivated land is given over to potatoes (8 per cent), flax and hemp (about 5 per cent) and vegetables.[23] The soil is rather poor (mostly *podzol*) and forests and swamps cover about 30 per cent of the territory. The population consists predominantly of farmers. Those who are not engaged in agriculture, work in lumber, food processing and textile industries and in the production of peat for fuel and as organic fertilizer. Several large-scale land-reclamation projects have been undertaken, usually in an attempt to increase the acreage of meadows.

The regional and district authorities were responsible for the evacuation of the rural population from the exclusion zone and from other heavily contaminated spots around it. Byelorussians from the exclusion zone were resettled in other parts of the Gomel region. The Ukrainian farming population was moved to the northern parts of the Kiev, Zhitomir and Chernigov regions. A few contaminated spots were found in the Bryansk region of the RSFSR. The official number of evacuees from the rural areas is about 65,000, but this is well below the real movement of the population during 1986 of more than 100,000. It was initially thought that people would be able to return to many of the evacuated villages after decontamination. The rural families in this group were not entitled to permanent subsidized housing in new settlements. There was a move in July 1986 to return villagers to one spot in the extreme southern part of the exclusion zone but nothing came of it.[24] In January 1987 Soviet newspapers reported for the first time that about 1,500 people had returned to 12 villages in the Bragin district (the southern and south-western parts of this district were included in the exclusion zone).[25] They had been evacuated in June 1986 so that special military chemical units could decontaminate their settlements.

According to unofficial sources, no children have been allowed to return to evacuated villages. From an interview with the chairman of the Gomel party committee, A. Prokhorov, published in in *Izvestiya*, it seems that the main reason for sending people back was to staff local industries. Medical and educational services were not restored and neither was trade. The work in villages like Gden', Karlovka, Ludvinovo, Ivanki, Paseka and others was carried out on a caretaker basis – in other words, workers returned without their families for short periods to fulfil specific functions. The rural areas in this district were relatively safe in the winter when all the fields were covered in about a metre of snow. Agricultural work does not seem to have been started up again in the spring. The level of radioactive caesium and strontium in Bragin district was well above the level that would have been safe for livestock farming.

However, independent observers who travelled through the exclusion zone in 1987 and 1988, contradicted the official statements that only adults had been allowed to return to Byelorussian villages (and only to those considered safe). The Ukrainian part of the exclusion zone was fenced off and there were police patrols around the Chernobyl plant and the two empty towns, Pripyat and Chernobyl (mainly to prevent looting which was quite common). But the Byelorussian border of the exclusion zone was open. The Ukrainian districts south of the exclusion zone enjoy a more prosperous agriculture than the Byelorussian districts north and north-west of the exclusion zone. The decision to evacuate the rural population to safer areas within the same regions meant that the Ukraine could absorb the evacuees in the Kiev and Chernigov regions fairly easily. The Byelorussian region of Gomel, on the other hand, found it far harder to absorb the peasants evacuated into the region. Moreover, the aid they were given to build new villages in safer areas was not very generous. After the frustration of a few months in cramped conditions, many evacuees ignored the danger and migrated back without permission.

The journalist, Yuri Shcherbak, visited both parts of the exclusion zone in 1987 and 1988. He recorded an interview with Vasily Samoilenko, deputy deirector of Gden' school. Gden' is a large village situated inside the 30 km exclusion zone:

> We were evacuated on 4 May, but some villages were only evacuated at the end of May. It was orderly . . . but the return, the resettling of villages took place in partisan fashion, so to speak.
>
> People began gradually to return. The collective farm drove a herd of cattle here, herdsmen arrived. Somewhere around October the village was resettled. And after the October holidays we began to the academic year . . .
>
> Only the medics work carefully in shifts and we have only half the teachers we need . . .
>
> On the Byelorussian side the zone is open. People drive around in their cars. Our collective farm has completely returned to its normal productive life. There are fifty-one children studying at the school. Three children did not return. Milk is delivered to the shop. There isn't enough of it but people have their own cows and they drink the milk those cows produce. I myself have a cow and drink its milk. Thank God, I'm still alive.[26]

There can be no doubt that the level of radiocaesium in such milk is very high, far higher than is permissible by any standard. It seems that no one cares about this; there is no alternative.

Nadezhda Samoilenko, the chemistry an biology teacher in Gden', conveyed the sense of having no option quite vividly in her interview:

> I'm sure I'm talking for many when I say that people would hardly have returned here if we had had somewhere else to live. They didn't promise to build us a village as they promised in the Ukraine . . . We are paid double salaries and told that our zone is clean. But I don't really believe that it is. If people were evacuated from a 30 km zone in the Ukraine because it

wasn't clean, then how come our zone in Byelorussia is clean? Do you know how many kilometres we are from the AES? Seventeen. In good weather one can see the station. How can it be clean here? We HAD to come back . . . we had nowhere else to go. If they had offered us houses and flats, do you really think we would have returned?

They promised us streets made of gold when we returned. Plumbing, roofs, asphalt. A club. The asphalt has never been laid. The plumbing was installed not long ago but it doesn't work properly . . . We try to keep local people informed, so that they stop their children from collecting mushrooms in the wood . . .[27]

Describing the same village in 1988, *Pravda* suggested that people had been able to return to Gden' because the decontamination measures had been successful.[28] It is clear from maps of the distribution of radioactive contamination in 1988 that the level of caesium-137 in the fields around Gden' was below 15 Ci/km$^2$. They were therefore considered comparatively clean. But they are located close to more contaminated areas and may suffer secondary contamination. *Pravda* admits that the people who returned without permission to their villages in the Byelorussian and Ukrainian parts of the exclusion zone have no idea about the level of radiation:

What is the level of radiation in these villages? The collective farmers who live there don't really know. They usually rely on the fact that the military dosimetrists who work in the zone tell them that 'one can live here but one must be careful'. One needs to take into account as well that the radiation contamination here is not even. The radionuclides settled in patches and there are large areas of the zone with normal readings.[29]

It is, in fact, impossible that the radiation level can be normal anywhere within the exclusion zone. Moreover, if there are 'patches', then there are areas where not only radiocaesium, but also radiostrontium and plutonium represent a serious source of contamination.

At first the evacuees shared the homes of their hosts or were housed temporarily in schools, clubs and other public buildings. A crash construction programme of government-subsidized housing was undertaken in Ukrainian villages which had absorbed evacuees. In some cases new settlements were established. By the winter 12,000 new village-type houses had been constructed for evacuees. A further 9,000 houses were built in 1987.[30] If the average rural family consists of four people this means that nearly 80,000 people were permanently resettled. The Ukrainian government allocated 15,000 apartments, most of them in Kiev, to workers at the Chernobyl plant who had lived in Pripyat and people who had been evacuated from the town of Chernobyl.[31] These people were expected to move to a new, purpose-built town, Slavutich, 50 km east of Chernobyl on the railroad which passes Yanov station near Pripyat.

There is a great deal of confusion about the exact number of people evacuated from rural areas, the number of villages affected, the number of new houses built for evacuees, and so on. According to the first Soviet report for the IAEA in August 1986 and the INSAG report, 135,000 people were evacuated from two towns (Pripyat and Chernobyl) and 73 villages. This implies that the evacuees were equally divided between the urban and rural population. In December 1986, the Central Committee and Soviet government gave the number of evacuees as 116,000.[32] In the second Soviet report for the IAEA, the number of evacuees was reduced to 115,000[33] and in 1987 the number of evacuated villages was reported to be not 73, but 179.[34]

More accurate figures were given about rural resettlement in Byelorussia in 1988. The second and third waves of evacuation took place predominantly in contaminated areas in Byelorussia close to the exclusion zone. Two years after the accident the Chairman of the Byelorussian Council of Ministers, M. V. Kovalev, told *Pravda* that 107 villages and other settlements had been abandoned in Byelorussia, 9,770 cottages had been built in non-contaminated regions for 24,700 people from contaminated rural areas; 412 villages and settlements in areas designated as 'strictly controlled' (from a radiological point of view) had been decontaminated and people had returned to them. Kovalev indicated that the direct and indirect costs of the accident to the Byelorussian government was 1.835 million roubles; 289 million roubles were allocated in 1988–90 to an assistance programme for people living in contaminated districts.[35]

However, in 1989 other villages in the Gomel and Mogilev regions of Byelorussia and the Zhitomir region of the Ukraine had to be evacuated and resettled in safer locations because their inhabitants were approaching the new maximal permissible dose of 35 rem per person. In an interview with *Pravda* in February 1989 Kovalev said that the situation in the contaminated areas had been discussed again by the Politburo. The Byelorussian government had asked for 700 million roubles more than had been allocated for 1989–90 to pay for further measures and resettlement. Twenty villages in Byelorussia and twelve in the Ukraine with a population of about 3,000 were included in the new evacuation plan.[36] Some of the evacuated villages in the Mogilev region were located as far as 150–200 km north of the accident site. Various methods of decontamination (very deep ploughing and the use of special chemicals to reduce the penetration of radiocaesium into the produce) were applied to one-fifth of the entire agricultural area of the republic.

At the end of 1989 pressure from the local population concerned about the health of their children made it necessary to include 79 more villages with a total of 7,000 people in the 1990 resettlement programme in Mogilev region alone. However, the local officials anticipated that eventually a further 271 villages located in the areas with concentrations of radionuclides above 10 Ci/km$^2$ (370,000 Bq/m$^2$) will have had to be relocated. The programme was expected to cost 3 billion roubles[37] (about $5 billion). If similar programmes are necessary for Gomel and Zhitomir region, which have about the same level of contamination, the human agricultural and economic cost of Chernobyl may double in 1990–5. In 1989 the local population, disillusioned by the official attitude began to invite freelance independent dosimetrists to the area. This practice produced several reports in which spots with radioactivity between 60 and 150 Ci/km$^2$ were registered in cultivated fields such as the state farm *Znamya* in Mogilev region.[38]

Resettling the evacuees was not without problems. Old people and pensioners who lived alone presented the main difficulty. Most of them did not want to be evacuated and in many cases force had to be used. The local procurator of Khoiniki described the difficulties of moving reluctant old people:

> We explained to them, told them, the deputy Minister of Internal Affairs tried to persuade them, but it was hopeless. 'What shall we do?' he asked Kachura, although he knew what answer the procurator would have to give . . . the law did not envisage a situation like Chernobyl. There are no legal grounds for resettlement. Kachura had previously telephoned Gomel and spoke to the *oblast* procurator. Naturally he had no answer. He telephoned the republican procuracy. But what could they say? Kachura decided that under no circumstances should people be left to die. If the law did not support morality, if it contradicted morality, there was something wrong with the law.
>
> 'Evict them!', Kachura answered, 'By force'.
>
> But I don't think that anyone would have been able to foresee the Chernobyl events and the legal complications that would ensue.[39]

The dilemma is quite clear. The correct, 'moral' response is far less clear. Resettling families with children was a necessity but it was uneconomic and far less essential to force pensioners to move. The carcinogenic effects of radiation cause a very rapid rise in the number of leukaemias among children, but adults and old people are more likely to suffer only from the 'late effects' of radiation which appear only 20–40 years later. There is a higher health risk in disturbing the traditional lifestyle of people in their sixties and seventies than in 100–200 rad of radiation extended over several years. Nobody has ever said this openly in the Soviet Union but, since 1988, old people who have returned to their abandoned houses in the exclusion zone have not been traced and moved away. In the spring of 1988 there was a spontaneous mass return of elderly people to their homes in the exclusion zone (a number of people had returned immediately after the evacuation in 1986). *Moscow News* described one village 'not far from Chernobyl';

> There are 27 residents: all are elderly men and women who refused to evacuate. Some left the Zone for two or three months but then returned home with their cows. They started breeding poultry and growing vegetables. In the fall, they harvested the potatoes they had planted before the accident.
>
> 'No, thanks, we are going to live out the rest of our days at home', said Anisiya Andreyevna, 72. 'What are we to be afraid of, dear fellow?'[40]

Of course, these people have no choice but to consume heavily contaminated products. The same Anisiya says: 'Our men also catch fish. I picked mushrooms last summer and took them to the troops camping out nearby. They also checked them. Then even their general had some mushrooms, so I don't think they can harm me. We have berries, pears and apples, too . . .'[41]

Whatever the general thought about the mushrooms, fungi use fallen leaves from the previous year as a growing medium and in 1987 mushrooms were particularly heavily contaminated with radiocaesium. People in the Ukraine and Byelorussia were advised against picking mushrooms. Similar advice was given to people in parts of France and Germany. Fish in the Pripyat river and its smaller tributaries were contaminated well above the level permissible for consumption.[42] But these rules were unimportant to people in their seventies. There was a danger, however, that they would try to sell their produce to soldiers and other people. They were living in villages devoid of shops and other services. They could not travel outside the exclusion zone because of roadblocks and radiation checks. But they could walk in and out of the zone through fields and forests, ignoring the danger signs which marked the zone. According to the report in *Moscow News* these pensioners should either be helped or moved, because this was not an isolated case:

> There are several such villages. People are abandoning their new houses . . . and returning home. Without permission or authorization. One can certainly understand them. Every time people bring them supplies of

bread, sugar and canned food, it is done against regulations. Neither the villages nor their residents have official status.

Two years have gone by. Everyone agrees: either everyone should be allowed to come back or these residents should be taken out of the Zone, and the houses torn down so that their owners stop worrying.[43]

Pensioners dominate the rural population in non-chernozem regions. The village to which 72-year-old Anisiya returned is typical. Before the accident there had been 48 households in the village. The 27 people who returned after the accident were probably those without children and grandchildren. It was reported at the end of the 1988 that the total number of villagers who returned to the Ukrainian part of the exclusion zone was 994. About 4,000 people returned to the Byelorussian part of the zone.[44]

A number of suggestions were made about the best way to replace the traditional livestock agriculture of the *Polesky* region with field crops of a kind that would not accumulate radiocaesium and other isotopes (for example, starchy varieties of potato, sunflower, sugar beet or the acreage of flax fields that were traditional for this area could merely be increased). Because of the shortage of labour, even in villages which had absorbed evacuees, none of the suggestions was adopted. Most crops in the Soviet Union (including such industrial crops as sugar beet, sunflower and flax) depend on the mobilization of urban people to work in the fields for critical periods of the season. It would be impossible to bring them to the contaminated districts around the exclusion zone. Although small towns in the area, such as Bragin, Khoiniki and Elsk, had been decontaminated, they were not considered entirely safe. There was already a problem with people who worked in local industry. Many of them working in the timber industry, making peat brickettes, or processing flax had to spend prolonged periods out of doors.

According to the rule which makes it obligatory to pay double salaries to people who work in hazardous conditions, (such as people in the Arctic regions and in copper mines), people working in areas contaminated by the Chernobyl accident were now entitled to extra pay. But in the case of Chernobyl, the amount of extra pay was decided by individual organizations and this gave rise to discontent. The procurator in Khoiniki, for example, was confronted by one couple who worked in different organizations in Khoiniki. They complained because the wife was paid double her salary, while the husband only received 70 per cent more. The procurator could not help them, since the amount paid depended on the financial situation of the ministry or department to which the organization belonged.[45]

In addition to the exclusion zone, the Soviet government also designated a 'zone of special strict control' and a 'zone of periodic control'. Dosimetric control of the population within the special zone was compulsory and extra payments were made to compensate for risks to health and to enable people to buy 'clean' food in the state shops. Despite the higher salaries and extra payments, people are still trying to leave the area. The exodus continued in 1988 and 1989.

In 1988 and 1989 contamination still affected agriculture seriously. A. Simurov was sent by *Pravda* to report on the local situation in Bragin district two years after the accident. He found that the way in which villages had been divided into those within the special zone and those outside it was causing many problems. The division had been based on dosimetric measurements, but it was difficult to explain to villagers why their neighbours received special attention and 'danger money', while their own village was treated as if nothing had happened. In some cases the border ran through fields. Farmers could claim extra payments when they worked in one part of the field, but not when they worked in the other. Simurov asked some farmers about their payments:

> 'On this side we receive double payment and on that side of the highway, the ordinary amount', the team leader replied.
>
> Other machine operators came up and joined the conversation . . . the villagers really did not understand how the state farm could be divided into different zones for payment.
>
> 'Before lunch', they said, 'we worked across the road. After lunch the whole brigade moved here. How can they work out our pay?'
>
> . . . There is an even more paradoxical situation on the state farm 'Kholmyansky'. The village driver, F. Maslakov, complained:
>
> 'Our little village "New Life" is situated between Novoel'nya and Kozel'. People in the neighbouring villages receive higher pay. Moreover for each person who buys produce from the shop a 30 rouble supplement is added. We get neither, although our private produce is also contaminated'.[46]

Simurov raised an important point. Whether or not a particular village or settlement was situated in the zone of special control and therefore subject to special financial help, there were restrictions on the use of locally produced food. Locally produced milk and meat could not be consumed. The problem probably arose because the radiological services decided where the borders of the special control zone should be (and therefore who was entitled to compensatory pay), while the medical authorities quite separately imposed restrictions on food consumption. The special payments and the distribution of clean food was the financial responsibility of the Byelorussian government and the regional authorities. Hundreds of villages and many thousands of people were affected by restrictions on the food they could consume, but were not entitled to any financial compensation. Many of the seemingly good decisions which had been made in 1986 had been forgotten: they were emergency responses and did not form part of a long-term programme. Simurov pointed out that:

> There is still no single comprehensive state programme in the country or the republic which extends, at the very least, to the end of the thirteenth five-year plan. Nor have appropriate financial and material resources been allocated . . . for supplying hermetic cabins for tractors, or special transport to carry goods and produce to settlements . . .[47]

People who went to the zone of special control on business from towns like Gomel, Mogilev or Minsk were also entitled to double pay. The local population call these extra payments a 'coffin supplement'.

The Byelorussian writer, Ales Adamovich, strongly criticized the policy of the State Committee for Agro-industry (*Agroprom*) because it continued to be more interested in production figures in 1988 than in measures to deal with the contamination of agricultural produce:

> This is very apparent from the behaviour of *Agroprom* which gets a direct profit from the callous practices which have revived in the affected areas of Byelorussia. Radiation stimulates the growth of some cereals . . . in some places there have been unprecedented harvests of grain. And *Agroprom* gathers the harvest, fulfils the plan and then does not know what to do with the produce.
>
> Byelorussia approached the All-Union *Agroprom* with a request to exclude the affected areas from all plans. And to destroy the thousands of tons of meat from radiated animals which have been forgotten in the freezers of the Mogilev and Gomel districts. Their answers can be summed up as bureaucratic moonshine.[48]

At first the evacuees tried to retain their original organizational structure (collective and state farms) and to preserve some independence. But this proved impossible. Their livestock was, as a rule, destroyed. Their machinery had been left behind. In 1987 an attempt was made to salvage some machinery. When the machinery was checked, however, 'The level of contamination was high. To decontaminate it would be difficult and expensive. And in any case, it was doubtful that one hundred per cent safety could be guaranteed. It was decided that it would not be used further. And the loss would be compensated by the State Insurance Organization.'[49]

Other important measures that had to be undertaken in the rural areas around the exclusion zone. Most important was the construction of alternative water supplies. The local population usually got its water from wells. More than 10,000 wells had been contaminated. Also, mechanics and tractor drivers were instructed to seal the cabins of their machines to prevent radioactive dust penetrating when they were working. The agricultural machinery industry was said to have designed special types of tractors with air filters for their cabins, extra air and pressure to prevent dust from penetrating, hermetically sealed doors, windows and roofs. These were to be delivered to the contaminated areas but few were ever completed.[50]

The first, military-style decontamination measures carried out in the summer of 1986 turned out to be insufficient. Decontamination should be a permanent process rather than a single event. To make it easier, traditional rural roofs had to be replaced and village roads had to be asphalted. In 1987 and 1988 more than 600 villages and settlements were in a state of periodic decontamination. More than 100,000 houses were affected by the measures undertaken.[51]

Another major problem turned out to be manure. The manure from grazing animals was found to contain high concentrations of caesium, strontium and other isotopes. Although this was not unexpected, it meant that the manure had to be collected and buried as nuclear waste. The local administrators did not know what to do and often asked how to store it.[52]

The problems in the Ukrainian sector of the exclusion zone and in less contaminated areas where agricultural work proceeded in 1987 and 1988 were different from those in Byelorussia. The initial radioactive plume which had created the most serious fallout containing comparatively large pieces of debris from the reactor core moved north and north-west from the reactor. The southern part of the contaminated area was affected by later releases with higher concentrations of radioactive strontium than caesium. In the northern sectors just outside the exclusion zone the ratio of caesium to strontium in the fallout in soil samples was about 10:1. In southern sectors the same distance from the reactor the ratio was about 0.5:1. In absolute figures the concentration of strontium-90 in the south was from two to three times higher than in the northern sectors.[53] Radiostrontium does not contaminate milk and meat as readily as radiocaesium does. None the less it is considered more radiotoxic because it replaces the calcium in the bones and remains in the body until death. It is also more strongly fixed in the surface layer of the soil and is not leached by rain. The main method of decontamination in the southern areas was therefore to remove the topsoil. *Pravda*

*Ukrainy*, reporting how this was done in the two years following the accident, indicated that 500,000 m³ was removed and buried as radioactive waste.[54] Although this may seem a vast amount, if that is all that was removed the land could not have been decontaminated. If 5 cm of the topsoil was removed, 500,000 m³ means that 1,000 hectares were treated. In fact, however, it is known that in fields around the nuclear plant often about 25–50 cm of topsoil was removed and buried.

*Pravda Ukrainy* also reported the return of old people to 15 villages which had initially been abandoned. This probably means that their return was the result of approved policy. The Ukrainian part of the exclusion zone is surrounded by a barbed-wire fence and patrolled by the military. It would be impossible to live in the zone without some form of government assistance. Here again the rural pensioners were a particularly difficult problem. With state pensions less than 40 roubles a month, they were destitute without their houses and private plots. Many of them were war widows. They either had to be housed in state institutions for the elderly or be allowed to return to their homes. It was difficult for local authorities to allow them to return to villages very close to the reactor, but those who came from the periphery of the zone were unofficially allowed to go home.

There was a smaller zone of special control in the Ukraine than in Byelorussia. There, too, people were not evacuated but they were entitled to special payments because of the health hazards. The exact location of the zone is not clear. According to one report, it was found that the produce from 22 Ukrainian villages which had continued normal farming in the 1986 summer season was too contaminated to be consumed. The villagers were provided with clean food and measures were taken to ensure that their produce was used economically and safely.[55]

The total number of rural people evacuated from the Ukrainian sector of the exclusion zone has not been reported. In general this sector was less contaminated than the Byelorussian sector. At first it was expected that many of the evacuees would be able to return to their villages after decontamination.[56] In May 1986 permanent evacuees were given a modest amount of financial aid. They were entitled later to proper compensation for their property (from 2,000 to 10,000 roubles, depending on the size of the family and other factors). The official figure for the number of evacuees may be used on the number of people who received compensation. But many more people were moved temporarily and therefore were not registered as permanent evacuees.

The exodus of people from the zone of special control became a problem for the authorities of both Byelorussia and the Ukraine. Despite double salaries and a 30 rouble supplement for each member of the family for the purchase of clean food, rural professionals such as teachers, doctors, agronomists and mechanics began to leave. By 1988 there was an acute shortage of professionals not only in villages, but also in local towns and regional centres. Young women formed the second largest group of people who left. They were afraid of having children while living in areas that had been designated as contaminated. The secrecy about the exact level of contamination, intended to prevent an exodus, merely stimulated one.[57]

The agricultural problems discussed in this chapter were predominantly local, involving the rural population evacuated from the exclusion zone and the farms in neighbouring districts, where people faced the grim prospect of living for many years under restrictive rules and regulations. But there were serious disruptions in milk, meat and vegetable production and sales in a far more extensive area of Byelorussia and the Ukraine.

The main reason why it was extremely difficult to resolve the agricultural problems caused by the Chernobyl accident was the poor state of Soviet agriculture in general. Any long-term schemes to rehabilitate the land and reprogramme agriculture to something less dangerous than livestock production require new investments and a new workforce. But it is difficult to recruit farmers from other areas to come and live in a contaminated environment. Despite active centralized help, the contaminated areas were left to heal their wounds with the help of local means. Many officials probably thought that time and Mother Nature would improve the situation in the long term. Waiting for better times may not be the optimal solution, but it is certainly the easiest and cheapest.

# 5

# The Health Impact in the Soviet Union

### INTRODUCTION

THE Chernobyl accident dramatically changed all existing perceptions about the safety of nuclear power stations and reactors in general. According to the registry at the Oak Ridge National Laboratory in the United States there were 284 major radiation accidents world-wide between 1944 and 1986 which resulted in significant exposure and fatalities from acute radiation sickness. This does not include any accidents which occurred in the Soviet Union, such as the Kyshtym disaster in the Urals. The 284 known accidents occurred in various countries: USA, Yugoslavia, Canada, Italy, and others, including the Marshall Islands, where radiation exposure resulted from nuclear weapons tests. These accidents affected 1,358 people, 620 of whom were 'significantly exposed'. There were 33 fatalities from acute radiation.[1]

The number of fatalities caused by Chernobyl officially still stands at 31, the number announced in August 1986. Twenty-four people were disabled by the accident, some of them so severely that they are invalids who cannot care for themselves.[2] The death toll may, therefore, increase in the near future. As a result of the accident, 600,000 people have been classified as having been 'significantly exposed' to radiation.[3] They have, therefore, been included on a special register of people whose health will be monitored for the rest of their lives. The register consists of people evacuated from the 30 km exclusion zone and other contaminated areas, and those who continue to live in a special zone of permanent strict control. Only some of the exposed emergency workers at the nuclear plant, the workers and soldiers who took part in decontamination, construction and repairs, firemen, policemen, medical personnel and other professional groups have been included and usually only those who live in the Ukraine. Officially, 238 people are said to have suffered from acute radiation syndrome. At a conference in Kiev in May 1988, however, the chairman of the Soviet Radiological Committee, L. A. Il'in, updated the dose estimates and reported that about 50,000 people had received 50 rad (0.5 Gy) or more, and some 4,000 people had received an average of 200 rad (2 Gy).[4] An exposure of about 100 rad or more can cause symptoms of radiation sickness and the number of people in this category could probably, therefore, reach 10,000.

It has become common to consider the radiation risk in numbers of possible radiogenic cancers. But this is not a very precise method. Radiation is not a specific carcinogen. It causes a multiple form of biological damage. As an expert on ageing and someone who has studied the phenomenon of 'radiation ageing', I believe that it is more meaningful to consider the general reduction in life expectancy as a result of radiation exposure rather than only to consider radiation-related cancer deaths.

It should be stressed that the initial Soviet and IAEA reports on the level of radiation exposure of the population and the projected health risks made in 1986 were much higher than the figures given later. The origin of the confusion has never been explained. To those with some knowledge of the state of Soviet nuclear medicine and genetics it is clear that, before 1986, Soviet medical genetics stressed radiation problems related to nuclear weapons and nuclear weapons tests. All health risk figures were normally increased by one, two or even more orders of magnitude compared to Western estimates. Radiation danger was considered a problem irrelevant to the Soviet Union. There was no proper agreed scientific method in the Soviet Union for making estimates. Different experts used very different approaches. The original Soviet estimates of future cancer risks which were reported at the IAEA meeting in August 1986 embarrassed the experts from other states who had intended to minimize the possible risks as they represented probabilities which would be difficult to verify statistically. None the less the original figures were included in all the IAEA documents in 1986.

The International Nuclear Safety Advisory Group (INSAG) of the IAEA described the health risks as follows:

> The spontaneous incidence of all cancers (for 135,000 evacuees) would not likely to be increased by more than about 0.6%. The corresponding figure for the remaining population in most regions of the European part of the Soviet Union is not expected to exceed 0.15% but is likely to be lower, of the order of 0.03%. The relative increase in the mortality due to thyroid cancer could reach 1%.

The number of cases of impairment of health due to genetic effects may be judged not to exceed 20–40% of the excess cancer doses.[5]

A year later the new Soviet report prepared for the second post-Chernobyl IAEA meeting reduced the figures of exposure of the Soviet population.[6] It also reduced the previous official number of evacuees from 135,000 to 115,000. No explanation was offered for the changes.

Since May 1986 there have been more than 150 scientific publications in Western medical and academic journals about the health impact of Chernobyl in various countries. The Soviet literature on this subject remains very limited, however. It is also very general. The only academic paper in the professional medical literature was published by A. K. Gus'kova. She and her team of doctors reported on cases of acute radiation sickness which were treated in the Moscow Radiological Hospital.[7]

The normal response to a serious nuclear reactor accident consists of a set of emergency measures and intermediate and long-term programmes. The emergency measures are, by definition, immediate. Everything that is required to put them into effect must be part of an existing, well-rehearsed plan, similar to Civil Defence measures in the case of a military alarm. The intermediate and long-term programmes depend upon a more accurate assessment of the situation and the actual number of people involved. Despite the fact that the Chernobyl accident was unprecedented and unexpected, the Soviet Civil Defence programme was designed to deal with potentially more serious problems. The medical events of Chernobyl were, therefore, not only a test of the nuclear energy network, but also of the military response to a possible war emergency.

## THE INITIAL ON-SITE EMERGENCY MEDICAL RESPONSE

The account presented in the Soviet Working Document and in the INSAG report of the emergency medical response to the Chernobyl accident gives only one side of the picture. Other accounts suggest that the emergency programme was not very effective. In fact, neither the local Pripyat and Chernobyl medical services nor the Ukrainian or Moscow specialized health services acted according to a co-ordinated plan.

All nuclear installations in the Soviet Union are securely fenced. At the end of a shift, everyone who works at the installation has to pass through a special medical dosimetric station. It is routine practice everywhere to ensure that workers do not have radioactive contamination. Dosimetric stations are equipped with simple medical and washing facilities. Normally a nurse or paramedic is on duty. At Chernobyl the plant shared a general medical service with the town of Pripyat. We now know that it did not have a doctor qualified in clinical radiology. There is, in the Soviet Union, a specialized medical service which is available for the many research and industrial centres which deal with military aspects of nuclear energy, reprocessing, manufacturing the radiochemicals and radioisotope equipment for general medicine such as the special apparatus for gamma irradiation of cancer patients. It is supervised and co-ordinated by an independent department of the Ministry of Health. It appears, however, that this service did not extend to civilian nuclear power stations like Chernobyl. Since workers there are not in daily contact with radioactive materials serious accidents are considered unlikely. Individual cases of radiation exposure, as when uranium fuel channels leak or are recharged, which may occur from time to time are dealt with in Kiev, Moscow or some other location.

It seems that the medical facilities of the Chernobyl plant and its dosimetric station were closed or even locked at the time of the accident. The duty nurse or health officer was probably expected to arrive towards the end of the night shift to check the workers as they left the premises. The Pripyat medical service was open, with only a small night staff. The main hero of that tragic night was 28-year old Valentin Belokon', the only doctor on duty. He had started his shift at 20.00 on 25 April, together with a paramedical assistant, Aleksandr Skachok. Dr Belokon' miraculously survived a rather acute form of radiation sickness (he was hospitalized the next day and was discharged from the Moscow hospital in October, five months after the accident). In June 1987 he described the events of that night and morning.[8] His interview, recorded for general readers rather than for those with specialized medical knowledge, remains the most reliable account of the response to the on-site radiation emergency.

Dr Belokon' is a general practitioner who has specialized in paediatrics. After midnight that night he was returning from a visit to an asthma case when he suddenly saw two lightning explosions at the site of the nuclear power station. Back at the town hospital he found a call from the station. He sent his paramedical assistant Skachok to find out what had happened. Fifteen minutes later Skachok called to tell him that there was a fire and that some people had suffered burns. Dr Belokon' sent two ambulances to the station and set off himself, passing Skachok's ambulance which was returning with flashing lights. It was transporting operator Shashenok, who died shortly afterwards from burns. Belokon' records that they had no dosimeters nor did they have respirators or gas-masks or protective clothing. He continued:

> Three people came up to me immediately . . . They brought a chap of about eighteen. He was complaining of nausea and severe headache and had begun vomiting. They worked in the third reactor and, it seems, had gone to the fourth . . . I took his blood pressure. It was 140 or 150 over 90, a little high. Then it leapt up and the chap became peculiar, somehow not himself. I took him to the first-aid section. There was nothing in the vestibule, nowhere even to sit, only two automatic mineral water dispensers. The medical room was shut. I took him to the ambulance. He became delirious before my very eyes . . . he showed symptoms of confusion, couldn't speak and began to mumble as if he'd had a drink or two, although he didn't smell of alcohol. He was very pale. People who ran from the building kept exclaiming 'How awful!' . . . then the chaps said that the dosimeters were hitting the top of their scales. But that was already later.
>
> . . . Another three people came to the ambulance . . . with headaches and the same symptoms – blocked throat, dryness, nausea, vomiting . . . I was alone, without the paramedic and I put them straight into the ambulance and sent them to Pripyat . . .
>
> . . . As soon as I'd sent them off the chaps brought the firemen to me . . . several men. They could hardly stand on their feet. I could only treat their symptoms . . . trying to relieve the delirium, the pain . . .
>
> When I had sent off the firemen I asked for potassium iodide tablets to be sent, although there probably were some in the station's medical room. At first Pecheritsa asked what I needed them for. And then, apparently, when they saw the firemen, they stopped asking, collected the potassium iodide and sent it. I began to give it to people.[9]

For several hours Dr Belokon' was the only doctor at the plant. The deputy chief doctor of Pripyat, Vladimir Pecheritsa, was dealing with the people brought from the site to the town clinic by ambulance. The ambulances where Dr Belokon' was working were parked near the damaged reactor. He soon began to feel ill himself:

> At six o'clock I began to feel a tickling in my throat. My head hurt. Did I understand the danger? Was I afraid? I understood. I was afraid. But when people see someone in a white coat nearby, it calms them. Like everyone else, I had no respirator, no protective clothing . . . Where was I to get a respirator? I would have grabbed one – but there weren't any. I telephoned the medical station in town: 'Do we have any [respirators]?' 'No, we don't.' So that was that. Work in an ordinary gauze mask? It wouldn't have helped . . .[10]

When Belokon' felt that he could not last any longer, he asked the ambulance driver to take him to the town clinic. There were already several doctors there. He was given a glass of spirits and advised to drink it but he already felt too nauseous to get it down. He could not find anyone to take potassium iodide tablets to his colleagues in the hostel where they lived. So he washed and changed and got a driver to take him there: 'I told them to close the windows, not to let the children out . . . I distributed tablets to the neighbours. Then our doctor . . . came to fetch me . . . I became delirious.'[11]

We do not know who replaced Belokon' at the nuclear power station. Reactor Unit 3 was shut down at 05.00, whereas Nos 1 and 2 continued to operate for nearly 24 hours after the accident, until 01.13 and 02.13 on Sunday 27 April, despite heavy contamination through their ventilation systems.[12] Some operators from Units 1 and 2 also began suffering from radiation syndrome. Dr Belokon' met one of them in the Moscow hospital. He reported that straight after the explosion their dosimeters had registered maximum radiation. They telephoned the chief engineer or the safety engineer to tell him. He asked what the panic was and told them to find the shift foreman and tell him to telephone a report. Meanwhile they were not to panic.[13]

At the time of the accident were were 176 operators, engineers and guards servicing the plant and 268 construction workers building Reactor Units 5 and 6 on a round-the-clock shift system.[14] At about 04.00 nearly 200 firemen arrived from Kiev and other towns and hundreds of policemen arrived from Kiev. It is not known how many people arrived to replace the night shift on Reactor Units 1 and 2 and to keep the cooling system of Unit 3 under control. The medical room located in the administrative building of the plant was opened at some time during the early morning. New teams of firemen from surrounding towns, sent to replace the first firemen from Pripyat who had been hospitalized, were checked for radioactive contamination after the fire on the roof had been extinguished. They were instructed to shower and change their clothes. They were also given iodine tablets (although after their work, rather than before as they should have been). Many people from this group later needed prolonged treatment in Moscow and Kiev hospitals.

Until the night shift ended at about 08.00 only those people who developed obvious early symptoms of radiation sickness were evacuated from the site, usually by ambulance. Those who were not directly involved in the emergency operations (drivers, reserve firemen, firemen who had completed their tasks) were given some protection in the civil defence underground bunker on site. It is possible that many people left the plant and returned to Pripyat without any inspection. The official Soviet report at Vienna described the situation on site very briefly and optimistically:

> Assistance was given to the first 29 victims leaving the site of the accident by themselves within the first 30–40 minutes by the middle-level medical staff on duty at the health station. The victims threw off their contaminated clothing and shoes even before entering the personnel airlock. Owing to the intense primary reaction, they were immediately sent to the hospital where health procedures and the first medical examinations were carried out.
>
> During the next four hours, first-aid teams which had immediately arrived on the scene provided assistance to the victims, removing them from the zone of production operations, carrying out preliminary health procedures in the personnel airlock and transporting persons suffering from primary reactions (nausea, vomiting) to the hospital. Persons who felt that their condition was satisfactory were sent home and, subsequently, actively summoned for examination in the morning of 26 April 1986. By 06.00 on 26 April, 108 persons had been hospitalized and, in the course of the day, another 24 persons from the group which had been examined were hospitalized.[15]

The authors of this report have conflated the situation in the Pripyat town medical station with that of the Chernobyl plant first-aid station. The clinic in Pripyat was, in fact, too small to deal with so many victims. Many of them were sent by ambulance and car to hospitals in Chernobyl and Polesskoye, the two nearest towns. Nobody was 'actively summoned for examination in the morning of 26 April'. There were no medical personnel to do this and more victims were arriving from the plant site. Outside medical teams (most of them from Kiev and Moscow) began to arrive in Pripyat only 12 hours after the accident. They included physicists, radiology therapists, laboratory assistants and haematologists.[16] From late afternoon on Saturday 26 April the medical emergency became a national task under the command of the Ukrainian Ministry of Health and the special radiological service of the USSR Ministry of Health. Dr Vladimir Pecheritsa was interviewed several months later for the Soviet television film on Chernobyl shown in 1987 (it was also shown by the BBC in Britain). He was criticized in the film for not raising the alarm in Pripyat among the general population or among the workers at the plant. He retorted that he had neither the means nor the authority to do so. He was not in control of organizational matters. All he could do was to report to his superiors.

Dr Belokon', hero of the emergency at the plant site, was released from hospital in the autumn. Although he has sustained lasting damage to his lungs resulting in permanent breathing problems, he has resumed his medical career. He now works as a surgeon in a children's hospital in Donetsk.[17]

### THE OFF-SITE EMERGENCY MEDICAL RESPONSE

In areas further from the site of the accident there were two main emergency tasks. First, the hospitalized victims had to be treated and the seriously ill had to be evacuated urgently to properly equipped specialized hospitals; secondly, the danger to the local population had to be assessed so that a decision could be made about evacuation. By Saturday 26 April it was already clear that the populations of Pripyat (45,000), of Yanov railway station (which served both the nuclear plant and Pripyat) and of a few small villages close to the reactor should be evacuated. Urgent decisions were required about how to organize it.

### Hospitalization

By 06.00 on Saturday 26 April, 108 people had been hospitalized in Pripyat. A further 24 people (including Dr Belokon' and his assistant) were admitted a few hours later. Specialized medical personnel arrived 12 hours after the accident and took charge of the medical emergency. It appears that they worked under Professor L. A. Il'in, a chief doctor of the Ministry of Health radiological service. The Ukrainian deputy Minister of Health, Dr A. N. Zelinsky, who had been the first to receive a report from Pripyat, was responsible for all decisions since his superior, Minister A. E. Romanenko, was in the United States at the time. The deputy Minister of Health of the USSR, E. I. Vorob'ev, and his assistant, Dr V. D. Turovsky, arrived with the government commission at about 18.00. The fact that it took as long as 12 hours for medical experts, including those who came from nearby Kiev, to respond to the emergency is explained by the initial miscalculation about the scale of the medical consequences.

At first the ministries in Kiev and Moscow decided that diagnostic procedures should be carried out in local hospitals to identify those likely to develop severe forms (third and fourth degrees) of radiation syndrome. Only they were to be evacuated.

Assessing the degree of radiation damage is a complex procedure which includes, among others, tests to measure the intensity of leucopenia and neutrophilic leucocytosis towards the end of the first 36 hours. This was why the emergency teams included haematologists, laboratory technicians and special equipment. But the most severe cases of radiation sickness could be diagnosed from simple clinical observation. More than ten people had obvious symptoms and were also suffering from severe skin burns (40–90 per cent of the body surface) which could prove fatal. They were thermoradiation injuries caused by hot radioactive particles in the aerosol and fumes which stick to the skin and are absorbed by the lungs, eyes and other wet surfaces and which cannot easily be washed away by water. These people clearly needed to be moved immediately to the specialized radiological hospital in Moscow without waiting for time-consuming blood tests. The description of this first evacuation was given by A. Yu. Esaulov, deputy chairman of Pripyat town council executive committee in charge of the local transport and medical services and roads and communications.[18] At about 15.00 he was ordered to organize the evacuation by V. Malomuzh, secretary of the Kiev region Party committee, now in full command of the entire operation (in the dual Party and government administrative system of the Soviet Union, the Party takes decision-making precedence in an emergency situation).

Representatives of the urgently formed high-level Government Commission had not yet arrived by plane from Moscow. The person responsible for the evacuation was Colonel-General Ivanov, Deputy Chief Commander of Civil Defence in the USSR. It was decided that his plane would be used to fly the seriously ill to Moscow. According to Esaulov:

> It was not easy to load the people. Documents had to be prepared for each person containing the case history and the results of the analyses. The main delay was in completing these personal affairs . . .
> We took 26 people in one bus, a red intercity 'Ikarus'. I told them to send two buses. Anything could happen. God forbid there should be a delay . . . And there was an ambulance because there were two severely ill people, stretcher cases with 30 per cent burns.
> I requested that the buses should not drive through the centre of Kiev. Because these fellows in the bus were in pyjamas. They were an awful sight. But for some reason they went through [the main street of Kiev] . . . We arrived at the airport. The gates were shut. It was night time, after 3 a.m. We hooted. At last . . . someone came out in slippers, wearing trousers without a belt. He opened the gate. We drove straight onto the runway to the plane. The crew was already warming up the engines.[19]

Thus these gravely ill victims arrived at Kiev airport more than 12 hours after the decision was made to send them to Moscow. It would have been more appropriate to send them by helicopter than by bus. If Esaulov's request to avoid the centre of Kiev had been heeded, it would have taken even longer to get them to the airport – the main street leads directly onto the bridge which must be crossed to get to the airport, which is about 40 km from Kiev.

When Esaulov arrived back at Pripyat with his bus convoy on Sunday morning there was a new order to evacuate all the hospitalized victims. The decision had already been made to evacuate the whole town and 1,000 buses had been commandeered from Kiev during the night. The second medical convoy consisted of four buses. It left Pripyat carrying 110 patients at about noon on Sunday. A special plane was waiting at Kiev airport. On its way back to Pripyat in the late afternoon it passed the long line of buses evacuating the entire population of Pripyat. (Intensive traffic between the Chernobyl site and Kiev during first few days, before the exclusion zone was established, caused many streets in Kiev to become heavily contaminated with radionuclides.)

The evacuation of Pripyat and Yanov did not mean that the local medical emergency was over. Several hundred people were still involved in emergency work at the plant. Moreover, not all the people with obvious signs of radiation sickness had been taken to Pripyat on the previous day since the local hospital did not have room to accommodate them. The hospitals in the surrounding towns of Chernobyl, Ivankovskoye and Polesskoye had also admitted patients. The largest was the district hospital at Polesskoye, about 40 km south-west of Chernobyl, in an area which had not yet been affected by radioactive fallout. Ordinary patients were discharged and the hospital was transformed into a temporary emergency medical centre. It became the base for the specialized teams from Moscow and Kiev. Various levels of radiation syndrome were diagnosed there.[20] People with acute forms of radiation sickness (those who had received doses of radiation higher than 200 rem or 2 Gy) were sent to a specialized radiological clinic in Kiev. But the Moscow radiological hospital (later known as Hospital No. 6) and the Kiev radiological clinic together did not have sufficient facilities to treat all the patients with radiation syndrome. A second hospital in Moscow was prepared for the purpose and several other hospitals and clinics in other cities took patients. Military personnel were checked and treated in military hospitals.[21]

The most serious cases of radiation sickness are known to have been treated in Hospital No. 6. According to the official Soviet report, 129 patients from Chernobyl were treated there.[22] A total of 135 people were airlifted to Moscow but some of them were probably not severely affected and were, therefore, discharged after detailed examination. The medical history of these patients is described in the Soviet Working Document. Seventeen of them had died by the time the report was compiled on day 50 after the accident.[23] One can assume that a further 12 fatalities were treated at the Institute of Roentgenology, Radiology an Oncology in Kiev, where Professor L. P. Kindzelsky was in charge of the Chernobyl patients. Their medical history is not well known and it was not included in the Soviet Working Document. Professor Robert Gale, from the University of California School of Medicine in Los Angeles visited the Kiev radiological hospital on 3 June, but he did not publish a medical account of his visit in his book on Chernobyl.[24] However, a credible account was given of the medical situation in another Kiev hospital by Dr Maksim Drach. As a student in his final year at the Kiev Medical Institute he was working as a senior paramedic in the intensive care section of the Cardiological Centre at the October Revolution Hospital. He began his shift on Sunday morning. At noon the section was urgently ordered to prepare 40 beds for accident victims from Chernobyl. They cleared the third floor of the hospital and prepared for blood transfusions and other procedures. Dr Drach says that:

> At six o'clock we were told that the first patients from Pripyat had arrived at admissions. The duty doctors from the department of radioisotope diagnosis and the intensive care unit went to admit them. We saw them. They were basically young fellows, firemen and people who worked at the nuclear power station. At first they went upstairs with their things. But then the frightened dosimetrist ran up shouting: 'What are you doing? They're irradiated!'
>
> They went back down, were measured and taken to wash not in the admissions unit but the department of radioisotope diagnosis, where all the water was collected in containers and taken out. This was wise because the admissions unit did not become contaminated. We gave them our operating pyjamas and they went upstairs like that.
>
> We didn't ask them many questions. There was no time. They all complained of headaches and weakness.[25]

Dr Drach's next shift was on 1 May. He found that there had been so many new admissions with radiation syndrome that another floor of the hospital had been taken over.

Radiation syndome causes an acute prolonged immunological deficiency. As long as it lasts patients must be kept in isolation in individual sterile wards or compartments to protect them from any possible source of infection. They also need frequent blood transfusions and intravenous feeding because the intestine epithelium is damaged. Each case is, in fact, unique and needs individual medical attention more complex than that provided in ordinary intensive care units.

Clinical aspects of the treatment of those who developed acute radiation sickness are very complex and specific and I do not plan to discuss the details here. The most interesting part of this generally very painful and grim story was an emergency attempt to use new methods of bone marrow transplantation to save some fatally ill patients. Professor Robert Gale arrived in Moscow to assist in the application of this experimental technique. The clinical details of this work (13 bone marrow transplants and 6 transplants of foetal liver which can be used as a source of haematopoietic stem cells) have been described by Gale.[26] In 1987 he was still optimistic about the prospects of this approach, despite the fact that it did not save the Chernobyl victims. Gale's Russian colleagues, however, later dismissed the method as impractical.[27]

## Preventative measures and the evacuation

The measures taken to reduce the radiation exposure of the local population and the timing of the evacuation were discussed at the IAEA post-accident meeting in Vienna in August 1986, at the Nuclear Safety Advisory Group in September 1986 and in the Soviet and Western press. The IAEA endorsed the actions taken, stating that they were appropriate and in full accord with the recommendations of the ICRP. The INSAG Report more or less repeated the description given in the Soviet Working Document.[28] Professor Richard Wilson from Harvard University, chairman of the American Physical Society for the Study of Severe Nuclear Accidents, visited the Chernobyl area in 1987. In his published report he also approved the actions of the local authorities and medical experts:

> The rules [of the ICRP] state that if the dose to an individual is expected to reach 25 roentgen-equivalent-man (Rem) integrated over time, evacuation should be considered; if the integrated dose is expected to reach 75 Rem, an evacuation plan should be implemented. During the day of 26 April, the radiation levels were only 10 mRem per hour in Pripyat, not enough to predict that the level required for evacuation would be reached. When, by 2100, the increased radioactivity release accompanying the graphite fire had caused the radiation level to rise to 140 mR per hour on the street nearest to the plant, evacuation was decided upon. It was decided to leave

people in their homes overnight, sheltered by the buildings, while transport was assembled. By this time the radiation levels had reached 1000 mR per hour on the nearest street.[29]

This description, however, contradicts journalists' reports, the evidence of evacuated Pripyat residents and material which became public at the trial of senior officials of the Chernobyl plant in August 1987. More importantly, the specific danger of the Chernobyl accident was not taken into account in the official versions of the evacuation. It came not so much from external radiation from gamma sources (which could be measured by dosimeters) as from radioactive aerosol and dust, called 'hot particles' (see p. 182).

On Saturday 26 April the residents of Pripyat did not receive any medical instructions by radio or any other local communication system which could reach every household. Only the few houses situated near the Pripyat clinic were warned, verbally. Moreover, contrary to the claims in the Soviet Working Document, all schools were working (schools in the Soviet Union have a six-day working week and Saturday is an ordinary school day). The ICRP rules, (which are generally accepted in the Soviet Union[30]) make evacuation compulsory if the integrated dose for the following day is likely to reach 75 rem. But they also insist that people, particularly children, should be sheltered and protected at much lower integrated doses. The environmental conditions in Pripyat and towns and villages north and north-west of the plant almost immediately after the accident required protective measures and clear instructions to the population. The initial explosion forced the radioactive cloud high into the air and Pripyat seemed to be spared, but the continuing graphite fire released radioactive aerosol which adversely affected the situation in Pripyat. The dynamic of radioactivity over Pripyat on 26–30 April (the first 100 hours) is shown in the Soviet Working Document (figure 5.1).[31] However, it is now known that the explosion also dispersed highly radioactive portions of the reactor core and pieces of graphite locally and as far as 6 or 7 km away. This created very dangerous spots of contamination well beyond the fenced-off area of the plant. The pattern of these spots was only established much later.

Nobody could predict the weather conditions. A small amount of rain over Pripyat would have made the situation catastrophic. It was already clear on Saturday that the radioactivity readings could only become worse the next day. With this knowledge, it would clearly have been better to carry out the evacuation as soon as possible. It was technically feasible to begin it in the late afternoon or evening of Satuday. In fact,

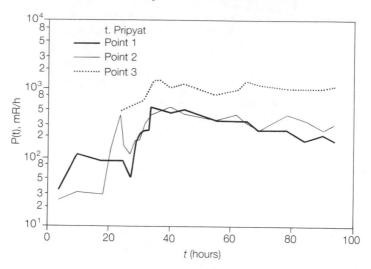

**Figure 5.1**   Dose rate change dynamics in the open country of Pripyat during the first four days after the accident (from *The Accident . . . Soviet IAEA Report*, Part II, Annex 7, figure 7.2.1).

Pripyat was entirely sealed off early on Saturday morning and police patrols prevented anyone from leaving the town.

There were 10,200 children in Pripyat who were particularly at risk. A local journalist, Lyubov' Kovalevskaya (whose article in *Literaturnaya Ukraina* on 27 March 1986 about the poor quality of construction at the Chernobyl plant was later widely quoted by the Western and Soviet press as a serious warning of the possibility of an accident) was in Pripyat on the fatal night of the disaster. Her interview about events in the town on Saturday 26 April 1986 was only published more than a year later, in June 1987.[32] Her report seems incredible but it has been independently confirmed by other witnessees. When the policy of *glasnost'* was applied to the general Soviet media in January 1987 vastly different accounts of the problems faced by the population and by people who were evacuated from the exclusion zone began to appear from those published in 1986. When Kovalevskaya woke up late on Saturday morning her mother reported strange sounds from the plant during the night. Kovalevskaya went outside:

> All the roads were covered in water and some white liquid. Everything was white, foamy, all the curbs . . . I walked further and saw a policeman here, another there. I had never seen so many policemen in the town. They weren't doing anything, just sitting in various places, at the post office, the

Palace of Culture. As if there was martial law. It was quite a shock. But people were walking about normally, there were children everywhere. It was very hot. People were going to the beach, to their country cottages, many people were already there, or sitting by the stream, next to the cooling reservoir. That's an artificial water reservoir next to the nuclear power station . . . Anya, my daughter, had gone to school. I went home and said 'Mama, I don't know what has happened, but don't let Natasha (my niece) out of the house, and when Anya returns from school, take her straight into the house'. But I didn't tell her to close the window . . .

I went back to the central square . . . The reactor was quite visible, one could see that it was burning and that its wall was broken. There were flames above the hole. That chimney between the third and fourth blocks was burning hot, it looked like a burning column . . . We knew nothing all day. Nobody said anything. Well, they said there was a fire. But about radiation, that radioactivity was escaping, there was not a word. Anya came back from school and said 'Mama, we had physical exercise outside for almost a whole hour'. Insanity.[33]

An equally incredible story was told by Aneliya Perkovskaya, secretary of the Pripyat town Komsomol committee. V. Malomuzh, second secretary of the Party Regional Committee, told the director of School No. 3 that everything should go ahead as normal that Saturday. So lessons took place normally, although the director cancelled outside events. Since it was Saturday:

. . . the children's cafe in the trade centre was filled with parents and children eating ice cream . . . people were walking about the town with their dogs. And when we went up to them and explained what was happening, their reaction was angry and unsure: 'It's none of your business' . . . I don't know whether they believed us or not . . .[34]

According to the Soviet Working Document, the INSAG Report and other official Soviet statements in 1986, no Pripyat residents developed any clinical effects of radiation injury. Professor Wilson later repeated the statement of Dr L. A. Il'in, chief of the Soviet radiological service, that no one other than power plant workers and firemen received a larger dose than the standards suggested by the evacuation plans.[35] But this statement is inaccurate. It is now known that the area between the nuclear plant and Pripyat, originally intended to be an uninhabited 'sanitary zone', had, over the years, been taken over by local families as allotments. Some spots in this area were heavily contaminated by pieces which had erupted from the reactor core and had been too heavy to rise with the radioactive cloud. Since there was no warning to the local people to stay indoors, some enthusiastic gardeners spent Saturday working on their plots. They were situated very close to the forest which Yuri Shcherbak, a Kiev journalist who covered the Chernobyl story for many papers, saw turning from green to red under the influence of highly radioactive dust. He later reported that he had met a woman from Pripyat in one of the Kiev hospitals during the May Day holidays. Like many others, she had worked on her plot that Saturday and sustained radiation burns on her legs.[36]

Soviet officials later claimed that they had not issued an official warning because they wanted to avoid panic. But there were surely better ways to avoid panic. The damaged reactor, the fire and the smoke over it were clearly visible. Many people realized what was going on. The absence of information in a situation which was so obviously an emergency itself created panic. There were more than 800 privately owned cars in Pripyat and roadblocks were set up to prevent them being used to take people out without authorization. This meant that the only way to leave was through the forest south-west of the town. But the wind was blowing radioactivity from the reactor in this direction that Saturday and it was this forest that was most severely contaminated.

> It is hardly surprising that in a situation of complete blackout of information, a number of people responded to rumours by rushing to leave via the road that led through the 'Red Forest'. Witnesses reported that along this road which was already 'shining' in the full force of radiation women wheeled prams . . .[37]

There are innumerable further descriptions of local ignorance. Several weddings were celebrated that Saturday night. In the villages close to the reactor site, particularly those to the north and north-west, the situation was even worse. Their wooden houses offered even less protection from the radioactivity of the initial cloud than the brick and concrete multi-storey blocks of flats in Pripyat. Pripyat was in the initial exclusion zone, which was 10 km in radius. But the zone was arbitrary and not based on real measurements of the distribution of radioactive contamination. Although it was probably sensible to carry out the evacuation in stages, beginning with Pripyat and Yanov and then extending the zone, the second stage was delayed for far too long.

The fact that the first stage of the evacuation only took place on Sunday afternoon would not invite criticism if proper measures had been taken immediately to protect the population. But in the absence of preventative measures, the entire population of Pripyat and Yanov (some 50,000 people) were needlessly exposed to radiation for 36 hours.

Some experts have argued that the doses were not really significant, but it must already have been clear that the main danger came from radioactive aerosol which made the idea of 'safe' doses of external radiation irrelevant. Moreover, children are vulnerable to radioiodine and its level was not measured separately.

Like many other countries, the Soviet Union has special rules and regulations which indicate the measures that must be undertaken when there is radioactive contamination of the environment resulting from an accident. Some of these rules are published.[38] others are classified circulars issued by the Ministry of Health and available only within the medical system. The Soviet report to the IAEA insists that all regulations were strictly followed, including the timing of the evacuation.

During the first few hours after the accident, the explosion forced radioactive debris very high into the air and it was carried out past the town by the wind. In the early morning of April 26 the radioactivity in the cloud above Pripyat was immense and almost unmeasurable. At ground level, the dose of external radiation was only 100 mR/h (see figure 5.1). It was dangerous in the long term, but the level did not, it was thought, demand immediate action. In fact, this was the very moment when evacuation should have been ordered. The reactor was still a radioactive volcano and the weather conditions and air currents were unpredictable. From 09.00 the situation began to deteriorate and ground-level radioactivity rose sharply. In the part of the town closest to the reactor (Kurchatov Street), the gamma radiation dose had reached 180–600 mR/h and was rising.[39] At this point the order was given in Kiev to mobilize buses and crews. More than 1,000 buses arrived in Pripyat at about midnight. Their drivers were ordered to remain ready to leave and await orders. They spent the entire night in a state of alert. Presumably someone still hoped that the local situation would improve. In fact, conditions were steadily deteriorating. None the less the evacuation did not begin until next afternoon. Between 26 and 28 hours after the accident there was a short drop in gamma radiation in some parts of town, so the evacuation was postponed. Two hours later it had risen again. At 14.00 on 27 April, when the level reached what later turned out to be its maximum, the command was finally given for the evacuation to begin. Thus the complex task was performed under the least favourable conditions, when the external radiation exceeded 1 R/h and when radioactive aerosol covered the town, so that everyone breathed air saturated with hot radioactive particles. It took a little more than two hours to complete the task. The local population would clearly have suffered significantly less health damage if the evacuation had occurred early that morning. Children and several hundred pregnant women were put at a particularly high risk.

It was pointed out later that stress and the traumatic experience of evacuation should be taken into account in assessing the public health effects of the Chernobyl accident.[40] From a technical and organizational point of view the evacuation was carried out well and it was much praised. However, the evacuees later complained about the lack of proper information. They were given to understand that they were being moved for only three days. A. Perkovskaya, the Komsomol secretary quoted earlier, reported that she and other Komsomol and Party leaders were explicitly told that people would be evacuated for a period of three days. They were told about the evacuation much earlier than the general public, at 01.00 on 27 April. She tried to justify the misinformation by explaining that everything had to be done as quickly as possible:

> When I got home in the morning, the neighbours began to arrive . . . I calmed them as well as I could. I didn't tell them that we were being evacuated . . . I managed to drink some coffee and at about 6 o'clock I went back to work . . . We were consulted about the text informing the residents of Pripyat. I can more or less reconstruct it from memory:
>
> 'Comrades, in connection with the accident at Chernobyl nuclear power station, the evacuation of the town is announced. Take your documents, essential clothing and food for three days . . . The evacuation will begin at 14.00'.
>
> This was announced four times . . .
>
> I think that it was right that they put it that way. Otherwise we would not have been able to conduct the evacuation so quickly and well.[41]

This account of the official announcement of the evacuation was later confirmed by other witnesses. It seems rather short and misleading. It said nothing about the radiation danger. Later, when it became clear that the town had been abandoned for good, there were numerous problems about possessions, documents and family papers that had been left behind.

Where were these 50,000 people taken? The Chernobyl accident was still a state secret. Outside the Chernobyl district no one knew about it. Swedish experts only detected the radioactivity on Monday 28 April, raising the international alarm which forced the Soviet government to admit the accident later that day. But the secrecy caused officials to make a further mistake. The buses did not travel eastwards towards non-contaminated areas nor did they go to Kiev or further away. The people of Pripyat were dumped in the neighbouring Polessky and Ivankovsky districts, west and south of Chernobyl district, distributed between villages in those districts, only about 40–50 km from the Chernobyl plant. When the exclusion zone was extended to a radius of 30 km, many thousands of evacuees were still living right next to it.

This was a great mistake. The rural districts were unable to accommodate nearly 50,000 extra people. Kovalevskaya, the Pripyat journalist, described how they were put in a village called Maksimovichi, only 6 km from the 30 km exclusion zone, But when the dosimetrists arrived later, they discovered that here, too, the radiation level was raised. She goes on: 'You can imagine the state of a mother who takes her child to the dosimetrist. He measures the child's shoes. "Contaminated". Trousers – "contaminated". Hair – "contaminated" . . . When I had sent my mother to Siberia with the children I began to feel better'.[42]

Perkovskaya who, as a Komsomol secretary, helped in distributing people amongst the various villages, explained:

> The thing is that there was no plan of evacuation and we didn't know which blocks of Pripyat flats or which micro-regions had been placed in which villages. I still can't understand what scheme was used, who was sent where. In Polesskoye we had a list of children. I would phone a village council and ask 'Do you have such-and-such parents? Their children are looking for them'. And they would reply 'We have such-and-such children without parents. We don't know where these children come from'. One would sit and phone all the village councils in turn. Sometimes it turned out that in some or other village a kind old granny was sitting with someone else's child and she'd not told anyone.[43]

The head of the equipment department of the Pripyat sector of *Atomenergomontazh*, G. N. Petrov, was evacuated with his family. He later told Grigory Medvedev:

> At exactly 2 p.m. on 27 April buses arrived at every entrance. We were warned by radio again: dress lightly, take as little as possible, you will return in three days.
>
> We were taken to Ivankova (sixty kilometres from Pripyat) and there we were distributed amongst the villages. Not everyone took us willingly.
>
> Many people who were put down at Ivankova continued further by foot, in the direction of Kiev. One helicopter pilot I know told me later that he could see huge crowds of lightly dressed people, women with children, old people, walking along the road and the roadside in the direction of Kiev.[44]

The second stage of the evacuation of Pripyat people included children and pregnant women. It took place in the middle of May when the first emergency was over and medical attention had been transferred to the people in a wider area around the plant. The accident had finally been acknowledged on 28 April 1986 and there was therefore no further need for secrecy. As a result, the second stage occurred without the blunders of the first.

It is difficult to conclude that either the on-site or the off-site medical reponse to the Chernobyl emergency was adequate and satisfactory. Neither international nor Soviet regulations were followed, usually because of political and bureaucratic interference and considerations other than people's health. The 'political health' of the system was given priority over public health. As a result, many more people were exposed to serious radiation risks than was inevitable in an accident of this scale. It was perhaps not surprising that the personnel of Unit 4 and the local firemen who first attended the accident suffered casualties. But the occurrence of radiation sickness among people who worked in other units at the plant, among firemen who arrived on the scene three to four hours after the accident, among policemen who guarded the territory and among the medical personnel who treated the victims was avoidable. Moreover, the population of Pripyat was needlessly exposed to radiation. An adequate response could have reduced the total number of cases of acute radiation syndrome from 238 to 30–35, particularly if even the simplest respirators had been available at the power station. Both the local and the specialized medical services can be criticized for not assessing the situation properly and not resisting outside administrative and political interference.

It is not only the evidence of ordinary witnesses and journalists that contradicts the legend that the health problems after the accident were dealt with quickly and fully. Even highly placed officials like Valery Legasov, the head of the scientific team on the government commission, spoke openly two years later about the very poor medical and dosimetric services in the exclusion zone. Legasov maintained that many people were needlessly exposed to radiation for rather routine operations:

> I remember how, in the first few days, when the commission was in Pripyat, there weren't enough protective respirators or dosimeters . . . At the station there were no automatic external dosimeters which would automatically have transmitted telemetric data about the radiation conditions in a radius of several kilometers. We had, therefore, to organize a large number of people to collect this information. There were no radio-controlled planes fitted with dosimetric equipment and therefore we needed a fair number of pilots and helicopter pilots to take measurements and collect information. And even an elementary hygienic regime was absent, at least in the first few days.[45]

Similar accusations were made during the trial of some of the Chernobyl plant officials in July 1987. One of the rulings of the court specifically mentioned that 'the absence of accurate information about the nature of the accident led to injuries of plant personnel and of the population of the surrounding areas'.[46] But the plant officials were not the only people who were held responsible. The Supreme Court also pointed to higher level organizations which were responsible for the poor safety standards applied to the personnel and to the general public. Among those who were singled out for further investigation were not only officials of the nuclear energy administration but representatives of the medical service, the radiation protection service and the local Pripyat administration 'who could not organize proper protection of the population from radiation injuries'.[47]

Inside the clinics and hospitals the doctors performed very well. They worked hard and probably achieved as much as possible. There no one could dictate what to do or how to do it. However, during the emergency and outside the hospitals the medical service performed very badly and doctors played a role in the overall cover-up. This cover-up extended well beyond the first two days, when the accident was still a state secret.

It was obvious immediately after the accident that the authorities intended to impose a long-term blackout on all independent studies of the radiation levels. All academic and university radiobiology laboratories which were not included in the special programmes and were not classified were prevented from measuring the environmental radioactivity. Two years after the accident Professor D. M. Grodzinsky, the head of the radiobiological laboratory of the Institute of Botany of the Ukrainian Academy of Sciences reported what happened in his laboratory in Kiev after the accident:

> As soon as the Chernobyl accident occurred the dosimeters in my laboratory registered an increase in radioactivity. We could only guess what had happened. Instead of explaining to us radiobiologists what had happened so that we could make recommendations to the population how properly to behave in the first hours after the accident, they sealed up our dosimeters. They told us that what had happened at Chernobyl was absolutely secret.[18]

More than two years after the accident the unauthorized possession of an individual dosimeter was still treated as a crime. Some engineers and physicists began to manufacture them from simple equipment and to sell them on the black market. Grodzinsky reported that people in Japan:

. . . go to the market with their dosimeters and measure the radioactivity of cabbages or fish . . . We not only don't have individual means of dosimetry, but any attempt to manufacture them is stopped . . . People lose their jobs so that they won't dare to make them. The explanation is the same . . . so as not to cause panic. And the fact that absurd rumours circulate because of the lack of information, or that people's health is harmed doesn't worry anyone.[49]

## THE EXCLUSION ZONE AND THE SECOND PHASE OF EVACUATION

The graphite fire in the reactor core and large releases of radionuclides, mostly in the form of a very fine aerosol, continued for ten days. For the first three days the winds blew the radioactive cloud in a north and north-westerly direction. On 29 April, however, weather conditions changed and so did the distribution of radioactive contamination. Areas to the south and south-west of the accident site began to be at risk. A few days later eastern areas were also affected. It became clear that there should be a further evacuation. It was inexcusable to delay 8 to 11 days before ordering it. The delay meant that people were exposed to much higher external and internal radiation doses than the residents of Pripyat. The worst situation was registered in Chistogolovka, Kopachi and Lelev, three small towns situated 5.5, 6 and 9 km from the burning reactor. Figure 5.2, which shows the dynamic of radioactivity over these towns and was presented in the Soviet Report for the IAEA, indicates that the maximum levels were reached on the second and third days.[50]

The very approximate estimates made by Soviet experts (on the basis of the false assumption that most Pripyat residents stayed indoors) indicated that the population of Pripyat was exposed to individual external doses of 1.5–50 rad for gamma radiation and 10–20 rad for beta radiation (usually to the skin). The doses of internal radiation of the thyroid gland were between 1.5 and 25 rad.[51] In some villages which were evacuated later, however, people were exposed to doses as high as 30–40 rad.[52] These estimates excluded the effects of consuming contaminated products. No attempt was made to give more accurate figures for farmers living in villages, but the official Soviet figures of the radiation exposure of the population of several towns (see table 5.1) make it clear that the radiation exposure (particularly the doses to the thyroid glands of children) was far too high, and it was ten times higher for the children of Lelev than for the children of Pripyat. According to

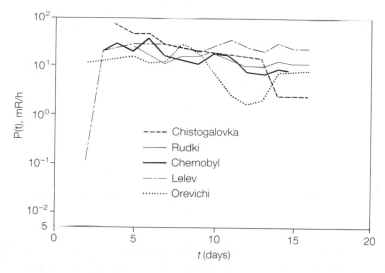

**Figure 5.2** Change of gamma radiation dose rate in the open country for some populated areas in the 30 km zone (from *The Accident . . . Soviet IAEA Report*, Part II, Annex 7, figure 7.2.3).

Soviet rules children with thyroid doses above 200 rad should be hospitalized.

The area within a 30 km radius around the Chernobyl plant was declared by government decree of 3 May to be an 'exclusion zone'. This decision made it clear that there would possibly need to be a second evacuation to include the rural population and their livestock. It was probably obvious to medical experts that any delay would cause a great deal of harm, but doctors were hardly able to carry out an evacuation on their own. About 90,000 people were evacuated between the eighth and the eleventh day after the accident from 170 towns, settlements and villages. The total number of people who were moved out of the exclusion zone finally reached 135,000.[53] The report for the IAEA considers that the population of the exclusion zone received a collective dose of 1.6 million rem, or about 12 rem per person before evacuation. This is considered within 'emergency permissible levels'. However, as Soviet calculations show (see table 5.2), the pattern of distribution of radiation exposure was extremely uneven. The population of about 20 villages and settlements which were closer to the damaged reactor (within a radius of 14 km which includes the town of Chernobyl) was more seriously affected. This table is based on the calculation of exposure to *external* radiation only.

Table 5.1 *Estimated doses to people in some of the populated areas in the 30 km zone around the Chernobyl nuclear power plant*

| Populated Area | Distance from Chernobyl plant (km) | Dose Rate 'D' (mR/h) | Dose from cloud of effluent | Dose to thyroid gland of children, (rad) | Dose from fallout over a time period of 7 days | |
|---|---|---|---|---|---|---|
| | | | | | Estimated | Measured |
| Chistogolovka | 5.5 | 12 | 10 | 120 | 8.4 | 3.2 |
| Lelev | 9 | 25 | 7 | 250 | 17 | 10 |
| Chernobyl | 16 | 8 | 1.2 | 80 | 5.6 | 3.0 |
| Rud'ki | 22 | 8 | 0.6 | 80 | 5.6 | 2.2 |
| Orevichi | 29 | 2.5 | 0.2 | 25 | 1.8 | 4.4 |

*Source*: The Accident . . . Soviet IAEA Report, Part II, Annex 7, table 7.2.1, p. 43.

Table 5.2 *Calculated doses from external radiation exposure of the rural population[a] in the 30 km zone around the Chernobyl nuclear power plant*

| Distance from Chernobyl plant (km) | Number of populated areas | Dose in rems from external radiation resulting from fallout for the period: | | |
|---|---|---|---|---|
| | | 7 days | 1 month | 1 year |
| 3–7 | 5 | 6–80 | 10–130 | 25–300 |
| 7–10 | 4 | 10–60 | 16–100 | 35–230 |
| 10–15 | 10 | 1.2–75 | 2–120 | 4–250 |
| 15–20 | 16 | 0.3–25 | 0.5–40 | 1–90 |
| 20–25 | 20 | 0.4–35 | 0.6–60 | 1.3–120 |
| 25–30 | 16 | 0.1–12 | 0.2–20 | 0.4–40 |

[a] Obtained taking into account the pattern of life of the rural population and the protection coefficients created by rural buildings. For urban conditions these values will be about half the size.

*Source*: The Accident . . . Soviet IAEA Report, Part II, Annex 7, table 7.2.2, p. 46.

The figures in table 5.2 were presented by the Soviet team in order to show that people were evacuated from the exclusion zone before anyone received a dose of 75 rem per person, which is the top limit, beyond which action is required. A dose of 100 rem per adult person would normally produce clinical signs of radiation syndrome and require hospitalization. The official explanation of why evacuation was delayed linked the level with projected doses after 1 month and 1 year. It was accepted by the IAEA, although it is not a convincing rational argument. The release of very high amounts of radionuclides continued until 5 May and it must have been clear from the very beginning that the situation would deteriorate. Even on 6 and 7 May the damaged reactor released 150,000 Ci and nearly 100,000 Ci, respectively, into the environment. This was considered an insignificant amount, but it was only insignificant in comparison to the 8 million Ci which had been released on 5 May.[54] The authorities were not yet able to provide the rural population with clean food supplies. The levels of radioactive iodine were almost certainly very high but they were not measured everywhere since there was a shortage of dosimetric equipment and qualified personnel. In a situation where it was impossible to monitor internal radiation or to prevent consumption of heavily contaminated food, it was important to evacuate the population as soon as possible. The doses of radiation to which people in the official exclusion zone were needlessly exposed cannot be considered harmless. The resultant damage to public health could easily have been reduced.

At the time it was thought that the 30 km radius of the exclusion zone (an area of about 3,000 km$^2$) gave a large safety margin and that people outside this zone were not at risk. Later, however, it was estimated that the radioactive fallout north, north-west and south-west of the reactor posed a serious threat to public health well beyond the exclusion zone. People were not given any medical advice in May and the rural population was actively engaged in seasonal agricultural activity. This area, situated for the most part in the Republic of Byelorussia, is known for its dairy farms. The fallout of radionuclides within the exclusion zone (which was in excess of 14 million curies) was mostly in the form of dust composed of hot particles. Despite intensive measures to fix it to the ground with chemicals that form a film or using water, secondary contamination through wind erosion was unavoidable. The official brief government statements about the situation in Chernobyl acknowledged on 7 and 8 May that there was 'some increase of radiation in the territory outside the zone close to the reactor'.[55] The official figures for 26 June which have already been mentioned in chapter 3 (table 3.2) indicate that an area as large as 5,230 km$^2$ (which included the exclusion zone) had an average contamination of above 1,000 Ci/km$^2$.[56] This is well above the level which is permissible for human habitation, particularly for rural populations.

It was later acknowleged that the largest part of the radioiodine that entered organisms during the first two months after the accident was through milk from grazing dairy cattle.[57] This is hardly surprising but it makes it very difficult to understand why the consumption of locally produced milk was not immediately forbidden to the rural population living close to the exclusion zone or in the zone prior to evacuation. In fact, at a time when market sales of milk in Kiev, Minsk and some other large cities had already been forbidden (after 1 May), the rural population around Chernobyl continued to consume locally produced milk, dairy products and vegetables simply because there were no alternative supplies. The Soviet report acknowledged the problem but offered no explanation:

> It should be noted that the above population [those evacuated from the exclusion zone and tested for radioiodine in the thyroid] consumed locally produced products prior to the evacuation (4–5 May) for 9–10 days, including milk and milk products, the proportion of which is significant in this region.[58]

The report also stated that:

> For prophylactic purposes all the children from the 30 km centralized evacuation zone were sent to summer sanitariums in the country. There is constant medical observation of children for whom the estimated thyroid gland exposure dose prior to complete clearance of iodine isotopes may exceed 30 rem.[59]

The evacuation of children who were also at high risk from the larger rural area was carried out much later (the exact date is unknown, but it was probably in the middle of May, at the same time as the Kiev children were evacuated). About 50 per cent of the population in these parts of the Ukraine and Byelorussia live in villages and work on collective and state farms. It is quite obvious that for a period of several weeks or even months after the accident the Ukrainian and Byelorussian medical services and the USSR Ministry of Health continued to apply criteria and rules designed for short-term emergencies and for avoiding *clinical* health effects. In other words, there was no clear policy aimed at avoiding such long-term health effects as cancer, a shortened life-expectancy and genetic effects. The permissible future integrated radiation dose remained as high as 75 rem (for the whole body) even after the first few days. Presumably, it was kept so high to avoid new evacuations and to minimize the economic and political impact of the accident.

When it became known at the beginning of June 1986 that the radio-active contamination was well above the permissible level in the area north and north-west of the exclusion zone and in more distant spots where local rain brought down radioactive particles, and that it could cause an unacceptable accumulated dose over a period of a few weeks or months, an attempt was made to decontaminate villages and towns without evacuating and resettling the population. The decontamination of one town, Bragin (population 7,000), situated about 80 km north of

Chernobyl, was described in *Izvestiya*.[60] A layer of topsoil and vegetation up to 10 cm in depth was removed from the streets, gardens and surrounding areas by special chemical units of the army and taken away to be buried. The streets were covered in a 'washable' asphalt. Old wooden houses and barns were destroyed. But agricultural use of the land in that area continued. The livestock was thus left untouched. To judge from the figures in table 5.2, the accumulated dose of radioiodine in the thyroid over seven days was close to 25 rad near the borders of the exclusion zone (29 km from the reactor). This means that people outside that zone (35, 40 and 50 km from the reactor) would get the same dose if they stayed in the area much longer.

The significance of an accumulated dose of radioiodine of 25 rad can perhaps best be understood by considering that after the most serious previous contamination of the environment after a reactor accident (at Windscale in Britain in 1957), the maximum level of accumulated dose in the thyroid glands tested was 16 rad for children and 4 rad for adults (160 and 40 mSv respectively). At that time this was considered a disgracefully high dose. The medical authorities were criticized for not conducting follow-up observations of these children in later years. The milk from a 500 km$^2$ area around Windscale was destroyed for several days (3 million litres of milk were lost). However, the Windscale disaster released about 20,000 Ci of radioiodine over four days, while the Chernobyl accident produced 7,300,000 Ci over a period of ten days, 350 times more than Windscale, and this includes only the radioiodine which was deposited within the Soviet Union.[61] There is no evidence that attempts were made to destroy milk in the area around Chernobyl, although some special methods of processing contaminated milk by making butter and cheese from it were considered and later implemented.

The Soviet Report states that:

> . . . for certain populated areas in the most contaminated parts of the radioactive path (the villages of Tolstyj Les, Kopachi and some others) people may have been exposed to 30–40 rem. However, even for these doses for external radiation exposure there is no danger of acute immediate somatic effects for those exposed.[62]

It seems strange that eight to ten days after the accident, when all the medical and other resources of the state had already been mobilized, the medical authorities still aimed to prevent the occurrence of acute radiation syndrome. The dose of 30–40 rem is one which is considered impermissible over the whole life of people who work directly with radioactive isotopes, for example, at reprocessing plants and reactors.

The maximum permissible annual dose for these people is 5 rem, but only if their life-long exposure does not exceed 25 rem. It seems inconceivable, therefore, that it was considered tolerable for people near and inside the exclusion zone to receive exposure of up to 30–40 rem (total body) within a few days.

As we have already seen, the evacuees were usually sent to neighbouring districts. Often their new places of residence also received increased levels of contamination, making it necessary to resettle them a second time. But the permanent residents of those neighbouring areas who had not yet accumulated high doses of exposure were left in place.

In May and June 1986 the Soviet media reported that the evacuation had been well organized and smooth. It was only in 1987 in the light of *glasnost'* that less positive aspects of the operation were revealed. Dr Maksim Drach, together with 40 other medical students from Kiev, was mobilized on 4 May to help with the second phase of the evacuation. He later recalled the problems produced by the livestock which was being evacuated:

> There were particularly difficult problems in trying to de-activate the horned cattle, since their fur had collected considerable radioactive dust. Those cattle that had managed to graze in the meadows and enjoy the fresh grass had also swallowed radioactive iodine and caesium. They were slaughtered at slaughter houses and the meat was collected in specially designated freezers where it was meant to rid itself gradually of radioactivity caused by iodine-131, an isotope with a short half-life.[63]

People leaving the exclusion zone were checked for exposure and allowed to proceed if their level was below a certain figure. Those who exceeded the level were sent to have the dust removed from their things. Drach noticed that:

> There were no people in the 20 to 50 age group. Why? We were told that they had . . . remained in the area to work. Thus the people leaving were predominantly old, bent grannies and grandpas and small children. We also measured the children's thyroid glands. We had instructions that if a thyroid gland registered a level twice that of the background reading, the child had to be hospitalized. I didn't see any such cases . . .[64]

> When the evacuation had ended we conducted medical examinations, comparing the results of blood analyses with other data. People who felt ill were admitted to hospital for further tests.

> On May 6 we were brought protective clothing: black overalls, hats, boots, respirators. They said that journalists were about to arrive.

> On May 8 we were sent back to Kiev . . . on May 10 I returned to classes as usual and went back to work at the October Revolution

Hospital . . . On about May 11 or 12 I noticed that I was sleeping a great deal, but I still felt tired. Usually I sleep for 5 to 6 hours and feel fine. Now I was sleeping for 8 or 12 hours, even 14 hours and still feeling tired. And I had become weak and filled with lassitude. They analysed my blood and admitted me to the eighth floor of our department.[65]

Yuri Shcherbak, who recorded this interview, added:

I remember the ward on the eighth floor of the cardiological wing where the students from Kiev Medical Institute who had worked on eliminating the consequences of the accident were admitted for tests. Maksim Drach, Dima Pyatak, Kostya Lisovoi, Kostya Dakhno and Volodya Bul'da. I went to the department with Professor Leonid Petrovich Kindzel'sky. The professor consulted the students, looked at their case histories, studied the results of their blood tests. Later Maksim Drach had occasion to meet Dr Gale who visited Kiev at the beginning of June.

Now Maksim Drach and his friends are well, they are in no danger. Before them are their final examinations.[66]

Shcherbak is wrong if he thinks that these young people are in no danger. They displayed symptoms of radiation sickness, which indicates exposure to levels of 100–200 rads (from 1 to 2 Gray). They were exposed to these doses by working in the zone for four days only, from 4 to 8 May. Their initial symptoms might have disappeared after two or three months in hospital, but very severe health risks remain (for example, cancer) both for them and for their children. Studies of life expectancy after radiation exposure show that a single dose of 100–150 rad reduces life expectancy by six to seven years. This is a very high price to pay for the inexcusable fact that these students worked in or near the exclusion zone without protective clothing and respirators. The first time they were supplied with such protection was on 6 May, when the evacuation was already over. Protective clothing was only considered necessary to impress the photographers.

### RADIATION PROTECTION OF THE GENERAL PUBLIC

While the situation in Pripyat on 26–7 April and in the entire exclusion zone on 8–10 May was considered a medical emergency, the instructions to the larger area north and south of Chernobyl which includes cities such as Kiev (population 2.5 million), Chernigov (population 300,000) and Gomel (population 500,000) and innumerable small towns and villages lying within a 150 km radius of the source of radioactive contamination were to continue 'business as usual'. The first time that the citizens of Kiev were given any medical advice was on 6 May, ten days after the accident. By then the level of radioactive contamination over Kiev had already peaked. The release of nearly 100 million curies of various radionuclides over ten days affected the whole of Europe. People in Eastern Poland were given potassium iodide tablets. East and West European farmers were advised to keep their livestock in barns temporarily and to feed them with the previous year's hay rather than with fresh grass. The EEC considered banning food imports from Eastern Europe. The only Europeans who knew very little or nothing about the radioactive levels were Soviet people, including those who lived in the most seriously affected areas of the Ukraine and Byelorussia.

Until 8 May the official Soviet position was that no one who lived outside the exclusion zone was in any danger. Moreover, the 30 km zone was said to have included a generous safety margin. Even when it was acknowledged on 8 May that there was some increase of surface radioactive contamination outside the exclusion zone, this was said not to pose any threat to public health.[67] On 12 May the radiation level in the air in Kiev was published (0.32 milliroentgen per hour). Although higher than the normal background reading, the level was said to present no danger. But at the same time it was reported that the permissible annual dose of absorbed radiation had been raised temporarily for Kiev from 0.5 to 10 rem. This new 'emergency' level had been introduced 'just in case', it was said, although it was not expected that the population would be exposed to such a high accumulated dose.[68] In fact, this was double the normal maximum permissible dose for people who work in the nuclear industry.

The authorities hoped that the new level would make it unnecessary to evacuate children from Kiev. The radioiodine content in the air over Kiev had peaked on May 1 and 2 and then begun to decline (see figure 5.3).[69] The Ministry of Health probably hoped that it would continue to decline sharply. But the local medical authorities had been advising people since 7 May that they should dust their apartments every day and keep their children indoors as much as possible. Broadcast on local television, this was said to be prophylactic advice. Special water trucks had begun washing down Kiev streets twice a day to prevent the accumulation of the fallout particles. One can assume that similar measures were taken in Chernigov, Gomel and in other towns and villages in the area.

In fact, a form of disinformation was occurring. Measuring the radiation level in the air in roentgens does not assess the danger posed by

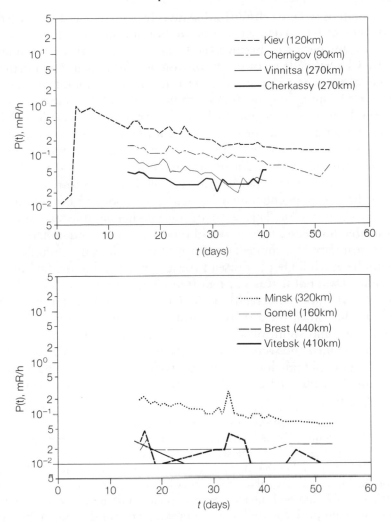

**Figure 5.3** Dynamics of the gamma radiation rate change in the open country of the Ukraine (a) and Byelorussia (b) regional centres close to the Chernobyl nuclear power station (from *The Accident . . . Soviet IAEA Report*, Part II, Annex 7, figure 7.2.3).

radioactive aerosol and dust. Roentgens measure gamma radiation, but not beta or alpha radiation. The dominant source of gamma radiation at that time was radioiodine, 0.32 mR/h is not a safe level for iodine in the air, particularly for children. But an even greater problem was the presence of insoluble hot radioactive particles in the dust.

We now know that there had been disagreement about whether the traditional May Day celebrations should be allowed. The Soviet Report to the IAEA (released in August 1986, but not published) indicates that radioactivity over Kiev began to rise a little on 29 April. In Kaliningrad, 1,000 km from Chernobyl on the Baltic coast near the north-west border of the Soviet Union, the concentration of radioiodine on 29 April was 4.9 Ci/km$^2$ in the air. In Kiev it was only 0.2 Ci/km$^2$. By the next day the level in Kaliningrad had risen to 10.5 Ci/km$^2$, while in Kiev it was 0.6 Ci/km$^2$ in the air close to the ground (the radiocaesium level was probably also high since it is as volatile as iodine, but Soviet sources do not give the level of either caesium-134 or caesium-137).[70] If one expresses the iodine level in Kiev in becquerels (the measure usually used for medical recommendations), 0.6 Ci/km$^2$ is about 20,000 Bq/m$^2$ (1 Ci = 3.7 × 10$^{10}$ Bq). This level of radioiodine in the air cannot be considered harmless, since it would render the meat and milk of grazing cattle unsuitable for immediate consumption. The surface radioactivity should be much higher because of the accumulation of the fall out from previous days, but it was not reported.) The Soviet medical authorities should have studied the trend of radioactivity carefully and recommended the cancellation of the 1 May demonstrations in Kiev and other cities north, west and south of Chernobyl. In fact, the demonstrations took place as planned and were presumably authorized at the highest political level. It was only much later that reservations were expressed about the decision. In 1987, for example, the writer Yuri Shcherbak (a trained doctor) commented:

> The first release of debris moved towards the north-west and west. On 30 April the wind changed direction and blew in the direction of Kiev. Radioacive aerosol was blown towards a city with a population of millions. I remember that day very clearly. I was in the Ukrainian Ministry of Health. I remember that the doctors became tense and worried. In the ministerial offices and corridors people spoke about the need to take extraordinary prophylactic measures. Proposals were heard about addressing the population with a special appeal to take precautions. But no one listened to these proposals until 6 May.
>
> Very many people blame the doctors now: why didn't they warn people? Why didn't they speak up sooner? I don't want to shield my colleagues – they have a number of sins on their conscience too. But it is only fair to emphasize that doctors don't have control of the channels of mass communication. And nor do they take the most important decisions. And decisions were needed. There should have been serious thought at the end of April already about the advisability of holding May Day demonstrations in Kiev and the area around the zone, and particularly demonstrations in which children participated.[71]

Shcherbak pointed out that demonstrations had been cancelled in the past because of rain, yet in 1986 the radiation level was not considered a sufficient reason. In the meantime, the radioactive contamination over Kiev rose to its maximum level on 1 and 2 May. Between the night of 30 April and the end of the day on 1 May the radioiodine level had risen from 2.5 Ci/km$^2$ to 10.3 Ci/km$^2$ or 370,000 Bq/m$^2$ – a very high dose.[72] These figures were given for 'ground air', not for surface fallout. According to normal Soviet rules, fresh milk should not be consumed if the concentration of radioiodine is higher than 3,700 Bq/litre. By the end of 1 May the level was as high as that per litre of air, but no action was taken. On 3 May the level was still as high as 2.6 Ci/km$^2$, whereas in Kaliningrad it had fallen to 0.24 Ci/km$^2$. As figure 5.3 demonstrates, the radioactivity in the Kiev air rose and fell for more than 30 days and this finally forced the authorities to take action.

As soon as some medical information was released on 6 May people began to press for an explanation about the possible dangers. Parents with small children were particularly anxious to leave the area. Thousands of pregnant women wanted abortions. After two weeks of mounting anxiety, the Ministries of Health and Education issued a joint instruction. All Kiev schools would close for the summer on 15 May. Children up to the age of 15, mothers and infants and pregnant women from Kiev and other cities and towns in the area (nothing was said about the rural population) would be evacuated for an unspecified period.[73] This was said to be a prophylactic measure, but no one had any illusions about the real danger.

The asphalt on the street was very radioactive for months (it probably still is). It accumulated particles from the reactor core and it was only on 6 or 7 May that they began to wash down the streets every day. But in any case even after that 'hot' radioactive particles melted the surface of the asphalt, sticking to the road and melting down rather slowly. Washing down the streets did not easily get rid of these particles; the asphalt should have been replaced to remove them. Measurements of radioactivity in Kiev were based on air measurements and at first no one thought to measure the road surfaces. Some unofficial reports indicated that asphalt surface radioactivity from 7 to 12 May was nearly 100 times higher than air radioactivity. The accumulation of fallout radionuclides was probably an important factor in the decision to evacuate children from Kiev on 15 May.

Children between the ages of 8 and 15 were sent to summer camps. This was not a difficult task because most Soviet schoolchildren spend time in these camps during the summer and the beds and tents were already available. Evacuating younger children, mothers and infants and pregnant women was far more difficult. Many hotels, rest houses, sanatoria and tourist facilities were taken over. The exact number of evacuees is not known but it was probably about one million. At first it was thought that they would be away for 40–50 days by which time the radiation levels were expected to have fallen to close to normal. In fact, this was an optimistic prediction and children only returned to Kiev at the beginning of September, in time for the new school year. The streets of Kiev, Gomel, Chernigov, Mogilev and other towns were vacuumed by dust-collecting machines and washed, sometimes as often as three times a day, until the winter, when the frost made it impossible to continue. There was no further danger from radioiodine (the half-life of iodine-131 is only eight days), but radiocaesium and radiostrontium, together with plutonium, are long-living and still presented a problem.

No figures were ever published of the accumulation of radioiodine in the thyroids of children outside the exclusion zone, although about 100,000 measurements were taken from children in summer camps and sanatoria. Between 7 and 21 May the general radiation level in Kiev fell from 0.32 mR/h to 0.18 mR/h.[74] The decline was almost entirely due to the fission and disappearance of radioiodine, which comprised about 40 per cent of the airborne radioactivity. On 1 and 2 May the radioactivity in Kiev had been at least ten times higher than on 6 and 7 May. The internationally acceptable environmental level of iodine for children must have been reached within a very few hours, particularly if the children were outdoors. In fact, most of the radioiodine they accumulated was probably consumed, particularly with milk and dairy products.

It was later well publicized that the sale of milk and dairy products was forbidden in Kiev markets (they are normally delivered to the markets directly from the collective farms and private peasant plots). Later the ban was extended to the sale of meat and some leafy vegetables. Only state shops were allowed to sell these products.[75] Similar restrictions were probably applied in other cities. But the ban was only applied after 1 May. As a result, there were cases of comparatively high exposures to the thyroids of children and adults in some towns and villages. The Soviet Report to the IAEA acknowledged this, but did not explain the delay in restricting market sales of milk:

> The relatively high thyroid gland dose burdens observed sometimes is evidently the result of the uncontrolled consumption of milk from cows for personal use despite the ban issued by the health authorities on 1 May 1986 on the consumption of whole milk with a radioiodine concentration higher than $1.10^{-7}$ Ci/l. This requirement was strictly adhered to within

the centralized milk supply. Furthermore, additional measures were taken for strict monitoring of the sale and consumption of milk from cows for personal use.[76]

The reason for the delay was probably political. Doctors were well aware of the dangers of radioiodine. But if market sales of milk, dairy products, meat and vegetables had been banned earlier, people would have suspected that their health was in danger. 'Business as usual' on 1 May would have been impossible. Since the markets would be closed on 1 May, it was easier to apply the ban from 2 May.

It was not only in Kiev that the situation was serious. Other cities, towns and villages outside the exclusion zone were in danger. The graphs in figure 5.3 show the dynamics of the changes in the gamma dose rates in the open air for eight regional centres of the Ukraine, Byelorussia and the RSFSR. It is noteworthy that the graph for Kiev represents the changes from the first day of the accident (showing a sharp rise on day 3 and a slow decline after day 10 with a few ups and downs until day 50), whereas the graphs for the other regional centres (Chernigov, Vinnitsa, Cherkassy, Minsk, Gomel, Vitebsk, Brest) start on day 15 after the accident. The first fourteen days of measurements are missing. In other words, the Soviet authorities have released figures demonstrating a decline in radioactivity from day 15 to day 50 after the accident for an area of the USSR in which dozens of millions of people live, but they have offered no figures for days 1 to 14.

It seems extremely unlikely that no measurements were taken. The most plausible reason for the reluctance to reveal them is that the figures were embarrassingly high. Judging from those for day 15 to day 50, the contamination in both Minsk and Gomel must have been particularly high. The pattern of decline for Gomel, for example, shows that it was the second most contaminated city. Radioactivity there was higher than in Chernigov, situated only 90 km east of the damaged reactor.

Radioiodine was not the only health hazard created by the accident. Radiocaesium causes contamination which, although probably less serious, is more durable. Because their isotopes are almost equally volatile, the area of distribution of iodine and caesium are very similar. Radiostrontium and plutonium also present very serious health hazards, but they are far less volatile and their fallout was limited to Soviet territory. Western experts have not attempted to project their possible effect. The Soviet medical response to caesium was even less satisfactory than the response to iodine. The standard for the 'permissible' level of radiocaesium was only issued by the USSR Ministry of Health on 30 May 1986, more than a month after the accident.[77] The level of caesium-134 and caesium-137 in food products only began to be measured at the end of May, when most of the radioiodine had already disappeared. The 'field' method of dosimetric control could not distinguish between different radioactive isotopes. More sophisticated measurements in research laboratories indicated the presence of other radionuclides in food, but in the Soviet Union, where more than 50 per cent of food products are unprocessed (in rural areas it is almost 100 per cent), it was difficult to have proper laboratory control over many isotopes. The Soviet Report to the IAEA indicated that tests on a number of types of foodstuffs revealed: 'the presence in food products of rare earth isotopes – cerium-144, ruthenium-106, zirconium-95, barium-140, lanthanum-140, cerium-141, ruthenium-103, niobium-95. The latter were found in significant quantities together with caesium in green vegetables ($1 \times 10^{-6}$ Ci/kg or more)'.[78]

The scale of the problem was, of course, enormous. Soviet experts had to take measurements of a territory which is nearly as large as the whole of Western Europe. A high proportion of the Ukrainian and Byelorussian population is rural, living traditionally off the land and consuming locally produced unprocessed food. It was almost impossible to implement health standards in the villages. There is usually a dearth of food, particularly fresh vegetables, in April and May, at the end of spring. Moreover, most farms do not have enough fodder or hay by then to keep animals indoors and prevent them from feeding on the meadows and pastures. The Soviet authorities had to choose one of two evils: immediate food shortages or long-term radiation problems. They seem to have chosen the latter, but the inevitable consequence was a restriction on information.

Dosimetric control and restrictions on private market sales of meat and dairy products remained in force in 1987 and 1988 in Kiev and other cities. The main concern had become radiocaesium. Private fishing in the Pripyat River and the Dnieper reservoir was not allowed. But maps of the radiocaesium contamination of areas outside the exclusion zone were not made public until 1989 nor were the permissible levels of radioactive caesium or strontium. The Soviet permissible levels of these isotopes in food products are very high (370 KBq or $1 \times 10^{-5}$ Ci for caesium-137), but apparently this only applies to short periods after accidents.[79] But even in 1987 international standards of permissible contamination of the environment in places of permanent residence could not be applied. The authorities introduced their own compromise standards, but they were not disclosed. People working in these areas received double pay to compensate them for the health hazards.

## THE LONG-TERM HEALTH EFFECTS

There is insufficient relevant information to enable an accurate assessment of the health consequences of the Chernobyl accident. The medical team which presented the report on the medical and biological consequences to the IAEA post-accident meeting in August 1986 did not try to minimize the consequences. Their estimate of anticipated extra cancer deaths within the Soviet Union was, in fact, much higher than Western estimates. The IAEA meeting therefore took the view that Soviet radiologists had overestimated the total collective radiation dose to the population of the western part of the USSR, perhaps by a factor of ten.[80] There were other experts, on the other hand, who thought that the Soviet figures were an underestimation.[81]

Robert Gale, the American bone marrow specialist who treated victims of the accident in Moscow, has said on several occasions that the accident will cause between 5,000 and 75,000 new cancers world-wide, nearly half of them in the Soviet Union.[82] In their later publications in 1987 and 1988, however, neither Gale nor Dr Gus'kova and colleagues commented on the possible more general health impact of the accident, despite the fact that much more accurate and reliable data on the radiation exposure of the population was already available. In his book about Chernobyl, Gale concentrated on the few attempts at bone marrow transplantation.[83] Most of the book describes his visit to Moscow, Armand Hammer's involvement and his talks with Gorbachev.

The National Radiation Protection Board of the United Kingdom (NRPB) has published a minimal assessment of the effect of the Chernobyl accident on Great Britain and the rest of the European Community (EC).[84] The report only considers the deposits of radioiodine and radiocaesium. It predicts not more than 1,000 extra cancer deaths in the EC, of which 100–200 will occur in the United Kingdom during the next 50 years. This is a very low estimate which is practically undetectable. The authors did not try to project this figure for Eastern Europe, Sweden, Finland, Austria or the USSR, where the deposits of radionuclides were much more significant.

Another very comprehensive study sponsored by the US Department of Energy came to a less optimistic prognosis, predicting from 14,000 to 39,000 extra cancer-related deaths in the next 50 years, most of them from the radiocaesium released in Chernobyl. At least half of these deaths will occur in the USSR and a third will occur in Western and Eastern Europe.[85] These higher estimates were the result of finding large quantities of radiocaesium at high altitudes. American experts calculated that not 1 million but 3 million curies of radiocaesium was released into the environment. They also used a different, more objective approach to the correlation between the dose of irradiation and biological effect. When Il'in and Pavlovsky published their new calculations, the American researchers recalculated their estimates for radiocaesium-related cancer fatalities. They concluded that the probable figure would be 17,000 of which 7,000 would occur in the USSR and 10,000 in the rest of Europe.[86] This is far higher than the estimate made by the Europeans themselves.

Other pessimistic estimates have predicted that there will be 50,000 deaths from thyroid cancer and cancer caused by radiocaesium alone.[87] In fact, cancer only accounts for a third of the cases of 'radiation shortening of life span'. It is thus clear that the health effects of Chernobyl are an area open to wide, divergent speculation. People who are opposed to nuclear power tend to make the highest possible estimates, while those in favour of it opt for the lowest possible figures. The lowest figure to appear so far in the literature about Chernobyl predicts from 200 to 600 extra deaths in the USSR and none elsewhere.[88] The highest estimate predicts 280,000 extra cancer deaths world-wide.[89]

A careful comparative statistical analysis of leukaemias amongst children evacuated from the exclusion zone, those in the rural areas around it, those in contaminated cities like Kiev, Gomel, Minsk and others and those in 'clean' cities and rural areas could help to clarify the picture of the future health effects of the Chernobyl accident. Preliminary figures for extra leukaemias, particularly among children, should already begin to be available in 1988 and 1989 if the promised proper monitoring is being conducted. But so far the figures have not been published. International experts were not invited to participate in the monitoring programme as was promised in 1986.

The heated debate about the possible future health effects of Chernobyl is understandable. The accident instantly and dramatically changed the previously very optimistic assessment of the health risks of nuclear energy.[90] If the lowest estimates are right, the safety record of nuclear energy remains better than that of coal, oil and hydroelectric power.[91] But if the highest estimates prove accurate, the outlook is vastly different. Without taking sides in this long-standing dispute, I would like to offer some factual material and information which can be verified or investigated further in due course.

As we have seen, two people were killed almost instantly by the accident and 29 people died later in hospital in the succeeding 50 days; 24 people became disabled invalids. They were among the 238 people diagnosed as having an acute form of radiation sickness, who had been exposed to radiation higher than 2 Gy (200 rem).[92] The number of people with a milder form of radiation syndrome (from 100 to 200 rem) was later reported to be more than 5,000.[93] According to Soviet regulations anyone who may have received a single dose of about 100 rem (1 Gy) must be hospitalized temporarily for comprehensive medical tests.[94] Practically everyone who was present on the site of the Chernobyl nuclear power station during the first few days (construction workers, members of the staff of Units 1, 2 and 3, firemen, medical personnel, military personnel, pilots) were exposed to doses in this range. Many people involved in emergency work in the exclusion zone, such as those who loaded sand and other materials for the air drops, medical personnel and those involved in decontamination, were also exposed to similar doses and were tested and treated in hospitals. There were a number of reports in the Soviet general media about the hospital tests and treatment and about the absence of proper dosimetric control during the initial emergency from 26 April to 5 May, when the reactor core was still burning. It is understandable that priority was given to the main objective of preventing a greater tragedy. At this stage it resembled a military operation. But many people were needlessly exposed due to poor organization and the absence of simple protective measures. Later, even highly responsible people needlessly exposed themselves. It was reported, for example, that Academician Yevgeni Velikhov, a member of the Government Commission, climbed up above Unit 4 on 27 April to inspect the damage. He exposed himself to 25 rem, 'which he is allowed by occupational standards once in a lifetime for emergency activities'.[95] On 18 July 1989 Velikhov told the 'Hearing' on the Ural nuclear disaster at the joint meeting of three committees of the Supreme Soviet of the USSR that the Japanese doctors in the Hiroshima medical centre estimated his exposure as between 30 and 50 rem.

The most striking description of ignorance or desperation which resulted in excessive exposure of young servicemen to high doses of radiation was given in 1989 by Grigory Medvedev in his 'Chernobyl Notebook':

> During my visit to Pripyat . . . I saw soldiers and officers picking up graphite with their hands. They had buckets and were collecting it by hand. They poured it into containers. There was graphite lying around everywhere, even behind the fence next to our car. I opened the door and pushed the radiometer almost onto a graphite block. Two thousands

roentgens an hour. I closed the door. There was a smell of ozone, of burning, of dust and of something else. Perhaps this was what burnt human flesh smelt like. Having filled their buckets, the soldiers seemed to walk very slowly to the metal containers where they poured out the contents. You poor dears, I thought, what an awful harvest you are gathering . . .

The faces of the soldiers and officers were dark brown: nuclear tan. The weather forecasters promised heavy rain, and to prevent the activity being washed into the soil by the rain, people were being sent instead of robots, because there were no robots. Later, when he heard about this, Academician Aleksandrov was upset. 'At Chernobyl they don't care about people. This will all be blamed on me'. But it's true that they didn't care about people when they promoted an RBMK reactor liable to explode for the Ukraine.[96]

Soldiers were sent to collect pieces of graphite from the reactor core and nuclear fuel by hand, without shovels. It would be obvious to any radiologist that in areas of such intense radiation, people cannot remain for longer than a few minutes. The radiation tan which Medvedev noticed indicates skin doses of radiation in excess of 400–500 rem. Most of these soldiers must have suffered acute radiation syndrome and some of them probably died. The military personnel who suffered radiation syndrome were treated in special military hospitals and no one knows how many people were taken there. The official casualty figures do not include soldiers. It is very likely that the soldiers who died were not listed as Chernobyl victims, but registered as the victims of an unspecified military operation.

The radioactive exposure of military personnel and the total number of servicemen who took part in the operation was not reported. The medical section of the Soviet IAEA documents only describes the fate of those who were evacuated from the accident site during the first two days. Later victims of radiation during the emergency period from 27 April to 10 May 1986 who were treated in different hospitals in Kiev, Minsk and Moscow are not included in the known figures of cases of acute radiation sickness. We do know, however, that nearly 400 unprotected helicopter flights to drop sand were carried out on 27 and 28 April. Each member of the crew received 20–80 rad of radiation during each flight. In 1989 the conditions were graphically described by chief engineer Anatoly Zayat', who took part in some of the flights:

> The first class military pilot, Colonel Nesterov, was the first to fly a helicopter on a 'bombing run' . . . He flew over the crater of the nuclear reactor. 150 metres was too high over the crater . . . 110 metres. The

radiometer registered 500 roentgen per hour . . . The helicopter hung over the crater . . . he opened the door. He could feel the heat from below. A mighty torrent of radioactive gas, ionized by neutrons and gamma rays, rose up. All this without repirators. The helicopter was not protected underneath with lead. They only began to think about that later, when hundreds of tonnes had already been off-loaded. At first, however, they stuck their heads out through the open door to aim at the nuclear crater and threw the sacks . . .

The first twenty-seven crews . . . soon had to be sent to Kiev for treatment. After throwing sacks from a height of 100 metres their level of radioactivity reached 1800 roentgens/hour. The pilots began to find it hard to breathe. Throwing sacks from that height had a significant effect on the active zone. The amount of fission fragments and radioactive dust from the burning graphite emitted rose sharply, particularly on the first day. People breathed all this. For a month afterwards uranium salts and plutonium were washed from the blood of these heroes, and they were given many blood transfusions. On subsequent days the pilots themselves began to put lead sheets under their seats and to put on respirators. This reduced the amount of radioactivity to which they were exposed.'[97]

As soon as the reactor started to cool down on 6 May, exposure of this kind ceased to be considered acceptable. Stricter radiological control was introduced: 25 rem was now the maximum limit of exposure, either in a single dose for some extraordinary task such as clearing the roof of the machine hall building or Unit 3 of large pieces of the reactor core, or accumulated over a longer period through decontaminating the buildings and the territory of the power station or constructing the walls of the protective structure. People who had accumulated 25 rem or more were relieved of doing any other task in the zone.[98] However, the acute shortage of monitors, dosimeters and radiometers made this rule purely theoretical. Most personal dosimeters were of the type which measure the dose *after* the working day is over. These personal dosimeters have to be read out in special laboratories.

About 50,000 people were later reported to have been exposed to doses higher than 50 rad (mostly during the initial emergency period and because of the delay before the second phase of evacuation took place).[99] The release of this figure in 1988 was probably prompted by the appearance of some of the clinical consequences of exposure. In fact, dosimetric control was very approximate. Few of the soldiers who were engaged in decontamination work had personal dosimeters with which to check themselves after the working day. The lungs, intestines and eyes of those involved in this work were most seriously at risk, since hot radioactive particles can produce very rapid effects. Active measures were taken to protect lungs (with respirators), but nothing was done to protect eyes.

The late medical and biological effects of radiation have been studied extensively. It is accepted that a single or extended exposure of 100–200 rem reduces the human life span by six or seven years due to an increase in cancer, cardiovascular disease, renal failure and other consequences.[100] Dr Gus'kova and her colleagues have previously maintained that the professional exposure of radiologists and roentgenologists to doses as high as 130–400 rem during their life span does not have any significant effect on their health, if they are compared to other medical professionals. But their study did not include a comparison of the incidence of cancer and it did not mention life span and mortality in general. It is, therefore, of limited value. But even that study registered an increased incidence of eye cataracts, arteriosclerosis and, particularly, of skin cancer on the hands of doctors and nurses exposed to radiation. About 3 per cent of their sample developed chronic radiation syndrome, particularly after the age of 50.[101]

Most of the people who were exposed to comparatively significant doses of radiation (between 10 and 70 rem) lived in the exclusion zone and areas close to it which were evacuated later. Military and civilian personnel involved directly in decontamination and repair of the site or within the exclusion zone were not included in the group for permanent medical follow-up examinations because they came from all over the country and returned home after their work at Chernobyl. Not everyone from Pripyat was evacuated. An interview with a Pripyat official, for example, indicated that: 'After the evacuation about 5,000 inhabitants remained in Pripyat. Some were people who were left there to work on the orders of various organizations. But there were others who refused to be evacuated and who remained in the town illegally, so to speak'.[102]

Official statements in 1988 indicated that several hundreds of thousands of people participated in dealing with the consequences of the accident.[103] In 1989 the approximate figure of 600,000 was disclosed. But it will rise because decontamination work is still continuing. In June 1986 there were about 2,000 people in an average, rather short shift of workers and soldiers involved in repair, construction and indoor and outdoor decontamination at the Chernobyl plant site.[104] The turnover of the work force was directly related to radiation exposure (the emergency maximum was 25 rem but the control was not very accurate). Violations of elementary protective measures were quite common, particularly the refusal to wear respirators. The Soviet documentary television film about Chernobyl ('The Bell of Chernobyl') showed this clearly. This was one of several reasons why screening it was forbidden for nearly a year. It was finally shown at the end of April 1987, by which time its director, Vladimir Chernenko, had died. One scene showed the workers digging the underground tunnel under Unit 4. None of them wore protective clothing or respirators. They were engaged in the kind of hard physical labour which is simply not possible in most protective clothing. Similarly, the workers who were clearing the highly radioactive debris from the roof and installing temperature-sensitive equipment in various places were not protected. In one of the novels written about Chernobyl they were depicted in space research protective suits borrowed from the Soviet Space programme,[105] but in the film they considered the speed at which they ran to be their chief protection. Radiation fields in some parts of the roof of the machine hall were between 10,000 and 20,000 R/h and one run of 30–50 seconds was considered permissible and high cash awards were given to each runner. 3,400 people took part in such runs. One minute or less of great effort and hospital bed after for checks of the dose. One of the people working on the film said bitterly:

> One of the many complaints about the film was particularly that the people who were dealing with the consequences of the accident in the first weeks were 'unsuitably' dressed. But what should the authorities have done? How could they immediately give people the necessary clothing when they weren't prepared for an emergency . . . It wasn't the film's business to 'cover up' the fact.[106]

For the many thousands of workers and military personnel who were involved in decontamination work outside the reactor site but within the exclusion zone and for some of the residents outside the exclusion zone the permissible maximal emergency exposure was also 25 rem. A special new clinical and research centre was established near Kiev in September 1986 to monitor the health of evacuees and of decontamination personnel. Called the All-Union Centre of Radiology, it was to include three institutes and clinics: clinical epidemiology, clinical aspects of radiation medicine and experimental radiology.[107] It was charged with the permanent observation of the 600,000 people (250,000 of them children) entered in the permanent medical register who would require periodic medical observation for the rest of their lives.[108] The Byelorussian government created its own Radiological Centre in 1988. It includes an Institute of Radiation Medicine, an Institute of Radiobiology and an Institute of Agricultural Radiology. It will supervise the 171,000 people living in the contaminated areas of Byelorussia.[109] There were distinct differences in the accumulated dose (and contamination through the food chain) between towns and villages.

In fact, the Ukrainian centre immediately produced a number of controversies. Construction began in September 1986 and the centre was completed in 1988. The intention has been to provide the most qualified treatment and the best preventative diagnosis for everyone who had been exposed to radiation. In reality the centre, under the directorship of the Ukrainian Minister of Health, Romanenko, immediately became a classified organization interested less in the pathology and long-term treatment of radiation effects than in statistical registration and computer analysis. Thousands of people who are treated in their local hospitals travel to Kiev for periodic examination but receive no treatment there. By 1988 people listed in the follow-up register lived all over the place. Demobilized soldiers had returned to their home areas, as had other people who had been involved in decontamination work. Some professional groups had organized treatment and rehabilitation for their own members. The police, for example, had established a special radiological hospital for affected personnel and they were reluctant to close it and transfer the patients to the new centre. As we have seen in chapter 2, the police were the third most severely affected professional group (after the nuclear plant operators and the firemen) and 57 policemen were treated for acute radiation sickness. Moreover, they retained the task of guarding the nuclear plant and patrolling the abandoned towns and villages, work which was still considered hazardous in 1988 and 1989. More than 1,500 policemen in the Ukrainian branch of the service suffered from lung and breathing problems (the most obvious result of inhaling radioactive dust particles).[110] But the centre has not yet released any scientifically valid information about the state of health of the 600,000 people on the radiation register.

In an interview on 26 April 1989, the third anniversary of the Chernobyl accident, Yu. Spizhenko, deputy Minister of Health in the Ukraine, said that of the 260,000 inhabitants of the Ukraine who had been checked at the Radiological Centre, 62 per cent had been classified as healthy and 38 per cent were found to require some form of treatment in hospitals, sanatoria and out-patient clinics. He maintained that there had been no increase in the incidence of cancer, but he did not disclose the nature of the health problems of those who were treated.[111]

The state of health of the evacuees will probably remain classified information for many years to come. The health of the pets they had abandoned was, of course, ignored. Nikolai Goshchitsky, an engineer from the Beloyarsk nuclear power station near Sverdlovsk, was sent to Chernobyl at the end of May 1986 to work on the decontamination of the machine and reactor buildings (Reactors 1, 2 and 3 were being prepared to restart). At the beginning of June, five or six weeks after the accident, he visited Pripyat. He described the abandoned animals he saw there:

> When they remembered about the animals, they began to shoot them – kindness demanded it . . . [But] in Pripyat they weren't shot. Here [they] crawled, half alive, along the road, in terrible pain. Birds looked as if they had crawled out of water . . . unable to fly or walk . . . Cats with dirty fur, as if it had been burnt in places . . .[112]

There were hundreds of dead birds and most of the animals were blind. Most pets, particularly dogs, were later killed by special teams of soldiers. Dogs and cats have the same radiosensitivity as humans. Their state indicated an accumulated dose of between 700 and 1,000 rem (extended to five weeks).

According to the Soviet Report to the IAEA, a 2 per cent increase of the natural incidence of cancer is predicted among those who will be monitored permanently. Under normal circumstances about 14,000 of the evacuees could expect to die of cancer within 70 years. A 2 per cent increase means that there will be 280 new cases of cancer-related mortality.[113] If one added to the evacuees about 500,000 people engaged in decontamination, repair work, road block inspections, servicemen and policemen who were exposed to the emergency level of radiation exposure, the number of estimated cancer-related deaths would rise to 1,700. About one million people now live in the special regime zone, where the permissible level of accumulated exposure has been raised to 35 rem.[114] In 1988 their average dose was already 9 rem per person. This will increase the figure of cancer-related deaths for the most exposed population to 2,500. But radiation damage is not a very selective mutagen or carcinogen and carcinogenesis causes only about a third of the cases of radiation-related reduction of life span. I estimate that this means that the total future mortality figure related to Chernobyl amongst the most exposed part of the population could reach from 5,000 to 7,000. Only one in a hundred of future deaths in this group will be directly due to Chernobyl, but the ratio will be different for different age groups (higher for those who were younger when the accident occurred). The incidence of cancer among the younger groups will be statistically measurable. There is likely to be a particularly marked increase in the incidence of cancer of the thyroid and leukaemia.

But the life expectancy of the entire group has been reduced by at least one or two years.

For people who live in the part of the Soviet Union that was most affected by the Chernobyl fallout, the figures given in the original Soviet report do not seem to me to be an overestimation. The actual contamination of the environment and food is not known, but the approximate estimate of the radioiodine contamination of milk, meat and other products given for 15 regions with a population of 75 million could also be an indicator of radiocaesium.[115] Market sales of milk and meat were forbidden in many regions, but it was impossible to prevent some radioiodine in the milk sold in shops. Standards were introduced for the 'permissible' level for milk that was to be sold. Milk which exceeded that level was normally processed into butter or cheese:

> The standards were designed to ensure that thyroid gland exposure of children (the critical organ for iodine-131) did not exceed 30 rem. This condition was observed by establishing the permissible content of iodine-131 in milk at $1.10^{-7}$ Ci/l. A similar standard was introduced in England in 1957 after the Windscale accident.[116]

In fact, this statement is not entirely correct. In the UK contamination above 3,700 Bq/litre meant that the milk was destroyed and milk with less than 3,700 Bq/litre could only be consumed after it had been mixed with clean milk during processing. It is not clear that milk with less than 3,700 Bq/litre was mixed with clean milk in the Soviet Union. Moreover, the rural population in the affected regions apparently often consumed milk with higher doses. There was no way in which the content of iodine-131 and caesium-134 and 137 in the milk of cows that belonged to individual households could be checked. There are about 8 million cows belonging to individual rural families in the affected regions (the regulations permit one per family). Rural evacuees combined their cattle with collective or state farm herds, but it was impossible to do that through the European part of the USSR.

The Soviet report indicates that in some regions (for example, the south of Byelorussia) the level of iodine was $10^{-6}$ Ci/litre in milk, or 37,000 Bq/litre and 370,000 Bq/kg in green vegetables.[117] Technical problems made it difficult to detect other radionuclides. There was no proper equipment for radiation measurement, particularly for beta radiation. The contaminated areas were too large and, in any case, the tradition of the local rural population (which numbered about 30 million people in the affected area) was to live off the land. This made it impossible to inspect their food for different radionuclides. The measurement of caesium-134 and 137 (beta and gamma radiation) began much later, when most of the iodine-131 had been destroyed (after five periods of its half-life only about 3 per cent of the initial iodine-131 remained in the food chain). The permissible level of radioactive caesium was only announced by the USSR Ministry of Health on 30 May, 1986.[118] Based on a 5 rem accumulated permissible annual dose, it was far higher than the international standard for radiocaesium. The actual levels of permissible contamination of food, expressed either in microcuries or becquerels, was not, however, reported. It was probably much higher than 3,700 Bq/litre for milk or per kilogram of meat.

In 1989 it was disclosed that meat from affected regions contaminated by radiocaesium was often distributed among many other meat-processing plants where it was added to the mince used to make a special kind of hard sausage (because people do not eat this sausage in large quantities). The level of radioactivity of this meat was kept secret. The news surfaced only when the workers in a Leningrad meat-processing plant started a strike, refusing to work with radioactive meat from Byelorussia. They sent a statement to the press when they started their strike:

> On the 2 March 1989 we, the workers of the raw materials plant of Sausage Factory No. 1 of Lenmyasokombinat flatly refused to process radioactive meat which has come from areas that suffered from the Chernobyl catastrophe.
>
> We started to receive this meat in August 1986. The workers were warned that a 'special batch' was arriving. It was not explained, however, that the 'special batch' was contaminated by radionuclides. The administration assured the workers that the contamination of the meat did not exceed the temporary permissible level determined by the Ministry of Health of the USSR and that processing the meat would not be harmful to our health. We do not believe this. The number of illnesses have risen in the workshop. Workers experience weakness and pains in the head. Small wounds and scratches fester and take a long time to heal. This is one of the reasons why the workers have firmly refused to process this meat.[119]

The officials at the plant told the reporter that the final products (after the mixture of contaminated meat with clean meat) were not contaminated above the temporary permissible level. No figures were given because they were classified. It also became clear that contaminated Byelorussian meat had not been sent to Moscow processing plants or used for export products.

Lithuania, Latvia and Estonia were not included in the analysis of radioactive contamination given in the Soviet Report. This was not because they were unaffected, but because of political sensitivities. The radioactive cloud affected Finland and Sweden and it must have passed directly over the Baltic republics. Together with the Kaliningrad region, they add 15 million people to the 75 million included in the report. Thus at least 90 million Soviet people were affected by the Chernobyl accident.

In 1988 the areas of significant radioactive contamination were established more accurately. There were several highly contaminated spots situated several hundred kilometres from Chernobyl, probably as a result of rain falling in these spots during the first ten days after the disaster, when the reactor was still releasing very large amounts of radioactive materials, gases and aerosol. The most accurate details about the real scale of contamination were released by the information department of the Chernobyl nuclear power station just before the second anniversary of the accident in April 1988:

> Eleven regions of the USSR, with a population at present of 17 million people, of whom 2.5 million are children below the age of 5, suffered some degree of radioactive contamination. As a result of determining the comprehensive doses, an area of strict control was established which now includes about a million people who live in the Gomel' and Mogilev regions and in parts of the Bryansk, Zhitomir, Kiev and Chernigov regions.[120]

It has already been mentioned that 20 more villages in the Gomel and Mogilev regions of Byelorussia and about ten villages in the Zhitomir region of the Ukraine were evacuated in 1989 because the accumulated doses of their inhabitants were approaching about 35 rem. They exceeded the maximum dose in three years. It is now established that there will be more villages in this situation in 1990, 1991 and later.

In 1986 and 1987 the Soviet medical officials issued assurances that the evacuees and those who lived in areas of strict control would not suffer any health problems. By 1988 their statements had become less categorical. It became usual to say, when the results of periodic medical observations were announced, that the examinations 'had not revealed any serious deviation from the normal health of the population'.[121] The thyroid glands of 150,000 children are being monitored, 160,000 people are being closely monitored for the level of radiocaesium in their bodies. The bland language used in reporting the results of this monitoring, that there are 'no clear and obvious clinical effects', often means that there *are* problems and also complaints from those affected.

In fact, in 1986 the medical authorities did not really have much information from large territories and they based their calculations on measurements from a few spots only. The figures for contaminated products were often exceptionally high and they did not yet know how much of the initial contamination would remain in the food chain. The retention of radiocaesium is very high in swamp areas, for example, and the retention figures for natural forests and swamps were probably used for agricultural areas. Similarly, the contamination of milk with radioiodine was extremely high in south-west Byelorussia. It is clear from the Soviet figures for the concentration of iodine-131 in milk in different regions[122] that Polyes'ye was an exceptional case. In some places in Polyes'ye milk contained up to 70–80 microcuries per litre, or close to 2,000,000 Bq/litre. This milk would be totally unsuitable for either consumption or processing; and, if the level of radioiodine was so high, the level of radiocaesium was probably about 300,000–400,000 Bq/litre.

In places where milk, meat and other products were so severely contaminated, people's exposure to radiation was probably as high as the level indicated in the Soviet Working Document for Polyes'ye, but it is unlikely that such levels were typical for the whole region. It is more likely that they were registered in a few 'hot spots' where rain brought down large amounts of radionuclides. The Soviet radiological services calculated the total release of radionuclides from the reactor for the Soviet Union only. The initial assumption was that most of the fallout was inside the USSR. Later measurements in other countries demonstrated that this was the case for non-volatile isotopes, but volatile radionuclides like radioiodine and radiocaesium were distributed world-wide (primarily in the northern hemisphere). The total release of radioiodine inside the Soviet Union was about 7 million curies and the total release of radiocaesium (isotopes 134 and 137) was about 1.5 MCi.[123] If all these 8.5 millions of curies of radionuclides had contaminated the Polyes'ye region preferentially, the incidence of future cancers could be as high as the level anticipated in the initial Soviet report, that is an increase of cancer-related mortality of 0.4 per cent.[124] This is an increase which could easily be measured, particularly for younger groups of the population. It is only five times lower than the increase predicted for people evacuated from the exclusion zone. It would mean 4,000–5,000 extra cancer deaths and three to four times more deaths from other radiation-related pathologies. The estimate would be even higher if other radionuclides were taken into account.

In July and August 1986 the Soviet medical service did not have the equipment to study the distribution of radiostrontium outside the exclusion zone. Strontium-90, the main health hazard due to its long half-life of 30 years, emits only beta radiation. Large, very simple detectors were being used which were too insensitive to detect beta or alpha radiation. Most of the preliminary territorial measurements were made from special low-flying helicopters which only registered gamma radiation. Strontium-89, which has a short half-life of 53 days, represented the main problem in 1986 because it was dominant in the mixture of two strontium isotopes (2.2. MCi of strontium-89 and 0.22 MCi of strontium-90) which was released from the reactor. Neither isotope is volatile and both were deposited within the USSR. Western estimates of the health effects of Chernobyl have not, therefore, taken them into account.

Plutonium, too, presented a problem only in the USSR (about 500,000 curies of various plutonium isotopes were released as well as 2.7 MCi of neptunium-239). The geographical distribution of these radionuclides was not disclosed, but their presence in some agricultural areas is obvious since special measures of deep ploughing have been recommended to reduce their level in the topsoil. Soviet regulations treat strontium-90 more seriously than caesium-137 because it becomes fixed in bones for the rest of human life if it gets into the food chain. It is therefore leukaemogenic, in other words dangerous and selectively malignant for bone marrow. Over a period of years the amount of caesium in the bodies of people living in Polyes'ye will decline, while the amount of strontium will increase.

No attempt was made by the Soviet medical team to calculate the health effects of the rest of the population of the European part of the USSR (estimated by the report to be 75 million people) of the caesium and strontium isotopes which may enter the organism through the food chain. Calculations were only made of the health effects of external gamma radiation and iodine-131. The external gamma radiation doubled the natural background level of radiation in 1986, but it was expected to be lower in later years. Soviet experts predicted that the rise in the cancer-related mortality rate amongst these 75 million people would not exceed 0.15 per cent and it could be as low as 0.03 per cent.[125] Mortality from thyroid cancer, not normally a high cause of death, will rise by 1 per cent.[126] This means 8,000 extra deaths on average from all non-thyroid types of cancer (9.5 million normal cancer deaths are projected for this population over the next 70 years). In the normal course of events the expected number of deaths from thyroid cancer would be 150,000. A 1 per cent increase means another 1,500

1 Academician Igor Vasilievich Kurchatov (1903–60), the Head of the Soviet Uranium Project, who directed efforts to develop the first Soviet nuclear reactors (1946, 1948), first Soviet atomic bomb (1949), first thermonuclear (fusion) bomb (1953), first Atomic Power station (1954), first nuclear power ship, icebreaker Lenin (1956), and initiated development of the Soviet fast breeder reactors programme.

2 Chernobyl reactor unit No. 4 on 26 April after two explosions and the fire. The smoke from the graphite fire was removed by special photographic 'censors' from this picture when it was shown a few days later on Moscow television.

3   The central hall of Chernobyl reactor unit No. 1. The top part of the reactor, consisting of 1,700 individual nuclear fuel pressure tubes, has a surface area of more than 100 m².

4   Daily spraying of the land surface with special film-making chemicals and other liquids took place to fix radioactive dust particles in order to prevent the spread of contamination. The streets of Kiev and other cities were washed daily with water.

5 Deactivation of houses in Pripyat town in 1986 after the evacuation of its 45,000 inhabitants. In 1987 some inhabitants were allowed to visit their flats to collect documents, family papers and some belongings left behind during the swift evacuation on 27 April. In 1989 the level of radioactivity was about 1 mR/h.

6 Decontamination of the Chernobyl site in 1986 was carried out mainly by Soviet chemical troops trained to operate in nuclear or chemical war conditions. Practically all Soviet chemical troops took part in the Chernobyl operation and in radiological control of the territory.

7   Radio-operated bulldozers being tested on an improvised testing ground outside the contaminated area before being used near unit 4. Their performance in areas of high radioactivity proved to be very poor; robots imported from West Germany for the decontamination of the turbine hall managed a very short effective life span in the high-level radiation conditions.

8   West German firemen washing down a truck on its arrival at Herleshausen on the border between East and West Germany, 5 May 1986, after the discovery of radioactive contamination. Such checks followed the spread of radioactive particles to some European countries in the wake of the Chernobyl disaster.

9 Pripyat river and the northern part of the 1000 km² Kiev reservoir became part of the post-accident 'exclusion zone'. Fishing was forbidden, and permanent control of water resources and flora and fauna contamination was introduced in parts of the Ukraine and Byelorussia. Compulsory checks still monitor the presence of radionuclides.

10 The President of the British Fire Services Association presenting the Order of Gallantry to the Commander of the Chernobyl Fire Brigade, Major Leonid Telyatnikov, for his bravery. Major Telyatnikov was among the few members of his brigade who survived after acute radiation sickness. Several of his colleagues were awarded only posthumously the order of Lenin and the gold star medal of Hero of the Soviet Union.

11　Pripyat from the railroad bridge, December 1987. The town is empty: 45,000 people were evacuated from it on 27 April 1986.

12　Chernobyl nuclear power station from the west, February 1987. The land around the station was cleared of forest apart from the tree on the left.

13 Unit 4 of the Chernobyl nuclear power plant, walled up and bound in reinforced concrete ('The Cover', unofficially known as 'The Sarcophagus'), May 1989. It took 400,000 tonnes of concrete, and was built in conditions of between 5,000 and 20,000 R/h of external radiation, by 200,000 men serving very short shifts. The other units of the plant were decontaminated and keep generating electricity.

14 After-effects of the Chernobyl disaster, Narodichni district of the Ukraine, August 1989. The first abnormal calves and piglets were born in the V. I. Lenin Collective Farm, about 100 km from the Chernobyl nuclear power station, a year after the disaster. Now the birth of freaks there has assumed a regular character: calves with deformed joints and extremities; some without hair. This calf has a cleft lip.

15 Photograph taken by Dr Vladimir Shevchenko, the head of the Laboratory of Ecological Genetics at the Vavilov Institute of General Genetics in Moscow, showing how the leaves of oak trees affected by the radiation from Chernobyl lose their symmetrical shape and grow round.

cases which, as the Soviet report suggests, 'do not change measurably the normal mortality in the affected regions.'[127]

Soviet experts used the NRPB (National Radiological Protection Board) method to calculate the incidence of cancer. For 30 million 'natural' cancers in the EC over the next 50 years, the NRPB estimates that there will be 1,000 new cases due to Chernobyl, as a result of a collective dose of about 80,000 man-sieverts (or 8,000,000 man-rem).[128] If one applies the NRPB method to estimate the dose effect of the radiation exposure calculated by the Soviet experts, about 18,000 extra cancer-related deaths in the European parts of the Soviet Union can be expected over the next 70 years. But if the method adopted by the US Department of Energy for the global fallout from Chernobyl is used,[129] the figure rises to nearly 50,000 extra cancer deaths. This is much higher than the actual prediction of 12,000–14,000 made in the US study for the European part of the Soviet Union. Because competent Western estimates of the future health impact of Chernobyl were much lower than their own, the Soviet radiological services reconsidered their preliminary findings and presented a very different set of figures at the IAEA meeting which took place in September 1987, more than a year after the post-accident meeting.

At the August 1986 post-accident meeting in Vienna many of the experts' questions remained unanswered. The Soviet medical team, headed by Professor L. A. Il'in and Dr A. K. Gus'kova promised to prepare a new report for the IAEA meeting in 1987 which was, in any case, intended to discuss the progress of Soviet countermeasures and changes in the safety systems of RBMK-1000 reactors. The meeting took place from 28 September to 2 October 1987 during the IAEA Conference on Nuclear Power Performance and Safety. A 23-page report was presented in Russian by L. A. Il'in and O. A. Pavlovsky.[130] It turned out to be less informative and specific than the 1986 medical report.

The description it offers of the radiation exposure of the evacuated population is essentially unchanged. But a very different assessment is given of the radiation exposure of the population outside the exclusion zone. Particular areas or hot spots, like Polyes'ye in the first report, are not identified. The estimated collective dose has been reduced from the figures given in the first report. The total past and future exposure of the whole Soviet population (280 million people) resulting from the Chernobyl accident is given as 326,540 man-sieverts (32,654,000 man-rem). This figure correlates with Western estimates of the Chernobyl-related exposure to radiocaesium and radioiodine for the rest of Europe (that is 200,000 man-sieverts, of which 80,000 man-sieverts relates to the EC countries).[131] But extrapolating a figure for the whole Soviet population which includes people in areas which were scarcely affected makes little sense. Moreover, the calculation is based on radiocaesium and radioiodine fallout and gamma radiation from cloud. It does not include radiation exposure resulting from strontium, plutonium or the other radionuclides which, because of their low volatility, were present only in the fallout over the Soviet Union. The result is that it is possible to conclude from the new report that the average exposure in the Soviet Union was not sufficiently serious to make much impact on future health statistics. No attempt was made to calculate the possible Chernobyl-related cancer increases.

A more detailed analysis of the information contained in the second report makes it clear that Chernobyl fallout affected two areas predominantly: Byelorussia (106,340 man-sieverts for a population of 10.01 million) and the south-west part of the Ukraine (80,660 man-sieverts for a population of 21.94 million). The central part of the RSFSR was far less affected (42,490 man-sieverts for a population of 29.8 million). It is also obvious that within these regions some smaller areas were much more seriously affected than others, and that 'hot spots' occurred where rain made the contamination higher by two or three orders of magnitude. This was the case in Western Europe and there is no reason to believe that it did not also occur in the Ukraine and Byelorussia. Southern Byelorussia was more affected than the rest of the republic whereas, in the Ukraine, areas to the west of Chernobyl and some spots south of the exclusion zone suffered more than the rest. But, even if one ignores these differences and averages the Byelorussia exposure for the total population of that republic, the total dose for a population of 10 million was the same as the exposure of the 400 million people in the EC. In other words, each individual in Byelorussia received on average an exposure 40 times higher than the average exposure experienced by an individual in the EC. About 40 per cent of the exposure was due to the consumption of contaminated food.

If one applies the NRPB method to calculate the health effects in the Soviet Union as a whole, the past and future exposure of the Soviet population to 326,540 man-sieverts will produce about 4,000 cancer deaths. If, however, one applies the American method, the number of future cancer deaths in the USSR caused by Chernobyl rises to 20,000. The Americans themselves estimated 14,000 deaths in the USSR (which they later reduced to 7,000), because they assumed that the radiocaesium fallout in the USSR was appoximately the same as in the rest of Europe and that the protection measures were effective.[132] If one took the exposure of the population to strontium and other radionuclides into account and, more importantly, the very poor methods of protecting the rural population, the estimate of future cancer deaths would be higher. While it is true that these extra deaths would not be detectable in the health statistics for the whole of the Soviet Union, in the most affected areas of Byelorussia and the Ukraine, where a population of between 10 and 15 million will be exposed to nearly 200,000 man-sieverts, a careful follow-up study would almost certainly find future late effects, particularly among younger people, and probably also an increase in leukaemia over a shorter period (from two to seven years after the accident).

At present about 1 million people have been tested and 600,000 included in a register for a closer follow-up study. According to the second Soviet report, no health effects have been identified so far. Although no supporting data are offered, it is not surprising no effects can be identified in a period of 15 to 16 months. Included in the preliminary follow-up register are 216,000 children. The register also includes evacuees, an unspecified number of people who worked in the exclusion zone after the accident, their future children and grandchildren. People from the affected populations of the neighbouring districts of Kiev, Zhitomir, Gomel, Mogilev and Bryansk have been selected for a shorter-term study. It would appear that only those who are shown by preliminary tests to have been exposed to a certain dose of external and internal radiation will be selected for long-term observation. The report does not, however, specify the qualifying dose. But it is clear that the size of the group which will be followed up is much larger than any other group ever studied for long-term effects of radiation. The largest previous group, the survivors of Hiroshima and Nagasaki, consisted of about 120,000 people. Whether the new Kiev and Minsk radiological centres created specially for the study will publish any factual data remains to be seen.

As far as one can judge from the new report, the people selected for follow-up who are not evacuees come from Kiev, Zhitomir, Gomel, Mogilev and Bryansk regions, where the average exposure in 1986 and 1987 was at the level of 10–15 millisieverts per person, but about 1 per cent of the population was exposed to doses 'above 50 millisieverts' through consumption of contaminated food from their private plots and livestock.[133] The report identifies them as pensioners, livestock farmers and farm machine operators. However most figures in this report are not relevant for a population in the zones of special control. By way of comparison, the highest average dose in the most contaminated part of Western Europe (South Germany) was 0.4 mSv.[134] The maximum annual dose permitted for professionals working in the nuclear industry is 50 mSv (or 5 rem). If rural districts in four regions in the Soviet Union give an annual dose of more than 50 mSv per adult who has not taken elaborate protective measures, the group that is most at risk – children – should be prevented from living in those districts.

Future cancer deaths related to Chernobyl are not the only expected health consequences. The Soviet follow-up programme will observe not only the future incidence of cancer, but also pregnancies, hormonal disorders, incidence of infections (to check the negative effect on the immunological system) and so on. Time alone will tell how these studies will be carried out and whether the knowledge obtained about radiation effects will be shared with the medical profession in other countries.

It should be stressed that the late effects of radioactive contamination depend not only on doses, but also on the form of radioactive particles in the aerosol. The health dangers of small, hot particles of insoluble material are greater than from gaseous and soluble radionuclides. The study of hot particles belongs to a special branch of radiology. They create greater problems for skin, lungs, eyes and other surfaces than gaseous material, because there is a 'killing area' close to a hot particle. The hot particles containing nearly 20 radionuclides which reached Sweden were, as a rule, very small (of the order of 2–6 micromillimetres) and did not contain plutonium.[135] But those that were identified and studied from the clothes and shoes of foreign students evacuated from Kiev and Minsk were much larger (of the order of 30–150 micromillimetres) and they apparently originated from the reactor core.[136] Their radionuclide composition reflected the composition of the melted core fuel elements and they contained plutonium among many other radioactive products. Hot particles were also found on the clothing of foreigners who visited Minsk in August 1986. There is a long-standing special research programme in the Soviet Union on the specific health effects of hot particles. The Institute of Biophysics (whose director is Professor L. A. Il'in) has identified plutonium as the greatest health risk, particularly when absorbed by the lungs in the form of hot particles.[137] Since plutonium and strontium remain fixed in the body for decades, it is clear that the medical history of Chernobyl will continue well into the next century.

The contrast between the original, detailed August 1986 report and the new brief report at the end of 1987 would not invite critical comment if the new report presented more information. Articles in the general media in 1987 indicated that new 'hot spots' of contamination were found in the winter of 1987, particularly in Byelorussia where special teams of radiologists, geneticists, haematologists and endocrinologists were sent in January and March 1987.[138] The consumption of local products in several more regions was restricted in 1987.[139] Many new spots and areas of elevated radioactivity were found in Byelorussia and the Ukraine in 1988 and 1989 when more dosimeters became available and better monitoring was introduced.[140] According to Western calculations, more than 80 per cent of radiation exposure was linked to the eating of contaminated food.[141] It is difficult to believe the accuracy of the Soviet calculation that only 40 per cent of the exposure in the Soviet Union was due to consumption, while 60 per cent was external radiation caused by fallout. The rural population of the Soviet Union is much larger than that of Western Europe and the consumption of processed food is far less common. While it is true that the rural population is more exposed to environmental factors, it is also true that control over food consumption is very poor in rural areas. It was very poor even for the organized army units that worked in the exclusion zone very close to the nuclear plant in the summer of 1986. For example, one report described how:

> Driving through Kopachi, we noticed people drinking and eating from their palms, from their mess tins, soldiers cutting bread and sausage. All of them, young and old, served at the command post and the baths. The baths were a dozen tank trucks with flexible hoses and sewage pits dug into the sand and covered over with film. They washed the cars returning from the station . . . creating a foamy stream of extremely radioactive dirt. Then they threw off their protective coats and rested, smoking, sucking their cigarettes with their lips, drinking and eating . . . Whenever we had the chance, we tried everywhere to persuade the soldiers to protect their stomachs and their lungs. Because we knew and they didn't that it was far more serious than the 'external' radiation about which they had heard. But we understood that their contempt for protective measures could not be eradicated. People are not at all prepared, they don't know the extent of the danger that radioactivity will penetrate their organs internally. People who did not respect or believe in protective measures or hygiene had to live and work in those conditions.[142]

The decontamination work continued in 1988 and 1989, but the practice of sending regular army units of conscripts, aged 18 and 19, has been discontinued. Older reservists are being sent instead, and only people over the age of 35 years are allowed to work in and near

Chernobyl.[143] They are less sensitive to the carcinogenic effect of radiation and less likely to transfer the genetic effect of radiation damage to future generations. The permissible dose of exposure has now been reduced to 5 rem per year.

In Soviet medical ethics secrecy is often justified as being kinder. According to this argument, people who suffer the risk of an increased incidence of future health problems feel better if they do not know about it. But in a case like Chernobyl secrecy causes exaggerated rumours which may do more damage. In Kiev, for example, where the radiation exposure was modest compared to that in and around the exclusion zone, lack of information produced various kinds of hysteria:

> In Kiev 'catastrophists' appeared and 'optimists' . . . In the hot days of May one came across strange figures in the town, covered from head to foot in old clothing, caps, hats or scarves covering almost half of their faces, wearing gloves and stockings . . . they were 'catastrophists' mobilizing all their resources of individual protection.[144]

The anxiety continued during the rest of 1986 and in 1987, 1988 and 1989 as well. It was largely created by confusing and contradicting official reports about the radioactivity level. People felt that they could not trust officials and they tried to find out for themselves. Bookshops sold out of books on radiology and radiobiology. Attempts were made to measure the level privately, despite the fact that possession of unauthorized Geiger counters or other dosimeters was a criminal offence (photographic methods, which are very inaccurate, were used instead). In fact, winds from the north blew dust from the contaminated areas and this meant that there were periodic rises in the level of radioactivity in Kiev and probably in other cities and towns.[145] Public anxiety was expressed in a number of ways, but reports only began to appear in May and June 1987, when *glasnost'* made it possible to print them. Women were said to have had dangerous abortions late in pregnancy, parents were said to be afraid to give milk and dairy products to their children. This produced rickets (through vitamin D deficiency), a disease which had not been seen in Kiev since the war.[146] There were cases of 'radiation phobia', with some people refusing to drink or wash in anything but bottled mineral water. Foreign visitors to Kiev confirmed the reports. The main worry in 1987 was about the water. There were quite reasonable fears that the spring thaw and floods would wash surface radioactivity into the Dnieper on which about 25 million people depend directly for their water supplies.

The attempt by medical and government officials to cover up the real levels of contamination in parts of Byelorussia and the Ukraine was almost certainly caused by fear that new waves of evacuation would be too costly and too politically difficult. Experts on radiation ecology had predicted that the main exposure had taken place in 1986 and 1987 and that the exposure in 1988 and 1989 would decline so much that it would not matter. But in 1989 it became clear that this was misguided. The government found itself in the embarrassing situation of having to declare a new evacuation in several villages nearly three years after the accident. Western experts could be misled with reduced figures of contamination and exposure; the Soviet public could also be calmed by issuing false statements, but it was impossible to prevent the biological effects of radiation exposure from showing up in some groups of the population.

Soviet methods of dosimetric control of the environment and food were inadequate and there were shortages of both qualified personnel and equipment. However, in the late 1950s Soviet radiologists had developed a comparatively accurate cytological method of measuring the effect of radiation exposure (Professor Gale praised it as an objective method when it was impossible to use traditional dosimetric measurement and it was essential to find the level of past exposure in a patient to assess his or her chances of survival). It has been described in a number of publications as well as in the Soviet IAEA report in 1986.[147] It is based on the measurement of the percentage of chromosomal abnormalities during divisions of cellular nuclei (mitoses) in lymphocytes taken from the blood of the affected person and stimulated by an activator to start cell divisions in culture. The original scale was made on the basis of observations of patients who had undergone whole-body irradiation for therapeutic purposes (patients with leukaemia during periods of remission). It was found that between doses of 1 and 5 Gy, there was a linear increase of chromosomal abnormalities in lymphocytes. A dose of 3.3 Gy normally produces nearly 100 per cent of recognizable chromosomal aberrations of one sort or another. A dose of 0.33 Gy should accordingly produce about 10 per cent of aberrations. The accuracy is lower, of course, at the lower range of radiation dose but, if the number of cells under observation is increased, the method gives satisfactory accuracy for the doses of radiation which those people who are on the medical register have experienced. If groups of inhabitants in the zone of special control accumulate doses in the range of 10–20 rem, some action is obviously necessary. Several hundred doctors, haematologists and other scientists were involved in these measurements of lymphocytes in blood samples and this made it difficult to cover up the findings. In fact, covering up would have been useless because clinical signs would have begun to show at a certain point.

In 1988 the Byelorussia government and medical authorities were faced with a difficult problem. Many villagers in contaminated areas of the Gomel and Mogilev regions were approaching the accumulated dose of 25 rem, previously considered the maximum permissible. A 'solution' was found by the Ministry of Health of the USSR, which established a programme of 'safe living' in the contaminated areas and raised the permissible level for the local population to 35 rem.[148] This was almost certainly done to avoid having to evacuate more people. Nevertheless, at the beginning of 1989 the Byelorussian Council of Ministers decided that 20 villages in the Gomel and Mogilev regions had to be evacuated because their inhabitants were approaching the accumulated dose of 35 rem per person.[149] More villages face the same prospect in 1990 and beyond.

Under public pressure a map of the contaminated districts was finally published in the local press.[150] It showed that some districts which faced evacuation were situated as far as 150–200 km from the exclusion zone. The Chairman of the Byelorussian Council of Ministers, M. V. Kovalev, stated that the average accumulated dose of people in the Byelorussia part of the special zone (171,000 people, 37,400 of them children) during the two years since the accident had been estimated at 9 rem per person.[151] He acknowledged that the contamination in Byelorussia was higher than had been originally estimated and that, in addition to the zone of special (and permanent) radiological control, a new zone of periodic control had been created where the average accumulated dose was about 3.3 rem per person in 1988. He did not say how many people were involved. What emerges is a clear picture of an increase in contaminated area, caused by erosion, normal ecological processes and human activity.

Similar problems appear to have emerged in the more densely populated Ukrainian sector. In March 1989 it was reported that 12 more villages would be evacuated in two districts situated close to the exclusion zone, because their inhabitants were expected to accumulate 35 rem per person.[152] New districts have recently been included into the area where there is restricted consumption of locally produced milk. In February 1989 *Moscow News* reported that in the Narodichi district of the Zhitomir region, at a distance of between 50 and 90 km from the Chernobyl plant, the contamination of topsoil exceeds 80 Ci/km$^2$ (or 3,000,000 Bq/m$^2$). This makes the land unsuitable for agriculture, but local people have no choice but to continue dairy farming because centrally supplied 'clean' food does not arrive in sufficient quantities. Despite health warnings, many people drink local milk and gather fruit and vegetables from their plots.[153] External radiation in some parts of the villages was 2 mR/h (more than 100 times higher than the Kiev level).

These new facts make the previous Soviet official estimations of the accumulated dose irrelevant. The Soviet IAEA report in 1987 (which was accepted by international bodies) established two areas of significant contamination, Byelorussia (106,340 man-sievert collective 50 year dose for a population of 10.1 million) and the north-western part of the Ukraine (80,660 man-sievert collective dose for a population of 29.8 million). If these figures are accepted as accurate, it would mean that these combined areas have suffered a health impact comparable with the population of Poland (150,000 man-sievert, or $1.5 \times 10^5$ Gy for a population of 36 million). Moreover, it would also mean that the Ukraine suffered less than Romania (92,000 man-sievert of $9.2 \times 10^4$ Gy for a population of 23 million). However, the new figures now published for the population of the zone of special control in Byelorussia and the Ukraine (nearly 1 million people), make it likely that this group alone will accumulate between 150,000 and 200,000 sievert (or grays) which is equal to the estimate for all of Byelorussia and the Ukraine in the 1987 detailed report. The size of the population under periodic control is not known and there has been no report from the Bryansk region of the RSFSR. However, it now seems likely that for the population of 40 million for which, in the Il'in and Pavlovsky report in 1987 an accumulated dose of 186,200 sievert was estimated in the next 70 years, the actual figure will be close to 1,000,000 sievert. And this is a conservative estimate.

CONCLUSION

It is quite obvious from the materials discussed here that the health impact of Chernobyl has been very serious and that it will remain serious for decades, indeed, for several generations. Many statements were made by both Soviet officials and Western experts claiming that the increase in the incidence of cancer which could be linked to Chernobyl fallout was so small in comparison with the existing rate of cancer, that it would be impossible to measure it by statistical methods to prove its Chernobyl origin. This is correct if the whole population of the

European part of the Soviet Union is considered. The incidence of cancer in modern industrial society has grown in recent decades. The causes of this growth (smoking, industrial pollution, increasing use of toxic and carcinogenic pesticides, increasing use of nitrate fertilizers, the wide use of X-ray for diagnostic purposes) are much more powerful than the past and future radiation exposure from Chernobyl fallout. But if the population of those districts of the Ukraine, Byelorussia and the Bryansk region, which were heavily contaminated by different radionuclides and now represent a zone of special and permanent radiological control, is compared with the population of other, 'cleaner' districts in the north-eastern part of Byelorussia and the south-eastern part of the Ukraine, the increase in the cancer rate (particularly in thyroid cancer and leukaemia) will be measurable, particularly in younger, more critical groups of the population.

It is almost certainly the case that the increase in leukaemia in the 250,000 children included in the medical register has already been detected, although it has not been reported. The register included 600,000 people in 1986, but it has certainly been made larger because many new hot spots were found in various parts of the Soviet Union and because of the problems which servicemen and workers who took part in the emergency operation have begun to face. There have been several reports in the Soviet press about medical and other 'privileges' given to Chernobyl veterans who have returned to their homes throughout the Soviet Union. It is clear from complaints about the difficulties of enjoying these 'privileges', that they concern health damage which was not immediately obvious but which may develop later.

In the Narodichi district of Zhitomir region in the Ukraine, 50–90 km from Chernobyl, clinical symptoms of radioactive contamination became obvious in 1989. The First Secretary of the district Party committee, Anatoly Mel'nik, reported that women in the district had been recommended not to fall pregnant. He also complained that, although people went to the Kiev Radiological Centre for check-ups periodically, the doctors there did not inform them about the state of their health. He also reported that in February 1989:

> . . . between one and two microcuries of caesium-137 were registered for 35 per cent of the inhabitants of the district, from three to five microcuries for more than 4 per cent and from five to ten microcuries for almost 4 per cent. The thyroid glands of more than half the children in the district have been affected, a considerable part of them to the second and third degree.
>
> . . . medical workers . . . have noted an increase in the number of chronic cases among the population, and deterioration in the postoperational

period among surgical patients. The mean annual number of cancer cases, notably cancer of the lip and mouth cavity, has doubled'.[154]

Ten microcuries means 370,000 Bq or 5,700 Bq/kg of human body. It is a very high dose, but it also indicates that the dose was probably ten to twenty times higher in 1986–7. *Izvestya* reported in 1989 that there were cases of even higher accumulations of radiocaesium in Khoiniki district of Gomel region (up to $13\mu$ Ci/kg).[155] This case is certainly only the tip of the iceberg of the health problems for the inhabitants of the special zone around the exclusion zone. But the zones of periodic control and people who live near the special zones should also be monitored closely for radiation-related health problems.

The top Soviet health officials, including the Minister of Health of the USSR, Evgeny Chazov, and his colleagues in the Ukraine and Byelorussia stated many times in 1986 and 1987 that the level of contamination in areas where people were allowed to live and to accumulate up to 35 rem of exposure represented no danger to health. The same position was taken by the Soviet Radiological Protection Committee. The main people in Soviet radiological protection, Like L. A. Il'in and A. K. Gus'kova, were, as young radiologists, directly involved in the cover-up of the medical problems which resulted from the Kyshtym nuclear disaster in 1958, when a very large area in the Urals was contaminated by radionuclides from nuclear waste disposal facilities. It took ten years before a limited number of ecological studies of the distribution of radionuclides in the soil–plant–animal chains were permitted in the contaminated area.[156] The medical history of the people who were evacuated from 32 villages and settlements has never been disclosed except for a passing reference in a review on Soviet radiology in 1967 to a classified report describing the treatment of 11 cases of acute radiation sickness.[157] Western hopes and Soviet promises that the medical history of Chernobyl will be available for international co-operation seem to have been premature.[158] The Soviet authorities have apparently decided that the costs of the political embarrassment and economic liability which would ensue from such a study would be higher than the medical benefits. This position suited the political leaders as well.

In January 1988 the Politburo reassessed the costs of Chernobyl upward, but it also made a statement about the health impact:

As a result of the extensive decontamination programme, the level of radiation on the site of the power station and its buildings has been reduced to a point where it presents no danger to the personnel that service the station. Detailed investigations which have been conducted indicate that no negative effects on the health of the population connected with radiation can be observed'.[159]

But exactly one year later it was necessary for the Politburo to consider the urgent task of finding money and resources for a new stage of evacuation from contaminated villages in the Ukraine and Byelorussia just because the damage to health was already evident.

As things stand now one cannot fail to be sceptical about Soviet official claims about the health impact of Chernobyl. No serious scientific studies have been published in the medical literature with valid statistics. There is no *glasnost'* about this aspect of the accident. It is, therefore, irrelevant to discuss the health impact in figures of possible cancer deaths in the next 70 years which might be attributable to Chernobyl. Whether the figure is 10,000 or 100,000 does not really matter. Signs of clinical problems are emerging which are clearly linked to the fallout, and particularly to the effect of large hot particles, and include thyroid deficiency, damage to lungs, lips, mouth cavity and other wet surfaces. Cases of leukaemia, thyroid cancer, and other forms of cancer which would normally be expected to occur at a certain level in any population group will inevitably be attributed to Chernobyl fallout by the population itself. The psychological attitude of people who live in the 200 km radius around the disaster site has been irreversibly changed. Inevitably, the mother of any child in that area who dies of leukaemia will blame Chernobyl, not Mother Nature, cosmic rays or rodon from the soil. It is useless to try to convince people living around the exclusion zone that their health has not been affected and will not be affected. The government and medical officials are afraid to publish accurate scientific figures of current and expected cases of leukaemia, decreases in immunological response, damage to thyroid and other problems which are already being recorded. But by keeping the figures (probably expressed in thousands) secret, they allow the general public to exaggerate the actual impact in their imaginations by several orders of magnitude.

# 6

# The Global Impact

THE Soviet authorities have consistently denied that the Chernobyl accident damaged the health, agriculture or economy of any other country. Western reaction to the radioactive fallout was treated as politically motivated anti-Soviet propaganda. This dismissive attitude was particularly strong in the first two weeks after the accident, when most information about the contamination came from Western sources. The 90-day ban imposed by the EC on the import of agricultural produce from Eastern Europe was considered a political boycott. The Soviet press insisted that radioactivity had not increased beyond safe and permissible levels in any other country. There could be no question of the Soviet Union compensating the farmers of Sweden, Austria, West Germany and other countries for their financial losses. Their claims were said to be groundless and hysterical.

It is true that some Western newspapers published false and exaggerated information. But this was hardly surprising given the brief, sanitized official statements issued by the Soviet government. At the end of April and throughout May 1986 the Chernobyl accident was the main news story in the world press, radio and television. Speculative and analytical articles appeared in mass-circulation popular scientific magazines, such as *Nature, Science, New Scientist* and *Natur*. The first book considering the global impact of the accident was published in Britain in June 1986 by a team of *Observer* journalists.[1] The first brief admission by Soviet scientists that food products outside the Soviet Union might be contaminated was only made in October 1987,[2] although concern was expressed at a meeting of the World Health Organization in June 1986. But the article claimed that the level was not more than 1 per cent of the dose that people receive from natural background radiation.

WHO and its regional office for Europe organized several discussions on the global impact of radioactive contamination from Chernobyl. The first took place on 6 May 1986. The aim was to analyse reports from various countries, to provide short-term recommendations and to raise longer-term considerations. There were wide variations in the amount of contamination permitted in different countries. WHO tried to establish international standards. At the first meeting experts reported the main areas of contamination in Europe:

> In the Chernobyl area (510 17'N, 300 15'E) the weather was at the starting time of the accident typical of a high pressure situation; winds were very weak and their direction varied strongly, a vast area of fog developed in the night. Higher in the atmosphere the wind field was more clear-cut than on the surface. Already at the height of 1.5 km the wind speeds were 8–10 m/s and they were blowing from the south-east or south . . .
>   The stream velocities varied between 30 and 60 km/h, which means that the emission plumes moved easily in good 24 hours from the accident area to Finland.[3]

With some simplification, the directions the plume took were grouped into five periods:[4]

1   Area: Scandinavia, Finland, Balticum.
    Emission during: 26 April; arrived 27–30 April.
2   Area: Eastern central Europe, Southern Germany, Italy, Yugoslavia.
    Emission: 27 April; arrived 28 April–2 May.
3   Area: Ukraine and eastwards.
    Emission: 28–29 April; arrived 28 April–2 May.
4   Area: Balkan, Romania, Bulgaria
    Emission: 29–30 April; arrived 1–4 May.
5   Area: Black Sea, Turkey.
    Emission: 1–4 May; arrived 2 May and later.

Seventeen maps illustrated how the plume directions changed over time and how new areas of the northern hemisphere were affected each day until 5 May. It was clear that even if the average level of radionuclide deposit in every country had not yet required action, local rain had contaminated some spots more seriously than others. As a result, rapid radiodosimetric scanning of the whole surface of Europe was required if urgent recommendations were to be made. But it was equally clear that the radiological protection services in many countries (particularly in France and Italy) were reluctant to undertake this work because they did not want to alarm the general public. Moreover, their own nuclear programmes and sometimes their tourist industries were at stake.

Thousands of American tourists cancelled their European trips because of the radiation scare.

The WHO reports were supplemented later by the findings of an independent air pollution research group at Imperial College, London. This group based its computer models on the meteorological and radiometric observations from weather stations across Europe and the USSR. Several other articles and reports confirmed the pattern reported by WHO:

> Scientists in southern Finland, Sweden and the north-eastern corner of Poland registered the arrival of the radioactive cloud on 27 April . . . By 29 April, the weather was rather stagnant. The cloud began to drift southwards over Poland, forming a wedge which thrust southwest across Germany during 30 April . . . Belts of rainfall led to a Y-shaped pattern of wet deposition. There was still clean Atlantic air over Britain and the northern coast of continental Europe.
>
> On the next day, from 30 April to 1 May, heavy rain led to a band of wet deposition of radioactivity from southeastern France across Switzerland, southern Germany, Austria and Czechoslovakia. On the following day, the material reached Britain, advancing in a northwesterly direction as a band with a sharp edge . . . Between 2 and 3 May, the main cloud cleared southeastern England with bands of rain affecting western England and Wales. The cloud had by then spread to cover most of southern Europe as well. On May 2, higher levels were again observed in the extreme north of West Germany . . . On 3 to 4 May, large parts of Britain were still within the cloud and further rainfall led to some relatively high values of deposited radioactivity, though by this time the cloud was more dilute.[5]

Other independent environmental and ecological groups and researchers made their own studies, but they did not have the resources and facilities to investigate extensive areas. Now, more than three years after the accident, we have extensive information about its effects on Sweden, the UK, West Germany, Italy and Austria. We know far less, however, about its effects on France, Belgium and Greece, where the governments did not sponsor comprehensive analysis. We also know very little about its effects on the neighbouring countries to the Soviet Union (Poland, East Germany, Romania, Czechoslovakia, Hungary, Bulgaria, Finland, Turkey, Yugoslavia), although we do know that they must have been severely affected. The contamination (and therefore the health and economic impact) was negligible in the more distant countries of the northern hemisphere such as the United States, Canada and Japan.

The initial concern in Europe was genuine. The total inventory of radionuclides in a RBMK-1000 reactor after more than two years in operation was calculated to be in excess of 2 billion curies (or $2 \times 10^{19}$ Bq), enough to contaminate a very large area. The graphite in the reactor core burned for 10 days and the danger of a full meltdown was real. It was only in August, when the Soviet report presented in Vienna gave the approximate figures of the radioactive releases that the anxiety of people in Western Europe was somewhat alleviated because, as an editorial in *Nature* put it, 'even the Chernobyl accident might have been worse'.[6]

A comprehensive picture of the global aspects of Chernobyl must be the task of international environmental and health bodies. This chapter examines the situation in a few selected countries and then summarizes some of the global aspects of the accident.

The first countries ouside the Soviet Union to be affected by the plume were Poland, Finland and Sweden. Sweden raised the international alarm and pressed Soviet officials for an explanation. It was originally assumed that Sweden suffered the most serious environmental pollution, because the first plume contained the highest concentration of radioactive debris. Some parts of the country were, indeed, more contaminated than anywhere outside the Soviet Union except Poland. Fortunately, however, they are sparsely populated areas and the health risk for the population was, therefore, comparatively low. Because of the effect on agriculture the greatest economic and health impact of the Chernobyl fallout was (and will be) felt in eastern parts of Poland and in southern parts of the Federal Republic of Germany (FRG).

Although the Chernobyl accident has produced comparatively few research publications in the Soviet Union, it has produced a special branch of research and dozens of interesting publications in Western radiobiological and radioecological literature. In the analysis that follows an attempt has been made to select the most essential and relevant information from these publications. Since the plume was first detected in Sweden, the analysis begins with the Nordic countries.

### THE NORDIC COUNTRIES

The radioactive plume was detected in Sweden at 07.00 on 28 April 1986, nearly 53 hours after the accident. Sweden was the first country to publish a detailed map of the fallout and to give advice to individual households about local contamination and necessary protective measures.[7] Swedish scientists were also the first to study the radionuclide composition of the plume and to discover that there had been a meltdown of the core. They estimated that the reactor had been operating for more than 500 days, which was an important indicator of the total inventory of radionuclides. They also published the first scientific article about the radionuclide composition and the possible overall release of radioactivity on 15 May.[8] Serious research work has probably never been made public so quickly.

By the time Soviet aircraft began monitoring the radioactive cloud on Sunday 27 April 1986 it had already crossed the Polish and Finnish borders. The stream of volatile gaseous and aerosol products at a distance of 5–10 km from the reactor in westerly and northerly directions showed gamma radiation activity of about 1,000 mR/h at an altitude between 200 and 1200 m.[9] But this was the residual tail of the plume. A significant part of the 20 million curies of radionuclides which had been released during the first two major explosions was already well beyond the reach of Soviet monitoring. It is likely that Soviet experts did not realize that the radioactive cloud was so large that there would inevitably be immediate alarm in neighbouring countries on 27 April. In fact, despite the existence of sophisticated radiation monitoring systems in both Sweden and Finland, the plume was not detected on that day because it was a Sunday.

Twelve nuclear power stations provide about 50 per cent of Sweden's electricity. Sweden also has a network of radiation monitoring stations which were created to monitor Soviet nuclear weapons tests (all Soviet nuclear weapons have been tested underground since the Partial Test Ban Treaty in 1963). Since the tests were conducted in *Novaya Zemlya*, an Arctic island close to the Scandinavian land mass, most of the Swedish and Norwegian monitoring stations are located in the Arctic regions close to the Soviet Kola Peninsula and the Barents Sea. They keep a continuous record of atmospheric and surface radiation to check Soviet compliance with the treaty. In the past they have successfully recorded several radioactive leaks from the *Novaya Zemlya* tests. The Chernobyl plume, however, arrived in Sweden from a completely different direction.

The giant plume of radioactive gases and debris formed a huge arc and on the day of the accident, 26 April, it swept to the north-west, over northern Poland and out over the Baltic. The first indication of the cloud appeared over the southern part of Sweden between Utlangan and Lund sometime between the evening of 26 April and 05.00 Greenwich Mean Time (GMT) on 27 April.[10] The central core of the cloud moved in a northerly direction over the Baltic but its periphery, with a range of activity concentration, enveloped almost all of Sweden.[11] The first alarm, however, was raised at 07.00 local time on 28 April 1986 at the Forsmark Nuclear Power Plant, 100 km north of Stockholm, when workers started their morning shift. Radiometric measurements showed a 10 to 150-fold increase in radioactivity in the air. It was assumed that there must be a leak in the plant. But two hours later independent observations at the hot cell laboratory at Studsvik, on the shores of the Baltic Sea 75 km south-west of Stockholm, reported an increase in radioactivity. Meter readings increased from the normal rate of 5–10 counts per second to 20–150 counts. Soon there were messages about increased activity in other areas. Within a couple of hours the Soviet Union was established as the source of contamination and it was confirmed that the release was not from nuclear weapons.

Scientists at Studsvik and in other stations immediately began to analyse various samples. By the end of the day 16 different radionuclides had been identified in air samples by using particle filters. The same nuclides were found in grass samples. The activity in the air was about 10 $Bq/m^3$ but at a height of 400 m it was ten times higher.[12] Autoradiography and electron microscopy revealed many hot particles, some with 1,000 counts per second. They were spherical, and between 1 and 20 micromillimetres ($\mu$m) in diameter. Some of them consisted of pure ruthenium (isotopes 103 and 106). Since ruthenium melts at a temperature of 2,250°C, this was definite proof of a meltdown of the reactor core. There were more volatile nuclides (iodine-131, caesium-134 and caesium-137, tellurium-132) in the fallout than non-volatile elements. But the proportion of non-volatile elements was surprisingly high, indicating very high temperatures in the reactor core and the absence of retaining barriers. The diagnosis was clear: a nuclear reactor accident of the worst possible type had occurred.

The Defence Research Institute, the National Institute of Radiation Protection, the Meteorological and Hydrological Institute and other organizations in Sweden began to analyse the air trajectory information. At 13.00 it was established that the accident had occurred in the Soviet Union, either in Latvia/Lithuania or in Byelorussia/Ukraine.[13] It was then that the Western media was informed about the accident, several hours before the Soviet authorities admitted that it had occurred.

In Finland an increased background radiation reading was noted in Kajaani (64°N, 28°E) at a measuring station of the Defence Forces during the evening of 27 April 1986. The observation was reported to the Operational Centre in Helsinki. But there was no sign of radioactive contamination at other observation points in Finland. In fact, Finland was not badly affected by fallout. The major part of the cloud appeared over Finland on 29 April 1986 at a height of 1–2 km. Some activity was washed to the ground by rain in central and southern Finland, creating random patterns of contamination with considerable local variation.[14]

The plume was discovered in Denmark on 28 April, after the news of the fallout had been reported in Sweden. Data from a self-recording ionization unit at Riso were analysed later, revealing that the cloud had arrived in eastern Denmark at noon on 27 April. The maximum intensity (0.01 mSv/h) occurred at 17.00, about 15 hours before the cloud was discovered in Sweden.[15]

The Norwegian authorities only began monitoring on 28 April, after the announcement from Sweden. Norway was little affected by the fallout. In some limited areas lettuce was contaminated. Later in 1986, however, it was discovered that reindeer meat and mutton were contaminated and the sale of contaminated products (including milk) was prohibited.

None of the other Scandinavian countries suffered as much damage as Sweden. When the initial cloud passed over Sweden on 27 April there was no precipitation. The milk in the area around Studsvik showed minor amounts of radionuclides (10 Bq/litre). But it soon turned out that other parts of Sweden were far more seriously affected. Rain fell around the town of Gavle (about 200 km north of Stockholm) on 28 and 29 April, causing severe damage. About 1,000 km$^2$ of land was so badly contaminated that all the grass had to be harvested and burned. Thousands of gallons of milk were poured away daily.[16] In some areas around Gavle the surface radioactivity was as high as 140,000 Bq/m$^2$, nearly 80 times higher than the radioactivity caused by all nuclear testing since 1945. The contamination increased in May and on 16 May some hot spots showed readings as high as 200,000 Bq/m$^2$, mostly caused by radioiodine and radiocaesium. Even after the radioiodine disappeared, radiocaesium continued to cause a problem. A map of the radioactive fallout in Sweden up to October 1986 shows a large area of about 1,000 km$^2$ containing between 10,000 and 40,000 Bq/m$^2$ and smaller, even more contaminated, areas (see figure 6.1). As a result, pastures and meadows were unsuitable for grazing and hay making.

At the end of May the Swedish authorities believed that, apart from the Gavle area, the rest of the country was unaffected. A few weeks later they discovered that the contamination was even worse in Lapland in the north. The Lapps (who inhabit the northern tundra regions of Sweden, Norway, Finland and the Kola Peninsula of the Soviet Union) are semi-nomadic reindeer herders who have lived in these areas for more than 10,000 years and who follow the regular migration of the

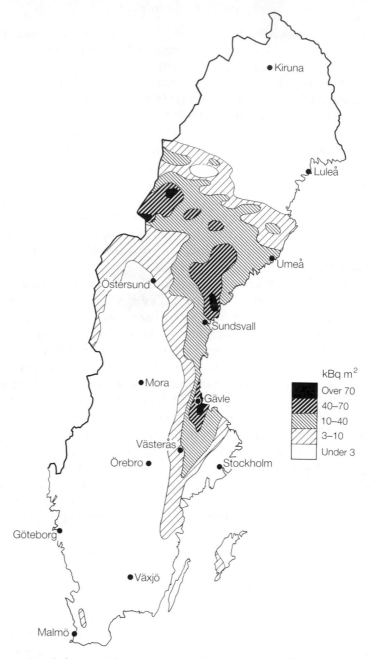

**Figure 6.1** Result from aerial surveys commissioned by the Swedish National Institute of Radiation Protection showing distribution caesium-137 ground contamination in kBq/m² ground surface on 19 September 1986 (quoted in *News and Views,* Information for Immigrants, Stockholm, November 1986, p. 3).

reindeer. They number about 70,000 and depend upon reindeer for food, clothing, implements and transport. In short, their entire income is derived from the reindeer herds. Moreover, reindeer remain the only renewable resource of the Arctic area.

Sweden had very stringent regulations about the amount of caesium-137 which is permitted in meat intended for consumption. By September, reindeer meat contained 4,000 Bq/kg, 12 times more than the permissible level of 300 Bq/kg. In October, when the reindeer changed to their winter diet of lichen scraped from under the snow, the level of caesium increased to 8,000, 16,000 and sometimes 30,000 Bq/kg. Lichen do not have roots and obtain all their nutrients from the air. They had, therefore, been heavily polluted. Moreover, they do not shed tissue in the way that other plants do. As a result it takes about nine years for the content of caesium-137 in lichen to reduce by half. It has been calculated that reindeer meat in this area will continue to have more than 1,000 Bq/kg of radiocaesium even after 36 years.[17] There are about 500,000 reindeer in Sweden of which 170,000 in Lapland are seriously contaminated and more than 300,000 elsewhere are less seriously affected.[18]

The Swedish government began to purchase the carcasses of contaminated animals to use as feed for fox and mink farms. Meat from about 50,000 reindeer had to be thrown away. Clean reindeer meat was imported for the Lapps to eat. Ironically, the main source was the Kola Peninsula in the Soviet Union, where the contamination level was much lower. The reindeer herds in Norway are less seriously contaminated than in Sweden. The help the deer herders, the Norwegian government raised the permissible level for caesium in reindeer meat from 300 Bq/kg to 6000 Bq/kg.[19] This was probably sensible as 300 Bq/kg is an extremely low level. The permissible level in Europe is 600 Bq/kg and in the US it is 1,500 Bq/kg. In 1987 Sweden also raised the permissible level to 1,500 Bq/kg. It was better to raise the permissible level for local consumption rather than take the risk of destroying the ancient traditions of the Lapp nation. If, as some officials had initially intended, the contaminated herds had been destroyed, the Lapps would almost certainly have had to be assimilated with the Swedes, Finns and Norwegians. Instead the Scandinavian governments helped them by providing commercial feed (free of caesium-137) for their reindeer and by developing feed high in potassium (potassium displaces caesium). Some reindeer were transported by truck to less contaminated areas of Finland. Although many Lapp families continued to eat reindeer meat, they were advised to give their children less contaminated food.

The effects on the reindeer indicate that the Soviet claim that Chernobyl caused no harm outside the borders of the Soviet Union is false. There were other effects in Scandinavia. Farmers around Gavle suffered long-term damage to their crops and livestock. In 1986 and 1987 green vegetables could not be cultivated in this area and pastures could not be used. In areas where the level of radiocaesium was higher than 10,000 Bq/m$^2$ (above 10 kBq/m$^2$ on the map shown in figure 6.1) in September 1986, the concentration of radiocaesium fell by four or five times in 1987 due to degradation of caesium-134 and the effect of the spring waters. Agriculture could therefore resume, but where the level was higher (20,000 Bq/m$^2$ and more), sheep and dairy farming continued to be affected in 1987 and 1988. The Swedish government had to continue compensating farmers and herders for their losses. In Sweden the economic cost of the Chernobyl accident was estimated to be well over US $100 million in 1986 alone.[20] Part of the cost came from loss of revenue caused by the decline in foreign tourism. Greatly exaggerated reports of the radiation levels in Sweden were published in various countries and extensive publicity was given to the plight of the Lapps. In the Lapp region between September 1986 and July 1987 there was heavy contamination of lake fish: their radioactivity varied between 2,600 and 28,000 Bq/kg.[21]

Strontium-90 and small amounts of plutonium were also identified in the fallout in Sweden. Sr-90/Cs-137 ratio in contaminated milk was only 1 per cent. In air and grass it was slightly higher (from 2 to 3 per cent).[22] But one unit of strontium-90 can give 5–15 times as large a dose contribution as one unit of caesium-137, particularly in children.

According to Swedish scientists the health risks to the Swedish population from the Chernobyl accident were not very serious. The collective effective dose commitment (for the next 50 years) was estimated to be about 10,000 man-sievert: 4,000–6,000 manSv were due to ground radiation; 2,000–3,000 came from internal radiation via food; the rest was inhaled.[23] The collective dose from hot particles had not been estimated by 1987 because it requires more complex calculations and research. As far as the radiation dose–cancer effect is concerned, Swedish authorities do not expect more than 100 extra cancer deaths caused by Chernobyl over the next 50 years. This figure will not be traceable in the statistics but it is based on the expectation that the population has followed the advice of the authorities that: '. . . people living mainly on reindeer meat may have to alter their living habits for several years in order to limit radiation doses. Those living to a great extent on the produce of forests, mountains and lakes may also have to reconsider their eating habits'.[24] In fact, it is unlikely that this advice was strictly followed but it is quite certain that the Chernobyl accident will be remembered in Sweden for a very long time. After the Three Mile Island nuclear accident in 1979, slightly more than 50 per cent of the Swedish population was against nuclear power. After the Chernobyl accident the proportion rose to 65 per cent.[25]

In 1988 and later, the Chernobyl fallout became an important topic for nuclear and environmental research, particularly in Sweden. The change of the isotope composition in the plume in samples collected from dry and wet deposition, from various distances from the reactor and from the initial and later releases, the transfer in foodstuffs and the behaviour in rural and urban areas all represented interesting problems for scientific study and made it possible to make predictions for various types of reactor accidents. Calculations showed that practically all the more volatile elements escaped from the fuel and the releases of radionuclides into the environment were substantially higher than originally reported in 1986.[26] Scientists paid particular attention to the hot particles and the changes that occurred in their character in the ten days of the graphite fire and the final heat-up period. Most of the particles represented fuel fragments (except for the carrier-free ruthenium particles). In Sweden the fuel fragment particles were between 1 and 20 $\mu$m in diameter. Some particles collected in Poland, however, were 10–30 times larger.[27] As shown in chapter 5, the local radiation exposure of the lungs due to the inhalation of hot particles is potentially a very serious danger, disproportionate to the comparatively small total-body irradiation.

## CENTRAL AND EASTERN EUROPE

Geographically, Hungary and Czechoslovakia are situated, along with East Germany and Austria, in Central Europe, not Eastern Europe. Eastern Europe is an established political designation. In analysing the effects of the Chernobyl accident, a political classification seems more appropriate than a geographic because the socialist countries of Central Europe have released very little information about the contamination they suffered and have not published a detailed assessment of their health risks. Austria, on the other hand, produced a detailed map of the pattern of fallout and particularly of the deposition of radiocaesium over its territory. Despite these differences, the two areas will be dealt with together in accordance with the way the radioactive plume moved about.

## Poland

Poland was more seriously affected by Chernobyl than any other country outside the Soviet Union. Eastern Poland was in the path of the initial plume which was undiluted when it reached Poland on the day of the accident. On 27–9 April almost all of Poland was covered by Chernobyl fallout when the wind changed to a westerly direction and moved towards western Czechoslovakia and Germany via Poland. Since the Polish authorities have never released reliable figures or maps of the contamination, it is difficult to present a comprehensive picture of the deposition of radioiodine and radiocaesium. Foreign diplomats took some measurements in Warsaw but did not find them high enough to warrant evacuating their families or other visiting nationals (foreign students were evacuated from Kiev and Minsk).

According to the British Embassy, the highest measured dose rate of gamma radiation in Warsaw was 0.4 microsieverts per hour and half of this value on 14 May 1986.[28] Allowing for radioactive decay and natural weathering, British experts believed that this level would not raise radiation above the permissible annual dose level for the public (5 mSv/year). However, the external gamma radiation in north-eastern Poland was ten times higher than this and it was even higher in border areas. Like other countries, Poland was not informed about the level of radioactivity on the Soviet border for 72 hours after the accident. But when the first figures were made available some spots (there were reports of serious contamination round the town of Mikolajki) showed levels as high as 105,000 Bq/kg of grass and well over 2,000 Bq/litre of milk.[29] The Polish government was the only European government which distributed iodine tablets to millions of children and made preparations to evacuate the population from heavily affected districts if it should prove necessary.

Restrictions were introduced on grazing cattle in both Hungary and Poland. But it was often impossible to keep farm animals indoors because of the shortage of hay and fodder. There were also restrictions on consuming milk produced by cattle grazing in pastures, but they applied to the level of radioiodine and not radiocaesium. Once the level of radioiodine had fallen and the panic had ended, the Polish authorities discontinued releasing contamination figures relating to radiocaesium and other radionuclides. Although Poland does not have any functioning nuclear reactors, two plants of 440 MWe each are under construction. One, near Gdansk, is expected to come into operation in 1991. The Chernobyl accident provoked some objections to the project, but they were not sufficiently serious to make the government change its nuclear programme.

Without maps showing the pattern of the fallout over Polish territory and data on measures taken to control food chains, it is practically impossible to make even an approximate assessment of the possible health impact of the accident. Polish agriculture is based on several million small individual farms. There is a chronic shortage of food in Poland. Any restrictions on the sale of milk and other food products would have brought hardship. Individual farmers ought to have been paid compensation by the government.

There were several unofficial reports of high levels of contamination in north-eastern districts which indicated that the milk there should proably have been destroyed because the radioiodine content was well above the permissible level.[30] But by the time these reports became known it was far too late for accurate measurements of this short-lived isotope. Polish representatives to the IAEA meeting in Vienna on 25–9 August, 1986 reported that the EC ban on food imports from Eastern Europe had resulted in a financial loss to Poland of about US $40 million. This was less than initially expected because the Soviet Union apparently purchased most of the meat exports that had been prepared for sale in the West.

An unpublished report on hot particles prepared by the Krakow Institute of nuclear physics indicated that border districts experienced the deposition of very large pieces of debris from the reactor core comparable to those collected in Minsk.[31] The hot particles found in Poland were often several hundred micromillimeters in diameter, larger than those recovered from other countries outside the Soviet Union. Later measurements summarized by US experts indicated that the highest levels of radiocaesium deposition outside the Soviet Union occurred in Poland. The Polish 'collective 50-year total body dose' was 150,000 person-grays, also higher than anywhere outside the Soviet Union. If the Soviet official figures can be believed, this was half of what was reported for the European part of the USSR.[32]

## Hungary

Hungary was less contaminated than Poland. The winds which blew the radioactive cloud in a northern and north-western direction on 26 and 27 April affected Poland, Germany and parts of Czechoslovakia and Austria, but they did not affect Hungary. When the wind direction changed on 29 April and began to move the radioactive aerosol south-westwards towards Moldavia and Romania, some radioactivity was brought to Hungary. Unlike Poland, Hungary already has two operational Soviet-made nuclear reactors of the VVER-440 type and two others are under construction. As a result, Hungary has a national radiation protection service. For reasons of credibility and impartiality, the Hungarian authorities co-operated with Austria in reporting radioactive deposits. In some districts, according to the official reports, fresh milk contained up to 2,600 Bq/litre of radioiodine from 1 to 4 May and its sale was banned. A week later the level had fallen to below the permissible level. Hungary's financial losses from the EC food import ban were greater than Poland's losses. The ban did not extend to Austria or Finland which had also been severely affected by fallout. But the reason was not political. Both Austria and Finland were prepared to allow the countries of the EC to measure the level of contamination in different agricultural districts or food-processing plants. The CMEA (Council for Mutual Economic Assistance) countries, on the other hand, refused any independent assessment of contamination. Hungary finally permitted Austrian experts to measure the contamination. In November it also published the level of surface radioactivity in the Debrecen region (between 2500 Bq/m$^2$ and 100 Bq/m$^2$ of beta activity from 1 May to 5 July) measured by the Institute of Nuclear Research.[33] After 25 May the radioactivity registered was not much higher than the normal background reading.

Hungary was the only socialist country to compensate its farmers for their losses. Livestock and horticulture farmers have received the equivalent of about US $10 million. The Hungarian Atomic Energy Commission prepared an official report for the IAEA on the radiation consequences of the Chernobyl accident,[34] but it has neither been published nor made available to independent researchers.

## Czechoslovakia and East Germany

Rain did not fall over Czechoslovakia and East Germany at the end of April and the first few days of May and therefore no protective measures against Chernobyl fallout were necessary. East Germany was excluded from the EC food import ban because neighbouring districts of West Germany were monitored and found comparatively clean. The Czech authorities introduced strict limits for the contamination of milk with radioiodine (1,000 Bq/litre) and there were a few cases in the middle of May when fresh cow and sheep milk from some areas was not recommended for direct consumption. The contaminated milk was not destroyed. No measures were introduced in East Germany to protect public health.

## Romania and Bulgaria

Romania and Bulgaria were badly affected by radioactive clouds after 29 April (the clouds moved on to Yugoslavia and Greece). The Soviet report for the IAEA shows that in some districts of Moldavia the contamination of milk was well above the permissible level, reaching 15–20,000 Bq/litre in some places.[35] Not surprisingly, the neighbouring districts in Romania also suffered. But the reaction of the Romanian authorities to the danger was even slower than that in Kiev. The first medical advice was given on 8–9 May. Children and pregnant women were told to stay indoors for some time and towns and cities were washed down frequently.[36] The authorities did not publish any figures to indicate the contamination by radioiodine or radiocaesium. The overall 50-year collective body dose in Romania was later calculated to be 92,000 person-Gy, the highest outside the Soviet Union after Poland.[37]

The authorities in Bulgaria prepared a report on the radiological situation after the Chernobyl accident but it was not made public.[38]

## Austria

Like other countries of Europe, Austria was affected by both the dry deposition of radioactivity (which was evenly distributed and not very serious) and by more serious wet deposition caused by rainfall and localized in spots which were not immediately found. In areas where there was rainfall the deposition of iodine-131, caesium-134 and caesium-137 was from ten to 100 times higher than in dry areas. The computer analysis of the distribution of the Chernobyl plume over Europe did not indicate that Austria was seriously affected. By the time the cloud reached Austria during 30 April–1 May, it had already been diluted and the release of radioactivity from the damaged reactor was low (the heat-up stage began on 2 May). But rainfall over several areas (Salzburg, Upper Austria and some parts of northern and western Austria) led to higher overall contamination than in Sweden, Norway or Finland.[39] The highest levels (over 17,000 Bq/m$^2$) did not affect large areas and are lower than the most contaminated areas in Sweden. But the area that was contaminated by levels of between 8,000 and

17,000 Bq/m$^2$ is larger and more densely populated. This means that the annual average dose to which Austrians were exposed was higher than the annual average dose to which Swedes were exposed.[40] The Austrians themselves calculated an even higher average dose – from 60–100 mrem/year.[41]

Austrian scientists carried out independent studies of the contamination of food products. The University of Vienna organized the sampling of cow's milk delivered to dairies and milk sold in supermarkets in the Vienna area. Pooled breast milk was also studied for the whole period of 1986.[42] The concentration of iodine-131 in cow's milk delivered to dairies in the first two weeks after the accident was between 0 and 3,550 Bq/litre. The level of radioiodine in milk in supermarkets was no higher than 200 Bq/litre. However, when the concentration of radioiodine began to decrease in May and June, the concentration of radiocaesium increased, reaching its peak in June (between 0 and 610 Bq/litre). Some increase was expected during the winter when the cattle began to consume hay and silage which had been contaminated in May. The presence of radioisotopes in breast milk was about ten times lower than in cow's milk. Nursing mothers were advised to continue breast feeding for as long as possible. The Vienna area, however, was not seriously contaminated and much higher concentrations of radio-caesium were found along the Austro-Hungarian border and in the Austrian Alps. The highest contamination was found in sheep's milk. Up to 41,800 Bq/litre was found in the most contaminated spots in May 1986.[43] Large amounts of leafy vegetables, especially spinach and green salad, were destroyed because of contamination up to 37,000 Bq/kg. Once the iodine peak was over, caesium became the main problem. In some areas honey contained higher amounts of radiocaesium than green vegetables and fruit.

The economic effect on agriculture in the mountainous parts of Austria and areas of high deposition was substantial. People in these areas received doses about ten times higher than the average for the country. In the Salzburg district, for example, the average environmental contamination in May 1986 was four times higher than in the Vienna area. Innsbruck was also seriously affected. The highest levels of beta and gamma radiation were registered in Hoheand Boden, where there were nearly 3,000 $\mu$R/h of beta and gamma radiation for several days in May.[44] The Austrian Ministry of Health and Environmental Control issued instructions to prevent cattle feeding on grass. The distribution of milk in schools was halted for some time and the sale of many kinds of vegetable was banned. Cattle and other livestock were screened at slaughter houses. In Salzburg, a tourist centre, a register of radiation levels was produced for each street.

Austria had built only one nuclear plant at Zwentendorf. After the accident the Austrian government announced that no further nuclear power stations would be constructed and that the Zwentendorf plant would be dismantled in due course. The government paid about US $80 million compensation to its farmers for their losses.[45]

## Summary of effects on Central and Eastern Europe

It is relatively easy to estimate the financial loss caused by the ban on food imports from Eastern Europe which lasted for most of the agricultural season in 1986: it has been estimated at about US $300 million. It is far harder to estimate the overall economic impact caused by control measures and restrictions. The losses were probably not very great because so few restrictions were introduced or enforced. The health impact of the Chernobyl fallout in Central and Eastern Europe will be higher than in Western Europe.

Indirect assessments can be made from the general comparison of soil contamination in different countries carried out by the Harwell Laboratory Environmental Study Group[46] shown in table 6.1. Soil samples were obtained from many countries of the world through colleagues and through the Foreign and Commonwealth Office. They were taken during May 1986 from undisturbed grassland, where possible to a depth of about 5 cm and from an area of about 900 $cm^2$. Some samples were obtained early enough to determine the presence of iodine-131. All the samples were analysed for two isotopes of radiocaesium, radioiodine and radioruthenium. Caesium-137 deposits attributable to Chernobyl were derived from the shorter-lived caesium-134 using the Cs-134/Cs-137 ratio in air of 0.6. Unfortunately, Poland, Romania, Sweden, Germany and Finland were represented in this analysis only by their capitals, which were less affected than other parts of those countries. But in general it is clear that there was a four to six times difference between the contamination of Eastern and Western Europe. Hungary, as seen in the table, suffered more than other countries but only in some spots. The table does not reflect overall contamination. The Hungarian border area, where caesium-137 was present in amounts as high as 23,000 Bq/$m^2$, will certainly be unsuitable for meat and milk production for many years if Western safety standards are used. If the authors of this study had been able to obtain soil samples from eastern parts of Poland and Romania which border

Table 6.1   *Radioactive contamination of samples of soil from different countries attributable to Chernobyl (European data only – from the world-wide collection of samples measured in Harwell AERE laboratory)*

| Sampling site | Caesium-134 (Bq/m²) | Caesium-137 (Bq/m²) | Iodine-131 (Bq/m²) | Ruthenium-103 (Bq/m²) |
|---|---|---|---|---|
| Bucharest | 2,600 | 4,300 | 31,000 | 17,000 |
| Sofia | 430 | 720 | 7,100 | 2,400 |
| Prague | 2,900 | 4,900 | 25,700 | 6,300 |
| Belgrade | 4,400 | 7,300 | 26,000 | 21,000 |
| Budapest | 5,300 | 8,800 | | 25,000 |
| Warsaw | 1,700 | 2,860 | 18,500 | 3,900 |
| Austro-Hungarian border | 14,000 | 23,000 | 71,000 | 24,000 |
| Austro-Czech border | 490 | 790 | 10,000 | 1,820 |
| Vienna | 700 | 1,150 | 12,500 | 2,700 |
| Ankara | 200 | 330 | | 1,120 |
| Athens | 190 | 310 | 9,900 | 2,000 |
| Bonn | 930 | 1,550 | | 2,700 |
| Rioms, France | 960 | 1,600 | 13,000 | 4,000 |
| Clevennes, France | 970 | 1,600 | | 3,800 |
| La Cardiere, France | 230 | 390 | | 1,050 |
| Remy, France | 175 | 290 | 1,850 | 800 |
| Cluny, France | 680 | 1,150 | 9,000 | 2,900 |
| Soissons, France | 155 | 260 | 4,200 | 580 |
| Reykjavik | 4 | 7 | 180 | 11 |
| Stockholm | 260 | 430 | 13,000 | 620 |
| Helsinki | 590 | 990 | 7,000 | 1,850 |

*Source*: Cambray et al. (1987) *Nuclear Energy*, 26 (2), 77–101.

Byelorussia and Moldavia, their measurements would probably have shown much higher readings of radioactivity.

### THE EUROPEAN COMMUNITY

The countries of the EC do not have a common policy on radiation protection. Each country imposes its own permissible level of contamination of food and other products and each has a different attitude towards nuclear energy. They did not make a common response to the Chernobyl accident and the resulting contamination of the environment. It is therefore necessary to consider the effects of the accident, and the response to it, in each individual country.

An attempt was made to co-ordinate studies of the fallout through United Nations agencies, NATO agencies and organizations of the EC. The British National Radiological Protection Board (NRPB) was asked to make a preliminary assessment of the radiological consequences of the accident to the population of the EC. The study was completed in March 1987 and distributed widely for comment.[47] A summary was published in April 1987 in all major European newspapers. However, the methods by which the NRPB calculated the health risks are not universally accepted. The radiological services in the United States consider them too conservative. Other independent radiology and radiobiology experts also use different methods to calculate health risks. The main areas of disagreement are indicated in this section. Although the way in which health risks are calculated are likely to change often in the future, the basic information about the level of environmental contamination in various countries will probably remain valid.

The general conclusions of the NRPB assessment did not cause alarm. They were far more modest than other, more rapid assessments made in 1986. The NRPB summarized its findings in a press release:

> The collective dose (the average dose times the number of people) in the EC is estimated to be about 80,000 man sieverts. This may be compared to the collected effective dose from natural background radiation of about 500,000 man sieverts every year.
>
> In some countries the restrictions placed on consumption of contaminated foods are estimated to have reduced doses to the most exposed individuals by about half.
>
> The lowest average doses per person were received in Spain (1–2 microsieverts) and Portugal (0.3 microsieverts), and the highest in West Germany, Italy and Greece (300–500 microsieverts). The average dose in the UK is 50 microsieverts – about one tenth of the figure for West Germany.
>
> Some individual doses were substantially higher than these average figures. For example, a few people in areas of high deposits of radioactivity, in NW England and parts of Scotland and Wales, received doses higher than 1000 microsieverts (similar to 1 year of natural background). Doses in parts of West Germany and Greece reached 2000–4000 microsieverts.
>
> Because of the presence of radioactive iodine in the deposit, the doses to thyroids, especially of young children, were up to 10 times those for the whole body.
>
> Over the next fifty years about thirty million people in EC countries will die of 'natural' cancers. The theoretical number of extra cancers predicted due to the Chernobyl accident is of the order of 1000. It will therefore be impossible to detect the health impact of the accident.[48]

Table 6.2 compares the possible health effect of the Chernobyl accident in different countries, as calculated by the NRPB and by American experts. The difference between the two sets of assessments is

*The Global Impact*

Table 6.2 *Collective effective doses*

| Country | Collective effective dose All time NRPB estimates | (man-Sv or person-Gy) 50-year exposure American estimates |
|---|---|---|
| Belgium | 940 | 880 |
| Denmark | 1,100 | 820 |
| France | 5,600 | 12,000 |
| FRG | 30,000 | 58,000 |
| Greece | 8,500 | 4,700 |
| Ireland | 950 | 1,800 |
| Italy | 27,000 | 52,000 |
| Luxembourg | 42 | 76 |
| Netherlands | 1,200 | 3,400 |
| Portugal | 2.3 | low |
| Spain | 57 | low |
| UK | 3,000 | 15,000 |
| Total | 78,000 | 148,700 |

*Sources*: M. Morrey, J. Brown, J. A. Williams, M. J. Crick, J. R. Simmonds and M. D. Hill, *A preliminary assessment of the radiological impact of the Chernobyl reactor accident on the pollution of the European Community* (Chilton, Oxon., National Radiological Protection Board, January 1987); L. R. Anspaugh, R. J. Catlin and M. Goldman, 'The global impact of the Chernobyl reactor accident', *Science*, 242 (1988), 1512–19.

striking. The NRPB calculations were done hastily, to coincide with the first anniversary of the accident[49] The American calculations, sponsored by the Lawrence Livermore National Laboratory, the Radiation Studies Programme, the Electric Power Research Institute and the University of California, are in line with the US Energy Department Report. They are probably more accurate. Paradoxically, the largest discrepancy between the two assessments is for the United Kingdom. The persistent reports in 1988 and 1989 about higher levels of radiocaesium in some parts of the United Kingdom suggest that the NRPB underestimated the level of contamination.[50]

There was considerable disagreement about the total release of radiocaesium from the Chernobyl reactor. The figures given by the Soviet Union (0.5 MCi of caesium-134 and 1.0 MCi of caesium-137, or about 13 per cent of the total inventory of radiocaesium in the reactor) were calcualted on the basis of radiocaesium deposition inside the Soviet Union only.[51] The Soviet authorities never attempted to calculate the world-wide distribution of radionuclides for the simple reason that they wanted to avoid liability. However, the Environmental Studies Group of the Harwell UK Atomic Energy Authority carried out an independent analysis of the radiocaesium fallout in Europe. This study was completed in 1987 and it concludes that the total release of caesium-137 was as high as 25 per cent of the total inventory.[52] Similar figures were reported by other independent European research groups which estimated that the amount of caesium-137 deposited outside the Soviet Union was between 2.2 and $5 \times 10^{16}$ Bq.[53] This is comparable to the Soviet figure for caesium-137 deposited inside the Soviet Union, mainly in European Russia ($3.7 \times 10^{16}$ Bq). The British figure of up to 25 per cent of the total inventory was thought later, when the global distribution of Chernobyl radioactivity was investigated, to be too low.

The United States Department of Energy (DOE) sponsored an extensive study of the health and environmental consequences of the Chernobyl accident. Preliminary results were distributed in January 1987 and a more comprehensive report became available in April 1987.[54] Most of the study was conducted at the Department of Radiological Sciences at the University of California, Davis by Professor M. Goldman's group. I visited this laboratory in May 1987 and looked through their background data. The DOE study did not take any official Soviet figures for granted. It analysed the figures of Chernobyl contamination by radionuclides reported world-wide and from all kinds of samples (including aircraft swipe samples on flights from Moscow, London, New York, Tokyo and other capitals). This is the most sophisticated and complete account of the fallout beyond the USSR. In 1988 the figures of this study were checked on the basis of all additional information that was available.[55]

The DOE study discovered, among other findings, that radionuclides from Chernobyl penetrated far higher altitudes than had earlier been assumed. The measurements were used to test a global model of the fallout cloud created by a computer model known as PATRIC, based at the Lawrence Livermore National Laboratory. PATRIC uses US Air Force weather data to produce a three-dimensional image of radioactive debris moving in space and time. Its results were compared to those from two European models, one based at Bilthoven in the Netherlands (GRID) and the other at Imperial College, London (MESOS). This study concludes that the amount of caesium-137 in the Chernobyl fallout was three times more than MESOS study assumed and 40 per cent higher than the GRID estimation. Roughly 1 million curies fell within Soviet borders, 1 million curies fell on the rest of Europe and 1 million curies spread throughout the northern hemisphere.

If one adds caesium-134 to this, at least 1.5 MCi of radiocaesium must have been deposited in Europe outside the Soviet Union. However, the US DOE and the US Environmental Protection Agency also used different methods to those used by the NRPB to assess the health impact of Chernobyl. The American method assumes a risk factor of 2.3 fatal cancers per 10,000 person-rem, which is higher than the risk factor used by the NRPB.[56] American experts use the wide and comprehensive experience they have acquired, particularly from the long-term results of the early and late effects of the bombs dropped on Hiroshima and Nagasaki. Using a risk factor of 2.3 fatal cancers per 10,000 person-rem, the number of expected extra cancer deaths in the EC from Chernobyl was expected to be from 5,000 to 6,000, less than might be expected from the amount of radiocaesium deposited, because the effective countermeasures taken in the EC reduced the risk. None the less the American estimates for the EC are much higher than those of the NRPB. But even if there are as many as 5,000 extra cancer deaths, they will not be statistically traceable in Western Europe in the next 50 years. But fatal cancers are not the only serious resultant health hazard. There will also be genetic problems, mental retardation and other health problems caused by the Chernobyl accident.[57]

The general descriptions and projections do not deal with the fact that there are a number of hot spots in Western Europe where serious problems continued in 1988, particularly for agriculture and food consumption. The rural population is a far smaller proportion of the population in Western Europe (only 3 per cent of the population is actively engaged in agriculture) than in Poland, Hungary, Romania and Yugoslavia (where about 10–20 per cent of the population is rural). In the next section only those countries that paid a high economic price as a result of loss of agricultural produce and the introduction of counter-measures are reviewed.

## Federal Rebublic of Germany

The NRPB and US studies found that the collective effective dose of the total population was highest for the FRG. But the major part of this dose was absorbed by people in south Germany where the average individual effective dose of internal and external radiation for 50 years was 1,000 microsievert, ten times higher than in the north. Critical individuals (infants and young children) received, on average, nearly 3,800 microsievert.[58] This was the highest dose in Western Europe. Moreover, in working out this dose, the NRPB took account of the protective countermeasures imposed by the German government (particularly in the food chains) which were thought to have reduced the possible health impact by 37 per cent (in France official countermeasures only reduced the health impact by 12 per cent and in Britain the impact was reduced by 25 per cent).[59] Thyroid doses caused by iodine-131 were also highest in the FRG (up to 30,000 microsievert in critical groups of the population in southern parts).

The German government published a very detailed official report of the effects of the accident in 1987.[60] Other studies were undertaken by German physicists and radiobiologists of the isotope composition of the fallout and the character of hot particles.[61]

The map showing the distribution of caesium-137 in the FRG calculated for May 1986 (figure 6.2) indicates that the main deposition was in south Germany along the border with Austria and Switzerland. It was caused by rain and heavy thunder showers which occurred in this area from 29 April to 2 May 1986. The deposition of caesium-137 reached 40,000–45,000 Bq/m² (50 per cent higher if caesium-134 is also taken into account) in some hot spots. In those spots there was also 45,000–55,000 Bq/m² of ruthenium.

Most green vegetables in the areas around Munich had to be destroyed because they were severely contaminated with 2,000–20,000 Bq/kg of iodine-131 and 2,000–9,000 Bq/kg of radiocaesium in 1986.[62] The permissible level of iodine-131 in milk was set at 500 Bq/litre and controls were strictly enforced. The official German report gives a great deal of information about the contamination of individual food products in different parts of the country in 1986. The average total effective dose per person was not considered alarming: 90 mrem for a child and 70 mrem for an adult in 1986, which was well below the natural radiation exposure of 200 mrem per year (1 rem is equal to 0.01 sievert). However, the average dose in the south was far higher than in the north. For example, in Munich, the dose was five or six times higher than the dose in Hamburg.[63]

Table 6.3 shows some of the general conclusions of the official German report. Like the NRPB report, a conservative approach was used in estimating the future health impact of the Chernobyl accident. The report concluded that, although the deposition in 1986 was serious because of the short-lived iodine-131, on average the Chernobyl deposition would add insignificant amounts to the radioactivity from natural sources for 1987, 1988 and later. Germany was affected by two waves of deposition (from the initial cloud and from the cloud formed during the heat-up period). As a result, substantial amounts of ruthenium-103, comparable to the amount of caesium-137, were deposited. Natural thyroid cancer mortality (0.01 per cent) may rise

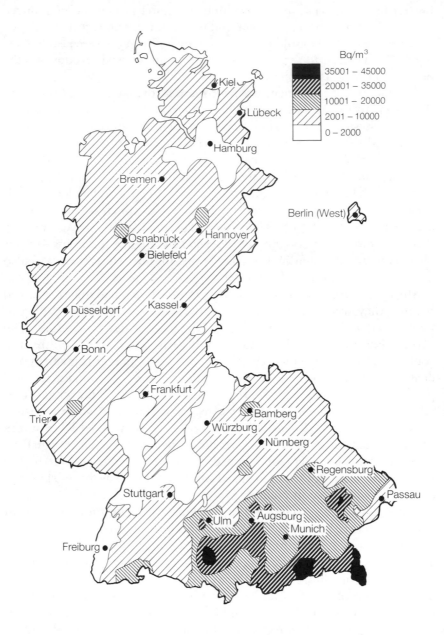

**Figure 6.2** Distribution of caesium-137 ground contamination (Bq/m$^2$) in FRG May 1986 (from *Auswirkugen des Reactorunfalls in Tschernobyl auf die Bundesrepublik Deutschland. Zusammenfassender Bericht der Strahlenschutzkommission. Stuttgart, Gustav Fischer Verlag, 1987, p. 47).

Table 6.3 *Average effective doses in the first year after the accident and in 50 years*

| Area | Effective dose first year | | Accumulated effective dose 50 years | |
|---|---|---|---|---|
| | (mSv) | (mrem) | (mSv) | (mrem) |
| Area north of the Alps | 1.2 | 120 | 3.8 | 380 |
| Area south of the Danube | 0.6 | 60 | 1.9 | 190 |
| Area north of the Danube | 0.2 | 20 | 0.6 | 60 |

slightly by not more than 1 per cent for children who are now between 1 and 10 years old (the rise will be less in the north). The mortality from cancer diseases attributable to Chernobyl is calculated on the basis of the median total effective dose for 50 years. It would vary from 0.01 to 0.05 per cent in the south and a third of this in the north. Statistically the increase will be too small to be registered. The report did not express the expected increased mortality in concrete numbers, perhaps because the number will be higher than for the rest of Western Europe.

Independent studies found that there were wide variations in contamination even within small districts in the FRG. Nuclear physicists at the University of Konstanz, for example, found that the gross beta activity at ground level in the state of Baden-Wurttemberg varied by as much as 30-fold.[64] They identified radioactive hot particles sticking to the grass which could not be removed by drying or vigorous shaking. They were also found in silos and barns. Near Konstanz the surface contamination was 10,000 Bq/m². The typical storage facilities of a small farm contained from 1 to 5 millicuries of radiocaesium (5 mCi is enough to spoil about 100,000 litres of milk if the permissible level is 500 Bq/litre). The grass and hay were so contaminated that they had to be destroyed to comply with the radiation protection laws in Germany and most other European countries. The Konstanz scientists suggested that beta-emitting hot particles might be permanently trapped in the lungs of individuals exposed to contaminated hay and they pointed out that the consequences were unpredictable because so little is known about the biological effects of hot particles. All that is known is that cells are destroyed in the area around a hot particle and that alpha-emitting particles are more dangerous than beta-emitting ones.

In a study comparing the distribution of caesium-137 around Heidelberg with other parts of the FRG and Austria, variations were found as broad as between 800–1,000 Bq/m² in 0–5 cm of soil to

20,000–24,000 around Munich and 33,500 $Bq/m^2$ near Salzburg in Austria.[65] The authors calculated that only about 500 $Bq/m^2$ of the radiocaesium represented the inventory from all nuclear weapons tests. In the whole of Germany there is five to ten times more caesium-137 as a result of the Chernobyl accident than the caesium-137 left from all previous nuclear weapons tests.

## United Kingdom

In the United Kingdom, as in other Western countries, there were both government-sponsored and independent studies of the Chernobyl fallout. Since the Chernobyl fallout could be distinguished from natural radiation (caused partly by radiation from natural sources and partly by the global fallout created by the nuclear weapons tests of the 1950s and 1960s), it could be used for research into ecological and food chains.

The United Kingdom was, for the most part, affected by fallout rather later than the rest of Europe. The Chernobyl cloud arrived on 2–4 May 1986. Rain in some western areas resulted in a high deposition of radioiodine and radiocaesium in Northern Ireland and the northern part of Eire (see figure 6.3). Studies of the radionuclide levels in soil, plants, food, animals, agricultural products and human tissue were sponsored by the National Radiological Protection Board, the Harwell Laboratories of the AERE and the Ministry of Agriculture, Fisheries and Food. A number of well documented reports emerged from this research.[66] In North Wales, Cumbria, Northern Ireland and Scotland, where heavy rain fell on 2 and 3 May, the surface contamination of grass by caesium-137 varied from 2,000 $Bq/m^2$ to 6,000 $Bq/m^2$. Some spots in Cumbria were more heavily contaminated (from 10,000 to 13,000 $Bq/m^2$ of caesium-137 plus caesium-134 and ruthenium-103 and radioiodine). In these areas the sale of sheep and lambs was banned (in Britain the permissible level is 1,000 Bq/kg). Since it took some time for radiocaesium to accumulate in animals, it was not until mid-June that levels of more than 1,000 Bq/kg in lamb and mutton became quite common (the accumulation of radiocaesium continues for up to three months and then it declines if the concentration of caesium in the environment also declines). Continuous measurements were made for each district and, where possible, on each individual farm. In Wales and Scotland the ban on sales affected 3 million sheep and lambs. It was not necessary to destroy the animals and wool production was not affected. The main economic loss resulted from the ban on sales and from restrictions on moving contaminated animals to new grazing grounds.

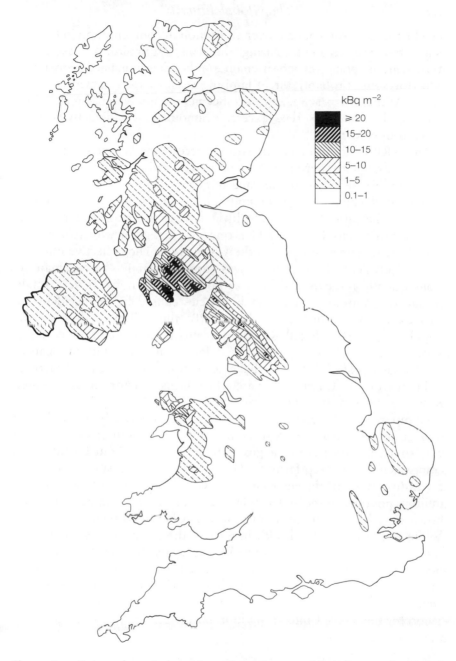

**Figure 6.3** Estimated total deposition of caesium-137 (kBq/m²) over the United Kingdom due to Chernobyl releases, calculated from a washout factor $6.5 \times 10^5$, the rainfall data and air concentrations (from F. B. Smith and M. J. Clark, 'Radionuclide deposition from the Chernobyl cloud', *Nature*, 322, 1986, pp. 690–1.

The British government paid over £4 million in compensation in the first year after the accident. During the 1987 agricultural season, the movement of about 300,000 sheep on 466 holdings remained restricted;[67] two (for some probably three) lambing seasons were ruined on these farms. At the end of 1987, 475,000 sheep could not be sent for slaughter because they had absorbed excessive amounts of radioactivity from grass in upland areas.[68]

The NRPB did not make any specific recommendations to the public after the first alarm in May 1986 (concerning radioiodine in particular). Even in more heavily contaminated hot spots the level of radiocaesium in the food chain (mostly in milk and meat) was very low and it increased the natural radiation by little more than 1 or 2 per cent.[69] The standard risk factor for the NRPB is one fatal malignancy for 100 man-Sv (which is 2.3 times lower than the US figures). The collective effective dose equivalent commitment was approximately 3,000 man-Sv. Consequently the expected health impact of Chernobyl is very small. About 100 non-fatal thyroid malignancies caused by the accident are also expected. According to the NRPB, the collective dose to the population of the United Kingdom from natural radiation is about 100,000 man-Sv, which gives a risk factor of 1,300 putative cancer deaths each year.[70] But as we have seen from table 6.2, the American estimates of the Chernobyl-related health risk factors in the United Kingdom are five times higher than this.

Compared to the effects on the FRG and Austria, both the health impact and the economic cost to the United Kingdom of Chernobyl is very small. By April 1987 the government had paid about £5 million in compensation to sheep farmers. The administrative cost of monitoring the radioactivity of the environment, livestock and imports was several million pounds. Some independent groups in the United Kingdom, however, take a far more serious view of Chernobyl-related problems. While it is true that the health impact of the accident was minimal, it was more serious than the 1957 Windscale reactor accident, the only previous reactor accident which resulted in significant releases of radionuclides. The Windscale accident caused a total effective dose equivalent commitment in man-sieverts of 150 man-Sv for Cumbria and 1,900 for the whole United Kingdom, far lower than the dose caused by the Chernobyl accident.[71]

## Other EC countries

As table 6.2 shows, the next most seriously affected country was Italy. Northern Italy bore the brunt of the contamination. In May 1986 the sale of fresh vegetables and milk was restricted in that area because of iodine-131. However, the iodine-131 decayed rapidly and it was only the amount of caesium-137 that put Italy in the same category as Germany.

The French authorities were extremely reluctant to issue any advice to the public. This did not prevent French scientists from monitoring the situation and publishing their results. The first scientific study of the level and composition of the Chernobyl fallout in France was published in June 1986.[72] By then the main problem was radiocaesium (earlier iodine-131 contamination of leafy vegetables had made it necessary to destroy large amounts of fresh vegetables in several districts). In June the concentration of caesium-137 on the ground around Paris was 400 times higher than in 1963 before the partial test ban treaty was signed. In absolute figures the level was not considered dangerous (between 2 and 41 mCi/km$^2$ or about 74–2,500 Bq/m$^2$). The radioactive plume was first detected over Paris on 29 April and 20 short- and long-lived radionuclides were identified. There was a second passage of the radioactive cloud over France between 10 and 19 May. Traces of plutonium-239 and 240 were also recorded.

The absence of heavy rain in France in late April and early May spared French farmers the problems caused by hot spots. Some independent anti-nuclear groups later claimed, however, that hot spots were found in south-east France. In some areas 90,000 Bq/m$^2$ were said to have been registered and, in Corsica, sheep milk was heavily contaminated by iodine-131 (in some cases up to 15,000 Bq-litre).[73]

The problem of Corsican sheep milk illustrates the unexpected and unpredictable consequences that occurred. In northern Turkey tea leaves were contaminated and this affected the export of tea. In Greece the sudden panic caused by Chernobyl led to an increase in the number of abortions in May and June 1986. In a few cases specific food products were more contaminated in 1987 than in 1986. Mushrooms, for example, drew nutrients in 1987 from the contaminated leaves of 1986 which had fallen in the autumn. When mushrooms are dried, the concentration of radiocaesium increases. As a result some dry mushrooms in late summer and autumn 1987 contained as much as 24,000 Bq/kg of radiocaesium. The West German and French authorities advised people to avoid wild mushrooms.[74]

THE REST OF THE WORLD

Fallout from Chernobyl was registered in every country of the northern hemisphere, but it was only in the Soviet Union and Europe that levels were high enough to affect human health and agriculture. The world-wide distribution of radioactive isotopes from a single source inside the Soviet Union was used for scientific research. The pattern of radionuclides in the United States and Japan was compared to the pattern in Europe, for example, and the change over time was monitored.[75] Other studies examined how much radioactivity reached distant areas in the form of aerosol and how much in gaseous form (the gas–aerosol ratio was found to be the same over Tennessee as over Sweden).[76]

The United States, Canada and Japan set up monitoring services to check tourists and students returning from Western and Eastern Europe and from the USSR. Several Japanese tourists were in Kiev at the time of the accident. Although they had detectable levels of radioiodine, it was not considered high enough to cause concern. In Japan and the United States there was concern that there would be a world-wide slowdown in nuclear energy development, similar to the one that had been triggered by the Three Mile Island accident in 1979. No new nuclear energy plants had been commissioned in the United States since 1979. The nuclear industry had hoped that the memory of the accident would fade with time. The Chernobyl accident dashed these hopes. Japan was in the middle of a very ambitious programme of nuclear power development. The Japanese Atomic Industrial Forum was so concerned about public reaction that Japan did not even send a delegation to Vienna for the IAEA post-Chernobyl review meeting in August 1986 in order to avoid having to report the results of the meeting back home.

CONCLUSION

Perhaps the most important global effect of the Chernobyl accident was an irreversible shift in public and scientific attitudes towards the safety of nuclear power. The use of nuclear power expanded significantly after the oil embargo in 1973 and the energy crisis of 1974–5. At that time various governmental studies concluded that nuclear power was safer than any other industrial project. The United States was the main exporter of nuclear reactor technology to the rest of the world. Most countries accepted the American safety estimates presented for a discussion of nuclear reactor safety in the United States Congress in 1973 and ignored the warnings of environmental groups and individual scientists. The Soviet leadership also accepted American safety estimates rather than sponsor research based on the Soviet safety record. According to the American study, there was a very low feasibility of a major reactor accident (partial meltdown of the core) and a maximal accident (massive release of radioactivity into the environment) was improbable.[77] Accidents linked to a breach in the third level of safety of the containment structures or safety systems which protect the public were considered impossible. It was expected that major accidents which would breach the second level of safety and lead to a partial meltdown of the core would happen only once in 10,000 years. It was accepted that minor incidents were quite common in operating reactors and nearly 600 such incidents (termed 'unusual occurrences') were registered for 1973 in all systems (control rods and drives, safety systems, instrumentation, emergency power supplies, pipes, pumps, valves, human errors and so on). Of these, 20 per cent were identified as 'potentially significant' and selected for additional review.[78]

Although the Three Mile Island accident in 1979 cast some doubt on these assumptions, a 'maximal accident' continued to be considered improbable because the containment structure was not breached at Three Mile Island and the reactor did not explode or release radioactivity into the environment. But after 1979 American scientists did not repeat their very optimistic 1973 safety predictions. Soviet authors, however, continued using them for public relations purposes. The figures indicated that if the annual chance of death from all types of cancer for Americans was 1:650, the death risk from cancer arising from radiation linked to nuclear effluents was 1:25,000,000. In other words, only about eight people die annually from cancer which can be linked to an operating reactor. This figure included the staff of nuclear plants who deal with radioactivity during their normal work. The death risk for the public from a reactor accident was calculated to be 1:10 billion (or one American in 50 years). Cancer from medical X-rays was much more common: for every one person who developed cancer from radioactivity released by nuclear plants, 250 people developed it from routine diagnostic X-rays.[79] It was also calculated that the average American received the following whole-body exposure (in millirems): 130 from natural sources; 4 from fallout after tests of nuclear weapons; 72 from medical diagnosis and treatment; 1.9 from commercial products; 0.1 from television screens; and 0.003 from commercial nuclear power facilities.[80]

Projecting to the year 2000, when nearly 30–40 per cent of electric energy was expected to come from nuclear plants, did not greatly affect the estimates. In the US the number of non-radiation fatal cancers was expected to be 486,000 annually: 1,310 from background radiation; 3,720 from medical X-ray; and 10 from nuclear effluents from reactors.[81] All these estimates (and many others) became irrelevant after Chernobyl, even if it was assumed that a Chernobyl-type accident could never occur in the West. There is no border protection from nuclear effluents, as the world-wide distribution of radioiodine and radiocaesium from Chernobyl proved. The American public was spared but, on average, American citizens received much higher doses of radiation from Chernobyl than the 0.003 mR which they expected from their own reactors.

For the 550 million Europeans outside the USSR the most reliable calculation of future radiation exposure from radiocaesium alone was 580,000 man-Gy.[82] This included the dose commitment from external radiation and from ingestion. The collective dose is calculated over 50 years, but about half of it has already been delivered, because the first years matter more. Even if the dose was spread evenly over 50 years, it would mean 2 mR per year per person in Europe in the next 50 years, nearly 700 times higher than the American estimates of possible radiation from reactors.

In Europe the fallout of radiocaesium resulting from the Chernobyl accident is higher than the fallout from nuclear tests in the atmosphere, because by 1986 the global fallout from such tests was well below the level in the early 1970s when the American figures were published. However, some areas in a number of countries were affected more seriously. In many hot spots in Europe (such as Lapland, parts of south Germany, the Austro-Hungarian border, east Poland) the mean exposure from Chernobyl fallout is up to 50 or even 100 times higher than average. For more than 3 million people the average individual dose commitment is about 10–20 mSv. This is less than the maximum dose limit over a lifetime of 70 mSv for an ordinary citizen. But it is within the same range and should not be considered insignificant.

A number of Soviet press statements ridiculed the 'radiation phobia' in the West and implied that the health danger from nuclear tests was greater than the danger caused by the release of radionuclides from Chernobyl. If one considers the general figures, this argument has some validity. The total amount of radiocaesium produced by nearly 20 years of atmospheric nuclear tests was 10–20 times higher than the total amount of radiocaesium released during the accident. But because nuclear test sites were located in remote, sparsely populated places and the Chernobyl fallout affected densely populated areas, the total radiation dose absorbed by people from nuclear tests and from the Chernobyl accident are, in fact, comparable. The atmospheric tests in the 1950s and early 1960s produced almost $10^{21}$ Bq of iodine-131, $10^{18}$ Bq of caesium-137 and about $5 \times 10^{17}$ of strontium-90.[83] The Goldman report for the US DOE indicates that the radiocaesium *dose* from Chernobyl to the northern hemisphere is about 60 per cent of the radiocaesium dose from the tests of more than 200 atomic and nuclear bombs.[84] However, Chernobyl caused more contamination in Europe than all nuclear weapons tests since 1945 combined.

For radiocaesium alone the cancer risk is nearly equal for the Soviet Union and for the rest of Europe because of the higher population density in countries west of the Soviet border. But people outside the Soviet Union were mostly spared contamination by other longer-lived isotopes (like strontium-90 or plutonium). Only Poland, Sweden and Finland, which were affected by the cloud during the day after the first explosion have to take other radionuclides into account, particularly because the ratio between caesium and strontium will change because of the lower rate of excretion of strontium from the human body than of caesium. In Sweden the ratio of strontium-90 to caesium-137 in May varied between 1:100 and 3:100.[85] In the fallout from nuclear tests this ratio was 0.6:1. In some parts of the exclusion zone around Chernobyl and in areas close by the ratio was 1:1.[86] It is likely that the danger of strontium-90 is detectable in eastern Poland but there are no figures to demonstrate this.

When one examines the contamination caused by Chernobyl great differences are obvious between Western and Eastern Europe not only in the general level of responsibility of governments in informing their own citizens, but in the technical level of their capacity to monitor nation-wide contamination and to take countermeasures based on the results. Although the Western European countries were not perfect, their response to the emergency was in all respects superior to that of Eastern European countries. Even the Soviet Union eventually released more information than its CMEA allies.

The total dose commitment (mostly from radiocaesium) will be corrected in the future on the basis of actual measurements of radioactivity in soil, water and food products, but it is unlikely that the corrections will greatly change the assessments that have already been made. It will also be possible to calculate the economic cost of Chernobyl to Western Europe from the compensation paid by governments for losses in sales, restrictions on grazing and other countemeasures. Of the Eastern European countries, only Hungary paid about US $10 million compensation to its farmers (about the same amount that the British government paid to affected farmers). The Austrian government paid nearly $70 million to its farmers, and the West German government paid more than $100 million. But this is only part of the loss caused by Chernobyl. If one adds the losses caused by the ban on food experts from Eastern Europe (in 1986 close to $300 million), the loss from tourism (particularly for Sweden, Austria and Italy) and the many indirect losses, the total cost of Chernobyl to Eastern and Western Europe is something between $1 and 1.5 billion in 1986 and 1987.

It is far more difficult to measure the health impact since it will extend over many decades and cannot easily be distinguished statistically from normal morbidity and mortality. The initial estimate by the NRPB for the EC was far too low. The American estimates divide the calculated global number of fatal cancers from the radiocaesium deposited after the Chernobyl accident (about 20,000) equally between the Soviet Union and the rest of Europe. This seems more realistic.[87] Although there were lower doses in Eastern and Western Europe than in the USSR, they are multiplied by far higher population densities.

Until 1986, the long-term epidemiological studies of radiation risks involved first, comparatively large groups of people who had survived the atomic bombs dropped over Hiroshima and Nagasaki. There are 80,000 people included in the register and their approximate collective dose was estimated at 22,000 Sv. A second group were workers at nuclear reprocessing plants. About 13,000 workers at Hanford in the United States (collective dose, 600 Sv) and 10,000 BNFL Sellafield radiation workers (formerly Windscale) (collective dose, 1,250 Sv).[88] A substantial number of people were affected by radioactive contamination as a result of the Kyshtym nuclear disaster in the Soviet Union in 1957 but if any study was made of their health problems, the results have never been published.[89] This is why Western experts are so anxious to take part in the medical follow-up studies. The experience of Western scientists could also contribute greatly to the Soviet efforts. It is already acknowledged that the real radiation health effect of the Hiroshima and Nagasaki bombs is much higher than estimated so far because the radiation doses were measured in 1945 at levels lower than they really were. The doses have recently been reassessed upwards. It has also become apparent that the late effect is far more serious than expected on the basis of previous observations.[90]

The Chernobyl catastrophe and its tragic consequences have given all those interested in the future of nuclear energy the opportunity to make more accurate analyses of the real danger of the nuclear choice made by governments on behalf of their citizens. As far as one can judge at present, the Soviet government has decided to prevent foreign scientists from using this opportunity. Moreover, Western governments are not anxious to press the Soviet Union to transform the global health effect of the accident into follow-up studies and international research which could prevent the health effects being lost in general future statistics of natural mortality. The effects can easily be covered up by secrecy and misinformation. Human radiology is a sensitive branch of science with political and economic implications. But, like all science, it should be free from the conspiracy of silence and fraud.

# 7

# The Soviet Nuclear Energy Programme

## INTRODUCTION: A BRIEF HISTORY OF THE SOVIET URANIUM PROJECT

THE first nuclear reactors in both the Soviet Union and the United States were created to produce plutonium for purely military purposes. It was only later that they were combined with steam turbines. If it had not been for the atomic bomb, using nuclear reactors as a source of electric energy would probably still be in the research stage. The technology is far too expensive for civilian use alone.

In the United States the nuclear programme is usually dated from 2 August 1939, a few weeks before the war started, when Albert Einstein wrote his famous letter to President Franklin D. Roosevelt warning of the danger that Germany might have the capability to use fission energy to produce a superbomb. Einstein was prompted by Niels Bohr's suggestion that a fission bomb was feasible. His warning led to the creation of the US Office of Scientific Research and Development in June 1941 and the Manhattan Project a year later. The first chain reaction of uranium-235 in a small reactor was achieved in a laboratory in Chicago on 2 December 1942.

The Soviet nuclear project also originated from a letter written by a physicist. Georgy Flerov, a young physicist who had begun studying radioactivity in 1939, had been drafted into the army in June 1941 as a military engineer. The Academy of Sciences of the USSR had been evacuated from Moscow to Kazan. Flerov visited Kazan for a few days and immediately looked at the latest physics journals to read about recent research in nuclear physics. He wanted to catch up on the developments that had occurred during the ten months he had been in the army. To his astonishment, he found no publications in the field of atomic physics. The names of well-known nuclear physicists had disappeared from the journals. Flerov reached the logical conclusion that all research on atomic physics in the United States, Britain and

Germany had been classified. He deduced that they must be working on an atomic bomb. In April 1942 he wrote to Stalin, pointing out that such a bomb could change the course of the war. He suggested that Stalin should take advice from nuclear physicists like Academicians Petr Kapitsa, Igor Kurchatov, Lev Landau and others.

Flerov's letter has only recently been published in full.[1] It must have impressed Stalin because he called several of the physicists to Moscow for consultations in the autumn of 1942. In November 1942 a nuclear project was launched. The first experimental reactor was built in Kurchatov's secret laboratory in 1946 and the first fission-controlled chain reaction occurred on 25 December 1946.[2] On 10 June 1948 the first military reactor large enough to make sufficient plutonium for an atomic bomb was launched. The first Soviet bomb was made and tested on 23 September 1949.

Although the Soviet Union was the third country to make an atomic bomb (the British bomb preceded it), it was the first to adapt nuclear reactors to produce electricity. Soviet nuclear scientists are proud of their pioneering role in the peaceful use of nuclear energy. An experimental nuclear power station, now known as Obninsk Atomic Energy Station (AES), began generating electricity on 27 June 1954. It was an integral part of the Physico-Power Institute, now the largest centre of reactor technology in the Soviet Union and responsible for the design and development of many subsequent types of reactor including the pressurized-water reactors for ships and submarines and the fast breeders. It is commonly thought in the Soviet Union that Obninsk AES was the world's first nuclear power station. It was here, they believe, that the problem of controlling the fission reaction of uranium, necessary to produce electric power, was resolved.[3]

In fact, many Western experts dispute this claim. The small, experimental Obninsk AES (about 5 MWe) had no commercial value. Its own electrical needs (for water pumps and other systems) probably consumed more than it produced and it drew electricity from the general grid of the Moscow energy network. They take the Calder Hall 50 MWe reactor as the first real nuclear power station. Calder Hall was switched into the British national grid on 17 October 1956, amid much international publicity. But even Calder Hall was merely the first power reactor that the public knew about. There was no publicity for the first American and Soviet power reactors.[4]

Obninsk, which is 100 km south of Moscow, is closed to foreigners. In 1954 it was not a town in the conventional sense, but a secret prison-camp facility where prominent Soviet scientists worked alongside

German physicists who were still prisoners-of-war. A prison labour camp was attached to the research centre. Construction and other work on the site were largely done by the inmates. The settlement had no name in 1954. It was merely a PO Box address, part of a vast empire of military atomic installations and research centres headed by Igor Kurchatov, the father of the Soviet atomic bomb and a legendary figure in Soviet science.

One of Kurchatov's biographers has described how public excursions to the first AES were organized after its existence was officially announced.[5] On 1 July 1954 the USSR Council of Ministers published an announcement 'Concerning the Inauguration in the USSR of the First Industrial Power Station using Atomic Energy'. It did not reveal the location of the plant and no further details were released for nearly a year.

Kurchatov had submitted a proposal to build a power reactor in 1949. Within a year he had received governmental approval to start work.[6] He appointed D. I. Blokhintsev, who directed the Obninsk Institute, to head the project although he himself supervised everything, including the emergency shutdown mechanisms. Nikolai A. Dollezhal and Anatoly A. Aleksandrov were members of the scientific team.[7] Dollezhal, who was an expert on power stations, completed the blueprints for the power turbine, while Kurchatov chaired discussions concerning the best model of reactor. The alternatives included the gas-cooled system. According to his biographers, Kurchatov himself chose the graphite-moderated, water-cooled model, apparently because it had already been successfully tested for military purposes. During this period plutonium production was the most important economic consideration and designers favoured the models which would yield the most plutonium.

No journalists were present at the inauguration of the first AES on 27 June 1954. It was only in 1967, seven years after Kurchatov's death that the event was described.[8] The prison research centre had been dismantled in 1955, when all the remaining German prisoners-of-war and deportees had been released and returned to Germany (a condition for the establishment of diplomatic relations between the Soviet Union and the Federal Republic of Germany). In the West it was public knowledge that German scientists had participated in the Soviet nuclear programme, but it only became known in the Soviet Union in 1987, when D. A. Granin published a biography of N. W. Timofeeff-Ressovsky, a prominent Soviet radiation geneticist who lived and worked in Germany from 1926 to 1945.[9] Granin described the work of a research team of German scientists in the Ural military nuclear centre where they were attached to the plutonium-producing facilities. In 1955 the 'laboratory was closed and the Germans were allowed to return home. This surprised them very much: they had expected to have to work much longer for the victorious power'.[10] The most prominent German scientists were Professors K. G. Zimmer and N. Riehl. Riehl had been closely involved in Germany's nuclear project in 1941–5. The US Institute of Information *Citation Index* shows a gap in Riehl's publications between 1941 and 1956.

The secret research facilities at Obninsk only acquired the name Obninsk in 1958, when the name first appeared on Soviet maps. Several other research institutes were established in the town. In 1962 the Research Institute of Medical Radiology was established and I was invited to set up its molecular radiobiology laboratory. I lived in Obninsk for nearly ten years. It was (and probably still is) a very pleasant town. Everybody who lives and works in an atomic centre like Obninsk acquires a more than superficial knowledge of the details of atomic energy, despite the obsession of local officials to preserve the secrecy of everything linked to atomic research.

Between 1974 and 1980, while living in Britain, I visited the principal nuclear research centres in the United States: the Argonne, Brookhaven, Oak Ridge and Los Alamos National Laboratories. At none of them did I see such elaborate security systems as those at Obninsk, where more than a battalion of professional military guards with dogs patrol a system of multiple fences and electrified wires separated by strips of freshly ploughed ground. Obninsk scientists were very active in the repair work at Chernobyl, helping to bring the other three units back into operation. However, when *Sarcophagus*, a play about Chernobyl by G. Gubarev, the science editor of *Pravda*, was rehearsed in Obninsk by a local amateur dramatic group, the local Party committee banned the play (it had already been published in Moscow and performed in Tambov and other towns.[11] The Obninsk Party secretary, A. V. Kamaev, maintained that it would be insensitive to stage such a play in the 'centre of Soviet atomic science'.[12]

Obninsk remained the only Soviet AES for nearly a decade. Turning an experimental nuclear power reactor into an economically viable, commercial power station proved difficult. In the 1950s the Soviet Union had more than enough sources of cheap energy. Constructing military plutonium-producing reactors (graphite-moderated) and power reactors for ships and submarines (more compact pressurized-water reactors with the same output) was considered more important than nuclear power stations. In March 1956 Kurchatov advocated the rapid development of power stations. In addition to the two models already tested (later known as the RBMK and VVER reactors), he was enthusiastic about small reactors which might be used by locomotives and even aeroplanes. He also wanted fast breeders to be developed as the most promising future source of energy.

When the Soviet nuclear energy programme was finally approved by the government sometime in 1956 or 1957, all three reactor types (graphite-moderated, pressurized-water and fast-breeder) were included in the programme. It was not because of economic efficiency, safety or institutional support that the RBMK was later given priority. In the late 1950s and the 1960s it was simply easier for Soviet industry to construct its less sophisticated design. The *diktat* of producers over consumers, pinpointed by *glasnost'* as the main weakness of the Soviet economy, was important in giving a technically obsolete model a new lease of life. The Ministry of Power and Electrification, responsible for running nuclear power stations, was given no choice: it could decide design and construction questions concerning turbines, but not reactors. There were also nationalistic reasons for giving priorities to the RBMK system: it was the only entirely Soviet system. Other designs would have entailed copying or imitating Western models.

### RBMK REACTORS

The acronym RBMK stands for 'reactor, high-power, boiling, channel-type (or pressure tube)' in Russian. The first reactor at Obninsk was not an RBMK because it was not a high-power model. The acronym only began to be used in 1973 when the first 1,000 MWe reactor was constructed. This was the first standard-type reactor. Previous graphite-moderated reactors had been designed individually, with different characteristics and power ratings. They represent stages in the development of the standard RBMK-1000 model.

The immediate successor to the 5 MWe reactor at Obninsk was completed near Troitsk in Siberia in 1958. It was intended to provide both plutonium and electricity for a separate plutonium producing and reprocessing plant. It was essentially a military project (and the modernized 600 MWe six-unit version is still used for military purposes). As authorized commentators explain, 'the principal expenses of this power station are covered by the cost of plutonium produced'.[13] Neither Obninsk nor Troitsk produced cheap electricity. It was at least ten times more expensive per unit than coal or hydroelectric energy. Not surprisingly, therefore, Soviet planners were rather unenthusiastic about nuclear energy. Kurchatov had numerous critics who opposed his proposals to build more and more nuclear power stations. Khrushchev was generally very enthusiastic about nuclear energy for ships and submarines, but he was sceptical about its use in civilian projects.

However, atomic scientists formed a powerful lobby in the USSR in the 1950s. According to Khrushchev's memoirs, Kurchatov wanted to be appointed special scientific adviser to the Chairman of the Council of Ministers and be the official spokesman for Soviet scientists.[14] There was no such position in the Soviet government system. Khruschev's chief scientific adviser was a prominent thermophysicist, Academician Vladimir A. Kirillin, Chairman of the Department of Science and Technology of the Central Committee of the CPSU. As an expert on thermodynamics and power engineering, Kirillin did not support nuclear energy. Moreover, Soviet uranium resources had not been properly explored and the military lobby argued that they should be husbanded for strategic purposes rather than squandered on the routine generation of electricity.

The nuclear energy programme really only began in 1958, when construction began on the first commercial atomic power station at Beloyarsk, near Sverdlovsk. With a power of 100 MWe, the Beloyarsk AES was also semi-experimental, and was used for dual military and civilian purposes. The key energy project of the time was the Bratsk hydropower station on the Angara river in Siberia which was expected to produce 4,500 MWe when completed. It was one of four hydrostations in the Angara cascade. The Bratsk and the Beloyarsk power stations were completed almost simultaneously six years later. The hydroelectric design was comparatively simple and seemed more durable. Moreover, 45 Beloyarsk-type stations would be required to produce the same amount of energy as the Bratsk station. It seemed far more sensible to concentrate on additional hydrostations than to accelerate the nuclear programme.

The Beloyarsk AES became operational on 26 April 1964. It was named after Kurchatov, who had died at the age of 57. The reactor was a larger, modernized version of the Obninsk reactor. It is now clear, however, that an increase in cost-effectiveness (by producing a better ratio between the output of heat and electric energy) was achieved at the expense of safety. The Obninsk reactor generated steam heat for the turbines in a separate circuit, uncontaminated by radionuclides. But this necessitated a special 'heat exchanger' and some heat was lost in the process. The uranium fuel elements often leaked and small quantities of contaminated water had to be disposed of periodically, but no contamination reached the turbines. Obninsk AES was considered so safe that it did not need a health-protection zone around it. A small square separated it from the apartment blocks of Lenin Prospect, the town's main street. The main disadvantage of the system was the high ratio between thermal and electric output (6:1). For every 30 megawatts of thermal power (MWt), only 4.8 MWe was produced (the ratio in modern RBMK reactors is 3:1). To prevent accidents the steam pressure in the pressure tubes was very low, 12 atmospheres (atm.). In the next generation of reactors, the quality of the pressure tubes and pipes was improved, allowing higher pressure and the introduction of a single-circuit system.

At Beloyarsk steam for the turbines was produced directly in the reactor core. The design gave a much better ratio between thermal power (285 MW) and electric capacity (100 MW).[15] It also used uranium fuel more economically. But the circulation of the same water first through the reactor core and then as steam through the turbine hall meant that much larger quantities of water became contaminated. Moreover, it was highly dangerous to produce superheated steam inside the reactor core fuel channels. This was the source of the 'positive void coefficient' which was the main cause of the Chernobyl accident. The Beloyarsk 100 MW reactor had fuel channels of a unique type: 730 of them were evaporative channels for the generation of steam; 268 were for superheating the steam. The temperature of the outlet steam (mixed with water) was 340°C, but its temperature on leaving the superheating channels was 500°C. This is much higher than the maximum steam temperature of 284°C in the RBMK-1000 reactors. The steam pressure in the Beloyarsk reactor was also much higher: 150 atm., compared to 83 atm. in the RBMK-1000.

Despite these very high pressures, the Beloyarsk reactor was built without protective containment. The reactor vault was designed to accommodate only a single coolant channel failure. Inadequate safety margins remained the major fault of all future Soviet graphite-moderated channel reactors. But the absence both of a containment structure, and of the single strong pressure vessel found in PWRs was often presented as an advantage. The truth, however, is that Soviet industry was incapable of manufacturing large steel pressure vessels in the 1960s and scientists had no choice but to pretend that they had found a simpler solution. But they realized that having hundreds of fuel assemblies in separate pressure channels, each individually controlled, made the system too complex. According to the official history of the Soviet nuclear programme, engineers had overcome the problem:

> Nuclear superheating effected directly in the reactor is associated with the well-known difficulties of controlling the process and particularly monitoring its course, with the required operating accuracy of very many instruments, the presence of a large number of tubes of different dimensions under high pressure, etc. However, all these difficulties are obvious to the scientists and engineers, and they have worked successfully to overcome them.[16]

This was far from the case. Moreover, subsequent increases in reactor size and power made the system even more complex. Each RBMK reactor behaves like several independent reactors. Operators have to observe signals from each individual pressure channel. In the early 1960s computer control of the system was rudimentary.

The unit cost of electricity from the first Beloyarsk reactor was still very high; far higher, for example, than the unit cost of electricity from the conventional thermal power stations around Sverdlovsk. The Ural region was rich in cheap coal deposits. Thus nuclear power stations could not be justified on the basis of energy needs alone. The main military reprocessing facilities were situated between Sverdlovsk and Chelyabinsk, in the Kyshtym and Kasly districts. After the Kyshtym nuclear accident and the contamination of a very large area with nuclear waste radionuclides,[17] it was probably thought advisable to site new reactors further apart, but not so far that spent fuel rods would have to be transported over long distances. This is probably why the second graphite-moderated reactor with a capacity of 200 MWe was already under construction on the same site well before the first was tested in operation. Scientists were experimenting and comparing different models and the design of the second unit was different. It was scheduled to go into operation in October 1967, in time for the fiftieth anniversary of the October Revolution.

The design of the second Beloyarsk reactor was simpler. Two-stage overheating was eliminated and the steam for the turbines was generated directly in the first circuit. Only one assembly of channels in the reactor core was required to produce superheated steam of about 510–20°C. However, the extremely high temperature of the steam turned out to be a disadvantage. Later it was admitted that: 'The increase of the working temperature in the reactor core leads to the necessity of using temperature-resistant materials which, in the majority of cases, is less favourable from the neutron-physics aspect and leads to a reduction of the overall utilisation efficiency of the nuclear fuel.'[18] This was the end of the Beloyarsk model. In 1968 the fast-breeder reactor was already under construction at Beloyarsk, where it was intended to work alongside the old reactors. However, the Beloyarsk 100 and 200 MW graphite moderated reactors operated until 1989, when they were stopped because of safety considerations.[19]

On the whole, the economic performance of the Beloyarsk reactors was very poor. The attempt to work at very high steam temperatures can only be explained by the need to use existing turbines, designed and built for coal or oil thermal stations which normally work at these levels of temperature and pressure. The nuclear energy industry was still part of the defence industry. It did not yet have the capacity to design and manufacture turbines specifically to suit the best model of reactor. It was calculated that the only way to produce nuclear-generated energy at acceptable cost was to raise the power of individual units to 1,000 MWe. Reactors of this power had already been licensed for operation in the United States, but they were either pressurized-water reactors (PWR) or boiling-water reactors (BWR) with massive, welded steel pressure vessels which could not be manufactured in the Soviet Union.

Forecasts were made in the United States in the early 1960s that there would be a growing need for nuclear energy to supplement fossil fuels. By the 1970s, it was predicted, nuclear-generated electricity would cost less than electricity from conventional sources. These projections stimulated many orders for large nuclear plants. The PWR was the most popular model. By 1962 the United States was well ahead in nuclear-generated electricity and there were 18 reactors on stream, as well as 13 large reactors producing plutonium. It was expected that by 1971 the combined nuclear-electric capacity would be over 8,000 MW. In the UK a high-power, gas-cooled graphite reactor (1,180 MWe) was under construction in the late 1960s. In fact, by the end of the 1960s the Soviet Union was well behind not only the United States but also France, West Germany and the UK, each of which had ten to fifteen reactors operating or in the final stages of construction.[20]

These were the circumstances in which Soviet atomic industry specialists decided to design a high-power version of the pressure-tube model: the design now known as the RBMK-1000. Although the disadvantages of the graphite-moderated channel-type model were already obvious, this was the only genuine Soviet design which had strong institutional support as well as its own industrial base. Anatoly Aleksandrov, a member of Kurchatov's original team, was now an academician and director of the Kurchatov Institute of Atomic Energy.

Nikolai Dollezhal, also an academician, was director of the Power Engineering Institute of the State Committee for the Utilization of Atomic Energy. The leading experts of the PWR programme were far less influential.

The construction of the Leningrad nuclear power station, consisting of two RBMK-1000 reactors, was already under way in 1964–5 when it became clear that the model that used superheated steam was not suitable. The ratio between thermal and electric energy had to be improved in some other way. The solution was found in the use of fire-resistant zirconium alloys. When they replaced steel or aluminium alloys in the fuel element claddings of uranium-graphite reactors, they improved the fuel cycle parameters by reducing the neutron absorption of the cladding. American experts, however, now believe that, although this improvement occurs, zirconium is unreliable from an engineering point of view. Their study of the Chernobyl accident indicates that the zirconium-to-steel welds are weak points in the RBMK piping system, prone to rupture with rapid rise of temperature.[21]

Once zirconium alloys were introduced, the reactor core had to be redesigned. The size of individual channels or pressure tubes was enlarged, and their number increased to reach 1,000 MWe with 3,200 MWt (the same ratio as in the American PWRs). Aleksandrov, Dollezhal and Petrosy'ants, who headed the project, presented an optimistic report of the prospects for the RBMK models, 'Leningrad Power Station and the Prospects for Channel Boiling Reactors', to the Fourth International Conference on the Peaceful Uses of Atomic Energy in Geneva in 1971, more than two years before the design was tested. Their confidence in the model was so high that two units were constructed more or less simultaneously and several more followed. The construction of the Chernobyl nuclear plant began in 1970, when foundations were laid for two reactors practically identical to the Leningrad station. Designs for the RBMK-1500 and RBMK-2000, the most powerful reactors in the world, were also completed well before the Leningrad power station became operational.

The first reactor in the Leningrad plant was tested in September 1973, but it took more than a year to put it into operation. In October 1974, the RBMK-1000 Unit 1 finally reached its projected power. The second unit went on stream at the end of 1975. The plant was declared a success. Producing 2 million kW of electric power, it was the largest in Europe at the time. It was, of course, named after Lenin (when Chernobyl station became the largest it, too, was called after Lenin).

The RBMK model had won the competition with the Soviet PWRs

(known as VVERs). The electricity it generated was calculated to be cheaper than that from the already operational VVER-440 model. The absence of a massive steel pressure vessel for the reactor core and a containment structure contributed greatly to the cost-effectiveness. These controversial design features, now known to be highly dangerous, were then presented as the main advantages of the model. They were said to be unnecessary: the design was completely safe without them. The existing protection would hold even if one or two (the worst case imaginable) of the 1,600 fuel channels ruptured. Nobody dared to suggest the possibility of a more general core explosion.

Temperature and steam pressure were greatly reduced (to 280°C and 65 kg/cm$^2$ before turbines) in the RBMK-1000, 1500 and 2000 without losing efficiency (the corresponding figures for the Beloyarsk station were 500°C and 90 kg/cm$^2$). A serious drawback was the size of the core, which was so large that a great deal of water in the first circuit was needed to cool it. Using low-pressure saturated steam for the turbines also meant that more water was involved in the process. In a Soviet textbook on the construction of nuclear power plants, 'the complex and bulky coolant circulation circuits and a large number of auxiliary systems' are listed as the system's major drawback.[22] Each RBMK-1000 has four main pumps circulating 37,600 tonnes of water per hour in the first circuit, not to mention several other, smaller pumping systems.[23] This is less than the total volume of water circulating in a VVER system with the same power output, but in the VVER most of the cooling water circulates in the second circuit. In the VVER-1000 model, where it is separate, the steam output is 1,469 tonnes per hour, while the RBMK-1000 reactor produces 5,800 tonnes of steam per hour.[24]

This significant difference creates a problem of circulating the contaminated water. In most Western nuclear power stations circulation water is normally recirculated in tall cooling towers, now a familiar feature of nuclear power plants. This is more expensive than the direct-flow water supply system which was standard in the first military graphite reactors in the Hanford reservation in Washington state (and probably in the first Soviet reactors in the Urals). Environmental considerations, however, made it impossible to use natural water reservoirs for nuclear power plants: water which circulates through the reactor core is always slightly radioactive, and heating it under pressure kills all water-borne biological life. Moreover, the radioactivity of the water increases constantly.

However, using closed cooling tower circuits for the RBMK systems would have raised the price of the electricity and made them less competitive with the VVER-1000 models. The designers decided instead on a very controversial simplification: a direct-flow water supply from purpose-built reservoirs near the reactor site and isolated from the nearest water system. The reservoirs would act as biological deactivators of radioactive water since the radionuclides precipitate to the bottom and are absorbed by silt. Cooling and decontaminating the water through artificial pools would require very large reservoirs. To cool one RBMK-1000, for example, the pool may be shallow (about 4 m) but it must be at least 5 or 6 km$^2$ in size. The first stage of the Leningrad plant needed a 10 km$^2$ pool, while the Chernobyl pool was about 22 km$^2$ because of the warmer climate in the Kiev region.

Since land belongs to the state in the Soviet Union and therefore costs nothing, the value of the area occupied by the pool did not have to be considered. Resettling local inhabitants involved trouble and expense, of course, but this was not something that concerned the designers. Clearly this particular solution would have been impossible in the more densely populated countries of Western and Eastern Europe, where land has a high commercial value.

The direct-flow water supply system of the RBMK-1000 is considered simpler than a recirculation system and it costs nearly 25 per cent less.[25] Certain environmental standards have to be observed; for example, waste water should not raise the temperature of the reservoir water above a certain limit and only a certain amount of radioactivity should be discharged into the water so that the silt can fix most of the radionuclides reasonably quickly. The reservoir water must be kept in motion with a natural water supply, such as a river, to compensate for evaporation and to prevent an increase in salinity. This means that a certain amount of radioactive material from the reactor core passes into the environment, and one of the tasks of the radiological services is to keep this within permissible limits.

Despite the insistence that the RBMK-1000 reactor was totally safe, the absence of pressure and containment vessels and the comparative fragility of individual channels (the danger of rupture is particularly high during the initial launch, when all 1,600 channels have to be tested simultaneously or in one half of the reactor) made it necessary to have a protection zone around the reactor much larger than for PWR or VVER systems. People cannot live or farm within a radius of 2.5 km around a RBMK-1000 reactor. Planners therefore suggested that they should be built in areas of little or no agricultural use. This was possible in the Leningrad region where agriculture is difficult. But in the rich black-earth region of the Ukraine it is difficult to find waste land. For centuries this area has been the granary of Russia and it could ill afford to sacrifice land along the rivers. But it was in the Ukraine that nuclear power station construction received the highest priority.

The large amount of water which circulates in a single circuit through the fuel elements and the steam turbines needs frequent replacement because it accumulates radioactivity which causes radioactive corrosion of the turbines. But heavily radioactive water cannot be discharged directly into the cooling ponds; it has to be evaporated in special evaporation systems and the radioactive sediment is then treated like nuclear waste. In the VVER (or PWR) reactors the water for the steam circuits in the turbines circulates in separate 'clean' circuits and has no contact with the reactor core. As a result less water has to be replaced and there is less evaporation. Experts consider that one of the main disadvantages of the RBMK-1000 system is the large amount of radioactive water which has to be disposed of daily. In 'Chernobyl Notebook', G. Medvedev describes the discussion in Kiev in 1972 when the decision was made about what reactor was suitable for the Chernobyl station, then under construction. The Minister of Energy for the Ukraine, Aleksei Makukhin, in whose office the discussion took place, played an important part in the decision. This was to be the first nuclear station in the Ukraine. Bryukhanov, the new director of Chernobyl, was in favour of the VVER system and so was Medvedev. Both maintained that it was safer. When Makukhin heard that the normal rate of radioactive emission would be 4,000 Ci a day, compared to the 100 Ci a day emitted from the Novovoronezh reactor, he was concerned. But the opinion of Academician Aleksandrov, who claimed that the RBMK-1000 was the safest and most economical reactor, influenced his decision. He was determined, however, that steps should be taken so that the first Ukraininan reactor was cleaner and safer than the Novovoronezh reactor.[26]

Thirteen years later it was already clear that Makukhin's optimism had been misplaced. By that time he had moved to Moscow. But when Medvedev met Bryukhanov in 1985, the director had a long list of complaints:'Bryukhanov complained that there were many leaks at the Chernobyl AES. The fittings weren't holding, the drainage was leaking. The amount of radioactive water was enormous and they were barely managing to process it into evaporated form. There was a great deal of radioactive dirt'.[27]

The RBMK-1000 became the most important type of reactor in the Soviet nuclear power industry. At the time of the Chernobyl accident there were 14 RBMK plants across the country providing more than half the country's nuclear electricity generating capacity. Several more were under construction. A more powerful RBMK-1500 plant was also in operation at Ignalina and a second one was under construction on the same site. The RBMK-1500 is very similar to the RBMK-1000 and has the same kind of core and the same number of channels. Its increased thermal capacity of 4,800 MWt is made possible by a new system of heat transfer from the fuel channels and a simplification of the circulation loop. Other technical innovations have made it possible to increase the steam volume. The electricity generated by the RBMK-1500 is potentially cheaper than that from a RBMK-1000 or VVER-1000. There are plans for RBMK-2000 and 2400 but construction has not been started.[28] They are projected to achieve a better thermal/electric power ratio by superheating up to 450°C but a new industrial base is required to build them.

The Ignalina plant was expected to be the most economical nuclear plant when fully operational. Until 1986, however, Chernobyl was more economical. With its four RBMK-1000 reactors, it was the largest nuclear plant in the USSR. Two additional reactors were under construction and they would have made it the largest plant in the world. Two more blocks were in the project stage to maintain this record into the twenty-first century. But the designers were not yet entirely satisfied. A project to develop a RBMK with an electrical output of 2,000 MWe by increasing the number of channels without modifying them was also undertaken to make more efficient use of the existing industrial base.

Thus although the design of the RBMK has been modified, no new technology has been introduced. The whole range of RBMKs derives directly from the early experimental, plutonium-producing reactors of the early 1950s. The main arguments used to support the technologically obsolete RBMK have always been its relative cheapness and its good safety features. It was recognized that the RBMK was accident-prone, but the accidents were never expected to amount to more than minor problems with individual pressure tubes. In principle, the VVER reactors were less vulnerable to accident, but any accident that occurred would be more dangerous, since it would involve the whole core. The Three Mile Island accident in 1979 seemed to confirm this assessment and it strengthened the Soviet commitment to continuing and modernizing the RBMK.

At first the Chernobyl accident did not seem to affect the nuclear energy programme. Official statements in 1986 confirmed that the reactors under construction (including Units 5 and 6 at Chernobyl) would be completed. But in 1987 the mounting criticism of the RBMK began to have an effect. The construction of Units 5 and 6 was postponed and later cancelled. But in 1988 the inevitable decision was finally made not to build any new RBMK reactors.[29] The RBMK programme was brought to an inglorious end.

## THE SECOND LINE: PRESSURIZED-WATER REACTORS

Pressurized water-cooled and water-moderated reactors (PWRs or VVERs from the Russian for 'water–water power reactors') were initially developed for nuclear submarines. The first small American 2.4 MWe PWR was tested on 30 March 1953 and used the next year for the USS *Nautilus*, the first nuclear-powered submarine. The reactor had to fit into a very small space, so a design was needed with a core of high-power density (heat output per unit volume) and which was easy to operate. Ordinary 'light' water was used both as the neutron moderator (instead of graphite) and as a coolant for the fuel elements. Heavy water, with deuterium, is an even better moderator but it is expensive and its manufacture consumes too much energy. The reactor consisted of uranium fuel elements immersed in water in a strong steel pressure tank or vessel. The pressure was required to keep the water from boiling. Steam for the turbines was generated in a boiler in a separate circuit, linked to the primary high-pressure circuit through a heat exchange system. Its simplicity of design has made the PWR the most popular system and it dominates the world reactor market.

The Soviet Union also needed reactors with a much higher power density than that provided by the graphite-moderated model. The inexorable logic of military competition meant that the USSR had to follow the US in building nuclear submarines. The first Soviet VVER was probably tested in 1954, soon after the first American test. Construction of the atomic ice-breaker *Lenin* began in 1956. It needed larger reactors than the *Nautilus*. Although the steel industry could manufacture steel pressure vessels for ships, constructing larger and heavier pressure vessels for power stations was a problem. Pressure vessels entail very complex engineering and consist of many different parts. Small vessels of welded steel for the first VVER power station were made in Leningrad and shipped to the site. The first power station with a VVER reactor (VVER-210) was started up in September 1964 about 50 km from Voronezh, at Novovoronezh. It was well behind schedule. Also, technical problems meant that the pressure vessels for more economical VVER-440 and VVER-1000 reactors remained at the project stage for many years.[30]

VVER reactors were required for export, primarily to CMEA countries. The Soviet Union had an obligation to provide these countries with energy, but it was important to reduce oil and gas exports to Eastern Europe and Cuba so that more of these resources could be sold for hard currency. RBMKs were not suitable for export and they would not have been licensed for operation in other countries because of their poor safety features, the absence of containment structures and the radioactive contamination of the environment through the discharge of radioactive water into cooling pools. The VVER-210 at Novovoronezh was connected to closed circulation towers, but its economic performance was rather poor. During 1965, its first full year of operation, only 54 per cent of projected output was realized and the unit cost of electricity was nearly double the average production cost from thermal power stations in European parts of the USSR.[31] In 1967 and 1968 the plant performed better, but its electricity still cost more than the average. A second, more powerful VVER-365 was brought into operation on the same site in December 1969. The electricity it generated was cheaper.

The main problem with VVER reactors is recharging. One-third of the fuel elements must be replaced annually, involving a complete shutdown of the reactor. The cooling period (waiting for the short-lived isotopes to decay) is rather long, so that each recharging process takes about 30 days (longer if the vessel needs repair).[32]

In 1970 when there were already two RBMK-1000s under construction, the prospect of building VVERs with the same power was still remote, owing to the absence of a suitable industrial base. RBMK-1000 reactors could be assembled from smaller parts, while the VVER-1000 required a single large, heavy and solid steel structure. To provide an industrial base for VVER systems *Atommash* (an abbreviation of 'atom machinery') was established to manufacture pressure vessels and other components.

*Atommash* was a key project in the Soviet energy programme. It was decided to locate it in Rostov region. The Party *obkom* secretary in the region was Ivan Bondarenko, a close friend of Brezhnev. The siting of *Atommash* was intended as a favour: it would give Bondarenko a higher profile and greater influence in Moscow. The decision to accelerate the nuclear energy programme had been taken in 1974, when the international price of oil rose sharply and export demands increased. Oil became the main source of foreign exchange after 1974. Poor harvests meant that large imports of grain and food were necessary. As a result, the replacement of oil by nuclear energy became a priority, not only because it was expected to be cheap but because it would help to increase foreign trade. In 1979, however, the Soviet Union's nuclear-generated capacity was still only 4,500 MW, 2 per cent of the total production of electricity.

The first two VVER-440s became operational in 1971 and 1972, well before the *Atommash* plant was completed. Their components, including pressure vessels, were manufactured at the modernized Izhorsky works in Leningrad. The new reactors at Novovoronezh were provided with containment structures made of reinforced concrete cells, 42×39 m. The parts for the first VVER-1000, planned for 1978 at Novovoronezh, were to be manufactured at *Atommash*. The pressure vessels were to weigh 500–800 metric tons each, too heavy to be transported by rail. They would be transported up the river by barge. In fact, the construction both of reactor and plant proved more difficult than expected. The plant was officially opened in 1978, but only part of it was in operation. The VVER-1000 was finally tested in May 1980, two years behind schedule.

Planners and builders had been in such a hurry to build *Atommash* that they had omitted to make a proper geological survey of the site. It turned out to be unsuitable for the plant and the new town of Volgodonsk. They were built below a hydroelectric dam across the River Don which had created the Tsimplyanskoye reservoir of nearly 2,000 km². The *chernozem* soil was poor protection against the pressure of the water mass above the level of the site. The area around the town gradually became a swamp. This was a fairly common problem with Soviet hydroelectric projects: the designers simply took no account of the environmental consequences of their projects. Raising the level of the rivers and transforming them into huge reservoirs gradually, over 10 or 15 years or more, affected the surrounding water-table. It is possible that when the geological survey for the *Atommash* plant was done, the water-table was still well below the surface, but by the time the project was nearing completion, the water-table had risen and problems became acute, hindering construction. By then it was too late. Volgodonsk was already a town of 100,000 people. So the problem was simply covered up.

According to the original plan, *Atommash* should have produced eight pressure vessels by 1980, as well as components for the primary circuits. In fact, only one or two vessels had been completed by 1983 when sinking foundations caused one of the plant's huge walls to collapse suddenly. The accident was so serious that it was reported in the Soviet press on 20 July 1983 and a commission was set up to investigate.[33] The Politburo held the Chairman of the State Construction

Committee, Ignaty Novikov, responsible and dismissed him. But there was little the new chairman, an experienced construction engineer, could do to solve the problem.[34] Volgodonsk now had a population of 134,000 and it could not easily or quickly be transferred to a safer place. All that could be done immediately was to scale down the construction plans for *Atommash*.

The accident called the whole programme of rapidly developing VVER-1000 plants into question. *Atommash* was regarded as the key to the accelerated development of nuclear energy and the plans for manufacturing and installing VVER-1000 reactors were now well behind schedule for both the 1981–5 and 1986–90 Five Year plans. It is thought that *Atommash* delivered its fourth pressurized vessel by August 1985.[35] It also had a programme for manufacturing giant steam generators, each weighing 320 metric tonnes. Smaller pressurized vessels (for VVER-440 models) continued to be manufactured at the Izhorsky works. They were also contracted out to the Skoda works in Czechoslovakia. The VVER-440 became a commercial model for Eastern Europe.

Both the cost of producing electricity from VVER reactors and the safety of the system were considered inferior to the RBMK. The core of the VVER-1000 reactor is about an eighth of the size of the RBMK-1000 core, but water flows through the reactor at more than twice the rate at which it flows through the RBMK and it therefore needs more powerful pumps. The larger volume of water is required because the power density of the core is much higher. It would require huge open reservoirs to cool the water. However, cooling it actively through cooling towers increases the cost of producing electricity and the reactor consumes a substantial part of the electrical energy it produces.

The pressure in the VVER-1000 primary circuit is higher than in the RBMK-1000 (160 atm.). Because of the higher density of heat production, VVER-1000 reactors are considered to be more prone to the interruption of the flow of cooling water through pipe rupture, pump breakdown, 'blackouts' and so on. Should this happen the standby diesel generators and emergency cooling would have to be started up extremely rapidly to avoid a serious accident. It was believed that if the water pumps were stopped by a blackout, the RBMK-1000 reactor would not reach the point of 'meltdown' because the natural circulation of water would be sufficient to prevent an accident or any damage to the core – as long as the control rods were moved down and heating was caused by accumulated fission products and not by a chain reaction with the generation of neutrons.[36] If a blackout stopped the water pumps of the VVER-1000, however, natural circulation would be insufficient to prevent an accident and it would be essential to switch over immediately to the emergency cooling system.

The perceived dangers of the VVER system led Soviet designers to provide it with a containment structure as well as a strong steel pressure vessel to house the reactor core itself. In the VVER-1000 the whole reactor system is separated from other buildings and enclosed in a steel-lined containment structure of prestressed reinforced concrete in the form of a vertical cylinder topped with an elliptical dome. It is made to withstand a 'worst case' accident of an explosion in which flying metal fragments might destroy the lining or depressurize the containment. To avoid this the circuit section is also protected by a reinforced concrete shield which usually serves as the interior wall.[37]

A sudden loss of coolant is considered less dangerous for the VVER than for the RBMK. Nuclear chain reactions can only continue in the presence of a moderator. In the VVER the coolant (water) also acts as the moderator. If it is lost the nuclear chain reaction is halted immediately. Meltdown of the fuel elements can still occur because of the fission radionuclides which produce heat, particularly at the end of the reactor fuel cycle. But a core meltdown is not an explosion. In the RBMK, a sudden loss of coolant does not stop the nuclear chain reaction in the uranium-235 because the moderator (graphite) remains. It can only be stopped by neutron-absorbing control rods. In fact, of course, the Chernobyl RBMK-1000 accident happened not because of heating and meltdown from accumulated fission radionuclides, as at Three Mile Island, but because of failure to stop the unexpected power increase from the chain reaction by immediately lowering the control rods. Because the core of the VVER-1000 is so much smaller, it would take less time to lower the control rods in the event of trouble. The VVER-reactors also have less complex controls and require fewer operators.

RBMK designers have always argued, however, that it is a safer reactor than the PWR or VVER systems, that each system has advantages and disadvantages and that both should therefore be refined and developed. This is the approach that was adopted. In 1986 there were fewer VVER-1000 reactors in operation than RBMK-1000s but the gap was narrowing. Six or seven were in operation and about 25 more were under construction or planned on 13 sites, half of them in the Ukraine.[38] The smaller VVER-440 was considered a success and 27 were operating in the Soviet Union, in CMEA countries and in Finland. A VVER-500 was designed which shared components with the VVER-1000 (there was no standardisation between the VVER-440 and the

VVER-1000 and the smaller model was expected to be phased out and replaced by VVER-500s).

Soviet energy experts, however, like their foreign colleagues, were well aware that global deposits of uranium were not unlimited. Their hopes were pinned on fast-breeder reactors. In this field at least, the Soviet Union was far more advanced than the United States, where economic and safety considerations had delayed the construction of fast reactors.

## FAST-BREEDER REACTORS

Most reactors use uranium as fuel. The first reactors were designed to use natural uranium which consists of a mixture of stable uranium-238 and fissile uranium-235. Although only uranium-235 is a fuel material, in raw uranium deposits it represents only 0.7 per cent of the mixture. Modern reactors normally use enriched uranium, produced by special enrichment plants. Although the process is complex and costly, it makes it possible to load more fuel material into the reactor core and to use the fuel elements for longer. The RBMK-1000 reactors use only slightly enriched uranium in which the content of uranium-235 is about 2 per cent. VVER and PWR reactors use more highly enriched uranium (between 3 and 4 per cent of uranium-235). This makes it possible to reduce the total amount of the uranium charge (66 tonnes in the VVER compared to 170 tonnes in the RBMK-1000). Fission of uranium-235 produces slow and fast neutrons. When some of the fast neutrons hit and fuse with uranium-238 nuclei, they generate reactions which release energy and which also form a new 'synthetic' element, plutonium-239. Plutonium was the principal product of the first military reactors. The first atomic bomb dropped over Hiroshima in August 1945 was made from uranium-235. The second, dropped over Nagasaki, was made from plutonium-239. The latter has certain advantages as fissile material and a much smaller 'critical mass' for explosion. With each fission, plutonium produces about 2.9 neutrons, whereas each fission of uranium-235 produces only 2.3 neutrons.

When uranium-235 mixed with uranium-238 is used as nuclear fuel, some of the neutrons transform or 'breed' uranium-238 into plutonium. However, the ratio between disappearing uranium-235 and accumulating plutonium-239 is less than one. By changing the conditions in the fission process, this ratio can be increased or decreased, but the best conversion ratio that has ever been achieved is about 0.7 (in graphite-moderated reactors, which is why they were so popular for military purposes). If plutonium mixed with uranium-238 is used as fuel, the conversion ratio can be higher than one. In other words, new plutonium is bred in larger quantities than it is spent.

Compared to plutonium, uranium-238 is very cheap. This is why nuclear physicists were so attracted by a system in which plutonium fuel converts uranium-238 into larger amounts of plutonium. Because there are limited natural deposits of uranium and many high-grade uranium ores have already been worked out, plutonium fast-breeder reactors were advocated as the most promising future replacement for ordinary nuclear reactors. In ordinary reactors, fast neutrons are slowed down by the graphite or water moderator in order to make better use of their energy. No moderator is required in plutonium reactors, since they use fast neutrons (this is why they are called fast-breeder or fast reactors). The first fast-breeder reactors were designed in the United States at the end of the 1940s and the first small, experimental prototype was tested in Idaho in 1951. Kurachatov initiated their development in the Soviet Union in 1950.[39] Similar experimental reactors were being built in Britain and France. The first prototypes for larger commercial reactors were built in Britain (Dounreay) in 1959 and in the United States (Detroit, Edison-Enrico Fermi-1) in 1963. The Detroit reactor later achieved notoriety when a frightening accident forced a permanent shutdown.

The first experimental fast-breeder reactor in the Soviet Union (called BN in Russian) about which anything is known was the 60 MWt and 12 MWe fast neutron reactor built in Dmitrovgrad in the Ulyanovsk region in 1965. It was used as a prototype for larger commercial fast breeders. Because fast-breeder technology was not considered entirely safe, the first commercial fast reactor with an electrical capacity of 350 MW was built a long way from large population centres, near Shevchenko on the eastern shores of the Caspian Sea in a semi-desert area with no fresh water. It was intended to generate power for the distillation of sea water into fresh water for the new town of Shevchenko which was built in this remote desert around the rich uranium mines. It is now the centre of uranium production.

Fast reactors use plutonium produced at a reprocessing plant. Because no moderator is necessary and fast neutrons are more efficient in a very compact core, fast breeders must have a very high density of heat energy generation in a very small core. The cylindrical core of the BN-350 in Shevchenko is at least ten times smaller than the core of the VVER-365 at Novovoronezh, and 50 times smaller than the 285 MWe Beloyarsk graphite-moderated channel reactor. It is obvious that if about the same amount of thermal energy (about 1,000 MWt) is released in the compact space of the BN-350, neither ordinary nor heavy water (water in which hydrogen is present as deuterium) is able to remove such intense heat, even if the flow is very rapid. It is also technically impossible to circulate tens of thousands of tonnes of water per hour through such a small core. Only molten metal has a thermal conductivity high enough to serve as a coolant in fast reactors. Liquid sodium was selected for this purpose. But using molten sodium as a coolant creates its own engineering problems. Any system in which thousands of tonnes of liquid sodium and water are circulating must be entirely leak-proof, because any contact between the water and the sodium would result in explosion and fire. Leakages of water from cooling circuits are common in all systems. The rupture of even a small pipe is a serious accident demanding immediate shutdown of the reactor. The water itself, however, does not represent a danger (apart from some radioactivity in the RBMK systems), but a leakage of sodium would be far more serious and the rupture of a pipe holding molten sodium could lead to disaster. None the less, sodium has some advantages as a coolant. It has a very high boiling point (990°C). This means that it can be used as a coolant under normal pressure, and this reduces the danger of a ruptured pipe. However, sodium reacts instantly and violently with many substances other than water. Moreover, it solidifies into a metal below its melting point (97.5°C), and this means that it must be kept heated even when the reactor is shut down.

Fast reactors pose other challenging technical problems which make the electricity they generate very expensive. Their main advantage – that they produce more plutonium than they consume – is itself not without drawbacks. The higher yields of newly bred plutonium accumulate only after the reactor has been in operation for many years. Both loaded and bred plutonium can only be extracted by complex and expensive reprocessing of spent fuel. The reprocessing produces a by-product in the form of millions of gallons of highly radioactive liquid waste ('radwaste') which must be disposed of in such a way that guarantees safety for centuries.

The Shevchenko plant is not considered a success, even in the Soviet Union. Many problems were caused by poor quality pipes and tubes. Leaks were common and the plant remained shut down for most of the first few years. The plant was started up in 1972, but it took four years of improvements, repairs and replacements before it was considered operational in 1976.[40] The cost of its energy was very high. The projected productivity of the plane was about 100,000 tonnes of distilled water per day. But with all the problems and with six loops of the primary cooling circuit needing nearly 20,000 m$^3$ of sodium per hour (and with six more sodium cooling loops in the second circuit), and similar quantities of water in the third circuit, the production cost of the distilled water also turned out to be very high.

The second Soviet commercial fast reactor had been under construction since 1968, well before the Shevchenko plant was in operation. The site, Beloyarsk, where two graphite reactors had already been built, was chosen largely on the practical grounds of finding employment for the thousands of qualified construction workers and engineers who already lived in Beloyarsk and who would be unemployed without a new project. The design was more modern than the Shevchenko project and the reactor was more powerful (1,470 MWt and 600 MWe). It was categorized as BN-600. However, as at Shevchenko, construction proved more difficult than expected. The plant took 12 years to complete and it only started commercial operations on 20 April 1980 (the government pressed hard for this starting date, to coincide with Lenin's 110th birthday).[41] At that time it was the largest commercial fast reactor in the world and its unveiling was hailed as a great achievement for Soviet technology, promising a future of unlimited energy supplies. The cost of the electricity produced by the BN-600 is not known but it is probably much higher than that produced by the RBMK and VVER reactors.

The main liability of Soviet fast reactors is that the reactor core needs recharging after a very short time (50 days for the BN-350 and 150 days for the BN-600). The replacement of fuel elements is the most hazardous operation in the reactor cycle and it takes several weeks each time. Another problem is that the temperature of the sodium in the first circuit is very high, 500°C, and the combination of a very high temperature and the intensive bombardment by fast neutrons rapidly corrodes the pipes, valves and other parts of the system.[42] Moreover, intense bombardment by fast neutrons makes some molecules of stable sodium absorb neutrons and convert into sodium-24, which is a radioactive gamma emitter. This is why a second circuit of sodium is necessary, with a heat exchange system between the two and an inevitable loss of energy in the process. Eventually a heat exchanger is also necessary between the hot sodium and the water (for the steam generator) and it requires a very sophisticated design to prevent any direct contact between the sodium and the water. Breeding new plutonium is a slow process. It takes about 20 years to double the original load, with many spent-fuel reprocessing operations. Soviet authors claim that the breeding factor of BN-600 is better than in French or British reactors. If it is, the improvement must be produced by increasing the power density in the core, which in turn creates more safety problems.

However, as with other reactors, the designers believed that more powerful fast reactors could be made commercially more viable. New BN-800 and BN-1600 projects were ordered. Regional leaders in Sverdlovsk lobbied in 1979–80 for construction to begin on the new BN-800 at the Beloyarsk site in order to keep the large workforce and design bureau employed (they had become redundant as soon as the BN-600 was completed). Their articles in the national press indicated that government circles had certain reservations about the project.[43] Although the 1981–5 Five-Year Plan called for the construction of new BN-800 and BN-1600 reactors, no new fast reactors have yet been built. The BN-800 was finally approved for the Beloyarsk site, but technical plans were only completed in 1984.[44] Construction work began in 1985 and it will probably take eight or ten years before the reactor becomes operational.

Nothing is known about the construction of the BN-1600, despite the provision in the 1986–90 Five-Year Plan for accelerated construction of fast breeders. The most highly advanced new French fast reactor (called the Superphénix), produces electricity twice as expensive as that produced by thermal nuclear reactors. In the United States, where construction is based on purely economic considerations, no fast breeders are being built. It seems likely that the ambitious Soviet fast-breeder programme will be adversely affected by the Chernobyl accident.

Soviet technology and industry have not yet attained the high level needed to deal with the complex problems of fast reactors. The liquid metal fast breeders require new, very high quality steels and other materials. Breeder technology is based on higher temperatures, much higher neutron density levels and plutonium fuel assemblies. The history of fast-breeder reactors in other countries is far from trouble-free and some accidents have been very serious or potentially disastrous. This makes it likely that the Soviet Union will adopt a cautious approach.

Apart from technical difficulties, fast breeders everywhere have a particular problem: they use plutonium as fuel. Plutonium is nuclear weapons material. Complex safeguards will be needed before any country except the main nuclear powers and their closest military allies are given a chance to buy and operate fast-breeder nuclear stations.

### NUCLEAR CENTRAL HEATING

The use of nuclear reactors to produce electricity is now quite common in many countries. However, the Soviet Union has a leading position in the construction of reactors exclusively to heat big cities. The idea was very attractive. Nuclear-generated electricity is widely used for heating in Europe and the United States, but only a small fraction of the total thermal energy from nuclear fission is actually used. The proportion of thermal energy to electrical energy in most reactors is 3:1, which is less efficient than in coal power stations, where it can reach 2:1.

The VVER systems were considered more suitable for central heating because locating reactors close to big cities required reliable containment structures. At first it was considered economical to use the same reactor to produce both electricity and heat. Later this idea was given up except for industrial heating systems, where high-temperature steam could be used directly. For cities, reactors dedicated to central heating were selected as the safer option. They were expected to operate with reduced pressure in the primary circuit and with the addition of a third heating circuit which would guarantee that no leaked radioactivity could reach domestic heating networks. The idea of nuclear heating was presented by Soviet experts at the Fourth UN Conference on Peaceful Use of Atomic Energy in Geneva in 1971.

Because of the rapid loss of heat in steam or water circuits, heating reactors need to be as close to their end-users as possible. This requirement made the idea unpopular in Western Europe and the United States, where there are strong anti-nuclear lobbies, the climates are milder and the economic advantages of nuclear heating would be wiped out by the reduction in property values caused by the close location of nuclear reactors. In the Soviet Union these problems did not exist: the government owns all houses and heating is free. The government, rather than the customer, is interested in reducing the heating bill. The first nuclear heating stations were tested in the remotest and coldest Arctic regions. In the early 1970s the first station was built in Bilibino, in the north-east. It was a small plant producing 48 MWt and designed to provide central heating and electricity to a mining settlement. In the European parts of the Soviet Union this would be uneconomic, but in distant Arctic regions the production costs of electricity from diesel-electric stations is 8–16 kopecks per kilowatt, nearly ten times the average for the country. It is also very difficult to transport diesel fuel to such remote areas.

In the Soviet Union coal and oil power stations are often used for dual purposes, as thermoelectric stations. Rapid urbanization and shortages of oil and coal for domestic use (because of transportation and pollution problems) compelled planners to consider the alternative of using nuclear reactors. It was decided that special thermal reactors of 500 MWt size should be built because it would be impossible to transport hot water from existing large nuclear power stations which are usually situated 50–100 km from major population centres. Thermal reactors, producing temperatures of around 150°C, were developed in the early 1980s. It was considered safe to locate them only 2 km or so from city boundaries. The first two reactors of this type (based on VVER models) were near completion in 1986 and their construction did not at first seem affected by the Chernobyl accident, but the attitude of the public has certainly changed and construction work is behind schedule. The idea of using nuclear stations to produce central heating arose from the assumption that such reactors are completely safe and can therefore be located very close to large population centres. This assumption is no longer commonly accepted.

The construction of heat-only nuclear stations was included both in the Soviet plans for economic development and in the plan for the technical and scientific progress of the CMEA countries (1985–2000). The USSR is desperate to reduce both its own domestic oil consumption and its exports of oil to East European countries. The export of nuclear reactors is seen as the only real way to do this.

Fourteen other heat-only reactors were at the planning or construction stage at the time of Chernobyl. However, it is now obvious that the programme is under reconsideration. Because the first plants were designed with very low pressure in the primary circuits, they were also designed without high-quality steel pressure vessels. Some reactor vessels were to be made with a wall thickness of only 2 cm.[45] This would hardly be acceptable in any other country and it is unlikely that it will remain acceptable in the USSR after Chernobyl. The designers of some of the new heat-only reactors were concerned that the third water circuit, which circulates heat through houses, should be completely safe from radioactive contamination. Despite the low pressure, leaks are possible. The problem was tackled in a very original way, by making the pressure in the second circuit (3 atm.) higher than in the first (1.5 atm.), and the pressure in the third circulating circuit even higher (6 atm.). This would make it impossible for leaks from the first or second circuits to penetrate the third. But a system of increasing pressures with decreasing temperatures is impossible if water is used in all three circuits. Organic liquids are therefore used in the first two circuits and water only in the third. However, the organic coolants which were first tested proved to be unsuitable.[46] Research into organic liquids is continuing but it is possible that inflammable substances of this sort will be unpopular after the Chernobyl fire.

Soviet nuclear research institutes have come up with several other ideas for heat-only reactors to generate high temperatures for the chemical industries. The CMEA plan for technical co-operation calls for the development of 'nuclear energy-technological stations with multi-purpose utilization'.[47] Little has been done so far, however, to translate this call into concrete projects.

The Chernobyl accident appears to have had serious effects on the thermal nuclear station programme. The two stations which were under construction to provide central heating for Minsk and Odessa became the subject of controversy and local concern. Construction was halted in 1987 and it was decided to turn them into traditional coal thermal stations. It is possible that the whole programme of direct nuclear heating will eventually be cancelled. The new safety regulations for such stations introduced in 1988 require that they should be located no closer than 5 km from residential areas (previously they could be 2 km away). The greater distance means less efficiency. There have been many changes in design. The programme was initiated nearly 20 years ago, yet not a single heating plant of this type has yet been launched in the European part of the USSR for commercial operations. A great deal of resources, money and labour have been wasted without any real practical results. Two 500 MWt heat-supply reactors which are being built at Gorky are expected to be the first in operation, but only after the International Operational Safety Review Team have certified them as safe. This is the first time the Soviet government has invited foreign experts to perform such a task.

## DEBATES ABOUT NUCLEAR POWER

Open debates, public hearings and inquiries about various aspects of nuclear power, such as siting, safety, disposal of nuclear waste and so on, are quite common in some countries. Conducted by independent organizations like Friends of the Earth and Critical Mass, or by government bodies and parliamentary commissions, they are published in newspapers, journals and books. In my own library I have a random collection of more than 30 volumes documenting debates which have taken place in the United Kingdom and the United States since 1973. There has never been this kind of open discussion in the Soviet Union. Information about safety, radwaste disposal and transport, economic records, uranium mining occupational health statistics and so on is classified. The public is not consulted about where nuclear power stations should be sited. The Chernobyl accident, however, finally brought an end to the *carte blanche* enjoyed by the bureaucracy and technocracy and to public apathy and silence.

In the Ukraine public concern has been accompanied by strong local nationalism. A group of Ukrainian writers set up an international 'Chernobyl Forum', for example, to discuss the problems of nuclear power and to stop the proliferation of atomic power stations in densely populated areas. The prominent Ukrainian writer, Oles Gonchar, publicly tested *glasnost'* with his angry questions:

> Why did these atomic power stations sprout on our soil, one after the other, almost back-to-back? Rovenskaya, Khmelnitskaya on the Dnieper river, Zaporozhe, and not far away, the South Ukraine station. Why do they dig great holes in our land, displacing villages, laying waste our meadows? And why are they now starting work on another at Chigirinsk, which has not yet been officially approved? We cannot see any end to this madness. A reactor is being built at Palesnya on the Crimean steppes, and there's a plan to build another plant on the upper reaches of the Disna river, the last Ukrainian river not yet poisoned by industrial waste, in the area which till now we always associated with the epic of Prince Igor. It is not the custom in our country to ask people whether or not they want their city to be renamed, or what they think of the power station in this region so precious to us. And of course, why should they ask?[48]

A few months after this protest and many similar objections expressed by Ukrainian writers, scientists and at meetings of groups of people who would be affected by the resettlement plans, the Chigirinsk project was cancelled by the government.

The Soviet Union is not the only country to practise nuclear power secrecy. France is the most obvious Western example of similar attitudes. The French government imposed a massive nuclear power programme without proper public consent. When asked about it, the director of Electricité de France, M. Remy Carle, made the notorious remark: 'You don't tell the frogs when you are draining the marsh'.[49]

There was little real debate in the Soviet Union even after Chernobyl. A few mildly critical articles appeared in the mass media, with complaints by some editors that neither nuclear power nor space research were subject to *glasnost'*. Disputes probably had occurred inside the nuclear establishment from time to time, particularly after the Three Mile Island accident in March 1979, but the public heard little about them. In 1979, the Soviet Union was about to launch its most ambitious nuclear energy programme to date, as part of the eleventh Five-Year Plan (1981–5). The problem of siting large nuclear power stations became the focus of disagreement. One group of scientists, headed by the President of the Academy of Scientists, Anatoly Aleksandrov, and probably supported by the Brezhnev leadership, favoured siting them in the European USSR, close to population and industrial centres. Their recommendations were based on economic advantage and the view that nuclear power was absolutely safe. A second group, represented by Academician Dollezhal and supported by influential government and Party officials, argued that clusters of nuclear power stations should be located in remote, sparsely populated areas of Siberia and the Arctic regions of the European USSR. They did not question safety standards, but based their argument on environmental and ecological factors and the folly of wasting good agricultural land. The dispute reached the public domain when an article by Academician Dollezhal and Y. Koryakin on the future of nuclear energy was published in *Kommunist*.[50]

Publication in *Kommunist* signified support by very influential senior Party officials. The authors did not challenge the general policy of rapid developments of nuclear power. They predicted that the rate of growth of nuclear power would reach 5–8 million kW per annum by the end of the 1980s and more than 10 million kW by the end of the century. They expected nuclear power to account for nearly 50 per cent of global power production in the year 2000, and more than 60 per cent in 2020.

Despite high construction costs, they approved in principle of the current practice of building nuclear power stations in the European part of the USSR. The benefits, they explained, were indirect, through savings on coal transport and reduced pollution. They also praised the performance of RBMK reactors and their capacity for producing a maximal power of 2,400 MW per unit. New VVER reactors, they maintained, were intended to supplement the RBMK systems. A three-prong approach (fast reactors represented the third prong) made Soviet nuclear energy options very flexible. However, they argued in favour of fast breeders for future energy needs in the USSR and elsewhere because they generate more nuclear fuel than they consume.

On the other hand, Dollezhal and Koryakin admitted that fast-breeder technology was proving more problematic than expected: the construction of economical, powerful fast breeders would not be feasible in the 1980s. Fast breeders needed very large nuclear reprocessing facilities to produce plutonium from spent nuclear fuel from all types of reactors. The process required operating with enormous amounts of radioactive material in conditions which could potentially be dangerous. It also generated vast quantities of liquid radwaste which had to be disposed of safely and was a costly operation. Large new reprocessing plants could not be located near population centres, but if they were located in distant parts of Siberia or European Russia, transporting spent fuel safely over long distances would create new problems. It was uneconomical and dangerous to separate the AESs from the reprocessing facilities by such distances, particularly given the inadequate rail and road networks. The solution was to build giant complexes, with reprocessing plants and power stations – in fact, the entire nuclear fuel cycle – on the same site, so that only electricity needed to be transported.

Dollezhal and Koryakin advanced several further arguments in favour of locating new nuclear power stations in Siberia, the Arctic or the Soviet Far East: abundance of water; saving fertile land in the European parts of the USSR (they calculated that the land required to build 50 nuclear power stations in European USSR would produce enough food for several million people); and reducing the amount of water that was lost through evaporation in the cooling process (by 1979 evaporation from nuclear-generated heat was already at the level of 2 km$^3$ per year).

To sum up, the authors argued that while nuclear stations themselves were safe, the piecemeal transportation of spent fuel, nuclear reprocessing, and the burial of nuclear waste were dangerous operations and making them safe would be enormously expensive. Their proposed solution, however, was itself rather problematic: huge complexes should be built, each housing a reprocessing plant and a large cluster of AESs producing 30–40 million kW or more. The problem was that even if the most powerful 2,000 MW reactors were used, the project would require 15 to 20 reactors on each site.

Although at first glance the article appeared to be a rather ambitious plan for the future use of fusion energy, it was taken as criticism of current policy. The suggestion that some parts of the nuclear fuel cycle might not be safe and the arguments about the loss of valuable land and water to nuclear power were interpreted as criticism of the current practice of locating AESs near population centres in the European USSR and support for the anti-nuclear and anti-hydro lobbies. In fact, of course, it was perfectly true that each AES with a RBMK-1000 reactor required an artificial cooling reservoir of some 20–5 km$^3$ for each 4,000 MW generated, a zone of 2.5 km radius. It also required land for the plant itself, as well as for living quarters and other facilities. Situated near rivers, the plants did occupy vast areas of agricultural land and several dozen villages and dozens of collective farms had been moved to make way for them. The Chernobyl plant, for example, took more than 4,000 hectares out of agricultural use. Not surprisingly, the agricultural sector objected to the resettlement plans.

The article by Dollezhal and Koryakin was quickly challenged. Aleksandrov, Director of the Kurchatov Institute of Atomic Energy as well as President of the Academy of Sciences, called an unprecedented press conference to refute their case publicly. Many diplomats and foreign journalists were invited to attend, indicating that it had been given top-level approval and suggesting that there were disagreements in senior scientific circles and anxieties among the general public. Aleksandrov maintained that atomic energy was among the safest industrial technologies, posing no threat to the environment or the population.[51] He was particularly critical of the comments Dollezhal and Koryakin had made about reprocessing and the burial of liquid nuclear waste. Dollezhal, he said, was a reactor designer and Koryakin was an economist. Neither were well acquainted with the broader aspects of nuclear technology. He dismissed the idea that there were problems with fast breeders. Toward the end of the century about a third of nuclear-generated electricity in the Soviet Union (or more than 10 per cent of total electricity output) would come from fast breeders. He ridiculed the suggestion made by Academician Peter Kapitsa that nuclear power stations should be sited on remote islands.

Foreign journalists believed that the article and the rebuff represented the beginning of a genuine public debate. In fact, it was the end of an abortive attempt at debate. From 1980 until the Chernobyl accident no further articles appeared which contested the official nuclear programme. V. A. Legasov, Aleksandrov's deputy in the Kurchatov Institute, was particularly active in asserting the complete safety of nuclear energy. The main academic journal in the field of nuclear power, *Atomnaya Energiya*, whose editorial policy was rigidly controlled, rejected any article which dealt with safety problems. For years radiation safety was discussed only in small, limited-edition annual collections of academic papers.[52] There were 12 issues between 1975 and 1987 and, among the several hundred papers published over more than ten years, there were no critical articles, reports of minor accidents or discussions of serious problems. Even the 1987 volume (sent to press in March, nearly a year after the Chernobyl accident) does not contain any articles about the accident or its implications for nuclear safety. The only paper that has been published in the Soviet technical literature on the technical problems of the Chernobyl AES was the general part of the Soviet official report at the IAEA post-accident conference in Vienna in August 1986.

Neither scientific debate about the future of nuclear energy nor anti-nuclear opinion among the general public was tolerated by the authorities in the years before the Chernobyl accident. Western campaigns against nuclear power were depicted as tools of the oil and coal industries anxious to preserve their positions in the market (Western anti-nuclear weapon campaigns, on the other hand, have been welcomed). The absence of debate insulated planners, scientists, designers, construction engineers and operators from criticism and enabled them to cover up minor and major accidents. It was this secrecy that led to the catastrophe of Chernobyl. Even after the accident, the only time there has been any professional debate about nuclear safety was in July and August 1987, during the two-week trial of the former director of the Chernobyl plant, Brukhanov, chief engineer Fomin and four other defendants. But apart from the opening and final sentencing sessions, the proceedings were held in camera. Only a few short extracts of the judgement were ever published.[53]

Even if there has been no professional debate *per se* since the accident, public pressure has meant that the general media has not been able to avoid discussion. Yet even here there was a long delay and real discussion only began in 1988. The initiative was taken by *Moscow News*, a newspaper which has a limited Russian language edition and is primarily distributed abroad in several European languages.[54] The discussion can be summed up as follows: economists have opposed the acceleration of the nuclear energy programme because it is too costly, arguing that it makes more sense to modernize existing thermal power stations and introduce energy saving methods in industry. Representatives of the planning and government bureaucracy have argued the reverse: the significant acceleration of atomic power is the *sine qua non* of future economic development. Andrei Sakharov has joined the debate on the pro-nuclear side, but he has suggested that new nuclear power stations should be located in special underground bunkers. Although expensive, it would solve the problem of safety.[55]

Heated debate about nuclear power stations began in the Ukrainian, Byelorussian and Lithuanian general press in 1988. But it was the posthumous publication of Valery Legasov's notes in *Pravda* that made it clear that nuclear energy experts have always had doubts about the safety and reliability of RBMK reactors. However, top officials of the Kurchatov Institute, the State Committee on Atomic Energy and the relevant ministries prevented their doubts being voiced. Legasov claimed that he had been very worried about the RBMK model, but his anxieties had been dismissed:

> As far as the RBMK reactor is concerned, reactor specialists had a poor opinion of it . . . for economic reasons, because it wasted a great deal of heat, because it required vast capital expenditure . . . I was concerned about the fact that there was so much graphite, zirconium and water in the apparatus. I also worried about the unusual and, to my mind, inadequate safety systems . . . only the operator could lower the safety rods – either automatically by pushing one of the buttons or manually . . . there were no other safety systems independent of the operator, which the conditions around the apparatus itself would bring into operation.[56]

The official designers of the RBMK model were Aleksandrov, Dollezhal and other top scientists; they were also its chief advocates. They had been given awards and prizes for its development. When the RBMK programme was finally cancelled in 1988 (the existing reactors were modified and were expected to remain in operation for some time), it became known that RBMK reactors had been introduced into serial, mass production under pressure, despite strong opposition from many experts in the relevant divisions of the Ministry of Power and despite opposition from within the Kurchatov Institute.

In July 1988 *Literaturnaya Gazeta* finally broke the silence about the main fault of the RBMK models – the 'positive steam void coefficient'. An article described how Dr Ivan Zhezherun, senior scientist at the Kurchatov Institute, had been writing to various officials since 1965, pointing out the inherent defect of the RBMK and warning of the possibility of explosion. Attempts had been made to silence him and to dismiss him from the Institute. He had accumulated more than 1,000 pages of correspondence with officials (including the Central Committee and Council of Ministers) in which he had reported that:

> All reactors of this type are in principle prone to explosion, because they have a significant positive steam coefficient of reactivity. In other words, the appearance of steam in the active zone of the reactor increases the amount of heat power discharged. This in turn causes an increase in the amount of steam . . . the power begins to grow rapidly and the reactor leaps out of control.[57]

This, of course, is exactly what happened at Chernobyl.

Zhezherun was too important to be silenced. He had been one of Kurchatov's main scientific assistants since 1944, a senior member of the team which constructed the first Soviet reactor in 1946 and the second in 1948. In those crucial years he was responsible for the neutron-physical tests and the selection of pure graphite and uranium for these reactors. He was also the author of the only scientific book about the history of the first reactors.[58] Although the public did not know his name (almost everyone who works in nuclear reactor research in the Soviet Union remains a 'secret' scientist), he was extremely prominent in the scientific world. On the other hand, Zhezherun confined his objections to the construction of RBMK reactors strictly to the privacy of the atomic bureaucracy. They could, therefore, simply be ignored. He could not make his criticisms openly to the public or use the general media. For one thing, even as a pensioner (he is 72 years old), he was under obligation to discuss the problem only with his former superiors; for another, he had no access to the media. *Literaturnaya Gazeta* admitted, in fact, that if he had tried to appeal to the media and to explain the dangers of the positive steam void coefficient, 'He would have been not on pension, but on a prison bench. And instead of being called fine words like "doctor of science", "laureate" . . . epithets like slanderer, blackguard, renegade would have been used about him . . .'.[59]

In September 1986 the administration of the Kurchatov Institute held a special 'Day of Information' to explain the official version of the causes of the accident. But there were no debates and those who attended were not permitted to ask questions.[60] As long as this kind of policy and practice of secrecy over scientific and technical problems continues within the Soviet nuclear energy establishment, the probability of future accidents cannot be excluded.

Since 1988 the USSR Academy of Science has begun to play a far more active role in the decision-making about the siting and safety of nuclear power stations. The retirement of Academician Anatoly Aleksandrov from the directorship of the Kurchatov Institute of Atomic Energy (because of his advanced age and also because of an embarrassing criminal investigation into the circumstances of the suicide of his deputy, Valery Legasov) made it possible to appoint a new director. Academician Evgenii Velikhov was elected director (the new, more democratic rules in the Soviet academic world allow for the senior members of an institute to choose by secret ballot between two or more nominated candidates). Velikhov was also appointed chairman of a special expert commission set up to study the soundness of the main projects of the new Ministry of Atomic Energy.

The first project investigated was the Crimean nuclear power station which was close to completion. Construction had begun in 1980 on the

Kerch peninsula, on the coast of the Azov Sea. It consisted of two VVER reactors of 1,000 MWe each. This was meant to be merely the first stage; two further reactors were planned for the site. In 1988 more than 500 million roubles were spent on construction, about half the estimated total cost of the project. The construction was well behind schedule. The local people and many independent experts were opposed to the project and they sent hundreds of letters to the authorities. The government seemed determined to proceed. The main objections to the station concerned the seismological instability of the site. The atomic energy authorities argued that a powerful earthquake was unlikely in this region and that minor tremors had been taken into account. However, the devastating earthquake in Armenia in December 1988 (most of the victims died because of the poor construction of their houses which had officially been declared safe for the area) made it impossible to proceed with the Crimean nuclear station without an independent expert review.

Velikhov's commission finally came to the conclusion that the project was unsound and that the station site was prone to more powerful earthquakes than had been taken into account. It did not object to the project in general, it merely made it clear that the geological survey done by the ministry and its predecessors was not objective. The ministry (and that means the government as well) refused to accept the findings of the commission. Because of the controversy, some members of the commission decided to make their objections public and they were published in *Pravda*.[61] This is the first time in the history of the Soviet nuclear energy programme that an independent scientific enquiry has made public its concerns about the safety of a nuclear power station. In theory the Ministry of Atomic Energy can ignore the opinion of the Academy of Sciences; in practice conflicts of this type cannot be ignored by the Committee on Safety in the Atomic Power Industry or by the Politburo which will make the final decision. The construction of the Crimean Atomic Power Station has been postponed. It will almost certainly be cancelled. This precedent will make it impossible for the Ministry of Atomic Energy to start any new projects without commissioning independent expert groups. This will slow down all new projects and many of them will be cancelled or postponed.


CONCLUSION

It is clear that the secrecy that has protected all Soviet nuclear power programmes since the first AES project was initiated in 1954 was a major contributory factor in the Chernobyl accident. There had been several previous accidents, but they were covered up at all levels. Operators and local engineers concealed small mishaps from their superiors. Often they were not even recorded in the operational log books. More serious accidents and shutdowns were covered up by nuclear plant administrators, because their bonuses and rewards depended upon good records. Construction and design faults were covered by the ministerial and atomic energy bureaucracies, which had vested interests in the good image of the nuclear industry. Really major accidents, like the Kyshtym nuclear disaster in the Urals in 1957, which led to a contaminated exclusion zone as large as that at Chernobyl, the fire at the Beloyarsk station in 1979 or the 1983 *Atommash* accident, were concealed by the government. Even the awards to the firemen and rescue workers were distributed secretly.

The new Five-Year Plan approved by the Supreme Soviet in June 1986, after Chernobyl, was unrealistic. It called for the addition of 41,000 MW of electric power from new nuclear plants and would have required nearly 40 new reactors to be in operation by 1990. In fact, four new reactors were licensed in 1987–8 and 16 to 17 were under construction in 1988–9. Each reactor, even when work proceeds according to schedule, takes more than five years to build. In the previous Five-Year Plan, 25 MWe of new nuclear power had been planned, but only 15 MWe was actually added. Acceleration during 1986–90 was necesssary if the targets of the more general 'Energy Programme of the USSR', adopted in 1983, were to be attained. But the plan bore little relation to reality. Some reactors already in operation have recently been shut down permanently (for example, the Armenian nuclear plant) and others which were under construction have been halted for modifications or cancelled (for example, the Kuban and Crimean plants).

The statement of accounts from the January 1988 Politburo meeting puts the economic cost of the Chernobyl accident at 8 billion roubles.[62] This is what it would cost to build 16 Chernobyl-type power reactors. In fact, this represents only a fraction of the real costs (which will continue to mount for several decades). But even if the losses up to the end of 1987 are estimated at 8 billion roubles, this is an underestimate. It excludes indirect losses and expenses. The methods by which the costs were calculated have not been disclosed, analysed or discussed. It is unclear, for example, whether they include the expensive modernization of the safety systems of existing reactors, the cancellation of projects which had already been started, or the design changes to reactors under construction and in the planning stage. The figure certainly excludes the cost of constructing a new town (Slavutich, 50 km east of the exclusion zone) for people who work at Chernobyl. In May 1988 a prominent economist, L. I. Abalkin, raised the estimate to 11 billion roubles but he did not reveal how he had reached this figure.[63]

If the costs of Chernobyl were properly calculated they would probably come close to the total amount that has been invested in the Soviet nuclear power industry since 1954. If that is the case, no one can claim any longer that nuclear power is economically beneficial to Soviet development.

# 8

# A History of Nuclear Accidents in the Soviet Union

INTRODUCTION

SOVIET nuclear technology may not be superior to nuclear technology elsewhere but the ability to keep accidents or mishaps in military and civilian nuclear facilities secret is certainly better. Nuclear energy projects at first belonged to the military establishment and were designated 'top secret'. Even when they were transferred to the civilian Ministry of Power and Electrification (when the first serial RBMK-1000 and VVER-440 models were developed), the reactor cycle technology (uranium rods, fission, reprocessing spent fuel, burial of nuclear waste) remained the responsibility of the Ministry of Medium Machine Building, which supervises military and civilian nuclear projects.

Although Soviet nuclear physicists represent the largest professional group in the USSR Academy of Sciences, their research institutes do not, as a rule, belong to the Academy. The leading nuclear research institutes (for example, the Kurchatov Institute in Moscow or the Physico-Power Institute in Obninsk) belong not to the Academy, but to the Ministry of Medium Machine Building and the State Committee for the Utilization of Atomic Energy which acts as its public relations office. Institutes like the Lenin Institute of Atomic Reactors in Dmitrovgrad, the High Energy Physics Institute in Serpukhov, the Instrumentation Scientific Research Institute in Moscow and others, are officially affiliated to the State Committee. Each institute supervises the work of the equipment it has designed. Malfunction or mishaps are usually, therefore, reported to the relevant research institute, but the information is treated as top secret.

The State Committee on Safety in the Atomic Power Industry was established in 1983. Its first chairman, Ye. V. Kulov, had previously been Deputy Minister of Medium Machine Building (he was dismissed after the Chernobyl accident). This committee now has representatives to supervise construction and operational works at every nuclear power station. It does not publish reports, however, and it also operates on the principle of secrecy.

Soviet commentators claimed that the Chernobyl catastrophe was the first accident in the Soviet nuclear programme. At the same time they dwelt on the numerous accidents which had occurred in the United States, the United Kingdom, Germany and other countries. Since their information came from open, easily available sources, most of it was accurate. The Soviet public was convinced that Chernobyl was the first accident in the Soviet Union. Some people even believed that the absence of accidents had made nuclear energy operators and officials too complacent. Before the accident (particularly after the Three Mile Island accident in the United States in 1979) many articles had been published claiming that total safety was enforced in Soviet nuclear establishments. It can be assumed that the authors of these articles were sincere since there was no public knowledge or analysis of previous accidents. As a member of the International Atomic Energy Agency in Vienna, the Soviet Union was obliged to report details of even minor or trivial accidents to the IAEA Safety Commission. These reports were considered useful to other member countries, as well as to the reporting country. But the Soviet Union had never reported an accident at a reactor or reprocessing plant. It only fair to add, however, that the IAEA did not press the Soviet government too hard for proper safety records.

It was, of course, a myth that the Soviet nuclear programme was 'totally safe', and it remained a myth not because it was impossible to discover the real facts, but because other governments were simply not interested in finding out. Minor (and more serious) accidents occur regularly in the nuclear energy industries of every country that operates nuclear reactors, but the way in which they are reported differs widely from country to country. The number of known accidents (per reactor or per billions of generated megawatts) in different countries does not reflect the quality of equipment nor the level of performance. Nor does it necessarily reflect safety standards. It is a function of the openness of the society and the attitude of its government to nuclear information.

The largest number of nuclear accidents and operational mishaps which have been described in the literature have occurred in the United States. This is because the United States is the country that is most open about nuclear-related accidents. Its nuclear energy stations are privately owned but supervised by a government body, the Nuclear Regulation Commission (NRC). This supervision and the many anti-nuclear, consumer and environmental groups make it difficult to cover up even minor mishaps. British nuclear power plants are fully controlled by the government and this makes them far less open to public scrutiny. However, the British press is free to discuss accidents. France depends more on nuclear energy (up to 70 per cent of its total requirement) than Britain or the United States. The French government tends to treat nuclear energy matters as highly classified information and there has never been a public enquiry into nuclear safety in France. Most other countries fall between the two extremes of France and the United States. The situation in the United States can, therefore, justifiably be taken as the best possible case.

Major nuclear accidents that have occurred in the United States are listed in open publications.[1] All minor accidents and mishaps have to be reported to the NRC and are also made public. Several independent groups constantly monitor nuclear safety. The Public Citizen's Reports on Nuclear Energy, composed and published annually by the Critical Mass Energy Project, record and analyse more cases than the NRC. They recorded 3,800 minor accidents and mishaps in 1980[2] and over 4,000 (at 74 reactors) in 1981.[3] The number jumped to 4,500 in 1982 and 5,000 in 1983. Between 1979 and 1987 about 26,000 mishaps were registered in the United States despite the tighter safety standards that were introduced after the Three Mile Island accident in 1979.[4] One can assume that similar numbers of minor accidents occur in other countries which build or use nuclear reactors. The only reason why we know less about them is that other countries do not allow such freedom of access to nuclear information. The nuclear industry itself (including individual plant managers) is not anxious to admit to accidents, particularly if they do not result in radioactivity leaks or the kind of damage to health which cannot easily be hidden. Yet, even if the public at large is kept ignorant, it would be comforting to know that the relevant experts discuss the accidents, analyse their causes and take necessary preventative or corrective measures. It would be far more serious if accidents remained both unreported and unnoticed.

Given the rather complex relationship of responsibility within the Soviet nuclear industry and the prevalent tendency to secrecy, cover-up is a particularly common phenomenon. It is, therefore, rather difficult to analyse Soviet safety records. I shall begin by examining cases that can be confirmed by valid sources.

## REACTOR ACCIDENTS

Before 1986 the Chernobyl AES was considered the best in the Soviet Union on the basis of its technical safety record. In July and August

1987, however, during the trial of the administrative staff of the plant, it emerged that there had been a number of previous accidents and emergency shutdowns. In a report of the last day of the trial Andrei Pral'nikov, special correspondent of *Moscow News*, quoted from the official court verdict:

> There were many unscheduled (emergency) shutdowns because of mistakes made by personnel. The causes were not always properly investigated and in some cases they were covered up. Out of 71 technical breakdowns in 1980–1986, no investigation into the causes was carried out at all in 27 cases. Many cases of equipment failure had not been registered in the operation logs.[5]

This brief statement gives only a glimpse of the problem. As mentioned in chapter 7 there were quite a few accidents at Chernobyl plant, particularly leaks of radioactive water because of poor quality of pipes and construction works. The safety records of the Soviet nuclear industry have never been discussed in the technical literature on nuclear energy. After the Three Mile Island accident in the United States in 1979 some scientists began to publish papers on safety problems, but they analysed the technical details of accidents at American or British, plants, ignoring the Soviet situation.[6] The most comprehensive technical history of Soviet nuclear science and technology prepared in 1981 for an English language edition by A. M. Petrosy'ants, Chairman of the State Committee for the Utilization of Atomic Energy, does not deal with safety problems *per se* and terms like 'accident', 'mishap' or 'safety' do not appear in its index. But there are, in fact, a few paragraphs buried within the 400 pages of text which indicate that there have been accidents and breakdowns. The section on the Novovoronezh plant VVER-210, for example, explains that '. . . when working-up the nuclear power station, everything did not proceed as smoothly as this might indicate. There were the inevitable failures and disturbances, originating during the start-up and adjustment work with obscure occurrences at first sight, which occasionally were not immediately explained'.[7]

One example given of these disturbances was the unexpected accumulation of radioactive cobalt in the water of the primary circuit. Radiocobalt is not a normal fission product and it can settle on reactor walls, pipes, etc. The reactor was not shut down while the source of the cobalt was sought. After the water in the primary circuit had been changed twice, the engineers discovered that a cobalt-containing stellite alloy in the main circulation pump was generating cobalt which was transformed into radioactive cobalt by neutron bombardment. Under normal circumstances the main circulation pump should not have been under heavy neutron irradiation. This means that there must have been a design fault. The problem was solved by replacing the stellite with another alloy.

A second problem in the same reactor was rather more serious. In December 1969 the water pressure inside the first water circuit suddenly dropped. The reactor was shut down as an emergency:

> After the total discharge of the fuel and the removal of the reactor stack, it was discovered that as a result of damage to the bracing of the thermal shield, it had dropped and was resting with its lower end in the elliptical bottom of the reactor vessel. Some components of the shield bracing to the reactor vessel were torn away. However, the shield was almost undamaged, with the exception of a few cracks at the welding points of the mounting brackets to the reactor vessel. It would be quite complicated to secure safely the thermal shield to the reactor vessel under high activity conditions. At the same time, a calculation of efficiency of the reactor vessel during the laid-down servicing period, with increased intensity of irradiation of its walls, confirmed the feasibility of the future operation of the reactor without the shield. Therefore the shield was cut up into sections and removed completely from the reactor.[8]

On investigation it was discovered that the thermal shield had collapsed under the influence of vibrational loads. Modifications were made to the reactor to prevent a repetition of the problem.

In describing the work of the first commercial fast-breeder reactor BN-350 at Shevchenko, Petrosy'ants describes technical accidents in a way that indicates that occurrences of this type were quite common:

> During operation the steam-generators with natural circulation started to leak through the steam pipe circuit, consisting of two evaporator and superheater sections. The cause of the leak was due to micro-cracks in the caps of the field tubes, manufactured by cold drop-forging. Because of this, the decision was taken to replace completely all the tubes, and to manufacture the caps for them by turning. Nevertheless, even after the repairs carried out in 1974–75, two cases of leaks were observed. An emergency shielding system for the steam generator, which ensures reliable discharging of the coolant even with large leaks, is strongly recommended.[9]

A number of accidents appear to have occurred in the Leningrad RBMK-1000 reactors. For example:

> Leaks from the primary circuit have been observed. However, they have developed relatively slowly and have never led to an instantaneous

rupture of large-diameter pipelines, although breakages of small pipes with a diameter of 1–2 cm have occurred as a consequence of corrosion and vibration. In accordance with this, measures have been taken to provide emergency cooling of the core and to eliminate failure of the fuel elements and the discharge of fission products into rooms of the nuclear power station and into the surrounding medium.[10]

There have also been ruptures of large-diameter pipes, which represent major reactor accidents. Petrosy'ants mentions one case only, but he does not give technical details nor say where it happened: 'As the analysis of the last rupture of a pipeline with a diameter of 300 mm showed, with a combined water space of the loop, a large mass of water and steam is discharged, which is difficult to localise without great additional expense'.[11]

It seems that rupture of water or steam pipes was a common occurrence and that is why some designers considered the RBMK-1000 model safer. It had very many autonomous water channels and any rupture was therefore localized.

Legasov was struck, the wrote, by the comments made by Nikolai Ryzhkov, Chairman of the Council of Ministers, during a special Politburo meeting on 14 July 1986. On the basis, presumably, of accident records which the government had, Ryzhkov said that it was more or less inevitable that this tragic accident had happened.[12] Legasov agreed with Ryzhkov's assessment:

> I remembered a case, for example, at one atomic station, when instead of doing the weld properly, the welder simply put the electrode on a seam in the main pipeline, welding it a little from the top. There could have been an awful accident, a rupture in a large pipeline, an accident of the VVER apparatus with complete loss of the heat conductor and melt down of the active zone, etc. It is just as well that the personnel was disciplined, attentive and careful because the leak which the operator discovered could not be seen even under a microscope. They investigated and discovered that it was simply a badly made pipe. They began to look at the documentation – it was all certified as required: that the welder had done a proper job, that the seam had been checked by gamma-defectoscopy . . . All this was done in the name of the productivity of labour, to weld more seams.[13]

Legasov maintained that major and minor accidents were endemic:

> Frequent leaks . . . badly working valves . . . all these took place every year. Decade-long conversations about training, five-year long, at least, conversations about setting up a system for diagnosing the state of the equipment, none of this was done . . . Anyone who has been in an AES

building site is amazed that one can do such highly responsible work at such shoddy building sites.[14]

It has only recently come to light that the most serious reactor accident before Chernobyl occurred at Kursk RBMK-1000 plant in 1980. It was described briefly in Annex 2 of the Soviet Working Document. Annex 2 is the longest (186 pages) and most technical of the seven annexes. The description of the Kursk accident is given at the very end (pp. 181–2), not to make a point about the possible danger of accidents but to illustrate that the safety devices are so well designed that even potentially serious accidents can be contained.

In 1980 the Kursk nuclear power plant suffered a total blackout, an event which puts any operational reactor in grave danger. According to the report, however, it proved not to be a serious problem for the RBMK system:

> A loss of power plant internal load is one of the most severe accident situations that can occur at the unit. When internal load is lost, the coolant is circulated through the core at the start of the accident by the running down main circulation pumps and thereafter by natural circulation . . .
>
> In the initial phase of that process, the decrease in the water flow rate is somewhat higher than the rate at which the reactor thermal power decreases; this results in a brief increase in steam content and reduction in the departure from nucleate boiling (DNB) ratios. DNB ratios – even in those channels which are under greatest thermal stress – is insignificant and poses no danger to the reactor, since in the initial phase of an accident the reactor is safely cooled by the running down main circulation pumps.
>
> The running down pumps have a significant effect on coolant circulation through the reactor only for the first 30–35 seconds of the transient regime. Thereafter the core is cooled by natural circulation.[15]

This was, of course, the accident scenario that was in the minds of those who were carrying out the fatal experiment at Chernobyl. 30–35 seconds did not give enough time to switch on the standby diesel generators. Whether natural circulation can cool the core effectively to prevent explosion depends on the stage of the fuel cycle. A shutdown reactor with freshly loaded fuel elements which have not yet accumulated significant amounts of hot fission radionuclides can probably be kept cool by natural circulation, but it is doubtful that damage to the reactor core or explosions of the fuel rods can be prevented in a reactor in the middle or at the end of its fuel cycle without active pumping of coolant. That is why the operators at Chernobyl were testing a device designed to increase the period when the pumps were still pushing water through by using electricity produced by the inertia of the turbines. Reading the description of the Kursk accident, however, one might almost think that the Chernobyl experiment was unnecessary:

> The safety of natural circulation regimes at RBMK units has been confirmed by accident situations which have occurred under real operating conditions at nuclear power plants. For example, at one unit of the Kursk NPP in January 1980 a total loss of station internal load occurred. During the transient conditions, readings from the thermo-couples of the fuel assemblies and from the flowmeter at the inlet to one of the reactor fuel channels were recorded. During the entire transient regimes, no increase in the temperature of the fuel element cans was registered and the flow through the channel recorded under natural circulation conditions was not less than 20% of the flow rate at nominal capacity . . .
>
> Experimental data on natural circulation regimes was correlated and compared with the results of calculations from the theoretical programs developed. In view of the good agreement between the results, theoretical predictions were made which showed that reliable and safe operation of RBMK-1000 units under natural circulation conditions is possible at power levels up to 35–40%.[16]

The way in which the January 1980 Kursk station emergency is described in the Soviet report makes it seem likely that accidents of the same type had occurred in other reactors without damage to the reactor core. The authors of the report maintain that RBMK reactors can work without main pumps and with only natural water circulation if their power level is reduced to 35–40 per cent. Graphs which illustrate this statement show that there was no great increase of steam pressure after the loss of the unit internal load (apart from a 30 per cent increase during the first 10 seconds). A total instantaneous cut-off of feed water, which happened somewhere according to the report, also did not create a dangerous situation. The pressure of steam in the separators did not drop for more than 80 seconds, nor did it rise more than 10–20 per cent. However, it was obvious that in both these cases the graphs presented in the Working Document did not depict real emergencies, but simulated computer 'theoretical transient regimes'. The model was probably programmed for fresh fuel, when thermal power dropped to nearly the same level as nuclear power within 80 seconds. But for reactors in which most of the fuel rods had been accumulating fission radionuclides for more than two years, as at Chernobyl, the computer models were irrelevant.

It is rather strange that descriptions of previous accidents were included in the Soviet report. Including them may have been an oversight caused by having to rush the report. Most of the text of Annex 2 does not appear to have been written specifically for the IAEA post-accident meeting. It seems to be part of a textbook for RBMK-1000 operators suitably adapted for the Vienna meeting. The signs of censorship are particularly evident in the Russian version, where several pages have missing paragraphs left blank (for example, pp. 10, 29, 35, 36, 37, 38, 40). In some places individual sentences have been removed from the text. The structural diagrams have been copied from a very large version and their reduction to A4 size makes them almost entirely illegible (see, for example, figures 2.10, 2.11, 2.52, 2.60, 2.61). The English version was translated in Vienna. It is better done and more professionally produced (it is typed with an electric typewriter, while a poor quality manual typewriter is used for the Russian version). The translators could do nothing, however, with the illegible diagrams and graphs, they were merely reproduced and marked 'other text illegible'. The mention of the Kursk accident probably slipped through the censorship in this way. But when the Soviet experts were asked about it during the discussion, they were reluctant to give details.

More than 400 technical questions remain unanswered in Vienna. Promises were made to provide more explanation later, but no further information has been made available about Kursk or about any other accident which involved complete loss of electricity in the power station, or the 'instantaneous cut-off of feed water'. It is, of course, bad enough when nuclear experts try to mislead the public and cover up serious accidents in the nuclear industry. It is much worse if young engineers who are training to become future operators of nuclear power stations are given false information about the possible consequences of the loss of coolant and about the likeliest outcome of a blackout of the power station: loss of internal electricity for its own needs. And it is lunacy to explain that after accidental stoppage of the main circulation pumps natural circulation is sufficient if the power level is reduced to 35–40 per cent or that the instantaneous cut-off of the cooling water will not lead to a major accident and produce overheating and possible melting of some fuel rods.

The occurrence of several accidents caused by operator error was mentioned in a *Pravda* article about the role of psychological studies for the development of safer systems of operation of nuclear power stations.[1/] The article described some of the results of an experimental study undertaken in 1985 by the Institute of the Psychology of Labour of the USSR Academy of Sciences in co-operation with the Institute of the Operation of Atomic Power Stations. Although the results of the study were never published, a report, 'An Analysis of the psychological peculiarities of the activity of the operational personnel of the AES and problems of professional selection', was prepared for the administration. Some of the observations were made at Unit 3 of the Chernobyl AES. The report claimed that the designers of the control and operational systems did not take many important safety factors into consideration. For example, important control panels and switches controlled by a single operator were located too far from one another, sometimes as much as 15 m apart. Psychological stress is quite frequent, particularly during changes of the plant regime. There are too many alarm and control signals for a single operator to make a proper assessment rapidly. Sometimes in an emergency several hundred alarms of different kinds flash on the control panels. The controls of a particular regime are situated randomly and have different control scales. False alarms are quite common. Statistical analysis of emergencies indicated that the most serious mishaps occurred during the night shift.

Although this study was done in 1985, no action was taken on the basis of its recommendations. The study does, however, suggest why the operators of Unit 4 switched off several systems to carry out their test on the night of 26 April 1986: they did not want to be distracted by too many alarms. Moreover, they knew from their operating instructions (similar to the instructions formulated on the basis of the Kursk accident in 1980) that the reactor would be safe even if the pumps circulating the water stopped entirely. Legasov explained what the effect was of these optimistic instructions:

> Before conducting experiments no thought was given to the possible consequences . . . There was complete contempt for the point of view of the designer and the scientific supervisor . . . no attention was paid to the condition of the instruments or the equipment . . . One station director said straight out: 'What are you worried about? An atomic reactor is a samovar. It's much simpler than a thermal station, our personnel are experienced and nothing ever happens'.[18]

It is only fair to point out that Legasov had not always displayed such a critical and honest attitude. If he had, it is unlikely that he would have been appointed head of the Soviet delegation to Vienna in 1986. Before the Chernobyl accident he was one of the most active supporters of the rapid development of nuclear energy and a vocal proponent of the safety of Soviet reactors. In an article on the lessons of the Three Mile Island accident in 1979, he maintained that it had no relevance to the Soviet nuclear energy industry because of the higher safety standards in the Soviet Union. The American accident had partly been the result of operator error. Legasov and his colleagues insisted that Soviet operators were fully trained before being allowed to control reactors and, 'unlike American AES personnel, they are recruited from specialists with higher education'.[19]

A detailed search through the Soviet literature on nuclear energy would probably reveal a few more details indicating that accidents have occurred in other reactors. But more important than these few hints is the secrecy and the habitual cover-up at all levels starting from the operators themselves. Essentially the secrecy originates from the general principle supported by scientists, designers and high officials that Soviet nuclear power stations are totally safe. There has been no exchange of information about accidents; emergencies and accidents have not been studied during operator training nor have they been simulated on the computer-operated control panels used for training. In fact, it emerged during the trial of the Chernobyl officials that no such purely training controls exist: 'So far there are no training controls where the operators are taught. The operators learn the instructions by heart and train at the work place "by sight" instead of mastering the things they need to do during a computer-simulated accident by practising at a control panel'.[20]

When operators are not trained how to deal with accidents and emergencies, any small mishap with which they do not know how to deal can develop into a serious problem. One cannot imagine pilots being trained without artificial simulation of emergencies and accidents in special simulator control cockpits. Nuclear reactors have no fewer controls and alarm systems than cockpits. It is now admitted that the senior operators and engineers at Chernobyl AES were poorly trained. But this only became clear after the trial.


REACTOR ACCIDENTS FOR WHICH THERE ARE NO RECORDS

Although the accidents mentioned in the previous section were not described in detail in Soviet sources, mention of them can be found in publications or statements. The very fact that their existence can be detected from accidental remarks suggests that they represent only the tip of an iceberg.

Mention was made in the last chapter of the unfortunate accident at the Atommash plant in 1983. Although strictly speaking it was not a reactor accident, it did have serious implications for reactor safety problems in general. The Politburo commission which investigated it found that the responsible officials had failed 'to ensure accident-free operations'. They were responsible for 'gross violations of design requirements'.[21] The commission did not disclose the nature of the accident nor did Legasov, although he maintained that Atommash had been very badly built.[22]

It is believed that nuclear safety was discussed by the Politburo in 1983 and that a special 'closed' letter was signed by Yuri Andropov, General Secretary of the CC CPSU (Central Committee of the Communist Party of the Soviet Union), and sent to Party organizations in many industrial centres to be read at closed Party meetings. This confidential letter listed some serious accidents in the nuclear industry. One, in which two people had died, was qualified as a potential disaster. It proved impossible at the time to discover any more details about this accident. A new Committee on Safety in the Nuclear Industry was established but its work was carried out in complete secrecy and it never published any reports or bulletins. In my research into the nuclear waste accident in Kyshtym in 1957–8 (summarized in the next section), it took more than two years of intensive study of Soviet literature on radiobiology, radioecology and other linked fields to establish proof of the nature of the catastrophe. It was only possible because the accident resulted in massive radioactive contamination of the environment. Until Chernobyl, nuclear reactor accidents did not have serious ecological effects and it was easy to cover them up. It is possible that an intensive study of all possible sources, including regional newspapers, would reveal some evidence. But after Chernobyl it is unnecessary to undertake this kind of detective work merely to prove the deficiencies of the Soviet nuclear industry.

In April 1979 the Minister of Power and Electrification, Pyotr Neporozhny, was asked by an American Congressional delegation about accidents in the nuclear industry. He admitted that several minor accidents had occurred over the past 25 years. In one case, a cooling line had fractured, spilling radioactive water onto the floor of a reactor vessel. In another, a steam generator ruptured and radioactive steam spread into the machine hall. He did not reveal when or where these accidents had happened and he insisted that the damage had been contained in every case.[23] His answer was in keeping with the official view that Soviet nuclear power is totally safe for people and for the environment.

When I lived and worked in Obninsk (from 1963 until the beginning of 1973) the first Soviet AES which had become operational in 1954 was still being used for experimental purposes. Between 1954 and 1973 several more nuclear reactors were built or tested in Obninsk, some at the large Physico-Power Institute which was responsible for designing small reactors for ships and submarines, others at the Karpov Institute of Physical Chemistry which was a research centre on reprocessing spent nuclear fuel. The Institute of Medical Radiology, where I worked, also planned to build a small reactor to study the effect of neutrons on tissues for biological and medical purposes, but it was decided that it would be too expensive and the Karpov Institute adapted one of its reactors to serve our needs.

A number of small-scale accidents occurred in Obninsk between 1963 and 1973 which were serious enough to cause human casualties that local residents knew about and to contaminate the environment. On several occasions the local river, the Protva, was 'closed' for recreation and signs were erected on its beaches temporarily forbidding bathing and fishing because of 'sanitary regulations'. This normally meant that there had been an emergency discharge of radioactive cooling water. The rules did not apply several kilometres downstream, presumably because the contamination was considered well diluted. It would have been difficult to 'close' the river downstream anyway, because most of the local collective farms and villages were dependent on the river for their water supplies, particularly for their livestock. Occasionally, the filters in the reactor chimneys gave cause for alarm and helicopters could be seen circulating over the institutes measuring the escaping radioactive gases.

Changing the fuel rods (particularly in the VVER reactors where a third or a half of the core had to be replaced periodically) was always an event which caused trepidation; the danger of the operation was well known. It was almost always the case that the reactor pressure vessel became contaminated and had to be washed by several different liquids, including alcohol. Cases of radiation sickness and fatal accidents were not uncommon. They were usually covered up and each institute had its own closed medical facilities to treat those exposed to radiation. But funerals at the local cemetery could not be kept secret. Once, in 1967, several freshly excised human lungs were brought urgently to the pathomorphology department in our institute for autoradiographic and radiometric investigation. Apparently several young men had died from inhaling highly radioactive aerosol or dust in the Karpov Institute. This case was also covered up.

The Obninsk Physico-Power Institute is probably the largest nuclear research centre in the Soviet Union, with a staff of over 5,000. The design work for the Beloyarsk nuclear power station and for nuclear reactors for ships was carried out there. The first Soviet fast-neutron reactor was also designed there. And it was there that sodium was first selected as the best coolant for fast reactors. Scientists in other countries were sceptical at first, but later they followed the example.[24] The Physico-Power Institute was also notorious for the high mortality rate among its research and engineering personnel. As a gerontologist I was particularly struck by the fact that, judging from the birth and death dates on gravestones in the local cemetery, people in Obninsk had a far lower life expectancy than in Moscow or in the Soviet Union in general.

In 1966 there were persistent rumours in Obninsk that there had been a meltdown in the reactor in the icebreaker *Lenin*. Soviet scientists believed that atomic icebreakers were the first application of nuclear power to normal shipping. In fact, the United States was the first country to use nuclear reactors for military submarines, while the Soviet Union pioneered the use of reactors for icebreakers, of which the *Lenin*, with a displacement of 16,000 tons, was the first. Construction work was started in 1956 and running trials were conducted in the Neva river in the centre of Leningrad in 1959.[25] In 1960 a great deal of publicity was given to the first voyage of the *Lenin* along the northern sea route. Each year its voyages were reported. In 1966, all mention of the ship disappeared from the Soviet press. For a few years no one heard anything about it and there were rumours that one of its reactors had suffered meltdown and that there had been some casualties. The accident was said to have happened during an Arctic voyage. Since the *Lenin* was the only nuclear icebreaker in the world at the time, its disappearance aroused curiosity outside the Soviet Union. Several years later it reappeared after 'modernization'. It is now known that the modernization was, in fact, complete reconstruction. All three of its VVER reactors (each with 90 MW of thermal capacity) were removed and so were its six steam generators. They were replaced by two new VVER reactors and four new steam generators which 'simplified the service and markedly increased the reliability of the whole power system'.[26] The entire dosimetric monitoring system was also 'modernized'. Since six years is rather a short life span for the original reactors, it is highly likely that 'modernization' was required because of an accident. What sort of accident occurred has never been disclosed. When the next icebreaker, *Arktika*, was launched in 1972, its trials took much longer (until 1975) and they took place not in Leningrad but in the Karsk Sea, behind Novaya Zemlya and far away from populated areas.

The Soviet Union now has well over 150 nuclear submarines (each of which normally has two VVER reactors). There were Western press reports about accidents on Soviet submarines in 1978, 1979, 1980 and later. There was an accident and fire in one submarine which resulted in its being towed to the deepest part of the Atlantic (off the American coast) and sunk in 1986, after Chernobyl. The American navy keeps records of such accidents but it does not disclose the results of its intelligence (which included an unsuccessful attempt to recover one of the Soviet submarines from the bottom of the Atlantic).

In 1978 the Charter 77 dissident group in Czechoslovakia reported two serious accidents at the nuclear plant at Jaslovske Bohunice in 1976 and 1977.[27] There was no official confirmation of the facts. There have also been rumours about unspecified accidents at Rovno and in the Armenian nuclear plant. In December 1978 a fire at the Beloyarsk nuclear power station about 50 km from Sverdlovsk caused panic in the city. The accident was later reported in the emigré journal *Possev* and it was also discussed in *Nature*.[28] According to the report, the fire began in the machine hall of the fast-breeder reactor BN600 which was in the final stages of construction. Several firemen were said to have lost their lives. The report in *Nature* was quickly denied, not by the Soviet authorities but by the British Fast Reactor Development Directorate. The author of the denial, R. D. Smith, maintained that since the BN600 was at least 12 months short of completion at the date of the reported accident, it could not have been in any danger.[29]

Some details of this mysterious accident have only recently become available. An article published in *Sotsialisticheskaya industriya* on 21 October 1988 described an accident about which 'there has been ten years of silence'.[30] The fire, it appears, was caused by an electric short circuit and it started in the machine hall of the two working reactors, in the vicinity of turbines two and three, not in the fast breeder reactor. The roof collapsed and broke the oil storage facilities in the machine hall. Burning oil made the fire uncontrollable. All the reactors except one were shut down and put on emergency cooling. The one that was kept in operation had to supply the electricity and heat for all other equipment. The control rooms in all the reactors were filled with smoke and the operators could not work in them:

> It was essential to control the work of the reactor, particularly the emergency cooling systems.

There was no time to waste. The firemen came to the rescue. In their oxygen masks (which, unfortunately, the station operators did not have) they lit the way with torches and accompanied the operators who groped their way to the control panels, took the readings of the instruments that were still working and rushed for the exit to breathe. Other operators made their way to the panels to make the necessary manual adjustments. Several of them lost consciousness and were dragged out. After a few minutes they rushed back into the smoke-filled control room. No one else could do their work . . .

Conditions kept deteriorating. By morning . . . the fire had enveloped the computer into which was fed all the information about the radioactivity of and around the reactors, the temperature regime including that of the turbogenerators. The computer analysed the technical processes and made recommendations to the operators. Once it went out of action it seemed as if we had lost all control over the processes in the reactors. At the time only the specialists knew this . . .

Everything possible was done to keep the equipment working, to prevent the reactors from coming to harm. It is up to the specialists to report how they managed to do this. Soon people seemed sure: nothing would happen to the reactors, their active zones would not be breached. None the less, the specialists raised no objections to the decision of the operational staff to prepare the people in the nearby settlement for evacuation.[31]

The author of this article was a firemen. He maintained that 1,200 firemen participated in putting out the fire (in other words, many more than at Chernobyl). At the end of his article he asks the reasonable question: 'Sometimes the thought comes to me: why weren't people told immediately about those who saved the Beloyarsk AES from tragedy? Perhaps if they had been the events at Chernobyl would never have occurred'.[32]

In his recently published 'Chernobyl Notebook', Grigory Medvedev described some earlier and previously unknown accidents. Some of them were so serious that if they had been properly investigated and reported, they would certainly have affected the Soviet nuclear programme. There was an explosion, for example, in the Leningrad AES in February 1974 in which three people died. Highly radioactive water was thrown into the environment. Eighteen months later there was another accident there and the active zone was partially destroyed: about 1.5 MCi of highly active radionuclides were emitted into the environment. Apparently this release was registered in Finland and Sweden, both of which asked the Soviet government for an explanation.

Medvedev also reports accidents at the Beloyarsk, Armenian and

Balakovsky nuclear power stations. Fourteen people died in the Balakovsky accident. There had also been a previous accident at Chernobyl: 'September 1982. The fuel assemblage in the first block of the Chernobyl AES was destroyed because of errors made by the operating staff. Radioactivity affected the industrial zone and the town of Pripyat and the repair team was exposed to radiation'.[33]

These small bits and pieces of information represent all that is known about accidents at Soviet reactors. If one compares this information with the records of almost any Western country, it would seem at first glance that Soviet safety records are excellent. In fact, they prove only one thing: the capability of Soviet officials and experts and of the Soviet press and censorship to cover up negative information and embarrassing accidents. Even the most serious nuclear accident in the world before Chernobyl, the Kyshtym disaster in the Urals, which is now well documented in the Western literature, has not been mentioned until recently in the Soviet press.

## THE KYSHTYM NUCLEAR ACCIDENT

The Kyshtym disaster was a nuclear waste disposal accident at a military nuclear facility. Since it does not concern reactor technology which is the subject of this book, it will be considered only briefly here. Reprocessing spent nuclear fuel is part of the plutonium-producing industry and a special field of technology. The Kyshtym accident (also known as 'nuclear disaster in the Urals') was the result of unsafe storage of reprocessed nuclear waste from military reactors and reprocessing plants which were in operation from 1948 in the area between the two old Ural towns of Kyshtym and Kasli, in the Cheliabinsk region. This site was selected by Igor Kurchatov for the first plutonium-producing industrial facility.

The main problem of the sequence of processes which are necessary to make the plutonium bomb is how to dispose of the nuclear waste which remains after the plutonium has been extracted. Once the plutonium has been extracted from the billions of curies of radionuclides that accumulate in a reactor at the end of its fuel cycle, a highly concentrated hot liquid solution of dozens of different radioisotopes remains. The methods that are used to bury or dispose of reprocessed nuclear waste or unreprocessed spent fuel represent the most difficult and controversial stage of the nuclear energy cycle. But in the late 1940s and 1950s, when making the bomb was an absolute priority, both the United States and the Soviet Union used primitive methods of disposing of nuclear waste. A number of accidents occurred in the United States, particularly in the Hanford reservation in Washington State, where American military reactors and plutonium-reprocessing plants had been in operation since 1946. Fortunately none of them developed into a real disaster, even if only because the area is a desert of about 750 square miles. The water-table is very deep and the contamination of soil, particularly by the disposal of liquid waste into trenches and underground waste tanks which often leaked, was localized in the surface layers.

It is not known exactly how nuclear waste is disposed of in the Soviet Union. However, during the autumn of 1957 there was a thermal or chemical explosion in the waste disposal site and huge amounts of long-lived radionuclides, mainly strontium-90 and caesium-137, were blown over a large area in a north-easterly and westerly direction. An area as large as 1,000–2,000 km$^2$ was heavily contaminated and evacuated. The level of contamination in the evacuated area reached between 2,000 and 4,000 curies per km$^2$. The number of evacuees (mostly peasants) was unknown, but it is estimated from maps that 32 villages and settlements were abandoned permanently. An exclusion zone was established and the contaminated district situated between several big lakes was hydrologically isolated by a system of dams and canals and turned into an experimental ecological reserve. From the numerous ecological, environmental, zoological and other studies carried out in this human-made radioactive 'natural reserve' I have been able to prove that the Kyshtym disaster occurred and have been able to attract the attention of foreign experts who have continued the study.

I had known a little about this accident since 1958. When I first mentioned it briefly in an article in *New Scientist* in 1976,[34] it was first treated as my fantasy or as a deliberate sensational falsehood designed to compromise the nuclear industry records. The heated debate about safe methods of nuclear waste disposal had just begun at that time. It took me more than two years to analyse most of the relevant Soviet scientific literature on radiation ecology, radiation genetics, zoology and marine ecology, in order to prove the existence of a geographically large radioactively polluted area in the Urals. Finally many documents which I was able to receive from the CIA through the 'Freedom of Information Act' showed that there had been a major nuclear accident in Cheliabinsk military-nuclear plant (known as Cheliabinsk-40) which resulted in many human casualties. This information was the basis for my book *Nuclear disaster in the Urals*, which is now well known and has been translated into several languages.[35] Although I shall not give a detailed description of the accident here, some facts are relevant to the present analysis.

The total amount of long-lived radioactive isotopes which were released into the environment during the Kyshtym disaster was larger than during the Chernobyl accident. Only about 4 per cent of the fission products in the fuel rods were released during the Chernobyl accident and non-volatile isotopes like strontium-90 represented a rather small fraction of the total release (about 250–300,000 curies). In the Ural disposal site the fission radionuclides were accumulated from many full reactor cycles and tens of millions of curies of strontium-90 were released into the environment. In the Ural exclusion zone the concentration of strontium-90 in the soil was at least ten times higher than the concentration of caesium-137. This was partly due to the distribution of radiocaesium over a larger area and partly because radiocaesium was extracted during reprocessing for industrial, medical and some unspecified military purposes.

Two major research projects were carried out by American government laboratories after 1979 to find out more about the Kyshtym disaster. The first was published by a team of experts of the Oak Ridge National Laboratory as a comprehensive report and as a scientific paper.[36] The second project was done by a group of experts from the Los Alamos National Laboratory in 1982 and it is available only as a report.[37] Its findings, however, have been widely cited in the scientific literature. American laboratories used satellite photographs of the area and located the system of dams, canals and other hydrotechnical works which were designed to isolate the most seriously contaminated area of about 1,000 km².

My explanation of the cause of the disaster, based on suggestions made by colleagues in the USSR at the end of the 1950s, postulated that the overheated primitive storage facility produced some kind of steam explosion and eruption when concentrated masses of hot radionuclides came into contact with water (either ground water or a water leak). Because an eruption of this type did not need very high temperatures or fires, the radioactive aerosol did not rise to very high altitudes and the winds distributed it locally, within the Ural geographical area. The Oak Ridge team suggested a chemical explosion. They based their suggestion on the methods of reprocessing which were common during this period and which needed the initial use of very large amounts of nitric acid. Large amounts of nitrates and particularly ammonium nitrates together with organic solvents in the nuclear waste created the possibility of a conventional chemical explosion. The Los Alamos team developed a different theory. They suggested that liquid waste was disposed of into a dry lake bed. The heavy metals would have settled onto the bottom of the lake, while the liquids would eventually disappear by ground absorption and evaporation. This method could contaminate the local Techa river and slowly affect a large area via the drainage processes and wind erosion. They also thought that a chemical explosion would have been possible in an abandoned, dried-up waste lake or pond.

In 1988, by courtesy of the Space Media Network, Stockholm, I was given an opportunity to study the satellite maps of the Kyshtym–Kasli area and to compare them with ordinary maps of the area before 1957. It is clear that a large pond (about 10 km$^2$) was created between Lake Kyzyltash (the Kyshtym nuclear complex is situated on the shores of this 30 km$^2$ lake) and the smaller Sikil'dim lake, 20 km south-east. This artificial pond is now in the process of being covered by some materials, as if a decision is being implemented to cover its bottom with sand or clay. The area around the pond is badly damaged, probably by bulldozers. It is very likely that this pond was specially built or converted for the disposal of liquid nuclear waste. Because of the high temperature of the radionuclides, however, the eventual evaporation of water created an explosive concentrated mixture. Eventually, after the eruption of a significant proportion of the hot nuclear waste, the attempt was made to cover the exposed bottom of the pond with sand and clay.

The work which has been done in the Kyshtym area since 1958, including the treatment of the evacuated population, must have given Soviet experts experience which proved very useful in Chernobyl. The Oak Ridge National Laboratory team believed that the Soviet experience was important to the international nuclear research community. They concluded their paper with an appeal to their Soviet colleagues:

> As scientists involved in evaluating hazards associated with radioactive releases to the bisophere, we urge the Soviet scientific community, which was engaged in the aftermath of the KA incident, to share all pertinent information with others concerned with achieving the safe development of nuclear energy. Soviet experience gained during the application of remedial measures on an unparalleled scale following this accident is clearly unique and would be invaluable to the world nuclear community.[38]

Their appeal remained unanswered. Perhaps the reason was that the Kyshtym disaster involved military nuclear facilities. After Chernobyl, however, willingness was expressed to share information about the measures they undertook there. Unfortunately, however, this spirit of co-operation did not extend to allowing Western experts to take part in solving certain problems, nor to permitting them to use the facilities for observations or to take independent measurements inside and outside the exclusion zone.

At the end of 1988 the Space Media Network made a short film about the Kyshtym disaster based on their satellite study. Only then did the new director of the Kurchatov Institute of Atomic Energy, Evgeny Velikhov, confirm that the accident had occurred. Without giving any details or explanations, he told reporters in Japan that no information had been published because the disaster had occurred 'at a military installation before the arrival of "glasnost" '.[39] When pressed he added: 'what happened, what damage occurred, should be made open. I will try to find out what happened'.[40]

In June 1989 the newly created Ministry of Atomic Energy (which incorporated most of the former Ministry of Medium Machine Building) officially informed the IAEA about the nuclear waste accident which had occurred at Kyshtym on 29 September 1957. The reason why information was suddenly released was the change that had taken place in the Soviet political system. In February and March 1989 elections had taken place to a new body, the Congress of People's Deputies. In many constituencies electors could choose between candidates who campaigned for alternative programmes. Several candidates in the Cheliabinsk region argued against nuclear power and promised to halt the construction of the South Ural fast-breeder nuclear power station which had begun in the Kyshtym area in 1987.

It had been clear for a number of years that the five military reactors which operated in the Kyshtym district to produce plutonium would have to be closed down and dismantled because of their age. The same problem had occurred in the United States, when the Department of Energy had decided to close down the entire nuclear site (which included nine reactors and a plutonium-extraction reprocessing plant) at the Hanford Reservation in the south-east corner of Washington state. The preliminary estimate indicated that it would cost between $100 billion and $150 billion over the next twenty years to repair the environmental damage.[41] In the Soviet Union it was intended to decommission the military reactors but retain the plutonium reprocessing facilities. The problem was how to employ the workers and technical personnel living in Kyshtym. The Ministry of Medium Machine Building began to build three BN-800, fast breeders that would both provide employment (since they would need their spent fuel reprocessed regularly) and supply the region with a new source of electric energy.

In December 1988 Gorbachev incorporated this decision into Soviet foreign policy. In his speech to the United Nations he announced that the Soviet Union intended closing down its five plutonium-producing military reactors permanently. He invited the United States to follow suit. But this meant that US officials could now ask for access to the Kyshtym site to test the seriousness of Soviet intent. The probability of a visit by US officials and the anti-nuclear stance of the newly elected deputies from the Chebialinsk region persuaded the Soviet nuclear authority to prepare and release information about the Kyshtym accident.[42]

The first official statement about the accident was made by the deputy minister of Atomic Energy, V. Nekipelov, at a press conference in Cheliabinsk at the beginning of June 1989. It was widely reported in both the Soviet and Western press. An American team composed of US Congressmen, a number of environmentalists and several journalists arrived at Kyshtym at the beginning of July. The *Washington Post* published a report on the visit. It is clear from what they were told and from the description of the accident given in the Soviet report to the IAEA that the explosion occurred in one of the large tanks which had been specially built to store nuclear waste. Evgeny I. Mikerin, an official of the State Committee for the Use of Atomic Energy who had been manager of the nuclear reprocessing plant at Kyshtym at the time of the accident, told the American group that:

> Radioactive wastes . . . were dumped into a series of stainless steel and concrete tanks located slightly more than a mile from the plant . . . To keep the wastes from becoming explosive due to a natural chemical reaction . . . they were cooled by a coil of water tubing along the interior wall of each tank. The designers of the tanks did not provide a mechanism for repairing the tubes in the event they failed . . .
>
> Sometime in 1956, the tubing in one of the tanks began to leak and was then shut off . . . faulty calculations by scientists . . . indicated that, despite the failure of the cooling tube, the wastes were stable . . .
>
> As a result, more than a year lapsed with little or no effort to devise a means of repair. During this period, the wastes began to dry . . . and highly explosive nitrate salts and acetate collected at the surface.
>
> By chance . . . a control device in the tank produced a spark which detonated the salts, and the resulting explosion obliterated the tank and all that it contained.[43]

The Soviet official report acknowledges that about 2 million curies were released from the tank. An area of about 1000 km$^2$ was contaminated to the extent of making it necessary to evacuate 10,180 people. But only 600 people were evacuated immediately. The remaining

9,580 were moved during subsequent months, some only a year and a half after the accident. According to the report, the 'maximum average' dose to which the population was exposed was 17 rad of external radiation, 52 rem of dose equivalent and 150 rem if the dose was projected for the intestine, caused by contamination of food products. The report insisted that there were no health or genetic effects caused by exposure and that the evacuees who had been monitored for more than 30 years after the accident did not show any increase in incidence of leukemia, cancer or other pathologies. People were evacuated from territory where the concentration of strontium-90 was higher than 3.1 $Ci/km^2$. However, there was a larger area, 15,000 $km^2$, with a population of about 270,000, where the contamination was between 0.1 and 3 $Ci/km^2$.

From a scientific point of view the report can be criticized in a number of ways. For example, it states that the first evacuation, 7−10 days after the accident, took place from territory where the concentration of strontium-90 was higher than 500 $Ci/km^2$. But if, as it also maintains, strontium-90 represented only 5.4 per cent of the radionuclides which were released (the major part of the contamination came from cerium-144 [66 per cent], with a half-life of 284 days and zirconium-95 [25 per cent] with a half-life of 65 days), the level of radioactivity in the territory must have been more than 10,000 $Ci/km^2$. That means that the distribution between external and internal (mainly from strontium-90) radiation must have been different from the one presented in the report. People who lived in the area where the level of strontium was between 18 and 65 $Ci/km^2$ were evacuated only after 250 days. Because strontium-90 is normally fixed in the bones, these people continue to be exposed to internal (highly leukogenic) radiation until the end of their lives. Experimental data which are easily available demonstrates clearly that it is extremely unlikely that people (particularly children) exposed to such high doses of strontium-90 could escape adverse health consequences.

On 18 July 1989 the first 'hearing' of three Supreme Soviet committees (the committees on ecology and the environment, on science and on military and state security) was devoted to the report of the Ministry of Atomic Energy and the Ministry of Health on the Kyshtym accident in 1957. The chairman of the sub-committee on nuclear ecology, Yuri Shcherbak, the author of the most reliable book about the Chernobyl accident, chaired the hearing. In July 1989 I was in Moscow for the first time since 1973 as a member of a British team attending an international seminar on global security. Unexpectedly, with only two days notice, Yuri Shcherbak invited me to take part in the hearing.

Although the first hearing only lasted for five hours, it began the process of reconstructing a true picture of the events. It became clear that the accident was far more serious and complex than the report suggested. There are many unresolved problems. The most serious problem is the fate of the huge pond which was used as a disposal site for liquid nuclear waste before the accident. It is 10 km² in size and it has dried up and is covered with some materials and concrete. Boris Nekipelov reported to the hearing that it contains about 120 million curies of radioactive materials, mostly long-lived radionuclides. There has been some contamination, particularly along the Techa river, because of careless long-term discharges of nuclear waste into the river. In a northerly and north-easterly direction about 1,000 km² was heavily contaminated by the explosion on 29 September 1957. But other areas have also been contaminated by various causes and there are now a number of 'hot spots' which represent a permanent source of secondary contamination. Nekipelov also acknowledged that about 70–80 tonnes of highly radioactive waste was in the storage vessel which had exploded and that about 20 MCi had escaped. Of this amount there was about 18 MCi of fallout close to the storage tank and 2 MCi rose up to a height of about 1,000 m and was blown in a north-easterly direction. So far only 200 million roubles have been spent on decontamination measures and this, of course, is entirely inadequate. The evacuees and people who continue to live in contaminated areas have been pressing hard for some sort of compensation. It is obvious that the consequences of the Kyshtym accident are far from resolved despite the fact that 32 years have elapsed since it happened.

### CONCLUSION

The secrecy about accidents in the nuclear industry is certainly not an isolated phenomenon in Soviet society. There is secrecy about all accidents. The government is directly responsible for the performance of all enterprises and it is also the source of all information. Not surprisingly, it is reluctant to expose its poor record, particularly on safety, to the public. In theory, socialism is supposed to take better care of the workers' welfare and work conditions. In practice, mortality and industrial accident rates are higher in the Soviet Union than in most other economically developed countries.

*Glasnost*' has begun to change the attitude of both the government and the public. The general media publishes far more information about industrial accidents. Newspaper and magazine editors have become more independent of the censors. Frequently they now take the initiative, introducing a type of investigative journalism into the Soviet Union. There has been little change, however, as far as the nuclear industry is concerned. In his 'Chernobyl Notebook' Grigory Medvedev commented on the negative effect of this secrecy on the performance of the industry:

> It was when N. S. Neporozhny was Minister of Power and Electrification that hiding accidents at nuclear power stations from the public became the norm. Accidents were hidden not only from the public and government, but also from people who worked in the country's AESs. This was particularly dangerous because lack of information about negative experience always carries the danger that it will be repeated. Maiorets, Neporozhny's successor as minister, continued the tradition of silence. Within six months of taking the post he signed an order forbidding the publication in the open press and in radio and television broadcasts of news about the negative . . . ecological effects of power installations on personnel and on the population and also on the environment (the effect of electromagnetic fields, irradiation, contamination of the atmosphere, water and land).[44]

These directives remained in force until the Chernobyl incident. It was only in 1987 that the media became bolder and demanded more direct access to safety records. Individual workers, engineers and other people who worked at atomic and other power stations wrote thousands of letters to the press about accidents and safety problems. The government responded by increasing the restrictions on reporting accidents. All technical details of accidents became classified information. The creation of a separate Ministry of Atomic Energy in 1986 put this branch of industry under strict regulations similar to those imposed upon the Ministry of Medium Machine Building which deals with military aspects of nuclear power. The electricity generation cycles of nuclear plants remain under the supervision of the Ministry of Power (because it is impossible to separate the input from nuclear power plants to the general grid from the input from other sources). Maiorets, for whom the only consequence of the Chernobyl accident was a reprimand, remains responsible for the generation of electric energy. He authorized new restrictions in 1989 on information about accidents. He has also forbidden the publication of internal correspondence and documentation on accidents, even when such correspondence and documentation has not been classified. *Izvestiya* recently complained that: 'Amongst others, we still cannot find out information about accidents and fires at energy and building installations of the Ministry of Energy of the USSR, about equipment being put out of action when this entails material losses, human victims or even non-catastrophic contamination of the environment'.[45]

This policy will do nothing to restore public confidence in nuclear power.

# 9

# Nuclear Power after Chernobyl

## INTRODUCTION

THE Chernobyl accident was not only the worst in the history of nuclear power, it was also the most expensive industrial accident in modern history. The cost to the Soviet budget is already acknowledged to be about 11 billion roubles (or £10 billion) in 1986–8 and its future cost will be well in excess of this amount. But its impact extends beyond past and future losses of life, property, and agriculture and pollution of the environment. It has had a profound effect on the development of nuclear energy as a viable alternative to energy obtained from non-renewable fossil fuels.

Economic development and the general growth in the world's population have enormously increased the amount of energy that is consumed. Future progress depends on the ready availability of energy. Many people and many governments believe that nuclear energy offers an alternative to fossil fuels, particularly if breeder technology can be developed and if economical methods of extracting uranium from the ocean are found. Optimistic estimates indicate that there is sufficient uranium in the ocean for about 100,000 years if the world's population remains at the present level.[1] Pessimists, on the other hand, (including some governments), argue against nuclear energy mainly because of the long-term consequences of nuclear accidents, the danger of accumulating nuclear waste fission products and the close connection between nuclear energy and nuclear weapons technologies. They believe that future energy needs should be met by developing renewable energy sources, growing special fuel crops, using solar, wind, tidal, hydro- and geothermal energy and conserving energy more effectively.

Between 1975 and 1985 nuclear energy supporters were in the ascendancy and the proportion of nuclear energy sources in the balance of energy of most industrial nations grew enormously. But the Chernobyl accident produced a dramatic change in people's perceptions of nuclear energy. The accident will certainly go down in history as an important landmark in the scientific and technological development of our civilization.

There have been innumerable serious and tragic accidents in the coal mining industry, in the history of oil extraction and in the construction of hydroelectric dams. A number of them, even in the last decade, have been more serious than Chernobyl in terms of the number of immediate casualties. Nuclear energy supporters often argue that Chernobyl will not change the future of nuclear energy any more than offshore oil platform accidents have affected the future of the oil industry. According to this argument, safer and more reliable reactors will be developed as technology reacts to the accidents. Safe nuclear energy will cost more but the overall cost of energy will rise anyway. The increase in the number of consumers and the decline in non-renewable energy resources make increased costs inevitable. Although recent vast finds of oil and gas deposits and new methods of exploration have postponed the increase, the new reserves will become depleted in a matter of decades. This means that nuclear energy has a future, even if its relative proportion in the total balance is static or even contracts for some time.

It is difficult to make convincing predictions about future alternatives. The situation differs from country to country and depends on size, population, resources, traditions, economic level and many other factors. Sweden has recently opted against nuclear energy and plans to close down all its nuclear power stations in the next century and to increase the development of renewable sources. Japan, however, cannot afford a similar decision. Japan (143,818 square miles) is smaller than Sweden (173,649 square miles), but it has a far larger population (110 million in Japan compared to 8 million in Sweden) and it has few resources for hydroelectric energy, no oil and poor coal deposits.

On the face of it the Soviet Union is fortunate. It is large and has rich energy resources. It still has vast coal deposits and it is the world's largest producer of oil and natural gas. It also has huge natural forests and great rivers with hydroelectric potential. Moreover, it is very rich in geothermal energy and oil-shale and peat deposits continue to be used. The Soviet Union is the largest exporter of various forms of energy (oil, gas, coal, electricity). In short, it seems the country most likely to be able to manage without nuclear energy. If technical, scientific and economic analyses indicate that the prospects for nuclear power are bleak because of the inherent dangers and the high cost, the Soviet Union seems to be in a better position to prevent the proliferation of nuclear power stations than France, Germany, the United Kingdom and many other countries including the United States.

The sudden expansion of nuclear power in Western countries in the early 1970s was not the logical outcome of normal technological progress, but a reaction to the oil and energy crisis produced by the OPEC oil embargo in 1973 and the resultant quadrupling of oil prices. Many industrial technologies which were dependent on cheap oil began to suffer. The result was a world economic recession, inflation and rising unemployment in 1974–8. The Western response was to invest in nuclear power and technologies that required less energy. At the same time new, offshore technologies for extracting oil and gas from the sea bed were introduced. This rapid response was very successful. By 1985 oil prices had begun to drop and in 1986 they virtually collapsed (from $34 a barrel to $10). Nuclear energy was an important part of the strategy.

Far from suffering from the 1974 energy crisis, the Soviet Union profited. As a net exporter of energy, export revenues from oil, gas and electricity increased. The availability of plentiful energy inhibited the development of energy conservation technologies. The USSR was the only country in the world which continued to increase its production of steel, iron and other metals in the 1970s and 1980s and to use oil in its power stations. The programme to accelerate the construction of nuclear power stations was not a result of the oil crisis, but an attempt to increase oil and gas exports to generate new capital and to purchase food abroad.

At first no one seemed to expect that one of the results of the Chernobyl accident and the reduction in energy production in other nuclear power stations due to technical reconstruction would be energy shortages. The loss of nuclear-generated electricity would be compensated easily from other sources. In fact, however, the Soviet economy suffered a severe energy crisis in 1987 because of Chernobyl. The absence of technological flexibility and the inefficiency of the centralized bureaucracy prolonged the crisis into 1988 and 1989. Acute energy shortages affected the fulfilment of the current Five-Year plan. Many of the consequences of Chernobyl were predictable, but acute energy shortages in a country so rich in traditional sources of energy were unexpected. This raises the question whether nuclear-generated energy is indispensable for future economic development. What strategy should be adopted for the future? Should the proportion of nuclear energy be reduced or should new, more effective sources of nuclear energy (for example, fast breeders) be developed?

### SOVIET ENERGY OPTIONS

In the current Five-Year plan the proportion of nuclear energy was expected to increase from 11 to 22 per cent of total Soviet energy output. The Chernobyl accident not only halted the whole programme of RBMK construction (both RBMK-1000 and 1500 models) but it also reduced the output of electricity from existing RBMK reactors because of the modifications that had to be made. The planned target could not be met. But apart from the technical problems, changing public attitudes to nuclear energy and nuclear safety made it necessary to cancel some VVER stations which were already built or under construction at sites now considered unsafe or unsuitable; for example, the Armenian nuclear power station, the Crimean nuclear power station, the Kuban station, the Chigirinsk nuclear plant in the Ukraine, plants in Azerbaijan and Georgia and several thermal nuclear stations. The construction of other plants was delayed because of new safety regulations.

One obvious way to compensate for these losses was to reduce energy exports. The proportion of fuel and electrical energy in total Soviet exports had risen from 19.2 per cent in 1973 to 54.4 per cent in 1984 (an increase from 15.8 billion roubles to 74.4 billion roubles).[2] In fact, it turned out to be difficult to reduce the sale of oil and gas to capitalist countries. Food imports and the purchase of high technology required the hard currency earned by energy exports, and falling oil prices meant that the Soviet Union had to sell more oil, not less. The Chernobyl accident occurred at a very difficult time, when falling oil prices and Soviet attempts to increase energy exports coincided with the long-predicted decline in production of oil from the Siberian oilfields. Moreover, the policies of *perestroika* and *glasnost'* exposed many problems in the Soviet coal and hydroelectric programmes.

In 1985, the total annual production of electricity in the Soviet Union was 1,544 billion kilowatt-hours: 13.9 per cent of it was produced by hydroelectric power stations and 10.8 per cent by nuclear power stations.[3] This was well below the American output of electric energy (2,469 billion kilowatt-hours in 1985, of which 15.5 per cent was generated by nuclear power stations and 11.4 per cent by hydroelectric power stations[4]). In both countries well over 70 per cent of electrical energy was produced from fossil fuels, mainly coal.

## Coal-generated electricity

The Soviet Union has the world's largest coal supplies, estimated at 6,790 billion metric tonnes. If current annual production (726 million tonnes) remains static, Soviet coal supplies could last for 8,000 years. However, the richest deposits are located in the remote, cold and sparsely populated areas of Kazakhstan, Siberia, the Arctic and the Far East. European coal deposits have been depleted and coal can only be extracted in very deep collieries (between 1,000 and 1,500 m deep). Safety is a severe problem and accidents are common. Increasing the capacity of the coal power stations situated in the European part of the Soviet Union is not feasible. More than 50 per cent of the coal requirements of the European part of the Soviet Union now has to be supplied by transporting coal from the eastern parts of the country over thousands of kilometres of a rather poor rail system. By 1979–80 the transport capacity of the Soviet rail system linking western and eastern parts of the country was saturated and any increase was considered unsafe. Coal represented more than 50 per cent of the country's cargo traffic.

Priority has been given to constructing very powerful coal power stations in Siberia and Kazakhstan and transporting the electricity westwards. The world's largest coal power complex, based on the very rich Ekibastuz coal field, has been under construction in Kazakhstan since 1981. Four vast power stations were planned of 4,000 MWe each. The size of the stations, each with an energy output of the whole Chernobyl plant before the accident, reflects the general attitude of Soviet planning. The complex was situated only 20 km from the main surface coal mining area, comprising open pits and area-strip and contour-strip mining with some pits producing as much as 50 million tonnes of coal annually.[5] In fact, when the first station (which burns more than 15 million tonnes of coal annually) was completed in 1986, it became clear that it was an environmental disaster. Ekibastuz coal is a low-grade high-polluting lignite with a very high ash content (up to 35 per cent). When the station began to operate it polluted a huge area around it (including the town built for the 150,000 miners) with dust and other pollutants. The local water reservoirs were affected. The completion of three other stations has now been delayed.

Similar situations have occurred in several other large-scale projects and the construction of high voltage electricity transfer lines is also behind schedule. These bottlenecks made it very difficult to respond to the Chernobyl accident by increasing the amount of electricity generated by coal power stations. The very severe winter of 1986–7 caused acute and serious shortages of coal for purely heating purposes in many large cities of the European part of the country, including Gorky, Moscow and Leningrad. More oil had to be used to compensate. The amount of coal-generated electricity can be increased by modernizing some old power stations which produce much less electricity per unit of coal than most Western thermal power stations. But this is a long-term project and it cannot provide for immediate needs.

Coal has traditionally been the cheapest source of energy in the Soviet Union. However, the low price of coal was sustained mainly by keeping the income of miners low and by reduced spending on social and other needs of the miners' settlements. The level of modernization of coal production was also inadequate. The unexpected but very powerful wave of strikes by coal miners in Siberia, Kazhakstan, Ural, Ukraine and Arctic areas in July 1989 have resulted in a sharp increase in the price of coal (between 200 and 300 per cent) in order to generate capital to increase the miners' wages and pensions and to improve their housing conditions and other social needs. The implications of these measures on the energy balance will have been felt essentially in the last quarter of 1989 and in 1990.

### Oil-generated electricity

There are many power stations in the European part of the Soviet Union located near oil refineries which produce oil-generated electricity by using heavy or 'black' oil products, called *mazut*. When motor and diesel petroleum is distilled, large amounts of residual heavy oils are left. They are used in the petrochemical industry, particularly for manufacturing plastic materials, but they can also be used for power stations. For example, 11.5 per cent of American electricity was produced from petroleum products in 1985. In fact, this represented a decline in the proportion of electricity produced from oil products, because it is not an economical way to use residual petroleum products.

Although there are no statistics available to indicate the proportion of Soviet electricity produced from fuel oil, it is almost certainly higher than in the United States. The 1986–90 Five-Year Plan demanded a reduction in the use of fuel oil in power stations. In the winter of 1986–7, however, oil and fuel oil had to be used to compensate for the loss of nuclear-generated electricity. As a result the Soviet Union found it difficult to fulfil the contract requirements of the CMEA countries for oil. There have been petrol shortages since then in the Soviet Union and

Eastern Europe. The oil industry was urged to reverse the decline in oil production which had been visible in 1984 and 1985. The situation improved slightly in 1986 and 1987, but not enough to remove the shortages. Production did not increase in 1988.

Soviet oil reserves are limited. Production peaked in 1983 at 616 million tonnes (12.4 million barrels per day). The 1986–90 target was to increase this to 630–640 million tonnes per year, but this level has never been reached. There is no long-term prospect of keeping production at this high level. After the Chernobyl accident the Soviet government temporarily suspended existing programmes to conserve oil, but this cannot be sustained for long. The current annual domestic requirement for oil in the Soviet Union is 500 million tonnes and it is likely to grow as demand increases. Generating electricity by burning oil or fuel oil is therefore not a viable option.

*Natural gas-generated electricity*

Until the late 1960s, when the world's largest gas fields were discovered in Siberia and began to be tapped, natural gas was used for domestic and heating purposes, but not for power stations. The largest of the fields, the Urengoi (about 100 miles long and 25 miles wide) contains more than 10 trillion m³ of natural gas. The Soviet Union has about 30 trillion m³ of gas reserves in Western Siberia, three times more than its oil reserves. There are other gas fields, such as in European Russia, at Bashkir, Stavropol, which have been exploited since 1948–52, but they are comparatively small and have become almost totally depleted.

Siberian gas is mainly used for domestic and direct heating purposes. It is transported to the cities of European Russia by five giant pipelines. One pipeline from Urengoi was built specially to export gas to Central and Western Europe. It is 3,500 miles long, reaching Prague, Warsaw, Budapest, Bucharest, Sofia, Vienna, Berlin, France and Northern Italy and capable of pumping more than 40 billion m³ of gas annually. It was built in 1981–5 to increase Soviet hard currency revenues. In 1985 Soviet production of natural gas reached 643 billion m³, more than double the amount produced in 1975 (289 billion m³).[6] However, the value of gas exports increased only modestly after the completion of the 'export' pipeline, amounting to 7.7 billion roubles in 1985; gas exports were often accompanied by a reduction in oil sales to the same customer.

Delays in constructing the Urengoi pipelines (caused in part by the US embargo on vital equipment like compressors) caused a surplus of extracted gas in the Siberian fields which was often lost or burnt. It seemed sensible to build gas-fuelled power stations near the fields. Although the area was very sparsely populated before 1960, several comparatively large industrial towns had been built in the area since then and they needed locally produced electricity. The largest town, Surgut, with a population of 230,000, has a large 2,730 MWe power station which operates from casing head gas. Several other power stations were built along the pipeline to produce electricity for compressor stations and local settlements. Large amounts of gas produced as a side product of oil extraction are still simply destroyed by burning it off in open giant torches.

Attempts have been made to use gas more for industry. Most newly built boilers and furnaces are designed to operate on gas. By 1990 natural gas will be a more important source of energy than oil, reaching 43 per cent of the total Soviet fuel balance (850 billion m³). In 1985, oil represented 39.8 per cent, gas 35.5 per cent and coal 22.8 per cent of the total fuel produced in the Soviet Union. Other fuel materials formed a small part of the balance (peat 0.3 per cent, oil-shale 0.5 per cent and firewood 1.1 per cent).[7]

The proven reserves of natural gas are not unlimited. They can support the current rate of gas consumption for about 60–70 years. Gas prospects are better than oil (at current production rates there is enough oil in existing fields for 10–12 years). Natural gas is also a valuable resource for the chemical industry. The very long pipelines which cross thousands of kilometres of permafrost are vulnerable to damage, leaks and accidents. The tragic explosion of the large cloud of gas leaked from a major pipeline between Western Siberia and the European part of the Soviet Union in June 1989 (with a loss of several hundred lives, more than 100 of them children) was the most powerful indication of the vulnerability of the long and poorly built pipelines. As a result of this explosion, the supplies of liquefied gas between two parts of the country was interrupted for several months. More than 600 different industrial plants and 140 million people were affected. Despite large deposits, the shortage of natural gas was chronic in the Soviet Union as a result of distribution problems by long-distance pipelines. This may explain why Soviet leaders and planners from Stalin to Gorbachev have been so enthusiastic about hydroelectric power, the only renewable source of energy and one which is economically very important to the Soviet Union.

*The problems of hydroelectric power*

A proposal to build a hydroelectric station on the Dnieper near Zaporozhie, where natural rapids had been an obstacle to navigation for centuries, had been under consideration since well before 1917. Its construction in 1932 was the most important achievement of the first Five-Year Plan of Industrialization. The water level of the Dnieper was raised by nearly 40 m by the dam of the hydroelectric power station and the rapids were flooded. The power station did not require the construction of large artificial reservoirs because the natural contours of the river could be used. The station had a capacity of 560 MW and was the largest hydroelectric power station in Europe at the time. It was destroyed during the war, but rebuilt and modernized in 1947.

The success of the Dnieper power station and the low cost of the electricity it produced convinced the Soviet leadership that hydroelectric power was the most promising way to fulfil the country's energy requirements. In 1939, the third Five-Year Plan incorporated plans for a cascade of power stations on the Volga river. Construction was delayed until 1948–9 and the seven hydroelectric power stations which comprised the cascade were completed in 1960. This was only the beginning. Between 1960 and 1980 not only the Volga, but other parts of the Dnieper, the Don, the Kuban, the Kama, the Volkhov, the Irtysh, the Angara and many other rivers were dammed to produce electricity. Plans to construct giant hydroelectric projects at Krasnoyarsk and Sayan-Shushensk in Eastern Siberia were included in the 1986–90 Five-Year plan. By then, however, environmental opposition had become vocal and the proposals were delayed.

In general, the Soviet hydroelectric programme is no longer considered totally successful. The total amount of hydroelectric power produced in the Soviet Union in 1985–6 was 216 billion kilowatt-hours, only 40 per cent of the projected output. Hydroelectric power forms about 13.4 per cent of the total energy output from all sources.[8] Moreover, hydroelectricity no longer seems so cheap when environmental and other consequences are taken into account.

Most of the rivers in the European part of the Soviet Union were unsuitable for generating power because they flow through the great Russian plain and steppe regions. The construction of dams transformed them into a sequence of very large artificial reservoirs of shallow water. The greatest problems they have produced include the loss of villages and towns along the rivers, the loss of land that has been flooded, the depletion of fish reserves and a deterioration in the quality of drinking water in the towns and cities situated near the rivers. To build the five hydrostations on the Dnieper after the first at Zaporozhie, for example, more than a million hectares of rich agricultural land had to be flooded. More than 1,000 villages and settlements along the river were lost. Moreover, the energy potential of the river was exceeded. Evaporation from the large reservoirs (from 1,000 to 2,000 km$^2$) and the increasing amounts of water used for industry, to supply the growing large cities and for irrigation have reduced the amount of water which reaches the downstream hydroelectric stations. As a result, the last two stations of the cascade are very unproductive. The Kakhovskaya station, the largest in the cascade, operates well below its design capacity for most of the year.

A similar situation occurs in the Volga cascade. The cascade system, particularly on rivers which run through flat plains (the Don and Angara are two other examples), is now known to be an engineering miscalculation. Although the inevitable loss of agricultural land and the need to relocate millions of people from flooded areas (6 million hectares in the case of the Volga Basin dams) had been taken into account, many of the long-term consequences of creating large, shallow artificial reservoirs had not been foreseen. In part this was because the environmental sciences were poorly developed in the Soviet Union and it took ten to 15 years after the construction of the dams for the problems to become apparent. A few examples of the problems will indicate how insoluble they are.

The reservoirs were built to be 1,000–2,000 km$^2$, but they have gradually been increasing in size as storms, waves and ordinary filtration wash away their banks and transform millions of hectares of surrounding land into swamps. At the same time, the reservoirs are becoming increasingly shallow because of sedimentation of silt. The result is that their surface area increases and the pressure of the water decreases, making them less satisfactory sources of generating electricity. The level of the ground water in areas around the reservoirs and dams has slowly been rising, damaging agricultural land and sometimes towns and cities too. The underground communications in many cities, including Gorky, Volgograd, Kazan, Kharkov, Ul'yanovsk and others, some of them with a population of more than a million people, have already been flooded and partially destroyed. The water of the Volga river used to take 30 days to run from its source in the north to the Caspian Sea. It now takes 200 days. The accumulation of industrial waste, refuse and the canal systems of nearly all the towns along the tributaries of the Volga, together with the stagnant water in shallow parts of the reservoirs, creates health hazards not only for humans but also for the fish stock. The fish resources of the Caspian, Azov and Black Seas have suffered severely from the loss of natural breeding grounds. Normal migration routes are interrupted by dams. The fish also suffer from hypoxia (lack of dissolved oxygen).

The Sevan cascade in Armenia presents typical problems. Sevan is a great mountain lake at an altitude of 2,000 m which serves six power stations. It has lost so much water, however, that the level of the lake is now half of what it was. The lake itself has shrunk (it was 1,360 km² before the cascade was built in the 1950s, the largest lake in the Caucasus). It is quite possible that the whole hydroelectric system will come to a halt. Many of the dams in this cascade were badly built and have become unsafe, particularly in earthquake-prone areas. Several fatal accidents have already occurred. The most recent disaster took place in Georgia in February 1987, when the dam on the Rioni river collapsed under the increased pressure of water caused by melting snow. More than 100 villages were washed away and several hundred people lost their lives. The prosperous agriculture of the valley was lost as the soil was washed into the Black Sea. The immediate human cost of this accident was far higher than the cost of the Chernobyl disaster.

Despite growing opposition from environmentalists and local people, the hydroelectric programme continues. The next project, a sequence of eight dams in the Vaksh valley in Tadzhikistan, is expected to produce 9,000 MW of electricity. But it will destroy agriculture in the valley. It will be the largest hydroelectric project in Soviet history. Moreover, it is planned for a seismologically dangerous area, where earthquakes are quite common. Some experts have argued that the Regun dam, which is intended to have a height of 345 m and will be the largest earthfilled dam in the world, could collapse if a serious earthquake occurred.

The Soviet media is very vocal in its criticism of the hydroelectric programme, publishing hundreds of articles and discussions containing valid objections. Local people, who previously would have been coerced quietly into resettlement, now resist projects which interfere with their traditional way of life. The future of the programme has been put in doubt by the opposition. Several projects were cancelled in 1988. Some people have even argued that many of the dams on the Volga and Dnieper should be destroyed to restore the natural flow of the rivers. In fact, it would make sound economic sense to dismantle poorly made hydroelectric stations. It has been calculated, for example, that the Kakhovskaya hydrostation required the flooding of 0.62 hectares (1.3 acres) for each kilowatt of power it produces.[9] Private consumers now pay 4 kopecks for a kilowatt-hour and industrial consumers pay one kopeck per kilowatt-hour. Destroying the rich black soil of the Ukraine cannot be justified for an energy output that is so small. It makes far more sense to use the land for agriculture. It seems illogical to sell energy from flooded fields and meadows and to import grain and meat from other countries.

Although the future of Soviet hydroelectric power is difficult to predict, the myth about its cheapness is certainly dead.

## Geothermal energy

In some regions of the Soviet Union it is economical to use geothermal energy. In 1987 more than 50 sources of geothermal energy were exploited, producing more than 60 million tonnes of hot water and 400,000 tonnes of hot steam.[10] This is equal to about half a million tonnes of artificial fuel units. Natural hot water is used for heating and other purposes in some districts in Tbilisi, Grozny and other towns and cities in the Caucasus regions. The total number of people who benefit from this cheap source of energy is 300,000.

The first small (11 MW) geothermal power station was built on the slopes of the Pauzhetsk volcano in Kamchatka in the Far East in 1967 to provide energy for a fish-processing plant. A larger, 200 MW station, using steam under pressure at a temperature of 250°C, is planned for the foot of the Mutnova volcano in the same region. There are also plans to increase the use of thermal resources in the Caucasus and other regions. But it will be many years before geothermal sources contribute significantly to the total energy supply. Research institutes have only now begun to initiate pilot studies. Some Soviet energy experts claim that geothermal resources could support power stations with a combined capacity of 150,000 MW in the future, with individual plants with a capacity of up to 1,000 MW. But most of the exploitable sources of geothermal energy are situated in the Far Eastern Arctic regions where there is little local need for energy.

## Summary

This brief review of the main non-nuclear sources of electricity in the Soviet Union shows that the only viable option for the future is coal. More coal power stations need to be built near the coal fields with proper absorption systems to control pollution. More use could also be made of gas, particularly in Siberia where huge amounts of natural gas emerging from oil wells are simply burnt as waste. There are substantial resources of geothermal energy, but they are located in distant zones of volcanic activity. The use of oil to generate electricity will continue to decline and the existing hydroelectric stations in the European part of the USSR will continue to reduce their output of electrical energy. The Volga cascade alone (including the Kama tributary) has resulted in the flooding of about 23,000 $km^2$ (8,400 square miles), an area equivalent to half the territory of the Netherlands. The contrast with the Netherlands could not be more striking. Over the last seven centuries the Dutch have reclaimed about 7,000 $km^2$ from the sea. In the last 30 years the Soviet Union has transformed more than five times that area from land into sea. Mismanagement and misuse of water reserves has become the most serious ecological problem in the Soviet Union. The cancellation of a project to divert the waters of northern rivers to replenish the water of the Volga and Don basins and the increase in territories under irrigation, together with the growth of industrial and population centres make it inevitable that the artificial reservoirs behind the dams will shrink and that the land will be reclaimed for agricultural use.

All these problems, together with the generally wasteful use of energy (which is partly due to the very low price of electricity, which has been kept at the same rate for more than 30 years) make it clear why the Soviet government was so enthusiastic about nuclear-generated electricity. It seemed the only viable option for resolving energy shortages and sustaining a stable level of energy exports to Eastern Europe. The current total amount of energy exported by the Soviet Union to Eastern Europe is 32 billion kilowatt-hour. Hungary is the main consumer (11 billion kW-h in 1985) and Bulgaria comes second. The export originates in the Ukrainian electricity grid. All the hydroelectric stations of the Dnieper and Dniester together do not produce enough electricity to meet the Hungarian demand alone. This is why so many nuclear power stations were located in the Ukraine. It is not surprising that the Ukrainian people have been very resentful about having to sacrifice so much land in order to satisfy another nation's energy requirements.

The Chernobyl accident has begun to make an impact on energy planning for the future. Several nuclear power stations have been cancelled because of poorly selected locations and because of the resistance of the local population. After the devastating earthquake in Armenia in December 1988 the government had to shut down the Armenian nuclear power station (which consists of two VVER-440 reactors) because it is situated in a seismically active zone. Officially it was built to withstand tremors up to 8 points on the Richter scale (the

December earthquake reached 7 points but the tremors which reached the power station were well below this strength). But when the earthquake occurred, anxiety was immediately felt about the nuclear power station situated 35 km from Yerevan. No one was sure that the construction 12 years ago had conformed to the specifications or that it had been well built.

The Soviet Union is still under obligation to supply nearly 90 per cent of Eastern Europe's requirements of oil and gas. Any change in this policy could create instability in those countires. This situation is untenable, however, and the only solution seemed to be the construction of nuclear power stations in those countries. But the recent Soviet decision to ask those countries to find their own locations and use their own technical skills to bury spent nuclear fuel has reduced their enthusiasm for nuclear energy. Until 1988 spent nuclear fuel from all the power stations built by the Soviet Union was buried on Soviet territory.

None the less, the belief that nuclear energy represents the main future source of energy in the USSR is still prevalent. The government has introduced a programme of modernization, improving safety and reviewing the locations of nuclear power stations. Personnel are being retrained and other measures have been taken in an attempt to ensure that a major accident like Chernobyl cannot happen again. Atomic scientists and the nuclear industry in general argue that the current setbacks are only natural in the development of a new technology. The first and second generation nuclear power stations which are now in operation are bound to be accident-prone and to have problems. But nuclear technology is not static, they argue, and new generations of safer nuclear power stations are being designed.

There is little research in the Soviet Union to investigate utilizing wind, solar or tidal power. The Soviet coastal line is very long, but much of it is in the sparsely populated Arctic and Far East regions. The climate does not lend itself to solar energy. However, there are discussions and ideas about developing solar power installations in the Central Asian deserts. Wind power could never supply more than a fraction of the country's electricity needs. The search for alternative sources of energy has, in general, been inhibited by nuclear dreams. It is only since the Chernobyl accident that debates have begun about alternative sources of energy.

Chernobyl was a shock. It changed the attitude of the whole country towards nuclear energy. It was a setback which delayed the implementation of the ambitious energy programme. But it has not really become a turning point in research and development priorities. It will be impossible, however, to rebuild the confidence of the people in a bright, nuclear future.

## THE ENERGY CRISIS AFTER CHERNOBYL

The loss of Reactor No. 4 at the Chernobyl station and shutting down Reactors No. 1, 2 and 3 reduced the Ukraine's electricity-generating capacity significantly. This partly explains why the attempts to clear the site, deactivate the buildings and restart Reactors No. 1 and 2 seemed so desperate. The Ukrainian power grid could not afford the loss of 4,000 MWe during the winter and it was important that at least two reactors should be ready to be restarted in October 1986 before the cold weather increased the demand for electricity. In the Soviet Union electricity is not normally used to heat homes directly, but houses in many regions of the southern Ukraine and Moldavia, particularly in rural areas, had been converted to electric heating in the 1980s. Some modern blocks of flats and government buildings were also heated by electricity, and it was also used on some livestock farms.

Reactor No. 3 was also restarted very quickly. Nonetheless, acute energy shortages developed during the winter of 1986–7. This crisis has been well documented in David Marples' book on the social impact of the Chernobyl accident.[11] Marples points out that the electricity crisis was caused more by the side effects of the accident than by the direct loss of generating capacity which ensued. The need to review the safety features of the other 14 RBMK reactors and their resultant temporary shutdown and refitting created many problems.

One of the modifications made to all RBMK-1000 and RBMK-1500 reactors was to increase the number of control rods kept permanently in the low position from 15 to 30. It was decided that the remaining control rods (more than 200) should be fixed in a raised position at a depth of 1.2 m into the core. This would reduce the amount of time required for an emergency shutdown. But it also made it necessary to reduce the power of each reactor by nearly 20 per cent.[12] The number of short absorber rods inserted into the core from below was also increased (to 32 on the RBMK-1000 model and to 40 on the RBMK-1500). The servodrives which move the control rods were modernized to reduce the time required for full rod insertion in response to a shutdown signal (AZ-5 button) from 20 to 12 seconds. It was also decided that higher enriched uranium (2.4 per cent of uranium-235) should be used, since this would reduce the positive void coefficient of reactivity. However, it also increased the amount of fission products in the spent fuel when the full potential of uranium fuel was used. The fuel cycle will probably be shortened to avoid this and fuel channels will be replaced earlier, before the maximum amount of uranium-235 is actually spent. If the burn-up is to remain the same, up to 80 additional neutron absorbers will be added in the core.

All these modifications significantly increased the cost of electricity generated by the RBMK reactors and reduced their maximal power from 1,000 MWe to about 800 MWe. This meant the permanent loss of about 3,000 MWe electricity from existing RBMK reactors. Modifications were probably also made to VVER reactors to improve their safety. Here too, the reactors had to be shutdown and this contributed to the shortage of electricity. In addition to the loss of nuclear-generated energy, the efficiency of the Dnieper hydroelectric cascade was reduced in 1987 to well below its maximum capacity because the spring flooding water was contaminated and could not be allowed to accumulate in the cascade reservoirs. Instead it was flushed out to the Black Sea. This reduced the pressure in the five dams of the cascade considerably. It is probable that about 2,000 MWe of the total capacity of the cascade was lost.

Apart from this direct loss of electricity, the completion of several new nuclear power stations was delayed in 1986 and 1987. Because of the accident their construction had to be modified and they were tested more vigorously and extensively. Those projects that were cancelled as a result of the accident and the decision to halt the whole RBMK reactor programme will only affect the energy balance after 1991 because it takes five to six years to build new stations.

Electricity shortages contributed significantly to the poor performance of the Soviet economy in 1987 (nearly zero growth in the winter and spring and the failure to reach the target growth rate in the summer and autumn). There were still electricity shortages in 1988. Explaining the poor performance of the economy in 1986–8, the Minister of Finance, B. I. Gostev, told the Supreme Soviet that budget losses during this period amounted to 40 billion roubles. The losses related to 'the elimination of the consequences of the Chernobyl accident' were responsible for more than 8 billion roubles.[13] Further losses were caused by a fall in the price of Soviet oil and the huge reductions in the production and sale of vodka and other alcoholic products because of the anti-alcohol legislation in 1985.

The situation was not expected to improve in 1989. The budget for 1989 was accepted in October 1988 with a huge deficit of 100 billion roubles (about £100 billion), 16 per cent of the total budget. In the 1989 economic plan the targets for nuclear-generated electricity were reduced. To compensate the production of an extra 36 million tonnes of units of fossil fuels (8 million tonnes of oil, 16 million tonnes of coal and 20 m$^3$ of natural gas) above the original targets was planned.[14] In order to stimulate the productivity of workers in these industries, their wages were increased. These targets are unlikely to be achieved in full. In fact, the Armenian earthquake in December 1988 made them irrelevant in one tragic stroke. Not only was 10 billion roubles allocated to rebuild and restore the destroyed areas but the Armenian nuclear power station had to be shut down because it was located in an earthquake-prone region. The government also decided to halt the construction of nuclear power stations in Georgia and Azerbaijan, at least until seismological reports on the areas where they were to be located could be obtained.

The decline in the output of electricity from the Sevan lake cascade due to water shortages and the increase in the Armenian population by nearly 300,000 refugees from Azerbaijan made the electricity shortages in the Transcaucasian regions rather desperate. There were also electricity shortages in the north Caucasus in 1988 and 1989, which made Saturday and Sunday work shifts necessary in most industrial plants to ensure a more even consumption of electricity throughout the week. There had been chronic electricity shortages in this area for some time and the Krasnodar nuclear power station was planned to meet the increasing demand. However, the area was found to be seismically active and construction had to be cancelled. Instead the site was designated for a coal power station which has yet to be built.[15]

Work on the third and fourth RBMK-1500 reactors at Ignalina in Lithuania had been stopped, although they were already at an advanced stage of construction. Under public pressure the third reactor was cancelled and there are proposals to close the station down altogether.[16] The Odessa and Minsk thermal nuclear power stations were cancelled. An IAEA team of experts inspected the Rovno nuclear power station and found many defects.[17] The Crimean nuclear power station which was almost completed in 1989 was not launched because of safety concerns and the discovery that the area was seismically active. The future of several other nuclear power stations, particularly fast breeders, which are either under construction or at the planning stage, is in doubt. Energy losses caused by cancellations were not compensated by an increase in other nuclear-generating capacity. The proportion of nuclear energy in the total energy balance still fluctuates around 12 per cent, well below the target. When the results of the 1986–90 Five-Year Plan are announced it will finally become clear how far the programme which was hastily pushed through the Supreme Soviet in June 1986 is from being fulfilled. By 1989 planned nuclear capacity had been reduced by 28,000 MWe.

Neither coal nor hydroelectric power could make up for the loss of nuclear energy. Problems had been accumulating in all branches of energy production. At the same time, the government failed to introduce a comprehensive plan to conserve energy, although it is clear that this is essential. There has been a great deal of talk about energy-saving technologies and a new generation of energy-saving domestic appliances. But a bureaucratic and centrally planned economy is insufficiently flexible to adapt rapidly to tasks that will help to reduce the acute shortage of electricity. Economists have calculated that Soviet industry consumes at least 40 per cent more electricity per unit of production than Western or Japanese industries (which have already responded to the 1973 world energy crisis). Although there is still an excess of electricity production capacity in the United States, American industry has found it necessary to reduce its consumption of electricity. Policy makers, industrial groups and environmentalists are urging an aggressive programme of energy efficiency and conservation because of environmental effects like global warming and acid raid.[18]

In the Soviet Union, however, the need to conserve energy results primarily from the shortage of electricity generating capacity. In the era of *glasnost'* new and influential environmental movements and local protest groups have emerged to oppose hydroelectric projects which require flooding, nuclear power stations and industrial pollution. As a result it is nearly impossible to compensate for the loss of nuclear-generated electricity by expanding other sources. At the same time the government is committed to improve housing for the whole population by the year 2000 by adding 30–40 per cent of new housing. This means a 30–40 per cent increase in the demand for domestic electricity and heating during the next decade.

The Soviet government has not yet found an answer to the energy crisis. It is likely to get worse unless prices are increased radically. Electricity has been too cheap in the Soviet Union for too long. For more than 30 years it has cost only 1 kopeck (less than a penny) per kilowatt for industry and 4 kopecks (3 pence) for domestic use. Unless the price is increased, there will be no incentives to save energy or invent new technologies. Ever since Lenin introduced the first programme of electrification in 1921, official policy has been directed towards increasing the production and consumption of energy. Increasing the production of electric power was believed to be the main index of technical and economic progress. Lenin's famous slogan, 'socialism is Soviet power plus the electrification of the whole country', remained an article of faith from the 1920s to the 1980s. Nuclear-generated electricity was essential to preserve the false notion that a per capita increase in the production and consumption of electricity could continue indefinitely. The Chernobyl accident was a severe setback to this notion. But policy makers and some energy experts in the Soviet Union (and in other countries) have continued to argue that the solution to the problem lies not in energy conservation and some limit to growth, but in the development of a new generation of more efficient, fast-breeder, plutonium-fuelled reactors and new designs for safer uranium-fuelled reactors.

The development and construction of entirely safe reactors that are economical is a very long-term project which might never be realized. It is more likely that higher safety standards can only be achieved by increasing the cost of reactor technology. Proper protection requires an increased redundancy of safety systems and many extra regulatory mechanisms with higher sensitivity and faster reaction speeds. It was more than three years after the Chernobyl accident, and nearly four years of severe electricity shortages, before the Soviet government began to realize that the only way to end the crisis is to increase the cost of electricity to the consumer. The New Year greetings sent to Soviet plants, factories and other industrial consumers in 1989 contained a message to prepare for sharp increases in the price of electricity. They were given a year to adapt their technology and their budgets. From 1 January 1990 the price of industrial electricity will rise from 1 to 3 kopecks per kilowatt. The price of coal will also rise from 13 to 26 roubles per metric tonne.[19] The private consumer will be given much less notice. This action cannot have been taken lightly. It will certainly reflect in higher prices for industrial goods. The hope is that it will stimulate the development and application of energy-saving technologies. But in a country where market forces do not play an important role in the regulation of supply and demand, the increased cost of energy may not have the same beneficial technological effect on the economy as it did in the West during the energy crisis in the 1970s.

## THE FUTURE OF NEW-GENERATION NUCLEAR POWER STATIONS

The difficulties of Soviet fast-breeder reactors were discussed in chapter 7. Initially the future of nuclear energy was thought to lie in fast breeders. This strategy was also adopted in other countries. The United States, which has the most open debates on the advantages and disadvantages of nuclear power plants, and where the state does not own electricity-generating nuclear power stations, was the first among the major nuclear powers to cancel its fast-breeder reactor programmes because they were uneconomical and unsafe.

In the 1960s and 1970s nuclear scientists everywhere considered it obvious that nuclear energy programmes would grind to a halt unless economic fast-breeder reactors were developed. It was thought that they would produce cheaper electricity than pressurized-water or gas-cooled reactors because they were not sensitive to the cost of raw uranium. Although the theoretical arguments seemed unassailable, the only way to prove the theory was to build large fast breeders and test them. However, there has been much stronger resistance to fast breeders than expected, largely on safety grounds. It was not disputed that fast breeders and solar energy were the only inexhaustible energy sources that were technically feasible for the first half of the next century. But the fast breeders were considered a great safety risk in the United States. The first 380 MWe fast-breeder reactor (with a projected cost of $3.6 billion) at Clinch River, Tennessee, was under construction for many years. Because of criticism of its safety features and opposition from local and environmental groups it was never completed. By the time the Chernobyl accident occurred it had already been postponed indefinitely. The accident destroyed the project completely because this type of fast breeder has a positive void coefficient, the main deficiency that caused the Chernobyl explosion. American commercial reactors are designed to lose power when the core loses the water which acts as both coolant and moderator. The loss of coolant in a fast breeder could, however, lead to a power surge. The speed of shutdown with the control rods should be much faster than in PWRs.

In the United Kingdom, where the government has owned nuclear and most other power stations, the belief in fast breeders was retained for much longer. There was an extensive research programme and a plan to build a prototype commercial fast-breeder reactor at Dounreay in Scotland. By 1988 more than £3.5 billion had been invested in the development of fast-breeder technology. This made Britain one of the world leaders in this field.[20] However, government plans to privatize electricity, including nuclear reactors, have produced dramatic cuts in the funding of fast breeder technology. It was assumed that fast-breeder reactors would not be commercially viable for 30–40 years and this made the programme difficult to include in privatization schemes.

The development of fast-breeder technology in West Germany began much later than in Britain or France. The first fast breeder, SNR-300, began to be constructed as an experimental prototype in 1972. After more than ten years it was ready for tests. It was found that the cost of the energy it produces is more than seven times greater per kilowatt than the cost of electricity produced by commercial pressurized-water reactors.[21] By 1988 the SNR-300 had still not been licensed for operation, although about DM 7 billion had been invested in it by then. The project became highly controversial, threatening the fate of the local government of North Rhine-Westphalia.[22] The Chernobyl accident increased local opposition and many changes had to be made to meet new safety standards. It is now only expected to be operational in 1992, 20 years after its construction began. By that time its design will be outdated and it will not breed enough new plutonium. The West German experiment with fast breeders can thus be considered a complete failure. The Japanese began building a similar model in 1987. It is possible that they may learn from the West German experience and try to remedy the shortcomings.

The only country apart from the Soviet Union that has built large fast-breeder reactors is France. In the early 1970s French scientists concluded that there will be a shortage of natural uranium before the year 2020.[23] French reliance on nuclear energy made the development of fast breeders a priority. It turned out later that they had been too pessimistic about the world's uranium resources. For one thing, the expected increase in the price of uranium (because of the shortage of fossil fuels and the depletion of uranium mines) did not occur, and rich new seams of uranium were discovered in various parts of the world in the late 1970s and early 1980s. The price of uranium actually fell below the previous level of $130 per kilogram and shortages of economically viable resources were postponed by 50–60 years. It is now believed that it will take 100 years before shortages occur.

The programme to develop liquid-metal fast-breeder reactors in France began in the late 1950s, when there were few known uranium resources. The first experimental reactor, Rapsodie, was designed in 1957. Construction began in 1962 and nominal power (20 MWe) operation was reached in 1967.[24] The construction of the next 250 MWe stage was also experimental. Construction of the Phénix, as it was called, began in 1968 and industrial operation was started in July 1974. The stability, manageability and safety records of this model satisfied French scientists and it became the prototype for the first commercial fast-breeder, the Superphénix, with a power of 1,200 MWe. At the time of its criticality tests in 1982 and commercial power operations in 1983, it was the largest fast breeder in the world. It was built at Creys-Malville, near Grenoble, and it became the symbol of French nuclear prestige.

Economically the Superphénix was not a great success. Moreover, embarrassing accidents (for example, the leakage of liquid sodium) occurred. Because the price of uranium dropped in the middle 1970s and the cost of reprocessing fuel for fast breeders soared, the electricity produced by the Superphénix was twice as expensive as that from ordinary reactors. In 1987–8 the Superphénix was shut down for repairs. It took 20 months to complete them and by the time the reactor was restarted in January 1989 they had still not yet been completed. By then a new Superphénix 2 had been designed. But construction work has not yet begun on the new model and the project has been shelved. A further fast breeder is at the design stage (with international co-operation) but it is unlikely to be built until the year 2000, if ever. The entire European fast-breeder programme is now in doubt and it has proved far more expensive than anticipated.[25]

As we saw in chapter 7, the Soviet fast-breeder programme has fared no better, to judge by the futile attempts to design and build commercially viable models (the BN-800 and BN-1600). Since no reactors of this type have been tested, it is impossible to analyse their economic characteristics. Nothing is known about the economic characteristics of the prototype, the BN-600, either.

Reprocessing nuclear fuel for fast-breeders and treating and burying the enormous amounts of liquid nuclear waste materials which are the inevitable side products of reprocessing and extracting plutonium are the main difficulties of fast-breeder programmes. Only states with nuclear weapons (USA, UK, USSR, France and China) can afford to develop a plutonium producing industry, because they already have the facilities for military purposes. If nuclear disarmament was ever to become a reality, reprocessing nuclear fuel to extract plutonium and the task of burying the consequent nuclear waste would rapidly become too heavy an economic burden. The amount of liquid nuclear waste accumulates in direct proportion to the amount of energy produced and there are limited possibilities of burying it safely. In the United States the production of plutonium for military purposes has already created so much nuclear waste and contamination (mostly from the Hanford and Savannah River facilities) that the cost of cleaning up the areas is officially estimated to be between $92 and $128 billion.[26] It is difficult enough to bury spent fuel rods from ordinary reactors and solid waste is easier to handle than liquid.

The Soviet fast-breeder programme also began early, when nuclear scientists were convinced that the scarcity of natural uranium would limit the construction of uranium-fuelled reactors. They were expected to replace uranium reactors at the beginning of the next century. Although this scenario has not been officially challenged in the Soviet Union, there can be no doubt that it will be. Safe, reliable and cheap energy is unlikely to be available from fast breeders in the next 40–50 years or more and, although nuclear fusion as a source of energy is theoretically feasible, we are far from finding a practical approach to the use of fusion. Existing facilities to produce fusion energy consume many hundred times more energy than they produce.

Because of the bleak short-term prospects of fast-breeder reactors and fusion energy, the Soviet leadership has expressed the intention of developing a new generation of nuclear power stations with better safety features and better economic performance. But what this means in concrete terms is not yet clear. Soviet researchers have not produced any viable projects except for the pressurized-water reactor models or VVERs which are essentially copies of the modern American PWR system. The State Committee on Science and Technology has declared an open competition amongst all research establishments for the best plan for an ecologically clean coal power station, in the hope that a decrease in the level of pollution produced by fossil fuel stations could be an answer to the energy crisis.

Soviet experts will probably follow all the new approaches to constructing safer nuclear power stations that other countries adopt. The American Nuclear Regulatory Commission is already looking towards a new generation of safer reactors which will replace the models of the 1960s and 1970s. The normal life span of a reactor is 30–40 years. With the end of the fast-breeder dream, the task of designing new, safer and more reliable reactors for the twenty-first century has become urgent. In the United States, Germany, Japan, Sweden and other countries, there are strategies to create disaster-proof reactors. Planning for the twenty-first century is probably furthest advanced in Japan, the country most dependent on importing energy. A programme of research, development and construction of advanced reactors has been adopted for the years 1990–2030. It is planned to have 35 nuclear power installations by 2030, producing about 137,000 MWe (compared to 24,000 MWe in 1985).[27] The American programme is less optimistic.[28] There is no programme for the twenty-first century in the Soviet Union. The Chernobyl accident made all previous programmes irrelevant and a new programme has yet to be created.

## CONCLUSION

There is no doubt that the Chernobyl disaster and its consequences in the short and long term are very important to the future of human civilization. Most people realize that it represented a serious setback to the development of nuclear energy. This particular accident also clearly had an adverse effect on the Soviet energy programme and the whole economic situation in the country. However, the global and historic aspects of the accident have not really been assessed.

It is common knowledge that the use of fire was an important step in the development of human society, dramatically changing the way humans lived and prepared their food. It meant that some tribes could move from tropical areas to moderate and cold climates. For millennia the main sources of energy were fire and horse power. The invention of the steam engine and other engines which use fission fuels and the first industrial revolution did not really change this. The ability to use energy in the form of electricity made a new technical revolution possible. Our modern civilization depends almost entirely on the use of electricity. But the generation of most electricity still requires energy in the form of fire and heat. The production of electricity by hydroturbines does not represent a new source of energy. Ancient civilizations also used natural sources of energy directly for water mills and windmills, for sailing ships, transporting barges and boats.

Nuclear energy produced by splitting or fusing atoms is the only entirely new and potentially unlimited source of energy. Using the energy of the sun or tapping geothermal energy are ways of using natural nuclear reactions. Because all sources of energy based on fire are limited and non-renewable (or are renewed too slowly to keep pace with humankind's needs), most scientists have linked further progress to nuclear energy. The Chernobyl accident does not mean the end of nuclear energy but it has certainly destroyed the idea that we can be almost entirely dependent on nuclear energy.

It will take several decades for the full impact of Chernobyl to be felt in Western economies. It is already reflected in the debates and decisions on future energy policies. But Chernobyl has not had an economic impact on Western Europe, the United States or Japan because their economies had already adapted to the energy crisis of 1973–85. The result was the 'electronic revolution' which was so successful that it finally forced down the price of energy. The economic impact on the Soviet Union and Eastern Europe was far greater because these countries had not yet passed through the energy crisis. As an oil- and gas-exporting country, the Soviet Union had been a beneficiary of the earlier energy crisis. Soviet oil wealth had postponed the need for technological reconstruction. The Soviet government is only now facing that crisis and it is doing so during the most difficult period of its economic development.

Western economies could adapt to energy shortages and create energy-saving technologies within a decade because of a combination of creativity, competition and the flexible nature of free enterprise economies and open democratic political systems. Soviet-style centralized economies, where governments do not simply regulate but also administer research, development and the production of almost all commodities, are simply not flexible enough to react quickly to unforeseen and uncontrolled situations. Their creativity is limited by political and economic restrictions. There is no real competition between producers and consumers are deprived of choice. This inhibits technical progress. It is unlikely that the Soviet economy, even under the more progressive and rational leadership of Gorbachev, will be able to pass through the necessary technological revolution within a decade. The energy crisis has already begun to have the same inflationary effect on the Soviet economy that the energy crisis of the 1970s had on Western economies, but the Soviet response is less visible and less positive. Attempts have been made to introduce some democratization and decentralization. However, the inflexibility of the political system and the previously uniform administration in the different parts of this very heterogeneous and multinational society slow down the pace of social and economic reform. What is clear, however, is that no matter how slow the process is, reform must take place.

Chernobyl has changed people's attitudes to nuclear energy in the West, but there has been no pressing need for immediate decisions about the future. There is sufficient time to adapt the economies to new realities and to find alternative solutions. In the Soviet Union (and in the countries linked to it economically), however, Chernobyl has precipitated an economic and a political crisis. It is unlikely that the Soviet Union will find an easy way out, even if *perestroika* goes ahead full speed. The only way to move forward now is to integrate with those Western economies which have already been restructured, even if this means sacrificing political and ideological dogmas.

# Glossary of Scientific Terms, Measurements and Abbreviations

## INTRODUCTION

SEVERAL different terminological systems are used in this book for units of radioactivity, radiation exposure and radiation doses. This is because there is no universal system common to all countries. Soviet official documents and most Soviet authors mainly use old terms like *roentgen* (R) and *curie* (Ci) to describe radiation exposure and the level of radioactive contamination of the environment. In most Western literature more modern units are found: *becquerel* (Bq) for radioactivity, *gray* (Gy) for absorbed dose and *sievert* (Sv) for dose equivalent. The existence of different terms and their abbreviations, together with their multiples and sub-multiples based on Greek names, kilo (k), mega (M), gigo (G), or milli (m), micro ($\mu$), nano ($\eta$), etc., may cause the non-specialist some confusion. Old units are still very much in use in some countries and in some specific fields of science (for example, in radioecology) which do not yet subscribe to the new International System of Units which was designed recently to unify radiation protection rules. Old units have been superseded but not eliminated by the new ones, even in most Western countries. The commercial production and sale of radioactive isotopes for research purposes, for example, still operates on the basis of curies and not becquerels. To reduce confusion, a table of units and conversion units is given at the end of this glossary, after each unit has been explained in alphabetical order.

**Absorbed dose:** The amount of radiation absorbed per unit mass of tissue or organ. It is normally expressed in *rad* or *gray* (100 rad).

**AES:** Atomic Energy Station, the abbreviation common in Soviet literature.

**Alpha radiation:** The emission of alpha particles which are high-energy helium nuclei (consisting of two protons and two neutrons bound together). Alpha particles are emitted by some radioactive isotopes. They do not represent a serious health problem as an external source of radiation because they have a very low penetrating capacity (they have a range in air of only 2–10 cm). Internally, however, this form of radiation has the highest mutageneity and carcinogeneity per unit. For the same number of becquerel, alpha emitters produce the highest level of radiotoxicity inside the body.

**Becquerel (Bq):** A basal unit of radioactivity, one radioactive disintegration per second. The unit is named after Henry Becquerel, the physicist who discovered the radioactivity of uranium.

**Ber:** Biological equivalent roentgen. A unit of radiation exposure often used in Soviet radiological literature. It is the same as *rem*.

**Beta radiation:** The stream of beta particles emitted by radioactive isotopes. Beta particles consist of electrons or positrons. Beta radiation from different isotopes have different amounts of energy and different penetrating capacity. Radioactive strontium (Sr-90) is an emitter of beta particles. In air, beta particles can penetrate from 8 to 10 cm (tritium decay) to several meters (radioactive phosphorus, P-32, or iodine, I-131, decay). Living tissue may be penetrated by beta particles for small distances, varying from several millimetres to 2–3 cm, rarely as far as 5–8 cm. Despite their higher penetrating capacity, beta particles (in equal quantities of Bq) are at least 20 times less radiotoxic than alpha particles.

**Boron:** The most powerful absorber of neutrons. Boron alloys are therefore commonly used for reactor control rods. Boron was used in the air drops on the Chernobyl reactor after the accident.

**BN:** The Russian abbreviation for a fast-breeder reactor.

**Breeder:** A reactor which produces more fissile nuclei than it consumes.

**BWR:** A boiling-water reactor.

**Caesium (Cs):** Non-radioactive caesium is widely used in the electronic industry. In reactors about 20 radioactive isotopes of caesium are formed, most of them very short-lived. Long-lived Cs-137 has a half-life of 30 years. It is the major isotope responsible for environmental contamination caused by nuclear bomb tests and reactor accidents (the American spelling is cesium).

**Curie (Ci):** A unit of radioactivity, named after Pierre and Marie Curie. One curie equals $3.7 \times 10^{10}$ Bq or 37 billion disintegrations per second. One curie is the decay rate of 1 g of radium. A megacurie (MCi) is a million curies. A millicurie (mCi) is one-thousandth and a microcurie ($\mu$Ci) is one-millionth of a curie respectively.

**Dose:** The amount of energy delivered to a unit mass of material by radiation.

**Dose equivalent:** The quantity obtained by multiplying the absorbed dose by a factor representing the different effectiveness of the various types of radiation causing harm to tissues. It is measured in sieverts (Sv); 1 Sv produces the same biological effect irrespective of the type of radiation.

**Gamma radiation:** A penetrating, high-energy electromagnetic radiation consisting of high-energy photons emitted at the speed of light by the nuclei of certain radioactive isotopes, in addition to the emission of beta or alpha particles. Because of the high energy involved, external irradiation by gamma rays causes severe harm to internal organs. Protection against gamma rays is provided by thick layers of concrete, lead or other materials. Isotopes that give off gamma rays include cobalt-60, iodine-131, and caesium-137. In air, gamma radiation can be detected several dozen metres from the source. This makes an aerial survey of the surface of a contaminated area possible.

**Gray (Gy):** A unit of radioactive exposure. One gray equals 100 rad. A whole body single exposure to 1 Gy produces a mild form of radiation sickness syndrome and may reduce life expectancy by three to five years.

**Half-life:** The time it takes for half the radioactive isotope in a given sample to disintegrate and, correspondingly, for the danger it represents to diminish by half. Isotopes with a short half-life, measured in seconds, hours or days, are considered generally less dangerous to the environment. Iodine and phosphorus have short half-lives. Strontium-90 and caesium-137 are the most dangerous waste products of nuclear reactors and nuclear explosions because they have half-lives of about 30 years. When the environment is contaminated by these isotopes, the danger can last for hundreds of years.

**IAEA:** International Atomic Energy Agency.

**ICRP:** International Commission on Radiological Protection.

**INSAG:** International Nuclear Safety Advisory Group.

**Iodine-131:** The most biologically hazardous radionuclide because of its volatility, rapid movement through food chains and selective accumulation in the thyroid gland. It is a gamma and beta emitter with a half-life of about 8 days.

**Isotope:** Form of an element. Variations of the same isotope have the same number of protons in their nuclei, but different numbers of neutrons. Unstable isotopes disintegrate and emit various forms of radiation.

**MCi:** The abbreviation for a megacurie or one million curies.

**MW:** Megawatt. **MWe**=megawatts, electric; **MWt**=megawatts, thermal.

**mR/h:** The abbreviation in Soviet literature for milliroentgen per hour. It is used to indicate radiation level.

**Neutron:** A neutral elementary particle (without a charge). Neutrons are ejected by nuclei at high energy during fission.

**Meltdown:** The consequence of the overheating of the reactor core, which liquifies the cladding and support structures of the fuel rods and also the fuel. It may lead to the collapse of the reactor core which burns through the reactor vessel and foundations due to its very high temperature (higher than 2,000°C). A full meltdown (known as the 'China syndrome') has only occurred in fiction.

**Moderator:** A material (for example, water or graphite) with nuclei of low atomic weight. In reactors it surrounds the fuel rods to slow down fast neutrons released in fission.

**NRC:** Nuclear Regulatory Commission (in the United States).

**NRPB:** National Radiological Protection Board (in the United Kingdom).

**Organ dose equivalent:** Dose equivalent imparted to a given tissue or organ. It is measured in sieverts (Sv).

**Plutonium (Pu):** An artificial radioactive chemical element used in nuclear weapons and as nuclear fuel. It is always warm because it emits alpha particles. Plutonium-239 has a half-life of 24,360 years. Plutonium-238 and 240 which were present in the Chernobyl reactor core in about the same amounts as Pu-239 have shorter half-lives (86 and 6,575 years respectively). A critical mass is reached if the amount of plutonium exceeds 300 g. An accumulation of plutonium in the human body in excess of 0.01 microcuries (370 Bq) is considered harmful. This corresponds to 0.0005 micrograms. Plutonium is the most radiotoxic of all radioactive isotopes.

**PWR:** Pressurized-water reactor.

**Rad:** Radiation absorbed dose. It is the unit commonly used to indicate the amount of radiation dose absorbed in a unit of tissue or organ. The amount of radioactivity in quantitative units (like curies or becquerels) to produce a rad per organ (for example, the thyroid) is different from the amount that produces a rad per whole body.

**Radiation or radioactivity:** In the context of this book it is the emission of energy in the form of neutron, alpha or beta particles or gamma rays.

**Radionuclide:** A radioactive nuclide, the product of fission in the reactor core.

**RBMK:** The Russian acronym for 'reactor high-power boiling channel type'.

**Rem:** Roentgen equivalent man. The dose received to produce the same biological effect as 1 rad of X-rays. In the case of beta or gamma radiation 1 rem is closely linked to 1 rad, but in the case of alpha radiation or fast neutrons much lower quantities of radiation (in Bq) are required to measure 1 rem. 1 rem is equal to 10 millisieverts.

**Reprocessing:** The mechanical and chemical treatment of spent fuel to remove fission products and recover fissile material.

**Roentgen (R):** A unit of X-rays and gamma radiation produced by radionuclides or Roentgen apparatus in medical practice. It is named after Wilhelm Röntgen who discovered X-rays in 1895. It is a qualitative physical unit and all other radiological units like rad, rem, Sievert and Gray are linked to it; 1 R of gamma rays is approximately the same as one radiation absorbed dose (rad) or 1 rem. Roentgen is the oldest dose unit and it indicates the amount of radiation that will produce in 1 cm$^3$ of air an amount of positive or negative ionization equal to one electrostatic unit of electric charge which can repel a similar charge at 1 cm distance with a force of 1 dyne. A dyne is a unit in the centimetre–gram–second system of physical units.

**Sievert (Sv):** A unit of radiation exposure, compensated to allow for extra biological damage by alpha particles or fast neutrons; 1 Sv is equal to 100 rem.

**Strontium (Sr):** Strontium-89 and 90 accumulate as non-volatile fission products in the reactor core. Sr-89 has a half-life of 53 days, while Sr-90 has a half-life of about 30 years and accumulates in the body, replacing calcium in the bones.

**Uranium:** The heaviest natural element. It emits alpha particles. Uranium-235 is fissile. There are sophisticated technical processes to increase the content of uranium-235 in the uranium fuel (to make enriched uranium).

**Void coefficient:** A positive or negative correlation between the amount of gas (steam) present in a liquid cooling system and the rate of fission in the reaction.

**VVER:** The Russian acronym for 'water–water power reactor'. It is the same as a PWR.

**WHO:** World Health Organization.

### INTERVENTION LEVEL OR ACTION LEVEL FOR CONTAMINATION OF MILK BY IODINE-131

*Figures for caesium-137 are similar. If there is an excess level the milk is not permitted for direct consumption.*

FRG = 500 Bq per litre
UK = 2,000 Bq per litre
USSR = 3,700 Bq per litre or 0.1 microcurie per litre (7,400 Bq in daily ration and 37 Bq/litre in drinking water.

In the USSR action level for strontium-90 is similar to iodine-131, but it is much higher for caesium-137.

### THE MAXIMUM PERMISSIBLE LIMIT OF ABSORBED DOSE OR DOSE EQUIVALENTS FOR THE POPULATION AND FOR WORKERS IN THE NUCLEAR INDUSTRY (RECOMMENDED BY ICRP)

0.1 rem = approximate annual dose from natural background

0.5 rem = permissible maximum annual dose for the general public

5.0 rem = permissible maximum annual limit for workers in the nuclear industry and for people dealing with radioisotopes (but not more than 25 rem per life).

In the case of accidents, special emergency doses can be introduced for workers and members of the general public. They are higher and are based on the expected possible accumulated dose. If the expected accumulated dose of external and internal radiation is likely to reach 0.25 Gy (25 rem), protection measures must be put into effect and the functioning of the general public must be restricted. If projections indicate a possible dose of 0.75 Gy (75 rem), the evacuation of the population is obligatory. It is not expected that the population will actually absorb these doses. The projections are designed to enable preventative measures to be taken.

### BIOLOGICAL AND CLINICAL EFFECTS OF WHOLE-BODY IRRADIATION

0.5–10 rem = undetectable increase of cancer incidence and statistically minor genetic effect

10–100 rem = detectable increase in cancer incidence and detectable genetic effect

100–200 rem = radiation sickness syndrome (danger of opportunistic infections)

200–400 rem = acute radiation sickness syndrome (danger of opportunistic infections)

400–600 rem = Lethal for bone marrow

600+ rem = lethal for intestine epithelium and some other tissues.

*Units of radioactivity and radiation exposure*

| Quantity | New name and symbol | Old name and symbol | Conversion factors |
|---|---|---|---|
| Exposure | | roentgen (R) | |
| Absorbed dose | gray (Gy) | rad | 1 Gy = 100 rad |
| Dose equivalent | sievert (Sv) | rem | 1 Sv = 100 rem |
| Activity | becquerel (Bq) | curie (Ci) | 1 Ci = 3.7 × $10^{10}$ Bq |

# Notes and References

## I A POST-MORTEM OF THE CATASTROPHE

1 V. Legasov, *The lessons of Chernobyl are important for all* (Moscow, Novosty Press, 1987), p. 32.
2 USSR State Committee on the Utilization of Atomic Energy. *The Accident at Chernobyl Nuclear Power Plant and its Consequences*. Information compiled for the IAEA Experts' Meeting, 25–9 August 1986, Vienna. Working Document for the Post-Accident Review Meeting. Draft. Part I: General Material; Part II: Annexes 1–7, August 1986 (hereafter referred to as *The Accident . . . Soviet IAEA Report*). Part I, p. 15. Part I was subsequently published in Russian in *Atomnaya Energiya*, 61 (5) (1986), Moscow.
3 Ibid., Part II, Annex 2, pp. 180–5.
4 Ibid.
5 A. M. Petrosy'ants, *Problems of Nuclear Science and Technology. The Soviet Union as a World Nuclear Power*, 4th edn. (Oxford, New York, Pergamon Press, 1981), p. 112.
6 *The Accident . . . Soviet IAEA Report*, Part II, Annex, 2, p. 135 and fig. 2.5.3.
7 Ibid., Part I, p. 15.
8 Ibid.
9 Ibid.
10 *Pravda Ukrainy*, 13 March 1984.
11 *Moscow News*, 8 August 1987, p. 12.
12 *The Accident . . . Soviet IAEA Report*, Part I, p. 15.
13 *Nuclear Power Safety Report*. Public Citizen Critical Mass Energy Project, Washington DC, 1979–1987. Annual reports of accidents and mishaps in American nuclear plants. Some of them include diesel generator malfunction or the inability of operators to put them into operation.
14 *The Accident . . . Soviet IAEA Report*, Part II, p. 135.
15 Ibid., Part I, p. 15.
16 Ibid., Part II, p. 117.
17 Ibid., Part II, p. 132.
18 Ibid., Part I, p. 15.
19 *Atomnaya Energiya*, 61 (5) (1986), pp. 301–20.
20 V. Legasov, 'Moi dolg rasskazat' ob etom', *Pravda*, 20 May 1988.

21 INSAG-1 Report. *Summary Report on the Post-Accident Review Meeting on the Chernobyl Accident.* International Atomic Energy Agency, Safety Series (Vienna, 1986).

22 Ibid., p. 17.

23 *The Accident . . . Soviet IAEA Report,* Part I, p. 15.

24 Y. Shcherbak, 'Chernobyl'. Dokumental'naya provest'. Kniga vtoraya', *Yunost'*, 10 (1988), pp. 23–4.

25 *The Accident . . . Soviet IAEA Report,* Part I, p. 16.

26 Ibid. (Russian version), p. 22.

27 Ibid. (English version), p. 16.

28 INSAG-1 Report, p. 15.

29 Shcherbak, 'Chernobyl', p. 22.

30 Ibid.

31 Legasov, 'Moi dolg rasskazat' ob etom'.

32 *Nature*, 323 (1986), p. 25.

33 Ibid., p. 26.

34 Ibid.

35 *The Accident . . . Sovet IAEA Report,* Part I, p. 16.

36 *Nature*, 323 (1986), p. 26.

37 *The Accident . . . Soviet IAEA Report,* Part I, p. 15.

38 Ibid., p. 17.

39 Legasov, 'Moi dolg rasskazat' ob etom'.

40 *Moskovskie Novosti*, 9 August 1987, p. 12.

41 *Nature*, 323 (1986), p. 26.

42 *The Accident . . . Soviet IAEA Report,* Part I, p. 17.

43 Ibid., Part II, Annex 2, p. 52.

44 INSAG-1 Report, p. 16.

45 *The Accident . . . Soviet IAEA Report,* Part I, p. 17.

46 Ibid., p. 20.

47 Ibid.

48 INSAG-1 Report, p. 26.

49 *The Accident . . . Soviet IAEA Report,* Part I, p. 20.

50 INSAG-1 Report, p. 26.

51 Ibid., p. 25.

52 Ibid.

53 *The Accident . . . Soviet IAEA Report,* Part II, Annex 2, Fig. 2.52.

54 Shcherbak, 'Chernobyl', p. 223.

55 Ibid., p. 23.

56 Ibid., pp. 23–4.

## 2 RADIOACTIVE VOLCANO

1 USSR State Committee on the Utilization of Atomic Energy. *The Accident at Chernobyl Nuclear Power Plant and its Consequences.* Information compiled for the IAEA Experts' Meeting, 25–9 August 1986. Vienna.

Working Document for the Post-Accident Review Meeting. Draft. Part I: General Material. Part II: Annexes 1–7, August 1986 (hereafter referred to as *The Accident . . . Soviet IAEA Report*). Part I, p. 12 (Part I was subsequently published in Russian in *Atomnaya Energiya*, 61 (5)(1986), Moscow.

2  A. B. Illesh and A. E. Pral'nikov, *Reportazh iz Chernobylya* (Moscow, Mysl', 1987), pp. 6–15.

3  Ibid., p. 13.

4  *Izvestiya*, 10 May 1986.

5  INSAG-1 Report. *Summary report on the post-accident review meeting on the Chernobyl accident*. (Vienna, International Atomic Agency Safety Series, 1986), p. 45.

6  Y. Shcherbak, 'Chernobyl', *Yunost'*, 6 (1987), p. 54.

7  *Izvestiya*, 7 May 1986.

8  V. Gubarev, 'Sarkofag', *Znamya*, 9 (1986), pp. 114–5. English translation by M. Glenny, *Sarcophagus* (Harmondsworth, Penguin, 1987).

9  INSAG-1 Report, p. 34.

10  *Moskovskiye Novosti*, 19 July 1987, p. 4.

11  Ibid.

12  G. Medvedev, 'Chernobylskaya tetrad', *Novy Mir*, 6 (1989), pp. 3–108.

13  *Izvestiya*, 7 May 1986.

14  N. Baklanov, 'Boleznennaya operatsiya', *Izvestiya*, 10 August 1988.

15  *Pravda*, 25 December 1986.

16  V. Legasov, 'Moi dolg rasskazat' ob etom', *Pravda*, 20 May 1988.

17  Ibid.

18  Ibid.

19  G. Medvedev 'Chernobylskaya tetrad', *Novy Mir*, 6 (1989), pp. 72–3.

20  Legasov, 'Moi dolg rasskazat' ob etom'.

21  *Pravda*, 25 December 1986.

22  Legasov, 'Moi dolg rasskazat' ob etom'.

23  Ibid.

24  *Moskovskiye Novosti*, 17 July 1988, p. 10.

25  Legasov, 'Moi dolg rasskazat' ob etom'.

26  *The Accident . . . Soviet IAEA Report*, Part I, p. 40.

27  Legasov, 'Moi dolg rasskazat' ob etom'.

28  *The Accident . . . Soviet IAEA Report*, Part I, p. 40.

29  INSAG-1 Report, p. 46.

30  *Izvestiya*, 1 May 1986.

31  *The Accident . . . Soviet IAEA Report*, Part I, p. 40.

32  A. B. Illesh and A. E. Pral'nikov, *Reportazh iz Chernobylya* and in V. Haynes and M. Bojcun, *The Chernobyl Disaster* (London, The Hogarth Press, 1988), pp. 17–18.

33  *Pravda*, 2 May 1986.

34  *Pravda*, 5 May 1986.

35 NTR (Bulletin of the All-Union Society) '*Znaniye*', 14 (22 July–4 August 1986), p. 3.
36 INSAG-1 Report, p. 36.
37 L. Devell, 'Characteristics of the Chernobyl release and fallout that affect the transport and behaviour of radioactive substances in the environment', Studsvik Report NP-88/1 (Studsvik, Sweden, 1988), p. 24.
38 INSAG-1 Report, p. 35.
39 Ibid., p. 39.
40 *Pravda*, 13 May 1986.
41 Legasov, 'Moi dolg rasskazat' ob etom'.
42 Medvedev, 'Chernobylskaya tetrad', p. 100.
43 L. A. Il'in, 'Diagnoz posle Chernobyla, *Sovetskaya Rossiya*, 31 January 1988.
44 Illesh and Pral'nikov, *Reportazh iz Chernobylya*, p. 49.
45 *Nature*, 321 (1986), p. 86.
46 B. Dubrovin, 'Blagorodnaya tsel', *Pravda*, 27 May 1986.
47 *The Accident . . . Soviet IAEA Report*, Annex 4, table 4.12, p. 18.
48 *Pravda*, 15 May 1986.
49 Ibid.
50 Ibid.
51 *Pravda*, 21 July 1986.
52 *Pravda*, 16 January 1988; Leonid Abalkin press conference as reported by TASS on 30 May 1988.
53 Legasov, 'Moi dolg rasskazat' ob etom'.

## 3 THE ENVIRONMENTAL IMPACT

1 USSR State Committee on the Utilization of Atomic Energy. *The Accident at Chernobyl Nuclear Power Plant and its Consequences.* Information compiled for the IAEA Experts' Meeting, 24–9 August 1986, Vienna. Working Document for the Post-Accident Review Meeting. Draft. Part I: General Material. Part II: Annexes 1–7, August 1986 (hereafter referred to as *The Accident . . . Soviet IAEA Report*). Part I was subsequently published in Russian in *Atomnaya Energiya*, 61 (5) (1986), Moscow.
2 INSAG-1 Report. *Summary report on the post-accident review meeting on the Chernobyl accident.* (Vienna, International Atomic Agency Safety Series, 1986), p. 33.
3 *The Accident . . . Soviet IAEA Report.*
4 Zh. A. Medvedev, *Nuclear disaster in the Urals* (New York, Norton, 1979). Additional information on the Ural nuclear disaster can be found in two studies sponsored and supported by the US government: J. R. Trabalka, L. D. Eyman and S. I. Auerbach, 'Analysis of the 1957–1958 Soviet nuclear accident', *Science*, 209 (1980), pp. 345–53 and D. M. Soran and D. B. Stillman, *An analysis of the alleged Kyshtym disaster*, Report LA-9217-MS (New Mexico, Los Alamos National Laboratory, January 1982).

5 Medvedev, *Nuclear disaster in the Urals*.
6 L. A. Il'in, 'Diagnoz posle Chernobyla', *Sovetskaya Rossiya*, 31 January 1988.
7 WASH-740, The Brookhaven Report. *Theoretical possibilities and consequences of major accident in large nuclear power plants* (Washington DC, US Atomic Energy Commission, March 1957).
8 *Pravda*, 28 October 1988.
9 *Izvestiya*, 15 June 1986.
10 Yu Israel, 'Chernobyl: proshloe i prognos na budushchee', *Pravda*, 20 March 1989.
11 INSAG-1 Report, p. 34 (table 2); *The Accident . . . Soviet IAEA Report*, Part I, table 1.
12 M. Goldman, 'Chernobyl: radiological perspective', *Science* 238, (1987), pp. 622–33.
13 INSAG-1 Report, p. 35.
14 *The Accident . . . Soviet IAEA Report*, Part II, Annex 5, fig. 5.1.
15 Ibid., Part II, Annex 4, table 4.12.
16 Yu. A. Israel, V. N. Petrov, et al., 'Radioaktivnoe zagryaznenie prirodnykh sred v zone avarii na Chernobylskoi atomnoi elektrostantsii', *Meteorologiya i Gidrologiya*, 2 (1987), p. 10.
17 Israel 'Chernobyl'.
18 *The Accident . . . Soviet IAEA Report*, Part II, Annex 4, Table 4.1.
19 Israel et al. 'Radioaktivnoe zagryaznenie' and Yu. A. Israel, V. N. Petrov and D. A. Severov, 'Modelirovanie radioaktivniykh vypadenii v blizhnei zone ot avarii na Chernobylskoi atomnoi elektrostantsii', *Meteorologiya i Gidrologiya*, 7 (1987), pp. 5–12.
20 *The Accident . . . Soviet IAEA Report*, Part II, Annex 4, pp. 5–6, table 4.2.
21 Israel, et al. 'Radioaktivnoe zagryazhenie' pp. 5–18.
22 Ibid.
23 V. G. Asmolov et al., *Avariya na Chernobylskoi AES: God spustya*. Soviet Report at the International Conference on Nuclear Safety, IAEA, 28 September–2 October 1987, Vienna, p. 24.
24 Ibid., p. 26.
25 Ibid., pp. 27–8.
26 Ibid., p. 13.
27 Ibid., p. 34.
28 Israel, 'Chernobyl'.
29 *Nedelya* (weekly supplement to *Izvestiya*), 29 (14–20 July 1986), p. 11.
30 Asmolov, *Avariya na Chernobylskoi AES*, p. 42.
31 L. A. Il'in and O. A. Pavlovsky, 'Radiological consequences of the Chernobyl accident in the Soviet Union and measures taken to mitigate their impact.' Report at the IAEA International Conference on Nuclear Power Performance and Safety, 28 September–2 October 1987, Vienna (IAEA-CN-48/33, Available on demand from IAEA Information Service Department.)
32 INSAG-1 Report, p. 26.

33  C. Walker, *The Times*, 25 April 1987, p. 7. See also *Literaturnaya Gazeta*, 15 April 1987.
34  *The Accident . . . Soviet IAEA Report*, Part II, Annex 6, p. 3.
35  Ibid., p. 4.
36  Ibid.
37  Asmolov, *Avariya na Chernobylskoi AES*, p. 34.
38  *NTR: Byulleten' Vsesoyuznogo Obshchestva Znaniye*, 14 (22 July–4 August 1986), p. 3.
39  Shcherbak, 'Chernobyl' p. 46.
40  R. Wilson, 'A Visit to Chernobyl', *Science*, 236 (1987), pp. 1636–40.
41  *Izvestiya*, 15 June 1986.
42  Ibid.
43  Ibid.
44  *The Accident . . . Soviet IAEA Report*, Part II, Annex 4, p. 18, table 4,12.
45  Ibid., p. 9.
46  Ibid., Annex 5, tables 5.8 and 5.9.
47  Ibid.
48  INSAG-1 Report, p. 58.
49  NTR, '*Znaniye*'.
50  INSAG-1 Report.
51  *Pravda*, 19 May 1986.
52  *Izvestiya*, 7 September 1986.
53  *Izvestiya*, 14 May 1986.
54  *Argumenty i Fakty*, 14 (1988), p. 8.
55  'Chernobyl area to be ecological reserve', *Science* (13 May 1988), p. 877.

## 4 THE IMPACT ON AGRICULTURE

1  L. Abalkin, Press conference, as reported by TASS on 30 May 1988. Earlier estimates of 8 billion roubles were calculated up to the end of 1987. See *Pravda*, 16 January 1988.
2  H. Hamman and S. Parrot, *Mayday at Chernobyl* (London, New English Library, 1987); V. Haynes and M. Bojcun, *The Chernobyl disaster* (London, Hogarth Press, 1988).
3  *Izvestiya*, 15 June 1988.
4  *Pravda*, 20 March 1989.
5  V. G. Asmolov et al., *Avariya na Chernobylskoi AES: God spustya*. Soviet Report at the International Conference on Nuclear Safety, IAEA, 28 September–2 October 1987, Vienna, p. 41.
6  Ibid., p. 40.
7  Ibid., p. 42.
8  Ibid., pp. 27–8.
9  Ibid., p. 24.
10  I would like to thank Mr Mats Thoren, Space Media Network, Stockholm, for kindly sending me the Landsat satellite photographs.

11 Asmolov et al., *Avariya na Chernobylskoi AES*, p. 24, fig. 4.1.
12 Yu. Israel, 'Chernobyl: proshloe i prognoz na budushchee', *Pravda*, 20 March 1989.
13 *Pravda*, 11 February 1989.
14 R. F. Mould, *Chernobyl: the real story* (Oxford, New York, Pergamon, 1988), p. xiii.
15 L. A. Il'in (ed.), *Rukovodstvo po organizatsii meditsinskogo obsluzhivaniya lits podvergeshikhsya deistviyu ioniziruyushchego izlucheniya* (Moscow, Energoatomizdat, 1985), p. 154.
16 USSR State Committee on the Utilization of Atomic Energy. *The Accident at Chernobyl Nuclear Power Plant and its Consequences*. Information compiled for the IAEA Experts' Meeting, 24–9 August 1986, Vienna. Working Document for the Post-Accident Review Meeting. Draft. Part I: General Material. Part II: Annexes 1–7, August 1986 (hereafter referred to as *The Accident . . . Soviet IAEA Report*). Part II, Annex 7, p. 64, table 7.2.7.
17 Ibid., p. 58.
18 *Nedelya*, 21 (19–25 May 1986), pp. 10–11.
19 *Nedelya*, 38 21–28 September (1986), p. 13.
20 *Radionuclide Levels in Food, Animals and Agricultural Products*. Post Chernobyl Monitoring in England and Wales (HMSO, London, Ministry of Agriculture, Fisheries and Food, 1987).
21 I. Moiseev, 'Tsepnaya reaktsiya', *Sel'skaya Molodezh*, 12 (1987), p. 3.
22 V. Kolinko, 'Radioactive echo', *Moscow News*, 8 (19 February 1989), p. 12.
23 Asmolov et al., *Avariya na Chernobylskoi AES*, pp. 40–1.
24 *Izvestiya*, 9 July 1986.
25 *Izvestiya*, 17 January 1987.
26 Shcherbak, 'Chernobyl', *Yunost'*, 6., p. 20.
27 Ibid.
28 *Pravda*, 8 October 1988.
29 Ibid.
30 *Izvestiya*, 15 December 1986.
31 *Izvestiya*, 16 January 1988.
32 *Izvestiya*, 15 December 1986.
33 L. A. Il'in and O. A. Pavlovsky, 'Radiological consequences of the Chernobyl accident in the Soviet Union and the measures taken to mitigate their impact'. Report at the IAEA International Conference on Nuclear Power Performance and Safety, 28 September–2 October 1987, Vienna (IAE-CN-48/33. Available on demand from IAEA Information Service Department), p. 4.
34 Moscow Radio, 24 April 1987.
35 *Pravda*, 22 April 1988.
36 *Pravda*, 11 February 1989.
37 N. Kolesnikova and N. Tolstik, 'Zalozhniki v svoem dome, *Nedelya*, 26 (1989), pp. 5–6.

38  Ibid.
39  Moiseev, 'Tsepnaya reaktsiya', pp. 2–3.
40  A. Pral'nikov and A. Fedorov, 'Entering the zone', *Moskovskie Novosti*, 17 (24 March 1988), p. 16.
41  Ibid.
42  *The Accident . . . Soviet IAEA Report*, Part II, Annex 6, pp. 3–6.
43  Pral'nikov and Fedorov, 'Entering the zone'.
44  *Pravda*, 8 October 1988.
45  Moiseev, 'Tsepnaya reaktsiya', p. 5.
46  A. Simurov, 'Vokrug zony', *Pravda*, 22 April 1988.
47  Ibid.
48  A. Adamovich, 'Chestnoe slovo ne vzorvetsya', *Moskovskie Novosti*, 17 July 1988, p. 10.
49  Ibid.
50  *Izvestiya*, 29 June 1986.
51  L. A. Il'in and O. A. Pavlovsky, 'Radiological consequences Chernobyl', p. 11.
52  *Izvestiya*, 15 June 1986.
53  Israel et al., 'Radioaktivnoe zagryaznenie', p. 13.
54  *Pravda Ukrainy*, 27 April 1988.
55  *Nedelya*, 38 (21–8 September 1986), p. 13.
56  *Pravda*, 15 December 1986.
57  Adamovich, 'Chestnoe slovo ne vzorvetsya'.

5  THE HEALTH IMPACT IN THE SOVIET UNION

1  C. C. Lushbaugh, S. A. Fry and R. C. Ricks, 'Medical and radiobilogical basis of radiation accident management', *British Journal of Radiology*, 60 (1987), pp. 1159–63.
2  L. A. Il'in, 'Diagnoz posle Chernobyla', *Sovetskaya Rossiya*, 31 January 1988.
3  Information and a report about the Kiev conference in May 1988 is given in *Klinicheskaya Meditsina*, 66 (8) (1988), pp. 155–7.
4  L. A. Il'in, 'The Chernobyl experience and the contemporary problems of radiation protection'. *Proceedings of the Scientific Conference on the Medical Aspects of the Chernobyl Accident, Kiev, 11–13 May 1988* (Moscow, Ministry of Public Health, 1988).
5  INSAG-1 Report. *Summary report on the post-accident review meeting on the Chernobyl accident.* (Vienna, International Atomic Agency Safety Series, 1986), p. 7. These figures are also given in USSR State Committee on the Utilization of Atomic Energy. *The Accident at Chernobyl Nuclear Power Plant and its Consequences.* Information compiled for the IAEA Experts' Meeting, 24–9 August 1986, Vienna. Working Document for the Post-Accident Review Meeting. Draft. Part II: Annex 7, August 1986 (hereafter referred to as *The Accident . . . Soviet IAEA Report*).

6 L. A. Il'in and O. A. Pavlovsky, 'Radiological consequences of the Chernobyl accident in the Soviet Union and the measures taken to mitigate their impact'. Report at the IAEA International Conference on Nuclear Power Performance and Safety, 28 September–2 October 1987, Vienna (IAE-CN-48/33. Available on demand from IAEA Information Service Department), pp. 149–66.

7 A. K. Gus'kova, A. E. Baranov, *et al.*, 'Ostrye effekty oblucheniya u postradavshikh pri avarii na Chernobyl'skoi AES', *Meditsinskaya Radiologiya*, 32 (12) (1987), pp. 3–18.

8 Y. Shcherbak, 'Chernobyl', *Yunost'*, 6 (1987), pp. 46–66.

9 Ibid., pp. 55–6.

10 Ibid., p. 56.

11 Ibid.

12 *The Accident . . . Soviet IAEA Report*, Part I, p. 28.

13 Shcherbak 'Chernobyl', *Yunost'*, 6, p. 56.

14 *The Accident . . . Soviet IAEA Report*, Part I, p. 12: *Atomnaya Energiya*, 61 (5) (1986), p. 307.

15 *The Accident . . . Soviet IAEA Report*, Part II, Annex 7, p. 1.

16 Ibid.

17 Shcherbak, 'Chernobyl', *Yunost'* 6, p. 57.

18 Ibid., pp. 57–8.

19 Ibid., p. 57.

20 *Izvestiya*, 7 May 1986.

21 *Krasnaya zvezda*, 3 June 1986.

22 *The Accident . . . Soviet IAEA Report*, Part II, Annex 7, p. 2.

23 Ibid., p. 3.

24 R. P. Gale and T. Hauser, *Chernobyl: the final warning* (London, Hamish Hamilton, 1988).

25 Shcherbak, 'Chernobyl', *Yunost'* 6, p. 64.

26 R. P. Gale, 'Immediate medical consequences of nuclear accidents; Lessons from Chernobyl', *JAMA*, 258 (1987), pp. 625–7.

27 Guskova et al., 'Ostrye effekty oblucheniya'.

28 INSAG-1 Report, pp. 54–6.

29 R. Wilson, 'A visit to Chernobyl', *Science*, 236 (1987), p. 1637.

30 L. A. Il'in (ed.), *Rukovodstvo po organizatsii meditsinskogo oblsluzhivaniya lits podvergshikhsya Deistviyu ioniziruyushchego izlucheniya* (Moscow, Energoatomizdat, 1985), p. 154.

31 *The Accident . . . Soviet IAEA Report*, Part II, Annex 7, Fig. 7.2.1.

32 Shcherbak, 'Chernobyl', *Yunost'* 6, p. 58–9.

33 Ibid., p. 58.

34 Ibid., p. 59.

35 R. Wilson, 'A Visit to Chernobyl', p. 1637.

36 Shcherbak, 'Chernobyl', *Yunost'*, 6, p. 63.

37 Ibid.

38 L. A. Il'in, *Rukovodstvo* and see *Normy Radiatsionnoi Bezopasnosti*

*NRB-76 i Osnovnye Sanitarnye Pravila OSP 72/80* (Moscow, Energoizdat, 1981).

39  *The Accident . . . Soviet IAEA Report*, Part II, Annex 7, p. 38.

40  G. F. Lawless, 'Chernobyl public health effect', *Science*, 238, (1987), p. 10.

41  Shcherbak, 'Chernobyl', *Yunost'* 6, p. 60.

42  Ibid., p. 61.

43  Ibid., p. 62.

44  G. Medvedev, 'Chernobylskaya tetrad', *Novy Mir* 6 (1989), pp. 80–1.

45  V. Legasov, 'Moi dolg rasskazat ob etom', *Pravda*, 20 May 1988.

46  *Moskovskie Novosti*, 32 (9 August 1987); p. 12.

47  Ibid.

48  M. Grodzinsky, 'Chernobyl' (interview), *Znanie Sila*, 8, (1988), p. 14.

49  Ibid., p. 16.

50  *The Accident . . . Soviet IAEA Report*, Part II, Annex 7, fig. 7.2.3.

51  *The Accident . . . Soviet IAEA Report*, Part II, Annex 7, p. 39.

52  Ibid., p. 44.

53  Ibid., p. 47.

54  Ibid., Part I, table 2, p. 41.

55  *Izvestiya*, 8 May 1986.

56  *The Accident . . . Soviet IAEA Report*, Part II, Annex 4, table 4.1, pp. 4–5.

57  Ibid., Part II, Annex 7, p. 48.

58  Ibid., p. 50.

59  Ibid.

60  *Izvestiya*, 15 June 1986.

61  *The Accident . . . Soviet IAEA Report*, Part I, p. 41.

62  Ibid., Part II, Annex 7, p. 44.

63  Shcherbak, 'Chernobyl', *Yunost'* 6, p. 66.

64  The many photographs published in the Soviet press and distributed abroad by *Novosti* and TASS indicate that the thyroid inspection was carried out with very large military dosimeters which have large Geiger counters in the form of a metal tube with a surface of 200 cm$^2$ or more. They can only be used to measure the radiation of large objects (like cars, car tyres, etc). They are not sensitive enough for reading thyroid gland activity because they have a very high count of background radioactivity and cosmic rays. Thyroid radioactivity should normally be measured with Geiger counters that have a small mica window with a surface of about 4 to 5 cm$^2$.

65  Shcherbak, 'Chernobyl', *Yunost'* 6, p. 66.

66  Ibid., p. 66.

67  *Izvestiya*, 8 May 1986.

68  *Izvestiya*, 12 May 1986.

69  *The Accident . . . Soviet IAEA Report*, Part II, Annex 7, p. 51.

70  Ibid., Part II, Annex 5, table 5.5, p. 8.

71  Shcherbak, 'Chernobyl', *Yunost'*, 7 (1987) p. 34.

72  *The Accident . . . Soviet IAEA Report*, Part II, Annex 5, table 5.5, p. 8.

73  *Izvestiya*, 13 May 1986.
74  *Izvestiya*, 23 May 1986.
75  Shcherbak, 'Chernobyl', *Yunost'*, 7 (1987), p. 34.
76  *The Accident . . . Soviet IAEA Report*, Part II, Annex 5, p. 50.
77  Ibid., Part II, Annex 7, p. 55.
78  Ibid., p. 57.
79  L. A. Il'in *Rukovodstvo po Organizatsii*, p. 154.
80  J. Maddox, 'Soviet frankness creates sense of solidarity', *Nature*, 323 (1986), p. 3.
81  V. N. Soifer, 'Chernobylskaya katastrofa, zagreznennost' okruzhayushchei sredy i nasledstvennost' cheloveka', *Kontinent* (Paris), 52 (1987), pp. 191–220. *Kontinent* is a Russian language journal published in France and Germany. Although mostly literary, it occasionally publishes scientific reviews by Soviet authors who cannot publish their work in the USSR. Dr Valery Soifer, Dr Sci, is a Soviet molecular biologist and geneticist. He has written several books and many research papers. He was an associate of Professor N. P. Dubinin, a well known Soviet expert on radiation genetics. His paper therefore has considerable professional value.
82  This estimate was given by Professor Gale during a television programme on Chernobyl (a telebridge between Soviet and American scientists) in October 1986. Because the programme was seen by millions of Soviet viewers and made a great impact, it was often mentioned in the Soviet press later, usually critically.
83  Gale and Hauser, *Chernobyl: the final warning*.
84  M. Morrey, J. Brown, J. A. Williams, M. J. Crick, J. R. Simmonds and M. D. Hill, *A preliminary assessment of the radiological impact of the Chernobyl reactor accident on the population of the European Community* (National Radiological Protection Board, UK, 1987).
85  E. Marshall 'Recalculating the cost of Chernobyl', *Science*, 236 (1987), pp. 638–9.
86  L. R. Anspaugh, R. J. Catlin and M. Goldman, 'The global impact of the Chernobyl reactor accident', *Science*, 242, (16 December 1988), pp. 1512–19.
87  Anonymous (1986) 'Chernobyl: the grim statistics of cancer', *New Scientist*, III (14 August 1986), p. 13.
88  This estimate was given by the Prime Minister of the Ukraine during his talk with a British Trades Union delegation on April 5, 1987. See *The Guardian*, 6 April 1987, p. 2.
89  R. E. Webb, 'The health consequences of Chernobyl', *The Ecologist*, 16 (1986), pp. 169–70.
90  Nuclear Reactor Safety Hearings before the Joint Committee on Atomic Energy. Congress of the United States, Part 1 (Washington, DC, 1974).
91  R. Wilson, 'Chernobyl public health effects', *Science*, 238 (1987), pp. 10–11.
92  *The Accident . . . Soviet IAEA Report*, Part II, Annex 7, p. 2.

93 L. A. Il'in *The Chernobyl experience.*

94 L. A. Il'in, *Rukovodstvo*, p. 157.

95 R. Wilson, 'A visit to Chernobyl', p. 1637.

96 G. Medvedev, 'Chernobylskaya tetrad', pp. 98–9.

97 Ibid., p. 83.

98 The amount of 25 rem for workers in the emergency services was only disclosed during discussions at the IAEA. In practice, their exposure was probably higher. According to the Soviet general rules of exposure in an emergency, an exposure of up to 50 Rem is considered a justified risk if it is extended for 30 days. It is operational for space flights. For manned space flights the Soviet rules allow a maximal dose of 2.5 Sv (250 Rem) if it is extended for 2.5 years. See Il'in, L. A. (1985), p. 155. The rules also indicate that if the work carried out in an emergency is directed towards saving the life of others, doses can be higher (they do not specify how much higher).

99 Il'in, 'The Chernobyl experience'.

100 C. D. Van Cleave, *Late Somatic Effects of Ionizing Radiation* (Springfield, Virginia, US Atomic Energy Commission, 1968).

101 A. K. Gus'kova, V. A., Soldatova, E. A. Denisova, N. I. Gorbarenko, I. A. Gribova, G. I. Kirsanova, and E. N. L'vovskaya, 'Otdalennye posledstviya professional'nogo luchevogo vozdeistviya' (Remote after-effects of occupational radiation action, in Russian with English summary), *Meditsinskaya Radiologiya*, 21 (4) (1976), pp. 34–40.

102 Shcherbak, 'Chernobyl', *Yunost*, 7 p. 44.

103 *Sovetskaya kul'tura*, 23 April 1988. Information was provided by the Department of Information of the Ministry of Atomic Energy which was affiliated to the Chernobyl AES.

104 N. Goshchitsky, 'Upala zvezda polyn', *Ogonek*, 38, pp. 25–8; 39 (1987), pp. 18–20. This is a documentary story about the emergency work at Chernobyl. The author mentions that the local emergency canteen at the reactor site had to prepare 2,000 hot meals daily.

105 V. Gubarev, 'Fantom', *Nauka i zhizn'*, 6 (1987), pp. 67–81, 7 (1987), pp. 56–71.

106 *Sovetskaya Kul'tura*, 25 April 1987, p. 5.

107 *Izvestiya*, 19 September 1986.

108 L. A. Il'in and O. A. Pavlovsky, 'Radiological consequences of the Chernobyl accident in the Soviet Union and the measures taken to mitigate their impact'. Report at the IAEA International Conference on Nuclear Power Performance and Safety, 28 September–2 October 1987, Vienna (IAE-CN-48/33. Available on demand from IAEA Information Service Department).

109 *Izvestiya*, 11 February 1989.

110 N. Baklanov, 'Boleznennaya operatsiya', *Izvestiya*, 10 August 1988.

111 *Izvestiya*, 27 April 1989.

112 N. Goshchitsky, 'Upala zvezda poly'n, p. 19.

113 *The Accident . . . Soviet IAEA Report*, Part II, Annex 7, p. 44.

114 *Izvestiya*, 11 February and 3 March 1989.

115 *The Accident . . . Soviet IAEA Report*, Part II, Annex 7, fig. 7.2.7, p. 64.

116 Ibid. p. 55.

117 Ibid.

118 Ibid.

119 *Sobesednik*, 17 (April 1989), p. 5.

120 *Argumenty i Fakty*, 16 (16–22 April 1988), p. 8.

121 Ibid.

122 *The Accident . . . Soviet IAEA Report*, Part II, Annex 7, fig. 7.2.7, p. 64.

123 Ibid., Part I, table 2, p. 41.

124 Ibid., Part II, Annex 7, p. 66.

125 Ibid., p. 63.

126 Ibid., pp. 65–6.

127 Ibid., p. 66.

128 Ibid., p. 27.

129 Goldman, 'Chernobyl: radiological perspective', *Science*, 238 (1987), pp. 622–33.

130 Il'in and Pavlovsky, 'Radiological consequences'.

131 M. Morrey, J. Brown, et al., *A preliminary assessment*.

132 Goldman, 'Chernobyl'.

133 Il'in and Pavlovsky', 'Radiological consequences', p. 21.

134 Morrey, et al., *A preliminary assessment*, p. 28.

135 L. Devell, H. Tovedal, U. Bergstrom, A. Appelgren, J. Chyssler and L. Andersson, 'Initial observations of fallout from reactor accident at Chernobyl', *Nature*, 321 (1986), pp. 192–3.

136 J. R. Bamburg, D. Bray and K. Chapman, 'Core fragments in Chernobyl fallout', *Nature*, 323 (1986), pp. 399–400.

137 Z. I. Kalmykova, I. V. Oslina, L. A. Buldakov, V. V. Kharunzhin, S. N. Sokolova, M. A. Okatenko, 'The absorbed doses and haematologic changes in dogs breathing submicron $^{239}$Pu dioxide', *Radiobilogiya*, 27 (1987), pp. 349–53.

138 V. Knizhnikov, 'Vokrug Chernobylya. God spustya', *Meditsinskaya Gazeta*, 22 May 1987, p. 3.

139 Ibid.

140 V. Rich, 'Continuing plans for evacuation', *Nature*, 340 (1989), p. 415.

141 J. Simmonds, 'Europe calculates the health risk', *New Scientist*, 114, (1557), (1987), pp. 40–3.

142 N. Goshchitsky, 'Upala zvezda polyn', p. 27.

143 *The Times* (London), 25 April 1987, p. 7.

144 Shcherbak. 'Chernobyl', Yunost', 7 (1987), p. 35.

145 *Izvestiya*, 24 July 1986.

146 *The Times* (London), 18 June 1987, p. 7.

147 *The Accident . . . Soviet IAEA Report*, Part II, Annex 7, pp. 15–17.

148 *Izvestiya*, 1 February 1989.

149 *Pravda*, 11 February 1989.
150 V. Rich, *Nature*, 337 (1989), p. 683.
151 *Pravda* 11 February 1989.
152 *Izvestiya*, 3 March 1989.
153 *Moscow News*, 8 (19 February 1989), p. 12.
154 Ibid.
155 *Izvestiya*, 30 July 1989.
156 For a review of the studies, see Zh. A. Medvedev, *Nuclear disaster in the Urals* (New York, Norton, 1979); J. R. Trabalka, L. D. Eyman and S. I. Auerbach, 'Analysis of the 1957–1958 Soviet Nuclear disaster', *Science*, 209 (1980), pp. 345–53.
157 K. Gus'kova, 'Osnovnye itogi i nekotorye zadachi issledovaniya v oblasti kliniki, diagnostiki i profilaktiki luchevoi bolezni cheloveka', *Meditsinskaya Radiologiya*, 12, (11) (1967), pp. 53–64.
158 *International Herald Tribune*, 25 June 1986, p. 3.
159 *Pravda*, 16 January 1988.

## 6 THE GLOBAL IMPACT

1 N. Hawkes, G. Lean, D. Leigh, R. McKie, P. Pringle, and A. Wilson. *The Worst Accident in the World. Chernobyl: The End of the Nuclear Dream* (London, Heinemann and Pan Books, 1986).
2 Yu, I. Moskalev, 'Itogi soveshchaniya ekspertov evropeiskogo regional'nogo buro VOS po otsenke posledstvii avarii na Chernobylskoi AES. Iyun 1986', *Meditsinskaya radiologiya*, 32 (10) (1987), pp. 87–8.
3 *Chernobyl Reactor Accident.* Report of a consultation 6 May 1986 (Copenhagen, World Health Organization, Regional Office for Europe), p. 4.
4 Ibid., pp. 6 7.
5 H. ApSimon and J. Wilson, 'Tracking the cloud from Chernobyl', *New Scientist*, III (1517) (17 July 1986), pp. 42–5.
6 *Nature*, 322 (1986), p. 672.
7 *After Chernobyl? Implications of the Chernobyl accident for Sweden.* Special issue of *News and Views*, Information for Immigrants, Stockholm, November 1986.
8 L. Devell, H. Tovedal, U. Bergstrom, A. Applegren, J. Chyssler and L. Andersson, 'Initial observations of fallout from reactor accident at Chernobyl', *Nature*, 321 (1986), pp. 192–3.
9 USSR State Committee on the Utilization of Atomic Energy. *The Accident at Chernobyl Nuclear Power Plant and its Consequences.* Information compiled for the IAEA Experts' Meeting, 24–9 August 1986, Vienna. Working Document for the Post-Accident Review Meeting. Part II, Annex 5, p. 1.
10 B. Erlandsson, L. Asking and E. Swetlicki, 'Detailed early measurements of

the fallout in Sweden from the Chernobyl accident', *Water, Air and Soil Pollution*, 35 (1987), 335–46.

11 C. Persson, H. Rodhe and L-E. DeGeer, 'The Chernobyl accident: a meteorological analysis of how the radioactivity spread to Sweden', *SMHI Meteorologi*, 24 (1986).

12 L. Devell et al., 'Initial observations', p. 192.

13 L. Devell, A. Aarkrog, L. Blomqvist, S. Magnusson and U. Tveten, 'How the fallout from Chernobyl was detected and measured in Nordic countries', *Nuclear Europe*, 11 (1986), pp. 16–17.

14 Ibid., p. 16.

15 Ibid., p. 16.

16 *The Observer*, 1 June 1986, p. 14.

17 D. MacKenzie, 'The rad-nose reindeer', *New Scientist*, 1539 (18 December 1986), pp. 37–40.

18 Ibid.

19 *The Daily Telegraph*, 24 December 1986.

20 *Chernobyl – its impact on Sweden* (Stockholm, National Institute of Radiation Protection, SSI-Raport 86-12, 1986), p. 4.

21 H. Svensson, 'The Chernobyl accident – impact on Western Europe', *Radiotherapy and Oncology*, 12 (1988), pp. 1–13.

22 *Radiation Doses in Sweden as a Result of the Chernobyl Fallout* (Stockholm, National Institute of Radiation Protection, SSI-Raport 87–13, 1987), pp. 7–8.

23 Ibid.

24 *After Chernobyl?*, p. 6.

25 L. Berman, 'Sweden's energy politics after Chernobyl', *Human Environment in Sweden*, 27 (New York, Swedish Information Service, December 1986).

26 L. Devell, 'Characteristics of the Chernobyl release and fallout of potential generic interest to severe accident analysis'. Report from Studsvik, presented at the American Chemical Society Symposium on Nuclear Reactor Severe Accident Chemistry, Toronto, Canada, 7–11 June 1988.

27 L. Devell, 'Nucleotide Composition of Chernobyl Hot Particles'. Studsvik report NP-87/119, Sweden, 1987; Internal Workshop in Hot Particles in the Chernobyl Fallout (Theuern bei Regensberg, FRG, 28–9 October 1987).

28 G. A. M. Webb, J. R. Simmonds and B. T. Wilkins, 'Radiation Levels in Eastern Europe', *Nature*, 321 (1986), pp. 821–2.

29 Rainbow Group in the European Parliament, *Report on Chernobyl*, chapter 3, 'Information policy and other measures' (1986).

30 V. Rich, 'Chernobyl: Polish fallout underestimated', *Nature*, 324 (1986), p. 603.

31 R. Broda, Gamma spectroscopy analysis of hot particles from the Chernobyl fallout (Krakow, Institute of Nuclear Physics, Report No. 1342/B, October 1986).

32 L. R. Anspaugh, R. J. Catlin and M. Goldman, 'The global impact of the Chernobyl reactor accident', *Science*, 242 (1988), p. 1516.

33  E. Csongor, A. Z. Kiss, B. M. Nyako and E. Somorjai, 'Chernobyl fallout in Debrecen, Hungary', *Nature*, 324 (1986), p. 216.

34  Hungarian Atomic Energy Commission, *Radiation consequences in Hungary of the Chernobyl accident* (Budapest July 1986).

35  *The Accident . . . Soviet IAEA Report*, Part II, Annex 7, fig. 7.2.7.

36  Rainbow Group in the European Parliament.

37  Anspaugh et al., 'The global impact', p. 1516.

38  Bulgarian Committee of Peaceful Uses of Atomic Energy. *Results of the investigation of the radiological situation in Bulgaria after the Chernobyl NPS accident* (in Russian) (Sofia, November, 1986).

39  R. H. Clarke, 'Radiological aspects of Chernobyl in Western Europe', *The NEA Newsletter* (Fall 1986), pp. 9–12.

40  Ibid., p. 11.

41  K. Irlweck, 'Actuelle messdaten nach dem Reaktorunfall Tschernobyl', *Acta Med. Austriaca*, 13 (4/5) (1986), pp. 107–13.

42  F. Haschke, B. Pietschnig, V. Karg, H. Vanura and E. Schuster, 'Radioactivity in Austrian milk after the Chernobyl accident', *New Engl. J. Med.* 316 (1987), pp. 409–10.

43  E. Henich, 'Chernobyl – its impact on Austria', *The Science of the Total Environment*, 70 (1988), pp. 433–54.

44  G. Galvan, 'Tschernobyl – praktische Erfahrungen am Beispiel des Salzburger Kriaenstables', *Acta Med. Austriaca*, 13 (4/5) (1986), pp. 103–6.

45  D. M. McKenzie and M. Glenny, 'From Polish potatoes to Turkish tea', *New Scientist*, 114 (1557) (23 April 1987), p. 48.

46  R. S. Cambray, P. A. Cawse et al., Observations on radioactivity from the Chernobyl accident. *Nuclear Energy*, 26 (2) (1987), pp. 77–101.

47  M. Morrey, J. Brown, J. A. Williams, M. J. Crick, J. R. Simmonds and M. D. Hill, *A preliminary assessment of the radiological impact of the Chernobyl reactor accident on the population of the European Community* (National Radiological Board, UK, 1907).

48  'First Assessment of the Effect of the Chernobyl Accident on Europe', NRPB Press Release, 4 (23 March 1987).

49  J. Simmonds, 'Europe calculates the health risk', *New Scientist*, 114 (1557) (23 April 1987), pp. 40–3.

50  Rob Edwards, 'Chernobyl fallout 40 times worse than admitted', *The Guardian*, 28 January 1989.

51  *The Accident . . . Soviet IAEA Report*, Part I, p. 41. The draft of the general material presented to the IAEA was later published in the Soviet Union in *Atomnaya Energiya*, 61 (5), November 1986, pp. 301–20. However, in the description of the main characteristics of the radioactive contamination many paragraphs from the draft were excluded from the published version. The impression was given that all the fallout occurred within the borders of the Soviet Union.

52  Cambray et al., 'Observations on radioactivity', p. 99.

53  H. M. ApSimon, H. F. Macdonald and J. J. N. Wilson, 'An initial

assessment of the Chernobyl-4 reactor accident release source', *J. Soc. Radiol. Prot.*, 6 (3) (1986), pp. 109–19.

54 Anspaugh et al., 'The global impact'.

55 E. Marshall, 'Recalculating the cost of Chernobyl', *Science*, 236 (1987), pp. 658–9.

56 M. Goldman et al., *Health and Environmental Consequences of the Chernobyl Nuclear Power Plant Accident*. Department of Energy Report, ER-0332, prepared by the Interlaboratory Task Group (Washington, DC, 1987).

57 M. Goldman, 'Chernobyl: radiological perspective', *Science*, 238 (1987), pp. 622–3.

58 R. H. Clarke, 'Radiologial aspects', p. 11.

59 Morrey et al., *A preliminary assessment*, p. 31.

60 Auswirkungen des Reactorunfalls in Tschernobyl auf die Bundesrepublik Deutschland. Zusammenfassender Bericht der Strahlenschutzkommission. (Stuttgart, Gustav Fischer Verlag, 1987).

61 K. Bunzl, W. Kracke and G. Vorwohl, 'Transfer of Chernobyl-derived $^{134}$Cs, $^{137}$Cs, $^{131}$I and $^{103}$Ru from flowers to honey and pollen', *J. Environ. Radioactivity*, 6 (1988), pp. 261–9.

62 Auswirkungen, p. 76.

63 Ibid., p. 125.

64 C. Hohenemser, M. Deicher, H. Hofsass, G. Lindler, E. Recknagel and J. I. Budnick, 'Agricultural impact of Chernobyl: a warning', *Nature*, 321 (1986), p. 817.

65 H. Dorr and K. O. Munnich, 'Spatial distribution of soil $^{134}$Cs and $^{137}$Cs in West Germany after Chernobyl', *Naturwissenschaften*, 74 (1987), pp. 249–51.

66 *A Compilation of Early Papers by Members of the NRPB Staff about the Reactor Accident at Chernobyl on 26 April 1986* (21 papers mainly dealing with how the accident affected the United Kingdom) (National Radiological Protection Board, October 1986; *Radionuclide Levels in Food, Animals and Agricultural Products*. Post-Chernobyl Monitoring in England and Wales. (HMSO, Ministry of Agriculture, Fisheries and Food, Welsh Office. London, 1987). Cambray et al, 'Observations on radioactivity'. J. D. Cunningham et al., *Chernobyl: its effects on Ireland* (Dublin, Nuclear Energy Board, March 1987).

67 B. Howard and F. Livens, 'May sheep safely graze?' *New Scientist*, 114 (1557) (1987), pp. 46–9.

68 B. James 'After the fallout, odd food in Europe', *International Herald Tribune*, 7 October 1987.

69 W. S. Watson, 'Human $^{134}$Cs/$^{137}$Cs levels in Scotland after Chernobyl', *Nature*, 323 (1986), pp. 763–4.

70 F. A. Fry, 'The Chernobyl reactor accident: the impact on the United Kingdom', *British Journal of Radiology*, 60 (1987), pp. 1147–58.

71 R. Clarke, 'Reactor accidents in perspective', *British Journal of Radiology*, 60 (1987), pp. 1182–8.

72  A. J. Thomas and J. M. Martin, 'First assessment of Chernobyl radioactive plume over Paris', *Nature*, 321 (1986), pp. 817–19.

73  *La Gazette*, 78/79 (publication du Groupement des Scientifiques pour l'Information sous l'Energie Nucleaire. Bimestriel, June 1987).

74  James, 'After the fallout'.

75  'Response to the Chernobyl accident in Japan'. *Atoms in Japan*, 30 (5) (1986), pp. 4–9; 'STA estimates exposure dose of Japanese from Chernobyl accident', *Atoms in Japan*, 30 (7) (1986), pp. 43–4.

76  E. A. Bondietti and J. N. Brantley, 'Characteristics of Chernobyl radioactivity in Tennessee', *Nature*, 322 (1986), pp. 313–4.

77  *Nuclear Reactor Safety*. Hearings before the Joint Committee on Atomic Energy, Congress of the United States, 93rd Congress, First Session, January 23, September 25, 26, 27 and October 1, 1973. (Washington DC, US Congress Printing Office, 1974).

78  Ibid., p. 545.

79  Ibid., p. 354.

80  Ibid., p. 366.

81  Ibid., p. 349.

82  Anspaugh et al., 'The global impact', p. 1516.

83  UNSCEAR, *Ionizing Radiation: Sources and Biological Effects* (report to the General Assembly of the United Nations, New York, 1982).

84  Goldman, et al., *Health and environmental consequences*, p. 575.

85  *Radiation doses in Sweden*, pp. 7–8.

86  R. Wilson, Harvard University, in a private communication.

87  Goldman, 'Chernobyl, pp. 622–3.

88  *The Work of the NRPB 1984/6* (National Radiological Protection Board, UK, June 1987), p. 35.

89  Zh. A. Medvedev, *Nuclear disaster in the Urals* (New York, Norton, 1979), J. R. Trebalka, L. D. Eyman and S. I. Auerbach, 'Analysis of the 1957–1958 Soviet nuclear accident', *Science*, 209 (1980), pp. 345–53.

90  L. Roberts, 'Atomic bomb doses reassessed', *Science*, 238 (1987), pp. 1649–51. J. Rotblat, 'A tale of two cities', *New Scientist*, 117 (1590) (7 January 1988), pp. 46–50.

## 7  THE SOVIET NUCLEAR ENERGY PROGRAMME

1  M. Chernenko, 'K istorii pervykh shagov sovetskogo atomnogo proyekta', *Moskovskie Novosti*, 16, 17 April 1988, p. 16.

2  I. F. Zhezherun, *Stroitel'stvo i pusk pervogo v Sovetskom Soyuze atomnogo reaktora* (Moscow, Atomizdat, 1978).

3  A. M. Petrosy'ants, *Problems of nuclear science and technology. The Soviet Union as a world nuclear power*, 4th edn (Oxford, New York, Pergamon Press, 1981), p. 343.

4  W. Patterson, *Nuclear power*, 2nd edn. (Harmondsworth, Penguin Books, 1983), p. 47.

5 P. Astashenkov, *Kurchatov* (Moscow, Molodaya Gvardiya, 1967), p. 167.
6 I. N. Golovin, *I. V. Kurchatov* (Moscow, Atomizdat, 1967), p. 77.
7 Ibid., p. 84.
8 Ibid., pp. 84–5. Astashenkov, *Kurchatov*, p. 167.
9 D. A. Granin, 'Zubr', *Novyi Mir* (1987), pp. 7–92.
10 Ibid., p. 46.
11 V. Gubarev, 'Sarkofag', *Znamya* 9 (1986), pp. 114–15. English translation by M. Glenny, *Sarcophagus* (Harmondsworth, Penguin, 1987).
12 V. Gubarev, 'No ne v Obninske', *Sovestkaya Kul'tura*, 28 May 1987, p. 3.
13 Petrosy'ants, *Problems of Nuclear Science*, pp. 103–4.
14 *Kruschev Remembers. The Last Testament*, tr. and ed. S. Talbott (Boston, Little Brown, 1974), p. 60.
15 Petrosy'ants, Problems of nuclear science, p. 107.
16 Ibid., p. 105.
17 Zh. A. Medvedev, *Nuclear disaster in the Urals* (New York, Norton, 1979).
18 Petrosy'ants, *Problems of nuclear science*, p. 107.
19 *Izvestiya*, 26 April 1989.
20 'Nuclear Reactor Development', *Encyclopaedia Britannica*, vol. 13, 1982, p. 321.
21 *Report of the US Department of Energy's Team Analysis of the Chernobyl Atomic Energy Station Accident Sequence*, (Washington DC, US Department of Energy, November 1986), p. 7.
22 V. Dubrovsky (ed.), *Construction of Nuclear Power Plants.* (Moscow, Mir Publishers, 1981), p. 92.
23 Petrosy'ants, *Problems of nuclear science*, pp. 118, 146.
24 Dubrovsky (ed.), *Construction of nuclear power plants*, p. 37.
25 Ibid.
26 G. Medvedev, 'Nekompetentnost'', *Kommunist*, 4 (1988), p. 97.
27 Ibid., pp. 96–7.
28 Petrosy'ants, *Problems of nuclear science*, p. 118.
29 *Argumenty i Fakty*, 15 (1988), p. 8.
30 Technical descriptions of the Soviet VVER can be found in Petrosy'ants, *Problems of nuclear science*, p. 118; Dubrovsky (ed.) *Construction of nuclear power plants*.
31 Petrosy'ants, *Problems of nuclear science*, pp. 130–1.
32 Ibid., p. 132.
33 *Pravda*, 20 July 1983.
34 *Pravda*, 31 July 1983.
35 G. Greenhalph, 'Soviet drive to nuclear power', *New Scientist*, 110 (1507) (8 May 1986), p. 198.
36 USSR State Committee on the Utilization of Atomic Energy. *The Accident at Chernobyl Nuclear Power Plant and its Consequences.* Information compiled for the IAEA Experts' Meeting, 24–9 August 1986, Vienna. Working Document for the Post-Accident Review Meeting. Draft. Part II,

Annexe 2, August 1986 (hereafter referred to as *The Accident . . . Soviet IAEA Report*).

37 Dubrovsky (ed.), *Construction of nuclear power plants*, p. 85.
38 D. R. Marples, *Chernobyl and nuclear power in the USSR* (London, Macmillan, 1986).
39 Petrosy'ants, *Problems of nuclear science*, p. 153.
40 Ibid., p. 162.
41 *Pravda*, 25 April 1980.
42 Petrosy'ants, *Problems of nuclear science*, p. 153.
43 *Izvestiya*, 14 December 1979.
44 *Ekonomicheskaya Gazeta*, 52 (December 1983).
45 Petrosy'ants, *Problems of nuclear science*, p. 231.
46 Ibid., p. 232.
47 *Izvestiya*, 19 July 1985.
48 Oles Gonchar, 'Otkuda yavilas' "Zvezda Polyn", *Literaturnaya Gazeta*, 9 December 1987.
49 G. Lean and R. Smith, 'The menace on our doorsteps', *Observer* Magazine, 11 October 1987.
50 N. Dollezhal and Y. Koryakin, 'Yadernaya energetika. Dostizheniya i problemy', *Kommunist*, 14 (1979), pp. 19–28.
51 *The Times*, 20 December 1989.
52 Yu. A. Yegorov (ed.), *Radiatsionnaya bezopasnost' i zaschita AES. Sbornik statei* (Moscow, Energoizdat; No. 12 was published in 1987, the previous numbers 1 to 11 in 1975–86).
53 *Moskovskie Novosti*, 9 August 1987.
54 *Moskovskie Novosti*, 10 January 1988, p. 10.
55 *Moskovskie Novosti*, 14 February 1988, p. 10.
56 V. Legasov, *The lessons of Chernobyl are important for all* (Moscow, Novosty Press, 1987).
57 S. Ushanov, 'Dva goda posle Chernobylya', *Literaturnaya Gazeta*, 20 July 1988, p. 12.
58 Zhezherun, *Stroitel'stvo i pusk pervogo*.
59 Ushanov, 'Dva goda posle Chernobylya'.
60 Ibid.
61 A. Yanshin, N. Glazovsky et al., 'Ekspertiza', *Pravda*, 11 January 1989.
62 *Pravda*, 16 January 1988.
63 L. Abalkin, Press conference, as reported by TASS on 30 May 1988.

8 A HISTORY OF NUCLEAR ACCIDENTS IN THE SOVIET UNION

1 H. B. Smets, 'Review of nuclear incidents', in Weinstein, J. L. (ed.) *Nuclear Liability. Progress in Nuclear Energy*, Series X, *Law and Administration*, vol. 3 (Oxford, New York, Pergamon Press, 1962), pp. 108–20; W. R. Stratton, 'A Review of Criticality Accidents' (Los Alamos Scientific

Laboratory Report LA 3611, US Atomic Energy, Commission, 1967). Also periodic reports of the US Nuclear Regulatory Commission, *Reports to Congress on Abnormal Occurrences*, vol. 3, 1980, vol. 4, 1981, etc. and other sources.

2  *Nuclear Power Plant Safety Scoreboard 1980*. Critical Mass Energy Project. Report (Washington DC, July 1981).

3  *Nuclear Power Safety Report, 1981*. Critical Mass Energy Project. Study Coordinator. R. A. Udell (Washington DC, 1982).

4  *1979–1987 Nuclear Power Safety Report*, Critical Mass Energy Project (Washington DC, 1987).

5  *Moskovskie Novosti*, 32, 9 August 1987, p. 12.

6  See, for example, N. S. Babaev, I. I. Kus'min, V. A. Legasov and V. A. Sidorenko, 'Problemy bezopasnosti na atomnykh elektrostantsiyakh', *Priroda*, 6 (1980), pp. 30–43; Yu. V. Sivintsev, *I. V. Kurchatov i yadernaya energetika* (Moscow, Atomizdat, 1980).

7  A. M. Petrosy'ants, *Problems of nuclear science and technology. The Soviet Union as a world nuclear power*, 4th edn (Oxford, New York, Pergamon Press, 1981), pp. 129–30.

8  Ibid., p. 133.

9  Ibid., p. 162.

10  Ibid., p. 116.

11  Ibid.

12  V. Legasov, 'Moi dolg rasskazat' ob etom', *Pravda*, 20 May 1988.

13  Ibid.

14  Ibid.

15  USSR State Committee on the Utilization of Atomic Energy. *The Accident at Chernobyl Nuclear Power Plant and its Consequences*. Information compiled for the IAEA Experts' Meeting, 24–9 August 1986, Vienna. Working Document for the Post-Accident Review Meeting. Draft. Part II, Annex 2, pp. 180–1. August 1986 (hereafter referred to as *The Accident . . . Soviet IAEA Report*).

16  Ibid., p. 181–2.

17  M. Vasin, 'Chelovek u pul'ta', *Pravda*, 17 October 1987, p. 2.

18  Legasov, 'Moi dolg rasskazat' ob etom'.

19  Babaev et al., 'Problemy bezopusnosh', p. 43.

20  *Moskovskie Novosti*, 32 (9 August 1987), p. 12.

21  *Pravda*, 20 July 1983.

22  Legasov, 'Moi dolg rasskazat' ob etom'.

23  *International Herald Tribune*, 5–6 January 1980, p. 9.

24  Petrosy'ants, *Problems of nuclear science*, p. 344.

25  One Soviet author on nuclear energy problems argues that this proves that the physicists were confident that the tests were entirely safe and posed no danger to the Leningrad population. See Sivintsev, *I. V. Kurchatov*, p. 60. This is a dubious assertion. A number of leaks of radioactivity from US ships

with reactors have been reported by Critical Mass and other independent groups.

26 Petrosy'ants, *Problems of nuclear science*, p. 262.

27 P. Wood, 'Nuclear power in Eastern Europe', *The Ecologist*, 10 (1) (1980), pp. 68–9.

28 V. Rich, 'Fire threatened fast reactor cooling system, says unofficial report', *Nature*, 283 (1980), p. 420.

29 R. D. Smith, 'Fast reactor safety and the fire at Beloyarsk', *Nature*, 284 (1980), p. 10.

30 V. Kamenshchik, 'V tu trevozhnuyu noch', *Sotsialisticheskaya industriya*, 21 October 1988.

31 Ibid.

32 Ibid.

33 G. Medvedev. Chernobylskay tetrad', *Novy Mir*, 6 (1989), pp. 3–108.

34 Zh. A. Medvedev, 'Two decades of dissidence', New Scientist, 72 (1976), pp. 264–7.

35 Zh. A. Medvedev, *Nuclear disaster in the Urals* (New York, Norton, 1979).

36 J. R. Trabalka, L. D. Eyman and S. I. Auerbach, 'Analysis of the 1957–1958 Soviet nuclear accident'. *Science*, 209 (1980) 345–53; and *Analysis of the 1957–1958 Soviet nuclear accident*, ORNL-5613 (Oak Ridge National Laboratory, 1980).

37 D. M. Soran and D. B. Stillman, An analysis of the alleged Kyshtym disaster, Report LA-9217-MS (New Mexico, Los Alamos National Laboratory, January 1982).

38 Trabalka et al., 'Analysis', pp. 345–53.

39 *Japan Times*, 7 December 1988.

40 Ibid.

41 D. Charles, 'Will these lands ne'er be clean?' New Scientist, 24 June 1989, pp. 36–7.

42 B. V. Nekipelov, G. N. Romanov, L. A. Buldakov, N. S. Babaev, Y. D. Kholina and E. I. Mekerin, 'Ob avarii na Yuzhnom Urale 29 sentyabrya 1957g'. Information Bulletin, Centre of Public Information in Atomic Energy, 30 June 1989 (report distributed among members of the Supreme Soviet of the USSR and to Soviet Newspapers).

43 J. Smith, 'Soviets describe accident at secret nuclear center', *The Washington Post*, 10 July 1989.

44 Medvedev, 'Chernobylskay tetrad', p. 11.

45 *Izvestiya*, 26 April 1989.

## 9 NUCLEAR POWER AFTER CHERNOBYL

1 J. H. Fremlin, *Power production. What are the risks?* (Oxford, New York, Pergamon Press, 1987) p. 69.

2 *Vneshnyaya torgovlya SSSR v 1974 godu* (Moscow, Statistika), p. 21; *Vneshtorg v 1985 godu* (Moscow, Statistika), p. 18.
3 *Narodnoe Khozyaistvo v 1985 godu. Statisticheskii ezhegodnik* (hereafter referred to as *Nar. khoz.*) (Moscow, TsU SSSR), p. 155.
4 *1987 Encyclopedia Britannica Book of the Year* (Chicago, Encyclopedia Britannica, 1987), p. 774.
5 *Pravda*, 14 June 1982.
6 *Nar. khoz.*, p. 157.
7 Ibid.
8 *Nar. khoz., SSSR za 70 let. Yubileiny statistichesky ezhegodnik, 1917–1987* (Moscow, TsU, 1988), p. 163.
9 *Ekonomicheskaya gazeta*, 13 (March 1988), p. 19.
10 *Izvestiya*, 14 August 1987.
11 D. R. Marples, *The Social Impact of the Chernobyl Disaster*, (London, Macmillan, 1988), pp. 90–5.
12 *The Chernobyl accident: a year later* (Vienna, IAEA, 1987), pp. 46–53.
13 *Izvestiya*, 9 March 1988.
14 Ibid.
15 *Pravda*, 14 February 1988.
16 *Izvestiya*, 9 March 1988. See also *Izvestiya*, 10 March 1989.
17 *The Times*, 23 December 1988.
18 M. Crawford, 'Electricity crunch foreseen . . . maybe', *Science*, 242 (1988), pp. 105–7.
19 *Moskovskie Novosti*, 8 January 1989.
20 'Fast reactor move hits European collaboration', *Nature*, 334 (1988), p. 278.
21 O. Keck, 'Fast breeder reactors: can we learn from experience?', *Nature*, 294, (1981), pp. 205–8.
22 S. Dickman, 'Fast breeder generates controversy', *Nature*, 334 (1988), p. 278.
23 C. P. Zakeski, 'Breeder reactors in France', *Science*, 208 (1980), pp. 137–44.
24 Ibid.
25 R. Milne and D. MacKenzie, 'Pace hots up for European fast breeder', *New Scientist*, 116 (1987), pp. 30–1.
26 M. Walker, 'US owns up on nuclear clean-up bill', *The Guardian*, 6 January 1989, p. 8.
27 'Nuclear Energy Vision. Perspectives of Nuclear Energy for the 21st Century'. Sub-committee on Nuclear Energy of the Advisory Committee for Energy, Ministry of International Trade and Industry, Japan, September 1986.
28 B. I. Spinrad, 'US nuclear power in the next twenty years', *Science*, 239 (1988), pp. 707–8.

# Index

Windscale accident 1, 68, 80, 155, 218
World Health Organization (WHO)
  monitoring the Chernobyl plume 190–3
  permissible levels of radioisotopes 111–12

xenon-133 45–6
xenon-135 27, 29, 77
xenon poisoning 27, 29

Yanov station 41, 136
Yemel'yanov, J. Ya. (nuclear physicist) 67, 71
Yugoslavia 193

Zayaz, A. (engineer) 168

Zelinsky, A. N. (Deputy Minister of Health
  of the Ukraine) 136
Zhezherin, J. (nuclear physicist) 258–9
Zhitomir region, contamination 77, 109,
  115–17, 120–1
  new evacuation in 1989–92 176, 181
Zimmer, G. G. (German radiobiologist) 229
zirconium-95 32, 60, 84, 107, 164
zirconium alloys 2, 7, 62, 335
zone of periodic radiation control 124
zone of permanent strict radiation control 91,
  124–5, 127, 129
Zvirko, M. S. (Chairman of the Atomic
  Energy Construction Committee) 51
Zwentendorf NPP 207